A Return to the Village: Community Ethnographies and the Study of Andean Culture in Retrospective

edited by

Francisco Ferreira with Billie Jean Isbell

INSTITUTE OF LATIN AMERICAN STUDIES

SCHOOL OF ADVANCED STUDY
UNIVERSITY OF LONDON

© Institute of Latin American Studies, School of Advanced Study,
University of London, 2016

British Library Cataloguing-in-Publication Data
A catalogue record for this book is available from the British Library

ISBN: 978-1-908857-24-8

Institute of Latin American Studies
School of Advanced Study
University of London
Senate House
London WC1E 7HU

Telephone: 020 7862 8844

Email: ilas@sas.ac.uk
Web: http://ilas.sas.ac.uk

Contents

	List of illustrations	v
	List of acronyms and abbreviations	ix
	Notes on contributors	xi
	Acknowledgments	xvii
	Introduction: Community ethnographies and the study of Andean culture *Francisco Ferreira*	1
1.	Reflections on fieldwork in Chuschi *Billie Jean Isbell (in collaboration with Marino Barrios Micuylla)*	45
2.	Losing my heart *Catherine J. Allen*	69
3.	Deadly waters, decades later *Peter Gose*	93
4.	Yanque Urinsaya: ethnography of an Andean community (a tribute to Billie Jean Isbell) *Carmen Escalante and Ricardo Valderrama*	125
5.	Recordkeeping: ethnography and the uncertainty of contemporary community studies *Rudi Colloredo-Mansfeld*	149
6.	Long lines of continuity: field ethnohistory and customary conservation in the Sierra de Lima *Frank Salomon*	169
7.	Avoiding 'community studies': the historical turn in Bolivian and South Andean anthropology *Tristan Platt*	199
8.	In love with *comunidades* *Enrique Mayer*	233
	References	265
	Index	295

List of illustrations

Figure

0.1	The peasant community of Taulli (Ayacucho, Peru). Photo: F. Ferreira.	2
0.2	Taulli's central village. Photo: F. Ferreira	2
0.3	A communal assembly at Taulli's central village, 2008. Photo: F. Ferreira.	10
0.4	Meeting at Taulli's medical centre, built in the 1990s. Photo: F. Ferreira.	11
0.5	Taulli's Carnival celebrations in the central village, March 2008. Photo: F. Ferreira.	12
2.1	Sectorial fallowing in Sonqo. Created by C.J. Allen.	83
6.1	In Tupicocha, newly invested presidents of parcialidades (ayllus) visit the community office in 2010 to form the new directorate. Photo: F. Salomon.	176
6.2	Tupicocha comuneros examining the author's work table. Photo: F. Salomon.	179
6.3	One stress factor that causes damage to the Tupicocha quipocamayos is the practice of twisting them into a single cable prior to transport and display. Photo: F. Salomon.	181
6.4	The 'simulacrum' or replacement quipocamayo displayed by parcialidad Centro Guangre in Tupicocha, 2007. Photo: F. Salomon.	181
6.5	In 2016, a display case inside the community meeting hall held a quipocamayo of ayllu Segunda Allauca. Photo: F. Salomon.	184
6.6	In Rapaz, the late Moisés Flores attends night-time balternos ceremonial inside Kaha Wayi, and in the presence of suspended khipu collection, New Year, 2004. He wears the formal dress of a balterno. Photo: F. Salomon.	189
6.7	Museologist Renata Peters (right, seated) in a 2005 working meeting inside the precinct with some balterno officers. Photo: F. Salomon.	190

6.8   Vendelhombre [ceremonialist] Melecio Montes (left) lifts the upper altar-cloth of Kaha Wayi's mountain altar, revealing a lower altar-cloth severely damaged by fungus. The lower cloth remains were repaired in 2005 by interweaving them with a fungus-proof synthetic fibre. Photo: F. Salomon.   190
6.9   Vice-president and Kamachikuq Víctor Gallardo examines khipu cords during conservation work inside the temporary site lab. Photo: F. Salomon.   194
6.10 Comunidad Rapaz allows visits inside Kaha Wayi in the daytime, but on rare occasions crowding can be a problem. This mass visit was organised by an NGO in 2005. Photo: F. Salomon.   194
7.1   San Marcos, 1970. Photo: T. Platt.   205
7.2   The alferez [ritual sponsors] and company coming up to San Marcos for Corpus Christi, 1971. Photo: T. Platt.   207
7.3   Tinku in San Marcos for Corpus Christi, 1971. Photo: T. Platt.   208
7.4   Liconi Pampa, 2013. Photo: Fortunato Laura.   210
7.5   Carbajal patriclan members, 1971: Curaca Agustín Carbajal (extreme right), Gregorio and Santiago Carbajal (at centre, seated). Photo: T. Platt.   211
7.6   Map of the great ayllus of Northern Potosí. Drawn by Esteban Renzo Aruquipa Merino (after Mendoza and Patzi, 1997; Harris and Platt, 1978).   214
7.7   Map of Macha territory, with moieties and cabildos (Mendoza and Patzi, 1997).   229
8.1   Tangor carguyoj with his servant and friends carrying chicha to the plaza for distribution to the whole comuna, 1969. Photo: E. Mayer.   239
8.2   Map of Cañete Valley (Lima, Peru) agricultural zones (Mayer and Fonseca, 1979; 1988, no page number)   242
8.3   Diagram of land management by production zones, Cañete Valley (Mayer, 1985; 2002, p. 389).   244
8.4   Maize terraces in Laraos (Lima, Peru). Photo: E. Mayer. 245

List of acronyms and abbreviations

AAA	American Anthropological Association
AFASEP	Association of Families of the Assassinated, Kidnapped, Detained and Disappeared (in Ayacucho)
AI	Amnesty International
ANASEP	National Organisation of Kidnapped and Disappeared Persons
APRODEH	Asociación pro Derechos Humanos (the Peruvian human rights organisation)
CCP	Confederación Campesina del Perú
CCPC	Closed Corporate Peasant Community
CIP	Centro Internacional de la Papa (International Potato Center)
CNRS	Centre national de la recherche scientifique
CONIAE	Confederación de Nacionalidades Indígenas del Ecuador
CORA	Chilean Agrarian Reform
COSUDE	Swiss Agency for Development and Cooperation
DESCO	Centro de Estudios de Promoción y Desarrollo (Promotion and Development Study Centre)
EC	European Commission
ESRC	Economic and Social Research Council
FADA	Federación Agraria Departamental de Ayacucho (Agrarian Federation of Ayacucho)
FAO	Food and Agriculture Organization (of the UN)
FICI	Federación Indígenas y Campesina de Imbabura (major peasant organisation in Ecuador's Ariasucu province)
FLACSO	Facultad Latinoamericana de Ciencias Sociales
FUNHABIT	Fundación Ecuatoriana del Hábitat
GIZ	Deutsche Gesellschaft für Internationale Zusammenarbeit GmbH (German Corporation for International Cooperation)
IEP	Instituto de Estudios Peruanos (Lima)
IMA	Instituto de Manejo de Agua y Medio-Ambiente (Institute for Water and Environmental Management)

INEI	Instituto Nacional de Estadística e Informática (Peru's Institute of Statistics and Information)
IPTK	Tomas Katari Polytechnic Institute
LSE	London School of Economics
MAS	Movimiento al Socialismo (Movement for Socialism)
MBL	Movimiento Bolivia Libre (Free Bolivia Movement)
MIR	Movimiento de Izquierda Revolucionaria (Revolutionary Left Movement)
MNR	Movimiento Nacionalista Revolucionario (Revolutionary Nationalist Movement)
MUSEF	Museum of Ethnography and Folklore (La Paz)
NGO	non-governmental organisation
NSF	National Science Foundation
ONERN	Oficina Nacional de Evaluación de Recursos Naturales (Office of Natural Resource Management)
PETT	Programa Especial para la Titulación de Tierras
PRATEC	Proyecto Andino de Tecnologías Campesinas (an NGO)
PRODERM	Proyecto de Desarrollo Rural en Microregiones (Project for Rural Development in Microregions)
PUCP	Pontificia Universidad Catolica del Peru (Pontifical Catholic University of Peru)
SAIS	Sociedades Agrarias de Interés Social
SANBASUR	Saneamiento Ambiental Básico en la Sierra Sur (Basic Environmental Sanitation in the Southern Highlands)
SEPIA	Seminario Permanente de Investigación Agrarian
SERPAJ	El Servicio de Paz y Justicia (the Catholic Church's Peace and Justice System)
Sendero Luminoso	Communist Party of Peru-Shining Path (more commonly known as Shining Path)
SINAMOS	El Sistema Nacional de Apoyo a la Movilización (National Social Mobilisation Support System)
SSRC	Social Science Research Council
UCLA	University of California, Los Angeles
UNAIMCO	La Union de Artesanos Indigenas del Mercado Centenario-Otavalo (Union of Indigenous Artisans for the Centenario Market of Otavalo)
VRAEM	Valley of the Rivers Apurímac, Ene and Mantaro (Peruvian coca-growing area located between the highland regions of Ayacucho and Cuzco)

Notes on contributors

Catherine J. Allen is a cultural anthropologist with an abiding interest in the connections (and disconnections) between the Andean present and the pre-Columbian past. She is professor emerita of anthropology at George Washington University where, from 1978 to 2012, she taught courses on South American cultures, the anthropology of art, symbolic anthropology and anthropological theory. Allen holds a BA (1969) in liberal arts from St John's College, and an MA (1972) and PhD (1978) in anthropology from the University of Illinois in Urbana, where she studied under the direction of R. Tom Zuidema. Among her academic awards are research fellowships with the Guggenheim Foundation, Fulbright Specialist Program, Sainsbury Centre for Visual Arts, Dumbarton Oaks, and the National Gallery's Center for the Advanced Study of the Visual Arts in Washington DC. She is the author of *The Hold Life Has: Coca and Cultural Identity in an Andean Community* (Smithsonian Press, 1988; expanded 2nd edn., 2002), based on her fieldwork in a Peruvian highland community. Her commitment to humanistic writing led to an ethnographic drama, co-authored with Nathan Garner, *Condor Qatay: Anthropology in Performance* (Waveland Press, 1996). Her most recent book is *Foxboy: Intimacy and Aesthetics in Andean Stories* (University of Texas Press, 2011). She lives with her dog Jimmy in Greenbelt, Maryland, a historic Roosevelt-era cooperative community.

Rudi Colloredo-Mansfeld is professor and chair of the anthropology department at the University of North Carolina, Chapel Hill. Since 1991, he has written and taught about community economies and cultural change in the context of globalisation. Much of his work has focused on indigenous peoples and provincial economies in the Andes. His publications include the books *The Native Leisure Class: Consumption and Cultural Creativity in the Andes* (University of Chicago Press, 1999); *Fighting Like a Community: Andean Civil Society in an Era of Indigenous Uprisings* (University of Chicago Press, 2009); and (with Jason Antrosio) *Fast, Easy and In Cash: Artisan Hardship and Hope in the Global Economy* (University of Chicago Press, 2015). His research has been supported by grants from the Fulbright programme, the Wenner Gren Foundation and The National Science Foundation. Since 2004, he has worked on local food issues in the United States, originally as a member of the Regional Food Systems Working Group at the Leopold Center for Sustainable

Agriculture in Iowa. He has served as president of the Society for Economic Anthropology, associate editor for sociocultural anthropology for *American Anthropologist* and on the editorial board of the *Journal of Latin American and Caribbean Anthropology*.

Carmen Escalante-Gutierrez is an anthropologist with a PhD in Andean studies from the Pontificia Universidad Católica del Perú in Lima. She is currently working as director of the Archivo de la Tradición Oral Quechua del Cusco, while doing a PhD in history at the University Pablo de Olavide, Seville in Spain. Her areas of study include rituals, gender, and oral history and traditions, and she has conducted extensive research and fieldwork in the central and southern highlands of Peru, mostly undertaken in Quechua-speaking peasant communities, located in high-altitude areas and lower valleys. She is married to Ricardo Valderrama with whom she has co-authored numerous publications, including the books *Gregorio Condori Mamani, autobiografía* (Bartolomé de las Casas, Cuzco, 1979) and *Nuestras vidas (abigeos de Cotabambas)* (Instituto de Apoyo Agrario, 1990), as well as many articles. Her own publications include *El Agua en la Cultura Andina* (SAMBASUR, 1999) and 'Huancavelica: Violencia y ciudadanía. Visión de los comuneros sobre la época de la violencia, 1980–2000' (PhD thesis, 2010).

Francisco Araujo-Ferreira is a researcher specialising in Andean ethnography and history, and his fields of interest include highland communities, political violence and cocalero areas, and related drug policies. Francisco completed studies in history and art history at the University of Santiago de Compostela (Galicia, Spain), before working for several years in museum jobs in the UK. While employed at the Victoria and Albert Museum, he completed an MA in Latin American studies at the University of London. He was then awarded a studentship from the British Arts and Humanities Research Council to undertake a PhD in Andean ethnography at Royal Holloway, University of London. Francisco completed his PhD in 2012 with a thesis entitled 'Back to the village? An ethnographic study of an Andean community in the early twenty-first century'. Francisco is currently an independent researcher in Galicia, while working as a teacher, translator and consultant.

Peter Gose is a Canadian anthropologist who pursued his graduate studies at the London School of Economics. He taught at the University of Lethbridge and the University of Regina but currently works at Carleton University, Ottawa. His early research as an ethnographer of the Peruvian Andes explored how peasant mortuary and sacrificial rituals articulate relations of production, property and political power. In the late 1980s, he turned to historical research on ritual and political power under the Incas. From 1993 to 2008, he did archival research on ancestor worship as a key mediating practice in relations of indirect colonial rule in the Andes. More recently, he has conducted archival research for a project on 'purity of blood' racism in Spain and its Andean colonies. His most abiding theoretical interests are in practice theory, hegemony theory, Marx and hermeneutics.

Billie Jean Isbell is professor emerita and graduate professor of anthropology at Cornell University, Ithaca, USA. Her area of expertise is the Andean region of South America. Her current interests include ethnography and fiction, the Slow Food Movement, innovative technologies for teaching and issues of global development. She served as the director of the Andean programme at the Cornell International Institute for Food, Agriculture and Development from 1990 until 2002, and also as director of the Latin American programme at Cornell from 1987 to 1993, and again in 2001-2. She has received awards, grants and fellowships from Woodrow Wilson, Fulbright, MacArthur, National Endowment for the Humanities (NEH), and was also awarded a Ford training grant for the interdisciplinary training of graduate students. Her most recent publications are: (in press) *Melody's Song with a Chorus of Transgender Voices* (University of Illinois Press); 'Lessons from Vicos', in *Toward Engaged Anthropology*, ed. Sam Beck and Carl A. Maida (Berghahn Books, 2013, pp. 132-57); (2011) 'Cornell returns to Vicos, 2005', in *Vicos and Beyond: A Half Century of Applying Anthropology in Peru*, ed. Tom Greaves, Ralph Bolton and Florencia Zapata (Altamira Press, 2011, pp. 283-308); and *Finding Cholita* (University of Illinois Press, 2009). Much of her work can be found on the website www.isbellandes.library.cornell.edu (created by means of a grant from the Olin Library Digital Collection, Wesleyan University, Connecticut).

Enrique Mayer is emeritus professor of anthropology at Yale University, USA. Born in the highlands of Peru to Jewish immigrant parents who had fled Nazi Germany, he completed his college education at the London School of Economics and received his doctorate from Cornell University. His professional career as a university teacher began at the Pontificia Universidad Católica in Lima, Peru. Enrique later moved to Mexico City, where he took charge of the anthropological research department at the Inter American Indian Institute. In 1982 he joined the University of Illinois faculty at Urbana-Champaign with a joint appointment in the anthropology department and the Center for Latin American and Caribbean Studies. In 1995, he became a member of Yale University's anthropology department. Professor Mayer specialises in Andean agricultural systems and Latin American peasantries. His best-known books are *The Articulated Peasant: Household Economies in the Andes* (Westview Press, 2002) and *Ugly Stories of the Peruvian Agrarian Reform* (Duke University Press, 2004).

Tristan Platt was educated at Oxford University and the London School of Economics, before studying Quechua at Cornell University. From 1970 he conducted long-term fieldwork in Northern Potosí, Bolivia. Between 1973 and 1983 he was a member of the research staff at the University del Norte, Arica, in Chile, the Museum of Ethnography and Folklore in La Paz, Bolivia and the Institute of Peruvian Studies in Lima. Co-founder of the Avances research group (La Paz, 1977–8), he published *Estado boliviano y ayllu andino: tierra y tributo en el Norte de Potosí* (Lima, 1982; republished La Paz, 2016). With Thérèse Bouysse-Cassagne and Olivia Harris he published *Qaraqara-Charka. Historia antropológica de una confederación aymara* (La Paz, Paris, St Andrews, London, 2006; 2nd edn. 2011). As a member of the University of St Andrews' anthropology department (1988, retired 2013, emeritus 2014) he directed the Centre for Amerindian Studies. In 1986 and 1999 he was directeur d'études at the École des Hautes Études en Sciences Sociales in Paris, and in 1993–4 he was research fellow at the University of Salamanca. Tristan Platt was the recipient of a Guggenheim fellowship in 1996. His research interests include anthropology and history, Andean ethnohistory, Andean childbirth, indigenous literacy and archives, Andean mining, Rothschild's quicksilver monopoly and the Andean-Amazonian interface. He is the author of numerous journal articles and book chapters and is currently collaborating with the Ibero-American Programme of the Universidad Pablo de Olavide, in Seville.

Frank Loewen Salomon is John V. Murra professor of anthropology at the University of Wisconsin-Madison – Murra, the late Andean ethnohistorian, was Salomon's doctoral adviser. Salomon gained MA and PhD degrees at Cornell University (1974, 1978) and joined Madison's anthropology department in 1982. He has been a senior fellow of Madison's Institute for Research in the Humanities, a past chair of its anthropology department, and in 2005 was elected president of the American Society for Ethnohistory. Recently, in 2014–15, he was a resident fellow at the University of Iowa's Obermann Center for Advanced Research. As a historical ethnographer, he discovered and analysed new sources about the Inca empire's northernmost realms, synthesised in *Native Lords of Quito in the Age of the Incas* (Cambridge University Press, 1986). In 1991 he published, with George Urioste, the first English version of the 1608 Quechua Manuscript of Huarochirí (University of Texas Press), the only known book documenting a pre-Columbian religious tradition in an Andean language. With Stuart Schwartz he edited the two South American volumes of the *Cambridge History of the Native Peoples of the Americas* (1999). In *The Cord Keepers* (Duke University Press, 2004) he studied a village which conserved the ancient khipu or knotted-cord script into modernity. A Spanish version, *Los quipocamayos*, was published in 2006. A complementary book, *The Lettered Mountain: A Peruvian Village's Way with Writing*, co-written by

Mercedes Niño-Murcia, concerned the acquisition of alphabetic writing and its Andean uses (Duke University Press, 2011). Both *The Cord Keepers* and *Ethnic Lords of Quito in the Age of the Incas* (Cornell University Dissertation Series, 77) were honoured with the Howard Francis Cline Prize of the Conference on Latin American History (1989, 2005), and the former also won the Hermine Wheeler-Voegelin prize for best book in ethnohistory (2005). Current research concerns the Peruvian village of Rapaz, famous for its repository of patrimonial khipus, for a work in progress, *The High Places: Ethnography at an Andean Mountain Altar.*

Ricardo Valderrama-Fernández is a professor of anthropology at the University of San Antonio Abad, Cuzco in Peru. He completed a PhD in Andean studies at the Pontificia Universidad Católica del Perú, in Lima, and has received grants and fellowships from the Guggenheim Foundation and the École des Hautes Études en Sciences Sociales in Paris. He is married to Carmen Escalante, with whom he has co-authored numerous books and articles, such as *Del Tata Mallku a la mama pacha, riego, sociedad e ideología en los Andes* (DESCO, 1988); *Nosotros los humanos. Testimonios de los quechuas del siglo XX* (Biblioteca de la Tradición Oral Andina, 1992); *Andean Lives: Gregorio Condori Mamani and Asunta Quispe Huamán* (University of Texas, 1996); and *La doncella sacrificada: Mitología del valle del Colca* (University of san Agustín, 1997). His own works include 'Sistemas de autoridad en una comunidad quechua contemporánea' (PhD thesis, 2007) and 'El Inca en la tradición oral quechua contemporánea', *Revista Andina*, 53 (2015).

Acknowledgments

We would like to thank everyone who has played a part in the production of this edited volume, particularly the chapter authors for their generous and outstanding contributions.

We are also grateful to the Institute of Latin American Studies (ILAS), School of Advanced Study (SAS), University of London, for publishing the book, and in particular Linda Newson, the ILAS director, for supporting this project from its early stages. Our thanks also go to the SAS publications team members for their patience and outstanding work, especially to Valerie Hall for her careful editing.

The Arts and Humanities Research Council of the United Kingdom funded the research that generated this book in Peru, as part of the multidisciplinary research project 'Inca ushnus: landscape, site and symbol in the Andes'. The project involved and received support and advice from both UK institutions (The British Museum, Royal Holloway University of London and the University of Reading) and the University of Humanga in Peru.

We are grateful to Eliot Jones for his excellent translation from the original Spanish into English of Valderrama and Escalante's chapter, and to ILAS for organising and funding this translation. Orin Starn's sympathetic approach to this project is much appreciated, and also his feedback, included in the introduction, on some key issues explored by this book. We must also thank several scholars, whom we approached and consulted about this project, especially Salvador Palomino, Paul H. Gelles, Henry Stobart, Inge Bolin, Regina Harrison, Florencia Zapata and Beatriz Rojas.

Reasonable efforts have been made to identify and contact copyright holders.

Last, but not least, this edited volume could not have been produced without the members of the Andean communities represented within its pages. We dedicate this book to them.

Introduction: Community ethnographies and the study of Andean culture

Francisco Ferreira

The idea behind this book was born out of curiosity in Taulli, a small peasant community of some 500 people, located in the Andean region of Ayacucho in the southern highlands of Peru.[1] It was 2008 and I was doing ethnographic fieldwork for my PhD research, surrounded by a beautiful and dramatic landscape of rugged mountains, deep ravines and sloping plains (see figure 0.1). During this fieldwork, I lived most of the time in Taulli's central village, a colonial *reducción* located some 3,300 metres above sea level (masl),[2] in a small room in one of the village's communal buildings kindly lent to me by the local authorities (see figure 0.2). When I was not working, interacting with local people, or exploring the community and the area, I used to spend much of my time writing and reading in this room, which I had transformed into a reasonably comfortable home.

I treasured my small library, part of it brought with me to Peru and partly bought later in urban centres such as Ayacucho City or Lima. Prominent in it were community ethnographies produced and conducted in the Andes in previous years and decades, particularly in the southern highlands of Peru, the geographical area of my research. Some of these ethnographies had formed an important part of my introduction to the anthropological study of Andean culture months before when I started my doctorate. As a newcomer to the world of ethnography and anthropology, I mainly followed the initial recommendations, for books mostly produced in the 1970s–80s, of my PhD advisers. I was struck by the quality of these works, the richness of the research and writing of their authors, and by the human dimension that they could powerfully invoke, highlighting intimate and privileged insights into the lives and key aspects of the culture of these communities and their members. I realised that these particular ethnographies transcended the boundaries set by

1 Peruvian peasant communites have a special legal status based on their communal features and ancient historial precedents. They are mostly located in Andean regions (see Robles-Mendoza, 2002).

2 The reducciones were Spanish-style villages established following the forced resettlement of native ethnic groups and communities. They were systematised in the Andes in the 1570s by Viceroy Francisco de Toledo (see Ravi-Mumford, 2012).

Figure 0.1. The peasant community of Taulli (Ayacucho, Peru). Photo: F. Ferreira.

Figure 0.2. Taulli's central village. Photo: F. Ferreira.

mere case studies. The insights they gave me helped me to grasp the central role that these rural communities have played in Andean culture. I also realised that they and the ethnographies about them are integral to the subdiscipline of cultural and social anthropology in the Andes.

During fieldwork, as I gradually immersed myself in the community's day-to-day life, I would go back to these ethnographies and recognise that elements of their content applied to Taulli. I also frequently identified with some of their authors' experiences. At the same time, I recognised that major historical changes had taken place since those studies were conducted, which would undoubtedly have caused major transformations within the communities under study. I sometimes wondered about these changes and how the authors would interpret them. As I developed affective bonds with the local people, the Taullinos, I also thought about the kind of bonds that these writers would have established and retained with these community members across the years.

Furthermore, at this stage I was already well aware that community ethnographies in general, and particularly those conducted in the Andes using certain theoretical approaches, had been subjected to heated scholarly debates and criticism. Such ethnographies have been the most paradigmatic form of anthropological study, particularly of indigenous cultures. However, in the 1980s–90s they came to be widely considered as too limited and subjective, in the context of wider academic changes (for example, the emergence of postmodern and revisionist trends, reflective and literary turns in anthropology). As a result they became largely discredited, losing their previous centrality. This was also the case within Andean anthropology, where community ethnographies have been especially important. This is because Andean culture has been largely rural and historically identified with highland territories in which most of the population was concentrated. In the context of Andean anthropology, the general criticism concerning these studies was coupled with the more specific theoretical and methodological debates and controversies outlined below. I recognised and shared some aspects of such criticisms and debates, but also found others to be unfair. Therefore, I also wondered what the authors of the ethnographies I was drawing on – some of whom had been directly involved in the debates mentioned here – would think about such criticisms, and how they would assess their community ethnographies retrospectively.

I remember going for a walk at midday one day in and around Taulli, just after reading and thinking about these issues. As I greeted the people I crossed paths with in Spanish or in my broken Quechua – the most commonly used language in this bilingual community – I became increasingly lost in my own thoughts, mesmerised by the surrounding landscape. I started to think that it would be really interesting to get together some of the authors of ethnographies that I had found so interesting and influential in an edited volume, asking them to elaborate on these different issues. I was busy then with fieldwork and my PhD research, but the idea stuck in the back of my mind as a potential and interesting project that I could undertake in the future, if the right circumstances and contacts could be worked out and established; as they eventually were. Moreover, during the following months, communities, their ethnographies, and their methodological and theoretical concerns, became central foci of my PhD due to my fieldwork experiences and readings. As a result, my thesis ended up being a community ethnography of Taulli that in part dealt with and reassessed the role and ongoing validity of these studies in the examination of Andean culture (Ferreira, 2012).

Over the next couple of years, I had the chance to meet personally some of the authors that had influenced me, and to discuss with them the idea for an edited volume that I had first conceived in Taulli. First, I met Catherine Allen, author of *The Hold Life Has* (2008, 2002a, 1988), in London in late 2010. This was at a conference hosted by the British Museum where we both presented papers. Her beautifully written and poetic ethnography of Sonqo (Cuzco region), which focuses especially on the symbolical and ritual dimensions of coca in this community, had been among my early readings and had impressed me profoundly. She was kind and sympathetic to the idea of the potential book, so we agreed to keep in touch about it. Some months later, in 2011, I also met Billie Jean Isbell, author of *To Defend Ourselves* (2005, 1985, 1978), at a seminar she gave at the University of London. Her exhaustive and comprehensive ethnography of Chuschi (Ayacucho), which focuses mainly on local sociopolitical organisation and ritual practices, had also been among my initial readings. Her book was particularly relevant for me because this community happens to be just a few hours away from Taulli. After the conference, I introduced myself to her and we ended up going to a nearby pub with fellow delegates. There, I took the opportunity to tell her about the book idea over a few pints, and she was also receptive to it. We also agreed to stay in touch. In late 2012, after finishing my PhD, I contacted Isbell and Allen again to discuss the project, which gradually took shape and evolved in the next few months. The support, contacts and prestige of Allen and Isbell were key to getting other authors on board, and to securing a publishing deal with the Institute of Latin American Studies at the School of Advanced Study, University of London, supported by Linda Newson, the institute director.

The result of this long process is this edited volume, which brings together several authors who have produced outstanding community ethnographies in the Andes, or who can offer privileged insights into this type of study and the contribution it makes to Andean anthropology. In their respective chapters, these authors reassess and reflect on key aspects of their works in light of contemporary anthropology, addressing some of the questions I asked myself in the mountains of Taulli. At a wider level the book aims to explore and consider the changing role of community ethnographies in the study of Andean culture, focusing especially on some particularly relevant theoretical approaches and periods. It also reflects on the past and present contribution and validity of these ethnographies, in an academic context that now widely perceives them as dated. By community, I refer specifically here to the territorial and administrative units formed by rural villages,³ and their corresponding lands and inhabitants, located in Andean highland areas.

In the following pages I offer a more detailed account of this book's origins, which will provide a better understanding of its theoretical and methodological context and concerns. A bibliographic review of community ethnographies in the Andes follows, and a personal interpretation of their evolution and contribution to Andean anthropology. The review focuses mainly on Peru, and to a lesser extent Bolivia and Ecuador. These countries correspond to a 'core Andean region'; with remarkable and distinctive common characteristics,⁴ where this book's contributors have conducted most of their research. The scope and validity of this bibliographic review to the wider Andean world is undermined by this geographical limitation. However, I believe that it is representative of a wider picture, and fills certain voids in the academic literature available in English covering community ethnographies in the Andes and their role in the region's anthropology. Finally, I introduce the different chapters and their authors, and make some final comments concerning the book's contribution to the field.

Personal experiences and emotional aspects of research are especially important in this book, as it touches on authors' deep feelings about and connections to the communities in which they have worked, and to the personal and biographical connotations of their work. However, it is not my intention to idealise, romanticise or fetishise these ethnographies in any way or the experiences of their authors. Instead, I wish to explore their contribution, advantages and also limitations. If some content in this introduction is already well known to specialists, it is because I have tried to provide a wide-ranging and engaging work that will also attract the general reader.

A personal introduction to community ethnographies and the Andes

In 2007 I was granted a scholarship from the Arts and Humanities Research Council (AHRC) of the United Kingdom (UK) to undertake a PhD on agricultural rituals in Andean communities in the geography department at Royal Holloway, University of London (RHUL). This PhD was linked to the multidisciplinary research project, Inca Ushnus: Landscape, Site and Symbol in the Andes, which studied architectonical platforms built by the Incas across their

---

3 Village as used in the book's title is synonymous with community, as its most paradigmatic setting.

4 These countries are enormously diverse geographically and ethnically, although they also share remarkable historical and cultural features. Many similarities can be found in their Andean cultures.

Andean empire, with a focus on the Peruvian highland region of Ayacucho.[5] The functions, uses and symbolism of these platforms were complex, but it seems clear they were considered sacred and used as altars or stages to perform state-related ritual practices and ceremonies, such as propitiatory sacrifices related to agricultural production. The project included the plan and funding granted to me for the ethnographic PhD, which would study how some of the concepts and practices related to the platforms, such as agricultural rituals and sacred space, function among contemporary Andean communities. The underlying idea was that understanding these issues in the present could suggest how they worked in the past, and in relation to Inca platforms. The pre-designed PhD plan outlined an established research focus and a methodology. It was planned that I would spend at least ten months carrying out ethnographic fieldwork in one or two rural communities in Ayacucho. I therefore began fieldwork with a pre-designed research focus and methodology.

I must confess that although happy to have the chance to do this research and participate in the project, I was also concerned because I had no formal background in ethnography or anthropology. Moreover, I was not particularly familiar with the contemporary Andean world and Peru. My previous academic and professional career had followed completely different paths: I had completed undergraduate studies in history and art history in Spain, before working for several years in museum jobs in the UK. However, I had just completed a part-time MA in Latin American Studies at the University of London, selecting colonial history as my major, so I had some knowledge of the Andean colonial past. I also had good initial advice from my PhD advisers, who recommended an extensive bibliography. Nevertheless, not having the above-mentioned formal background in the field represented a big personal challenge, causing me to be insecure throughout the research process and contributing to its prolongation. I tried to use this lack of an orthodox background as an opportunity to offer a kind of outsider's look at the anthropological issues my thesis dealt with, one that I have also tried to replicate in this book while still aiming to be anthropologically sound. I therefore aimed to combine my fieldwork's participant-observation with a kind of academic participant-observation of Andean anthropology. With those initial concerns in mind, I started navigating the relevant literature with the unavoidable clumsiness of a beginner, but also with the necessary curiosity of someone embarking on a journey of discovery.

5   The project, funded by the AHRC through its Landscape and Environmental Programme, ran from 2007–10. It brought together scholars from different disciplines (archaeology, physical and human geography, history, anthropology and geology) and institutions from the UK (RHUL, University of Reading and the British Museum) and Peru (University of San Cristóbal de Huamanga, in Ayacucho City). Further project information at www.britishmuseum.org/research/research_projects/complete_projects/featured_project_inca_ushnus.aspx (all web links included in the book were functional in July 2016).

This initial bibliography included several community ethnographies, mostly monographs based on single communities in the southern Peruvian highlands, although there were also some from other highland areas in Peru and Bolivia. Soon I realised that most were based on fieldwork undertaken before the 1990s, even if some were published long after. In the case of Peru, this was partially understandable taking into consideration the armed conflict between the Maoist guerrillas of Sendero Luminoso [Shining Path] and the Peruvian state that took place in the 1980s–90s. '*La violencia*' [the violence], as the conflict is graphically known in Peru, reached the scale of a civil war, causing massive and traumatic human rights violations, deaths and population displacements.[6] Most of the victims were Quechua-speaking peasants from Ayacucho, where the conflict actually originated, and also neighbouring Andean regions that were caught between the army and the guerrillas. The conflict also made fieldwork impossible in many parts of the Peruvian highlands, and it also became traumatic for ethnographers and other researchers who had worked in affected communities when their long-term subjects of study, who were also friends and acquaintances, became victims of violence, dislocation and disruption.

Moreover, the conflict had a far-reaching impact on the study of Andean culture in Peru and, by extension, beyond. It is important to take into consideration that other Andean countries have also suffered – more or less extreme – armed conflicts and violence, affecting ethnographic fieldwork and research, especially in Colombia due to its own internal conflict and drug-related problems. For example, Tristan Platt (personal communication) argues that Bolivia was 'driven by violence' from the Chaco War (1932–5) until democracy was restored in 1982. This gave fieldwork in the country 'a particularly tense and dangerous context', especially during the period of military dictatorships (1964–82), which was marked by torture, massacres, disappearances and mass movements. Violence has therefore often been a constant and important factor in Andean anthropology, becoming a central theme of study in recent decades. Nevertheless, the Peruvian armed conflict of the 1980s–90s had a particular impact on the sub-discipline, due to the country's geographical and academic centrality and the fact that the conflict was more recent and virulent than others had been, coinciding and becoming interrelated with wider academic changes and debates as explained below.

As I learned more about the wider historical and academic context of Andean anthropology, I realised that community ethnographies had played a fundamental and central role from the start (the mid 1940s) until the early 1990s, at least. During these decades, scholarly approaches to these studies, and

---

[6] Human rights violations committed during the conflict were extensively researched and reported in the nine-volume *Final Report of the Truth and Reconciliation Commission* (2004), available at www.cverdad.org.pe/ingles/pagina01.php.

to Andean anthropology more generally, could be divided, following Olivia Harris, roughly between 'short-' and 'long-termists', depending respectively on a predominantly social change and development focus or on historical continuities and cultural phenomena.[7] However, it is important to consider that this division long-/short-termism is relative and not mutually exclusive (but rather complementary), referring to predominant tendencies rather than neatly defined perspectives; and that there have been overlapping and more flexible approaches.

Gradually, I began to develop a better knowledge of the background and evolution of such division. From the 1960s, Andean anthropology had been influenced by the work of leading ethnohistorians, particularly John V. Murra, R. Tom Zuidema and John H. Rowe, who revolutionised the study of the Andean past. They focused on distinctive aspects of Andean culture and introduced a whole set of theoretical references. They also discovered new documental and ethnographic sources to increase understanding and interpretation of the Inca empire and other Andean societies of the past. Andean culture and communities have presented remarkable historical continuities across time so, particularly during the 1960s–80s, anthropologists linked to or influenced by the aforementioned ethnohistorians tended to focus on those distinctive aspects of Andean culture. They also applied the same theoretical references, looking for historical continuities and logically becoming the main long-termists of this period.

I define these decades as a 'Classical Period' of Andean anthropology, because of the noteworthy progress and distinctive characteristics gained with both long- and short-termist approaches. By the early 1990s, this was followed by what I define as a 'Revisionist Period'. This revisionism was the result of wider changes in academia, and led to a rejection of 1960s–80s long-termism by a new generation of scholars, who criticised its followers of overemphasising historical continuities, and idealising and essentialising Andean cultures and peoples. Following emergent academic tendencies, these critics defended instead a hybrid and processual view of culture. Some even rejected the 'Andean' concept itself as an artificial academic category, and community ethnographies as a too limited and subjective research methodology and setting. As a result, long-termism and these studies became largely discredited from the 1990s onwards, and there was a certain thematic, methodological and theoretical fragmentation of Andean anthropology, leading to it becoming increasingly assimilated within the wider discipline. Nevertheless the rejection

---

7   Harris (2009, pp. 1–2) defined the followers of these two approaches as, respectively, 'those who focus on the present conjuncture and have a more social and political agenda, engaging with the problems of Andean peoples'; and 'those who focus on long-term processes and continuities'. She mainly used this division to characterise Andean anthropology in the 1960s–90s, while I am applying it to a wider chronological context.

of this long-termism paradoxically took place at the same time as some of its central elements became increasingly integrated in Andean peoples' discourses about themselves, and also in state policies directed to them. This academic evolution along with its related controversies and paradoxes is explained in more detail below, but is introduced here as a key theoretical reference point for this edited volume.

As I became familiar with the literature, I realised that I was trending towards a kind of scholarship which was generally considered to be outdated. My research was partially based on looking for continuities with the past through community-based fieldwork, and this approach closely resembled that of the 1960s–80s long-termism that had been rejected in the context of 1990s revisionism. What a dilemma! Furthermore, the community ethnographies I had been reading, following my PhD advisers' recommendations, were also considered outdated by many. Yet to people approaching ethnography from outside anthropology's disciplinary core, as I initially was, such studies still seemed a valuable product.

With these thoughts in mind, I travelled to Peru for the first time in 2007 to participate in an archaeological field season of the wider research project, along with other members. During four weeks we excavated several Inca platforms located in *puna* [high-altitude areas] around Ayacucho City. The experience was challenging and fulfilling, and I was positively impressed by my first contact with the Andes and its peoples. My main duty during these weeks was to carry out ethnographic research about the platforms around the excavated sites, although I also looked for a community in which to undertake my own fieldwork later on. Following the advice of Cirilo Vivanco, an archaeologist from the University of Huamanga who was a project member, I travelled to the River Qaracha basin and visited several of the villages he had suggested. The river is located some 100 to 150 kilometres south of Ayacucho City, and is characterised by the presence of peasant communities on both sides, characterised by very poor socioeconomic conditions and very rich cultural traditions. These traditions and the existence of several anthropological studies, mainly community ethnographies conducted there in previous decades,[8] made the area interesting for my research.

The final community I visited was Taulli, which was particularly hard to get to and also exceptionally beautiful. Some local people welcomed me in the central village and told me about fascinating local customs and legends. This was the place! Some months later I returned to Peru and moved to Taulli soon

---

8 For example, several students of Zuidema conducted community ethnographies around the area in the late 1960s and early 1970s, in places like Huancasancos (Quispe-Mejía, 1968), Sarhua (Palomino-Flores, 1970) and Chuschi (Isbell, 1978) among others. These studies followed Zuidema's structuralism and were the result of a wider research project (see Isbell, chapter 1 here).

Figure 0.3. A communal assembly at Taulli's central village, 2008. Photo: F. Ferreira.

after. Once there, I introduced myself to the people in a communal assembly, asking for and being granted permission to live among them (see figure 0.3). I spent some 16 months in Taulli in 2008-9, soon beginning to develop strong bonds with local people, establishing relationships of mutual respect and friendship that consolidated with time. My original fieldwork plan was to focus on local celebrations and ritual life, and on their links with agriculture and concepts such as sacred space. I did follow this plan (for example, Ferreira, 2014) but, as I immersed myself in local life and increasingly engaged with Andean anthropology, Taulli gradually acquired wider implications than my original research aims, which I then systematically reoriented.

One fieldwork experience to cause this reorientation was being struck by the level of change the community and its entire area have gone through in recent decades, particularly since the armed conflict of the 1980s–90s ended. The warfare badly affected the whole area and region, causing massive human suffering and disrupting life in local communities to a traumatic degree. It also brought major changes for these communities and peoples in the longer term, contributing to new social processes and changing and accelerating pre-existing ones to unprecedented levels. In Taulli I was able to trace and assess these developments through the testimonies of local peoples, and through comparison with earlier anthropological literature on the area. For example, I found that the conflict brought a much deeper interrelation of the community with coastal and urban areas, due to massive population exodus which altered local migration patterns and life experiences. It also brought unprecedented state intervention into the community, mainly through the introduction of new public services and works (for example, communications, infrastructure,

Figure 0.4. Meeting at Taulli's medical centre, built in the 1990s. Photo: F. Ferreira.

welfare services) (see figure 0.4). This tendency started in the 1990s, as part of the state's counterinsurgency strategy, increasing since then in a context of political democratisation and economic neoliberalism. I could see that this state intervention is largely insufficient and ineffective overall, although it has brought some considerable improvements to the community, such as increasing health standards and education opportunities.

In this context of far-reaching social change, I also found that local traditions, such as those related to religious and ritual practices and social organisation, continue to offer local people a strong sense of identity and social cohesion, as well as some important practical advantages (see figure 0.5). Moreover, these traditions have been dynamically reinvented to serve as a primary channel through which Taullinos experience and accommodate change. At the same time, I found that many aspects of the 1960s–80s long-termism commented on above were useful, sometimes fundamental, to understanding and interpreting many aspects of local life.[9] As a result, I came to believe that in Taulli many aspects of 1960s–80s long-termism continue to be perfectly valid and useful, and also compatible with a hybrid and processual interpretation of Andean culture.

Drawing on these fieldwork experiences and observations, and on my readings and thoughts about these topics, I finally decided to produce a community ethnography of Taulli as my PhD. I analysed the far-reaching social changes the community has been experiencing in recent decades, and

9   For example, the focus on distinctive expressions of Andean culture (such as syncretic religiosity, particular forms of sociospatial organisation) and strategies of ecological adaptation (for example the need to complement and diversify production across different ecological zones), or particular theoretical concepts (such as reciprocity, redistribution).

Figure 0.5. Taulli's Carnival celebrations in the central village, March 2008. Photo: F. Ferreira.

how traditional aspects of local life worked their way in and adapted within a context of change. At a wider level, I used this case study to examine the situation of Peruvian peasant neighbourhoods in the early 21st century; and to reassess the role contribution, and current validity of community ethnographies in the study of Andean culture. To do this I developed a bibliographic review of such Andean ethnographies as part of my thesis (Ferreira, 2012, pp. 70–94), which will form the basis of the section that follows.

Community ethnographies in the core Andean region: a review

This bibliographic review focuses mainly on monographs based on single communities, written in or translated into English and Spanish. However, I also include other relevant community-based ethnographies and formats, such as articles, edited volumes, comparative and regional studies, and examinations of wider administrative and ethnic units. As outlined above, I mostly focus on those produced in Peru and, to a lesser extent, in neighbouring Bolivia and Ecuador, as a core Andean region with distinctive common characteristics. The review does not pretend to be exhaustive for obvious questions of context and length; and I am sure that I have involuntarily and unfairly neglected high-quality community ethnographies, conducted in these and other Andean countries and languages. However, it seeks to be representative as well as both useful and engaging for readers. I distinguish some precedents and four periods in the evolution of these studies. Such periodisation is based on my readings and interpretations of primary and secondary sources and particularly the important work on Peru by Ramón Pajuelo included in *No hay país más diverso* (2000).[10] This book, edited by the late and great ethnographer Carlos Iván Degregori, is an epochal summary and assessment of anthropology in Peru from the perspective of Peruvian scholars. As such, it is a fundamental reference point for approaching Peruvian anthropology, and has been an important source for this bibliographic review.[11]

Earlier ethnographic documents and immediate precedents

Academic anthropological study of Andean culture and communities started in the 1940s. However, it is possible to identify earlier precedents and studies including some from the period immediately preceding that decade. Degregori (2000a, pp. 25-30) traces the earliest precedents to colonial writings by conquerors, clergy, chroniclers and mixed-race individuals and so on; and others to those of European travellers from the 18th and 19th centuries (for example, Alexander V. Humboldt, Antonio Raimondi). These authors were the first to try to understand and explain indigenous Andean cultures to western audiences. In fact, the existence of such rich earlier precedents, particularly those of the early colonial period resulting from the conquest's unique circumstances, provides one of the most distinctive characteristics of Andean anthropology, the importance of the past as a fundamental reference point. As pointed out by Harris (2000a, p. 1), this factor has differentiated Andean anthropology from that of other regions, where the focus has been unequivocally on the present due to the lack of historic documents and sources.

Some of the most remarkable colonial precedents resulted from the notorious campaigns of 'extirpations of idolatries' conducted by colonial powers. They took place in the late 16th and early 17th centuries, and sought to extirpate pre-Hispanic religious beliefs and practices among Andean people. These campaigns mainly targeted rural communities, and paradoxically produced invaluable historical documents about the beliefs and practices they sought to destroy. For example, the compilation of local myths and religious beliefs from the Huarochirí community, in the highlands of Lima, in the document *Dioses y hombres de Huarochirí* (Arguedas et al., 1966 [1598-1608]). Written in Quechua between 1598 and 1608 by an anonymous Andean author, probably

---

10 Pajuelo distinguishes four periods: 1) Early studies, 1900–30 (Pajuelo, 2000, pp. 128-31); 2) The golden age, 1940–60 (ibid., pp. 132–41); 3) The great transformation, 1960–80 (ibid., pp. 142–55); and 4) Thematic diversification, 1980s–90s (ibid., pp. 156–64).

11 This book, ed. Degregori (2000), also includes: Ávila (2000a and b), Degregori (2000a and b), Golte (2000) and Roel-Mendizábal (2000). For other references on community ethnographies in the Andes, especially Peru, see Urrutia (1992) and Fonseca (1985); on the evolution of Andean anthropology see Harris (2009; 2000a); Starn (1994; 1991); Osterling and Martínez (1983); Salomon (1982); Valcárcel (1985 [1980]); and, focused on Peru, Degregori and Sandoval (2008).

Cristóbal Choquecasa, under the orders of the Spanish priest Francisco de Ávila, it offers unique insights into community-level mythology and religiosity (see Salomon, chapter 6, here). Rodrigo Hernández-Princípe (1923 [1621-2]), extirpator in the Peruvian region of Ancash, also came surprisingly close to a community perspective in his 1622 report about Recuay, in which he gave a detailed description of local religious practices and beliefs. Other early colonial precedents include administrative documents that can provide valuable ethnographic information about Andean communities. A particular example would be the census, such as the 1562 *visita* of the Huanuco and Chucuito regions of central and southern Peru, which includes information on local ethnic groups from the household level upwards (Ortiz de Zuñiga, 1972 [1562]).

The immediate precedents can be traced to the first three decades of the 20th century, and are linked to the Indigenist movement that emerged in Peru at the time and had its heyday in the 1920s. This mainly intellectual and cultural movement revalorised Andean culture and peoples through idealising their pre-Hispanic past. It also led to a new interest in the study of contemporary Andean peoples and communities, and to the emergence of pioneering institutions and authors,[12] such as the scholar Luis Valcárcel. This revalorisation coincided with fundamental changes and the beginning of key historical processes in several Andean countries. For example, the start of massive emigration from highland territories to urban and coastal areas;[13] or the legal recognition of indigenous communities in Peru, under Augusto B. Leguía's government (1919-30). This recognition, achievable only on an individual basis, started with the 1920 Constitution and was based on Andean communities' historical rights and traditions,[14] affecting them almost exclusively.[15] This legal status brought some important advantages (recognition of communal organisation and territorial boundaries, certain legal protections), so it was systematically sought by Peruvian highland territories from then onwards. Similarly, Bolivia and Ecuador also legally recognised their own Andean communities, in 1938 and 1945-6 respectively, and had their own equivalents to indigenism.

12 Osterling and Martínez (1983, pp. 344-5) review these institutions.
13 This emigration was the result of increasing demographic pressures on highland regions and would change the configuration of national societies from then onwards. For example, Bertram (2002 [1991], p. 8) argues that the Peruvian Andes only reached pre-Hispanic demographic levels around the 1950s.
14 During the colonial period, Andean communities had a special legal status and recognition that provided them with certain autonomy and protection. This was lost during the early republican period, facilitating massive land usurpations and abuses, especially by haciendas.
15 98% in the 1990s (Robles-Mendoza, 2002, pp. 19-20), mostly in the central and southern highlands (85% according to Castillo-Fernández, 2004, pp. 22-3). Amazonian indigenous settlements in Peru achieved legal recognition as native communities in 1974.

As Pajuelo (2000, p. 128) explains, earlier monographs exploring Andean communities appeared from the 1900s.[16] The first ones were done by lawyers and agronomists, interested in the legal status of land property or by changes in agriculture in these areas. Others approached them in terms of supporting or rejecting their existence (ibid.), normally from ideological perspectives (for example, Andean communities as socialist societies that must be protected or abolished, depending on the author's ideology). Hildebrando Castro-Pozo (1979 [1924]) was one of the first authors to present fieldwork-based ethnographic descriptions of some of these. He was a socialist member of the Indigenist movement, who worked as head of the Peruvian Sección de Asuntos Indígenas (Indigenous Affairs Section) undertaking fieldwork in the regions of Jauja and Junín. He presented a positive image of the communities, considering them to be continuations of pre-Hispanic *ayllus*.[17]

Significantly, these were also the decades in which academic community ethnographies appeared. Their main pioneers were a generation of scholars who established the modern foundations of anthropology in the early 20th century. They rejected the initially racist and colonial connotations which had marked the discipline since the 19th century, and set about exploring indigenous cultures through immersing themselves for long periods in their communities, learning their languages and studying their social systems through ethnography: the description and interpretation of other peoples' lives.[18] One of the main pioneers was Bronislaw Malinowski (1922), with his classic study of the indigenous peoples of New Guinea's Trobiand Islands. There, he developed the main ethnographic fieldwork technique of participant-observation, the combination of and balance between an insider's subjective participation and an outsider's objective observation.

As a result, from the 1910s–20s onwards, anthropology and ethnographic fieldwork predominantly came to be associated with western anthropologists going into 'isolated' villages or communities of 'distant' indigenous societies, considering them as a microcosm of the whole. The selection of the community as the basic unit of anthropological study was a logical development from the idea of intensive long-term fieldwork. However, as Petti J. Pelto and Gretel H. Pelto point out, 'the use of a particular village to characterise a whole culture can be deeply misleading, or lead to stereotypes' (1973, p. 244). Early scholars

16 Pajuelo (2000, pp. 128–31) offers a complete review of these earlier studies.
17 Ayllu is an ancient and complex Andean concept that mainly refers to kinship, ethnic group or diverse sociospatial internal divisions of ethnic groups and communities, so it was often identified with the latter.
18 A direct precedent of this approach can be traced to the field guide written by French philosopher, Marie Joshep de Gerando (1800), which recommended the study of 'primitive' peoples within the context of their social systems, through being integrated into their communities and learning their languages.

had a functionalist approach to fieldwork, trying to understand a whole society through the study of its different parts, and how they fit together. Ethnographers soon realised that the understanding of some aspects of a given society often come through the understanding of other completely different aspects, which can help to make sense of previously incomprehensible customs and practices.

The earlier pioneers of this academic approach in the Andes were foreign scholars who started undertaking community-based fieldwork. Frank Salomon (personal communication) explains that the first to attempt modern international ethnography in the region was the French author Paul Rivet, who worked mainly in Ecuador from 1905 onwards. According to Orin Starn (1994, p. 15), early foreign scholars were few and generally shared a dislike for the indigenous peoples they were studying, despite denouncing their exploitation. However, Pajuelo (2000, p. 132) states that it was the arrival in the 1930s of foreign authors, like Harry Tschopik to Peru and Alfred Métraux to Bolivia, which marked the beginning of the scientific exploration of Andean culture.

Initial period (mid 1940s–mid 1960s)

Academic study of Andean anthropology began after World War II, with a series of landmark events, such as the publication of the *Handbook of South American Indians*, edited by Julian H. Steward (1963 [1946–50]), whose second volume of 1946 was dedicated to the Andes.[19] Foreign scholars and institutions, such as the Smithsonian and Cornell University, started several projects in which future generations of scholars from Andean countries were trained (for example the Virú project in 1946, Peru-Cornell in 1952); while new institutions were created by national or foreign initiatives. In Peru, José Luis Bustamante's democratic government (1945–8) was important in this process, integrating figures from the Indigenist movement (for example Valcárcel as culture minister), and facilitating the creation of organisations such as the Ethnology Institute of the University of San Marcos (1946), the Institute of Ethnological Studies (1947) and the French Institute of Andean Studies (1948). The latter, still a key research establishment, is deeply linked to the important role that French scholars – originally around the Parisian Musée de l'Homme, founded by Paul Rivet – have played in Andean anthropology, especially in Bolivia. Founding these institutions decisively influenced the development of this field of study in Peru, an evolution differing from that in other countries. In this sense, Tristan Platt (personal communication) compares Peru and Bolivia, arguing that the former 'had and has a "proper" academic context for research and publication', while the latter 'always had a

---

19 It presented fieldwork-based work by pioneering authors (e.g. Valcárcel, Mishkin) and earlier works by key future scholars (e.g. Murra, Rowe). Pajuelo (2000, p. 132) considers it to be the 'starting point' for Andean communities' anthropology.

very unstable academic context'. Platt also explains that much of the work in Bolivia 'was done outside academia', published first 'in mimeographed form', and 'of course, in Spanish', responding often 'to immediate political situations and demands'.

Jorge P. Osterling and Héctor Martínez (1983, pp. 345-6) argue that there was not much interest in theoretical issues during the initial period, and anthropological work followed a practical and empirical approach. According to Degregori (2000a, p. 39) there were three main fields of study to begin with: folklore, communities, and applied anthropology projects, which were mostly community-based. In this context, Andean rural territories and peasants became dominant themes, such that Pajuelo (2000, p. 132) defines these decades as the 'golden age' of community studies in the region. Paradoxically, these origins of Andean anthropology, focused mainly on community ethnographies, coincided with a time when anthropologists elsewhere became increasingly interested in other types of settings and methodologies. New schools wanted to overcome the limitations of single-community ethnographies, developing alternative methods such as regional sampling and comparative approaches. As a result, in the 1950s–60s fieldwork methodology was increasingly refined and developed by new schools and authors. For example, Benjamin Paul (1953, p. 442) proposed a combination of different research methods to maximise the objectivity of ethnographic fieldwork, such as examining existing written materials like archives, observation-participation and interviews. Others introduced new techniques such as mapping, inventories and census work. Nevertheless indigenous cultures and peoples and community ethnographies remained central research foci while basic research methods remained essentially the same, involving participant-observation, gathering data, maintaining detailed records of events, and developing ideas and theories that have to be cross-checked and tested through different methods.

In the context of Andean ethnographies, descriptive approaches were dominant, firstly of individual communities in isolation, later frequently as part of wider projects or areas. An example of the former is the ethnography conducted by Elsie Clews Parsons, a pioneer of feminism and a follower of Franz Boas, in Peguche, situated in the northern Ecuadorian Otavalo region (Parsons, 1945). It was researched in 1941, and published after the author's death, with Murra's editorial help, becoming one of the first modern anthropological monographs published about the Andes. As other ethnographic research of the period in Latin America had done, the book shows how Indian culture has evolved after mixing and fusing with European traits. An example of a wider-ranging study is the Huarochirí-Yauyos project (1952-5), organised by the San Marcos University Ethnology Institute under the direction of José Matos

Mar. It compared 28 communities with each other and related them to their regional and national contexts (ed. Matos Mar, 1958).

An earlier division between 'short-' and 'long-termist' approaches to Andean cultures and communities can be traced to this initial period, with the predominant foci depending on either social change or historical continuities respectively. The former can be theoretically linked to schools such as *desarrollismo* [developmentalism], and particularly to applied anthropology, whose projects were directed to provoke social change and development in certain communities or areas, with the aim of spreading their positive effects. Javier Ávila (2000a, p. 415) criticises such applied anthropology, arguing that it was a strategy of containment for revolutionary ideologies in the context of the Cold War.[20] He also explains that, although the projects were supposedly based on the respect of the beneficiaries' cultures, they were actually based on paternalistic and prejudiced positions that considered cultural assimilation as the ultimate goal and ideal (ibid., pp. 416-7).[21] In the case of Peru, Degregori (2000a, pp. 41-2) argues that the most remarkable aspect of these projects was how massive and spontaneous peasant movements and revolts in many ways surpassed the objectives. Taking place between the late 1950s and mid 1960s, these mostly took the form of occupation of hacienda lands by Andean communities claiming that these lands had been taken from them. Significantly, they managed to almost eliminate the previously dominant hacienda system without any anthropological influence. Nevertheless, these and other projects and initiatives resulted in abundant community ethnographies that generally focused on the study of social change.[22] They tended to look at settlements considered to be examples of 'progress', a term that encompasses the gradual overcoming of traditional ways through acculturation and integration into national life and the market economy. Examples of this approach in Peru are the community ethnographies of Paul L. Doughty (1968) in the Huaylas district (Ancash), and Richard Adams (1968 [1959]) in the Muquiyauyo community (Junín).

---

20   Most 20th-century revolutions (such as Mexico, Russia, Vietnam) had important peasant components, so great attention was paid to this collective during the Cold War (Ávila, 2000a, pp. 423-4).

21   The most famous was the aforementioned Peru-Cornell project (1952-72), which focused on the Vicos hacienda (Callejón de Huaylas, Ancash), rented by Cornell University. The project was relatively successful (e.g. former workers became land owners, living standards increased), but it did not meet the expectations created by the level of investment and effort. See Ávila (2000a, pp. 418-21), who also reviews similar projects from that period. Also see https://courses.cit.cornell.edu/vicosperu/vicos-site/. Several contributors to this volume also refer to the project in their chapters.

22   Valcárcel (1985 [1980], pp. 22-3), then director of San Marcos University Ethnology Institute, explains that the plan was to combine the study of continuities and change, but that in the end the latter predominated.

In contrast, long-termism in this period could be theoretically linked to American culturalism, and identified with authors such as those linked to the *Handbook of South American Indians* (for example, Mishkin, Tschopik, Kubler, Valcárcel). These scholars were generally more interested in long-term historical continuities, and in other classical anthropological themes such as kinship and ritual life,[23] as exemplified by the work Tschopik (1955) carried out in Chucuito, an Aymara community in Lake Titicaca (Puno). Frank Salomon (personal communication) argues that 'even "classical" ethnographers arrived in countries that already had projects not defined by the discipline of sociocultural anthropology'; and that 'what Harris calls "long-termism" is largely a product of convergence with them', as well as a 'product of the salience of Inka as canonical theme in Western theories of the state since the seventeenth century' (more on this theme below). Degregori (2000a, p. 43) affirms that during this period the focus on social change was highly significant, although community ethnographies predominately concentrated on historical continuities. In these studies, Andean communities were often considered to be practically frozen-in-time,[24] especially those where communal traditions and native languages had been better preserved.

These contrasting dominant approaches, with the focus on communities considered to be either progressive and acculturated or ageless and immovable, resulted in a simplified, misleading dichotomy. This simplification therefore undermines the validity of and interest in studies conducted under such premises. However, more nuanced and flexible approaches already existed, as exemplified by the work of José M. Arguedas, who set out to examine historical continuities and cultural phenomena in a context of social change. For instance, in his article (1956) about the community of Puquio (Ayacucho), significantly called '*Una cultura en proceso de cambio*' [a culture in flux]. It is already possible to identify in this initial period a geographical divide – which would continue – between a long-termist focus on areas considered to be more 'traditional', such as the southern Peruvian highlands and Bolivia, and a short-termist focus on areas considered to be more 'modern' or 'acculturated', such as the central, northern and coastal highlands of Peru and those of Ecuador. During this same period, wider academic developments influenced Andean anthropology and the study of highland communities. For example, authors such as Robert Redfield and Eric R. Wolf offered new interpretations of and approaches to Latin American peasants, exploring among other topics the

---

23 Salomon (personal communication) explains that the *Handbook*'s editor, J.H. Steward, was 'interested only in a highly abstracted long evolutionary term, but some of his contributors … [adopted] diachronic [perspectives] more in the vein of historiography.'

24 For example, the Peruvian newspaper *La Prensa* sponsored a notorious 1955 expedition to the community of Q'ero (Cuzco), made by a prestigious multidisciplinary team to study local culture. The expedition was presented as 'a journey to the past' (Pajuelo, 2000, p. 141).

rural/urban or tradition/modernity dichotomies. Amid these, Wolf's (1955, 1957) categorisation of 'open' and 'closed corporate' peasant communities had an important impact in the Andes, particularly in the subsequent period.[25] Meanwhile anthropology in Andean countries turned to important historical processes that were going on at the time. For instance, as Harris (2000a, p. 6) explains, in Bolivia interest was focused on the effects of the 1952 revolution and the resulting land reform. At the same time the new field of interest in Peru was emigration from Andean to coastal and urban areas, especially to Lima. Emigration was reaching massive heights at the time, leading to the beginning of urban anthropology there (see Golte, 2000; Sandoval, 2000).

This was also the period when a new generation of scholars emerged in Andean countries, changing the study of the past via a new academic perspective, ethnohistory. Most important among them were the aforementioned Rowe, Murra, and Zuidema, who eclipsed previous dominant – and ideologically partisan – approaches to the study of the Inca empire.[26] They pointed out the flaws of the colonial chronicles (for example biased Spanish perspectives, privileged Inca versions), using alternative written sources (for example administrative records, census reports). Furthermore, they introduced new theoretical influences and a multidisciplinary approach that incorporated archaeology and especially ethnography.[27] As a result, the study of the Andean past became intimately linked to the study of its present, through the search for continuities and the comparison with colonial sources. These scholars had a great influence over Andean anthropology in subsequent years, when their historical and comparative approaches became key reference points for the study of contemporary Andean peoples.

'Classical' period (mid 1960s–80s)

I have defined this as a classical period of Andean anthropology because of the quality and quantity of the work produced, and the advances that took place in knowledge of past and present Andean cultures and communities. This was a

25 Wolf (1955) employed the corporate community category to characterise Andean and Mesoamerican rural areas. Later, he compared communities in Mesoamerica and Java, using the 'closed corporate' concept to define their defence mechanisms against externally induced change (1957).

26 Some authors considered the Inca empire to be 'socialist', comparing it with the Soviet Union, especially during the 1920s period (e.g. Baudin, 1961 [1928]).

27 Murra introduced the theoretical influence of the French Annales School, and Karl Polanyi's concepts of reciprocity and redistribution in pre-capitalist societies; as well as a focus on ecological adaptation. Zuidema introduced structuralism, giving it a Dutch School historical perspective gained from his studies at Leiden with P.E. Josselin de Jong. Meanwhile Rowe, who was trained in classics and art history, introduced a strict interpretation of data in contexts such as texts, textiles and archaeological sites. These scholars came from Europe or the USA and started to work in the Andes during this period, influencing ethnohistorians from foreign lands (e.g. Wachtel, Duviols) and Andean countries (e.g. Rostworowski, Pease).

direct result of the historical contexts, at a time of radical politics (for example, Latin America becoming a Cold War battlefield) and rapid social change. In Peru this transformation is exemplified by General Juan Velasco's revolutionary military regime (1968-75), which in 1969 enhanced the greatest land reform ever in Latin America. This wider context also brought important changes within academia, such as the increasing influence of emerging ideologies and theoretical schools (for example, Marxism, dependency theory, structuralism, cultural ecology) and thematic diversification (such as emigration, social movements). As Harris (2000a, pp. 6-7) explains, by the late 1960s a radical version of modernisation theory emerged in Latin America, and political mobilisation led to a renewed interest in Marxist theory. This brought 'a radical and much-needed rethink of the political and economic relations within which peasant communities were embedded' (ibid.). As a result, by the 1970s Marxism dominated many universities in Andean countries, especially in Peru, although its influence was problematic. Degregori (2000a, p. 46) defines the dominant Marxism of the 1970s as 'manual', criticising its dogmatic character and negligence of culture and empirical investigation, particularly fieldwork. Nevertheless, this historical and academic context contributed to new sensibilities towards and interests in subaltern peoples such as indigenous groups and peasants.

On the other hand, Andean anthropology acquired a new dimension academically speaking, resulting from the framework ethnohistorians provided to approach the contemporary Andean world from the study of its past. Murra can be considered as the main author behind this. He wanted to interpret the Andean past in its own terms, beyond western paradigms, identifying a series of key concepts (such as reciprocity, redistribution) and institutions (for example, ayllu, *ayni*),[28] whose particular expressions he deemed common and exclusive to this world, specifically to the core Andean region. He used these as the main tools to explain and interpret the Andean past. This approach, which Golte (2000, pp. 209-11) defines as '*substantivismo*' [substantivism],[29] became particularly influential in the study of contemporary Andean cultures and communities due to their striking historical continuities. Moreover, Murra identified particular strategies of ecological adaptation among past Andean peoples, who accessed as many ecological zones as possible, complementing

---

28 Ayni is another key, complex and ancient Andean concept used mainly to define different types of reciprocal relations, such as work-exchange systems between families in Andean communities.
29 The term substantivism was coined by Karl Polanyi in his book *The Great Transformation* (1944). Salomon (personal communication) notes how its use here refers to debates generated by Polanyi's work in the 1950s.

and diversifying economic activities, resources and production.[30] His theories were highly successful and ecological adaptation became a main research focus for Andean studies in the 1970s–80s. Soon, other authors started to look for evidence, variations or the persistence of such strategies in past and present Andean ethnic groups and communities, with more or less success and originality.

Zuidema was also a key influence. Linked to the structuralist school, he focused on the exploration of Inca kinship, calendar, myths and Cuzco's sociospatial organisation (for example, 1964). Harris (2000a, p. 9) compares him with Claude Lévi-Strauss[31] for his 'seemingly intuitive grasp of what fragmentary references in the sources of indigenous beliefs and practices might signify'. Harris also summarises the influence of these two authors:

> Murra's highlighting of key aspects of Inca social and economic organization, and Zuidema's sensibility to symbolic forms together provided powerful tools for understanding the cultural practices of indigenous peasants in the Andes. Their work is historical but at the same time indicated a preference for understanding the quality of lived experience in the past, rather than the dynamic of historical transformation. Their work also encouraged the strategy of cross-referencing sixteenth- and twentieth-century materials. (ibid.)

Many anthropologists started to apply their theoretical approaches to contemporary Andean cultures and communities, focusing on historical continuities. As Harris (ibid., p. 10) points out: 'The emphasis on continuities from the 16th to the 20th centuries and on unique features of Andean civilization proved a powerful and influential combination, which by the early-1980s became identified in shorthand as *lo andino*' (the Andean). As a result Andean peasants became a distinctive field of study within anthropology, although Andean ethnography has had a small impact on the wider discipline 'suggesting a degree of localism and introversion' (ibid., p. 1). In a similar vein, Starn (1994, p. 16) talks about limited public diffusion and insularity within the discipline resulting from lack of participation in broader scholarly debates, and from more emphasis on some exclusive concepts. Nevertheless, this kind of approach was not exclusive to the Andean world. From a critical perspective, Les W. Field (1994) links it to a 'cultural survival position' (or school) in the wider context of the ethnographic study of indigenous cultures

---

30 Murra developed his theories and ideas over a long period, but his *Formaciones económicas y políticas del mundo andino* (1975) is the principal work to compile, summarise and articulate them. Van-Buren (1996) critically traces the influences of Murra's work.

31 Lévi-Strauss's structuralism was based on the assumption that the human mind works through a universal logic of dualities or binary oppositions (e.g. life versus death).

in Latin America.[32] He also argues that this school tended to identify particular indigenous cultures, assigning them 'fixed cultural traits, particular language, worldview and its rituals, social organization and leadership' (ibid., p. 237).

During this period anthropological approaches to Andean culture and communities were increasingly complex and elaborate, and the differentiation between long- and short-termism reached new dimensions. The former can logically be associated with those that were more influenced by ethnohistorians and their approaches, while the latter remained more associated with concerns about developmental and social change. It also became influenced by emerging ideologies, particularly by Marxism, and interested in key political events and changes of the period, such as the Peruvian land reform of 1969.

In an ideologically polarised context, tensions had been increasing between long- and short-termism since the late 1960s. This was partially the result of a certain confrontation between ethnohistory and Marxism-influenced leanings, even though they were not necessarily mutually exclusive. As Harris (2009) points out, some authors accused others of romanticising indigenous cultures and over-emphasising historical continuities; while the latter criticised the former for the limited temporal validity of their approach, and for a tendency to neglect non-material aspects of life such as religion and culture. As an example of this confrontation, Enrique Mayer (2005, p. 11), a prestigious author linked to the long-termism approach and also a contributor here, recalls how, in the 1971 International Congress of Americanists, celebrated in Lima, the French anthropologist Henri Favre criticised Murra and Zuidema for influencing their students in adopting a 'romantic and selective interpretation' of life in Andean communities, as 'continuities from the past'. Mayer, who also mentions that episode in his contribution to this volume, explains that he, a student of Murra, and B.J. Isbell, a student of Zuidema, attended the congress together. Significantly, as I show below, Favre's accusations have much in common with others that emerged later, in the context of 1990s revisionism, demonstrating the long history of these academic debates.

Assessments are contradictory as to which tendency dominated these decades. Harris (2009), a self-defined long-termist, affirms that her option dominated, while Pajuelo (2000, p. 143) asserts that there was more interest in change than in continuities. My view is that long-termism tended to dominate among foreign authors, who generally had a more pan-Andean vocation, while short-termism was more dominant among writers from Andean countries, who generally tended to more national perspectives and greater engagement with

---

32 Field (ibid.) traces the theoretical roots of this school to Boas in the USA, who 'tightly bound language, material culture, and cultural identities together', and to British structural functionalism, 'which imagines social relations as a homeostatic organism in which individual and collective behaviors are defined by cultural norms and values in order to maintain social equilibrium.'

politics.³³ Nevertheless, it is again necessary to keep in mind that this division is relative in relation to predominant propensities rather than to neatly defined schools or ideologies. Over and above that, more flexible and overlapping approaches exist. For example, Ávila (2000a, pp. 193–4) explains how during the 1970s–80s an emergent generation of Andeanists set out to break the gap between ethnohistory and Marxism (for example, Alberto Flores-Galindo, Manuel Burga, Steve J. Stern, Karen Spalding).³⁴ They introduced the study of mentalities and offered new visions of contemporary Andean peasants (and communities) as a product of dynamic resistance and continuous readaptation.

Community ethnographies started to decline within anthropology during this period, as the discipline went through important changes, especially from the 1970s. New schools and tendencies emerged as a result of the 1960s political and social context (for example, counter-culture, feminism, radical politics). One of these, political economy, was influenced by Marxism and set out to look at the effect of global capitalism in practically any context, moving away from traditional ethnology and community ethnographies. Tristan Platt (personal communication) points out how these changes were experienced in Britain, and how they affected such studies:

> I think it is important to remember that the queries about the isolated nature of local ethnographies began already in the 1960s and 1970s. That was when the London Alternative Anthropology Group was founded, which gave rise to [the journal] *Critique of Anthropology*. Certainly many of us then were aware of these criticisms and the real limitations of local ethnography in the 1970s. We did not need to wait for the postmodern fashions of the 1980s and 90s, which was a de-Marxified (neoliberal?) version of what had already gone before. We were demanding a politico-economic presence in social anthropology … This meant that, although those of us who began in the 1960s and 70s continued to believe in the value of local ethnography, we were sure that it could not stand on its own, but had to take into account the history and political economy of the wider society, the growth of capital, etc.

In the context of Andean anthropology, community ethnographies maintained a central role, although not as much as before following increasing thematic diversification. Degregori (2000a, p. 44) notes how there was an evolution from more descriptive to more interpretative approaches, and also a tendency to broaden projects, studying communities within certain microregions or areas. Importantly, during these years significant attempts were also made to systematise information provided by the previous ethnographies

---

33 Long-termist authors were often linked to leading ethnohistorians, who had a wider international profile, attracting many foreign scholars. A divided core (European-North American world)/periphery (Andean countries) can be perceived here, as scholars from Andean countries rarely have the international projection of their foreign peers.

34 Pajuelo (2000, p. 156) identifies several Peruvian works that combine both approaches, e.g. Alberti and Mayer (eds.), 1973.

(such as Dobyns, 1970; Fuenzalida-Vollmar, 1976 [1969]; Matos Mar, 1965); to explore the historical origins and evolution of Andean communities (for example Arguedas, 1978 [1968]; Hurtado, 1974); and to define their nature. For example, Fonseca (1985, pp. 73–5) explains different interpretations of Andean communities in the 20th century as:

- continuities of pre-Hispanic ayllus (for example Castro-Pozo, 1979 [1924])
- mere transplants of European institutions, basically by Marxists who considered the colonial regime as a form of feudalism (such as Mariátegui, 2005 [1928]; Díaz-Martínez, 1985 [1969]; Hurtado, 1974)
- a product of conquest (such as Wolf, 1957; Fuenzalida-Vollmar, 1976 [1969])
- an original product of cultural syncretism (for example Arguedas, 1978 [1968]).[35]

An example of short-termist approaches to community ethnographies in this period is the project, 'Proyecto de estudios de cambios en pueblos Peruanos' [Studies of change in Peruvian villages], carried out by the Instituto de Estudios Peruanos. It set out to study 27 communities in the Andean valleys of Chancay (Lima) and Mataro (Junín) in the second half of the 1960s, with the collaboration of Cornell and several Peruvian universities. As with others discussed from the previous period, the project's philosophy consisted of identifying communities considered to be positive or negative examples of progress, largely understood as integration into the market economy and elimination of traditional lifestyles. The resulting ethnographies examined the factors that created or hindered social change and the above concept of progress in these communities and areas. An example of this is Degregori and Golte's ethnography of Pacaraos (Lima) (1973). The authors present Pacaraos as a negative example, considering it as involving a process of 'structural disintegration', caused by its 'conservative' character and 'weak integration' (ibid., p. 5). They also compare it, negatively, with other communities (Lampián and Huayopampa), studied as part of the same project, that were considered to be undergoing a process of modernisation through the introduction of commercial crops. This study introduces key theoretical references of the period, such as dependency theory, Murra's ecological adaptation hypothesis, and Wolf's concept of closed corporate community. However, it still presents a concept of progress as acculturation, and a general rejection or negligence of traditional culture that is common in short-termist ethnographies of this period.

---

35 Fonseca's work on this topic has recently been republished in an extended version (Fonseca and Mayer, 2015).

In contrast, long-termist approaches to community ethnographies during these decades tend to focus on traditional aspects of local culture, and to present positive and often idealised images of them. As already noted, these approaches were influenced by the theoretical framework offered by ethnohistory, with its new interpretative tools, leading to a qualitative leap forward in the study of Andean culture and communities. As a result, the ethnographies produced employing these approaches often transcended their particular case studies, becoming key references for the examination of the particular themes, and sometimes even classics. These were among those that formed part of my introduction to Andean anthropology, and of my library in Taulli, and some of their authors have contributed to this volume.

The aforementioned Isbell (1978) and Allen (1988) are among these. The former's ethnography of Chuschi (Ayacucho) has become a key reference work in the study and understanding of local ritual life, kinship and sociospatial organisation of Andean communities. Isbell theoretically combines influences of Zuidema's structuralism, Murra's ecological concerns and Wolf's concept of 'closed corporate community'. She argues that traditional social organisation and rituals serve as mechanisms by which Chuschinos' *comuneros* (in the sense of communal organisation members) 'defend' their 'closed' society against the influence of unstoppable social change, revealing the tensions and contradictions that result from such a dynamic. For example, in the context of an internal social division between *comuneros* [in the sense of commoners] and *vecinos* [neighbours as notables].[36] Similarly, Allen's study of Sonqo (Cuzco) is a key reference work in the understanding of the role of coca in Andean culture. She argues that coca is the major ritual vehicle which serves as a bridge between the world of the people and their land in this community, and as a 'link between the social and the spiritual', using concepts such as reciprocity and dualism to explain local society and religious and ritual life (1988, p. 17).

Other classical community ethnographies from this period to take this theoretical approach are the study on the agricultural use and wider connotations of astronomy in Misminay (Cuzco) by Gary Urton (1981), and the exploration of religious pilgrimages in Qamawara (Cuzco), by Michael J.

---

36 Many highland communities of the core Andean region have demonstrated internal social divisions between such groups, widely identified as indigenous and mixed-race respectively, in the 20th century. Vecinos would not participate in communal organisation, becoming intermediaries with the state through the near-monopoly of commerce and public jobs (such as teachers, political authorities), accumulating local lands and resources, and establishing dominating relationships with comuneros, who tended to be monolingual native language speakers and illiterate. In many communities this internal social division would have a spatial dimension, according to divisions in neighbourhoods or ayllus that would belong exclusively or predominately to one group or another. Many ethnographies have also made this division their central focus of study, and several have demonstrated how, at least in the late 20th century, it was based more on different self-perceptions and conceptions of life than in real past or present ethnic differences (e.g. Gose, 2001 [1994]; Sallnow, 1987).

Sallnow (1987). The former is a seminal work in the rich and complex field of Andean ethnoastronomy, in which the author examines astronomical observation and the correlation of solar and lunar cycles in relation to the agropastoral sequence of yearly tasks in this community. Urton looks for continuities from and differences with Inca times, by comparison with colonial chronicles and Zuidema's studies of Inca astronomy. The latter is a basic reference work for approaching Andean pilgrimages as a key aspect of past and present religiosity in the region. The author argues that pilgrimages are part of 'certain religious structures and processes' that 'are endemic to central Andes society and have continued to manifest themselves, transformed, to the present day', mingling Christian and pre-colonial beliefs (Sallnow, 1987, p. 26). This ethnography also demonstrates the wider dimensions of these pilgrimages, such as their commercial links (through markets and fairs), or their role as a channel through which participants strengthen and renew their social bonds, in the context of a sacralised landscape.[37] Another good example of community ethnography from this period, the authors of which have also contributed to this volume, is the study of Yanque Urinsaya produced by Ricardo Valderrama and Carmen Escalante (1989). This focuses on an examination of irrigation, and its social and ritual dimensions, in the Colca Valley of Arequipa – nowadays very touristy. It is a seminal work in this key field of Andean agriculture and culture. The authors explore the intimate relationship between local social organisation, the cult of water, and the management and maintenance of local irrigation, stressing its environmental sustainability and the ideological universe and system of values that underlie this activity.

Other excellent community ethnographies generally following similar thematic approaches are based on fieldwork undertaken during this period, especially the 1980s, although they were published later on and incorporated wider theoretical references. One example is the Huaquirca (Apurímac) ethnography produced by Peter Gose (2004; 2001; 1994), another contributor here. He focuses on the local vecinos/comuneros internal division, which is interpreted as a class division rather than an ethnic one from a Marxist-influenced perspective. Gose also explores local agropastoral rituals, as deeply

---

[37] Other interesting community and community-based ethnographies produced in this period which follow similar approaches are the works of Urton (1990, 1984) on myths, ethnohistory and spatial organisation in Pacariqtambo (Cuzco). In Bolivia, examples include Harris's (2000b) articles on the Laymi ayllu (Northern Potosí); Bastien's (1978) on the ritual life of the Kaata ayllu (mid-western Bolivia); and the study of traditional authorities among the Yura ayllu (Potosí) by Rasnake (1989 [1988]). Generally, all these predominantly long-termist studies present highly interesting ethnographic information, and rich and elaborate interpretations of local culture. However, some of them tend to present more idealised and ageless visions of these cultures, veering towards neglecting or underestimating social change (for example Bastien, 1978), while others present more flexible approaches to them, and to the dynamics between change and continuity, generally resulting in more convincing and nuanced works (for example Harris, 2000b).

interrelated with the cult of ancestors and mountain spirits, and as part of ancient wider religious and social beliefs. Another example is the study of the Cobanaconde community (Colca Valley, Arequipa) by Paul Gelles (2002 [2000]). It focuses on local irrigation, which combines traditional and state management, presenting particularly rich ritual and symbolic dimensions, linked to an internal dual sociospatial division. The author shows how Andean traditional beliefs and ritual practices are compatible with globalisation and transnationalisation processes, and addresses contemporary academic concerns.

Revisionism, diversification and assimilation (1990s–present)

During the 1980s, postmodernism emerged in academia, as a whole set of ideas and tendencies that emphasised the subjectivity of experiences and knowledge. In the context of anthropology, a new generation of scholars advocated for new ways to study culture. Some questioned the authority and legitimacy of western approaches to and studies of non-western cultures, considering them as prejudiced, stereotyped or charged with postcolonial connotation (for example, Said, 1979). The validity of anthropological knowledge and ethnographic fieldwork was also questioned (for example Clifford, 1988), as it was even argued that ethnographies are just another form of creative writing that privilege their authors' perspectives. As a result, many anthropologists retreated from this type of fieldwork during the 1980s–90s, turning towards more theoretical perspectives and alternative methods; and community ethnographies generally came to be considered as outdated. Above all, ethnography acquired a much more self-reflective approach (reflexivity), and this kind of writing took a literary turn towards a more nuanced engagement with the subjects of study and, at least theoretically, an increasing political and social awareness.[38]

The 1980s decade was also a time of dramatic historical change in Andean countries and Latin America more broadly with processes of democratisation from military regimes, economic and debt crisis in a context of neoliberal reform, armed conflicts in countries like Peru. This led to a widespread neoliberal hegemony in the 1990s that has persisted in many countries since then, and in most of the world, and also had an impact on academia. For example, Linda J. Seligman (2008, p. 325) points out how studies of peasants and the peasant category diminished dramatically since that decade among scholars of Latin America.[39] She argues that these studies corresponded to a particular moment in history, and resulted in rich and varied debates surrounding the subject

---

38 Paradoxically, as Degregori (2000a, p. 56) points out, this radical critique of ethnography went on at the same time as other disciplines (such as cultural geography, pedagogy) increasingly incorporated it as a methodology.

39 According to her this took place due to a combination of factors such as 'the peculiar construct of the category of peasant', 'the failure of both reform and revolution' in previous decades, and 'the conditions of violence that made field research difficult' (ibid.).

that challenged existing notions of economic and political systems and how they worked (ibid.). For her, Latin American anthropology in general, and Peruvian in particular, have been shaped by debates that have emerged from these studies (ibid., p. 326). However, she also makes the critical comments that 'the concept of peasants was invoked as a political instrument, transformed sometimes into a utopian ideal that blinded many scholars to significant transformations in the ways that rural inhabitants in general were making a living, constructing their identities, and drawing on a wide range of political resources in the process' (ibid., p. 325). Such evolution logically contributed to a decline in the study of rural communities and peoples, Andean and others. It therefore contributed to a corresponding decline in community ethnographies as a research methodology and setting.

In the context of Andean anthropology, postmodern tendencies were increasingly influential, leading to a reaction against the dominant paradigms of the classical period by a new generation of scholars in the early 1990s. This reaction was mainly directed at long-termist approaches, and was linked to a rejection of community ethnographies as a methodology, culminating in heated criticisms and revisionism. Starn best exemplifies this revisionism in the series of articles he wrote during this period (1991; 1992a; 1994).[40] Then a young scholar starting his career, he criticised 1960s–80s long-termism identifying it with the concepts of the Andean and Andeanism. His censure stemmed from Edward Said's book *Orientalism* (1979), which disparaged dominant western views of oriental societies as a certain kind of prejudiced exoticism. In a similar vein, Starn linked long-termist approaches to Andean culture with an idealisation of the native, and the 'proclivity for presenting contemporary peasants as noble inheritors of pure and ancient traditions' (1994, p. 16). Specifically, he used Isbell's classic ethnography of Chuschi as a central example of this approach. This choice was highly symbolic because Shining Path had perpetrated its first violent action in Chuschi in 1980, not long after Isbell's work had been published in 1978. Starn criticised the inability of Isbell and other ethnographers to perceive the conditions that led to the armed conflict in Ayacucho, where abundant fieldwork and community ethnographies had been conducted in previous years. Starn blamed the focus on historical continuities and on the essentialisation of Andean culture for this inability, using Isbell's presentation of Chuschi as a closed corporate community to illustrate his

---

40 These articles are successive reelaborations of the same ideas, and they attracted both heated criticism and support. The Peruvian journal *Allpanchis* dedicated a special issue to this debate in 1992, including a Spanish version of the first article and several responses, while the 1994 article revisited the polemic, including further feedback.

point, and rejecting this type of study as having a too partial and subjective research methodology and setting.[41]

Meanwhile, and also following revisionist perspectives, other authors criticised more key aspects of that 1960s–80s long-termism, such as Murra's theories of ecological adaptation (Van-Buren, 1996), or the idea of an Andean 'exclusiveness' (for example Stanish, 2001). This criticism reached the Andean concept itself, which Starn (1994, p. 16) defined as 'an artificial occidental invention' associated with 'a topical view' of 'a timeless Andean World', arguing that there was never a singular Andean tradition. Field (1994) contextualised this period's revisionism as part of a wider 'resistance school' emerging at the time in the 'analysis and representation' of Latin American indigenous cultures and peoples. The followers of this school, he stated, brought an 'anti-essentialist' perspective, and a new focus on 'the processual nature of indigenous identities' (ibid., p. 237). Field also traced the theoretical references of this school to Nestor G. Canclini's concepts of hybridity in Latin America (2001 [1992]), and to the critiques of western approaches to ethnography, by James Clifford (1988) among others.[42] As a result of these leanings, Andean anthropology in general, and community ethnographies in particular, gradually lost most of the previous period's idiosyncrasy, tending to merge with wider anthropological concerns and tendencies. A certain amount of fragmentation has been caused by further diversification of the discipline in recent decades. I have therefore defined this ongoing period as one of revisionism (in the 1990s), and of assimilation and fragmentation (since the 2000s).

My personal view of this academic evolution is that 1990s revisionism rightly identified and criticised negative aspects of the 1960s–80s long-termism (for example, pointing out tendencies towards romanticisation and essentialisation). However, I also believe that the overall rejection of this entire perspective was deeply unfair and academically nihilistic, as it dismissed valid

41 Frank Salomon (personal communication) points out how Eric R. Wolf, who created the concept of closed corporate community in the 1950s, paradoxically 'predated' 1990s revisionism by demanding 'a general alteration of scale' in his *Europe and the People without History* (Wolf, 1982). This book explores the historical trajectory of modern globalisation, challenging the long-held anthropological notion that non-European cultures and peoples were isolated and static entities before the advent of European colonialism. It also emphasises the role of the people silenced by western history as active participants in the creation of new cultural and social forms emerging in the context of commercial empire. Salomon also points out how some British social anthropologists, especially Africanists of the decolonising era, had also adopted a 'rising scale' since the 1970s for different reasons.

42 Field (1994, p. 237), a follower of this school, argues that indigenous identities are continuously redefined by their self-identified protagonists, in the context of 'a struggle for resources' waged between hegemonic sectors of the nation-state and 'the social organizations of indigenous communities'. Field also argues that indigenous cultures with 'little or no connection' to pre-colonial societies have been extensively moulded by colonialism, and that 'the resistance struggle itself has become the primary characteristic of Indian ethnicity' (ibid.).

and useful aspects of it, and negated its overall positive contribution to the study of Andean culture. For example, regarding the much-criticised concept of the Andean, I found it to be a valid practical category established on the basis of some objective elements (for example, historical and cultural similarities across the core Andean region). As such, it can be considered no more artificial than any division in academic disciplines in that they are merely practical categories introduced to help approach the study of our world. It is also my perception that this revisionism and the rejection of community ethnographies were influenced by certain academic fashionability. It should be taken into account that this could also be linked to wider academic dynamics, and the way new vogues and schools tend to emerge – with greater or lesser justification and fairness – as a reaction against pre-existing ones. In my view such dynamics often present a certain 'ritualistic character', with hints of Marxist dialectics, which would benefit from anthropological examination in its own right.

I believe that, in the particular case of Starn's articles, some sections of his critiques certainly provide the basis for valuable insights, being also partially interpretable or understandable as youthful rebellion against conventional or mainstream wisdom. However, I also believe that his focus on Isbell's community ethnography is especially unfortunate and misleading, as he homed in on the parts that fitted his argument, neglecting those that did not. For example, Starn does not mention the fact that Isbell's central argument includes the idea that the closeness of Chuschi's society was a kind of illusion that local comuneros tried to maintain in a context of unstoppable social change; that she dedicated a whole chapter to local emigration to Lima, as a key factor of ongoing transformations in the community; or the fact that this study actually and vividly showed deep social and political tensions at the local and regional level that contribute to explaining and contextualising the subsequent violence.[43]

Several contributors to this edited volume refer critically to this notorious academic polemic in their chapters. I therefore thought that it would be interesting and fair to give Starn the opportunity to offer his own reassessment, mirroring the contributors' retrospective perspectives. I contacted him and he kindly agreed to participate in this retrospective exercise, answering the questions reproduced below:

> ***What do you think of your critiques to 'Andeanism' in retrospective? What parts would you maintain or change if any?*** I wrote the original 'Missing the Revolution' essay in 1989. I was 29, in another life. There was certainly an Oedipal dimension to it all, the angry young anthropologist raging against his disciplinary fathers (and mothers). And, of course, I was influenced by the moment in anthropology and the academy. That was the era of the so-called 'postmodern turn' in anthropology and the rising

---

43 Sendón (2006) offers a much more detailed review of this polemic (in Spanish).

influence of poststructuralist and postcolonial theory. It was also a decade, it should be remembered, of war and crisis in the largest Andean country, Peru. I was living in Lima when I wrote 'Missing the Revolution'. The spectre of such sometimes world-destroying upheaval made the staid conventions of Andean 'community' ethnography seem all the more inadequate to me. Are not we all, like it or not, the products of our times? I know I was.

I would like to think I am wiser now, although, like many in middle age, I sometimes wish I had the same energy and conviction of my younger self. If I were to write the essay again, I would be more generous. I would also do a better job of contextualising the development of Andeanist anthropology. And yet, I do not regret the essay at all. I think it did need work in shaking up a somewhat in-grown, unreflective subfield. The problem of what I called 'Andeanism' was real in anthropology and in general; you still see it all the time in the exoticising imagery of the tourist brochures and the adventure channel shows. I worry, in fact, that some new scholarship around 'alternative ontologies' and 'Andean cosmovision' recycles the same old tired tropes of a timeless indigenous other imagined in opposition to the modern west. Anyone who travels across the Andes knows it is an area unlike any other in the world. It has never been, however, ... [an] island ... [unscathed by] history and modernity. I do not quite understand why we can still be so stubborn sometimes about projecting our own wishful fantasies of a noble, untouched, ancient way of life on to the mixed-up, often very difficult 21st-century realities of Andean peoples.

Is your thinking still the same about community ethnographies as a methodology, and Andean communities as a focus of study? If not, what do you think now and why? I did a kind of 'community ethnography' for my dissertation. It was a study of the *rondas campesinas*, or peasant patrols, in a dusty Andean foothill village in Piura. There is certainly a place still for village-based ethnographies, albeit ones freed from the old conventions. But it is now impossible to imagine the village ethnography should or could any longer be the only form of anthropology about life in the region. As anthropology has metamorphosed from studying the primitive to studying just about everything, that has been reflected in the Andes. So now we have the ethnography of punk rockers, soap operas, elite enclave neighbourhoods, the cocaine trade, shantytowns, street kids, the police, mining and much more. There's no returning to the old anthropology that limited itself just to the village or the tribe. And I think this pluralisation of the topics of investigation in Andeanist anthropology, if we can still even call it that, is very much a good thing.

In any case, as a result of this revisionism, 1960s–80s long-termism became largely discredited in the 1990s. Some authors who were linked to it continued their work undisturbed by the polemics, while others turned more towards history and other academic concerns, or engaged to varying degrees with self-criticism. Isbell addresses these polemics in chapter 1, where she also explains how she was deeply affected and haunted by the armed conflict. As a consequence she worked extensively on this topic, and also faced and exorcised her related demons through theatre and ethnographic fiction.

Academic criticism and the discrediting of 1960s–80s long-termism took place at the same time as many of its key aspects became popular, and were appropriated, in other spheres. For example, development policies and legislation towards Andean regions and communities incorporated an emphasis on concepts like reciprocity and Andean cosmology, as part of an increasing attention to and sensibility towards local cultures and traditions. Moreover, Andean peoples started to appropriate these elements in discourses about themselves, and, as Salomon (personal communication) argues, Andean cultural anthropology gained a whole new intellectual frame as a result (see Poole, 2008). Similarly, Xavier Ricard-Lanata (2005, p. 11) points out that the academic revisionism of 'the Andean' paralleled the concept's increasing popularity in international politics (for example, initiatives of economic regional integration like the 1997-founded 'Andean Community of Nations') and social movements (for example, emerging indigenous movements claiming a pan-Andean identity, especially in Bolivia).

Despite the decline of peasant studies, and the critiques to community ethnographies, the latter continued to be produced during the 1990s, even though they were less abundant and lost much of their previous importance. These ethnographies generally show a continuity of the division short-/long-termism, and some of its related problematic (for example respective emphasis on change/cultural phenomena) and geographical divide (respective focus on acculturated/traditional regions). They also demonstrate a predominance of short-termist approaches, which tended to be influenced by the revisionism of these years, and to present new thematic and theoretical foci and references, examples of which can be found in the ethnography of Ariasucu (Otavalo) in Ecuador, produced by Rudolf J. Colloredo-Mansfield (1999), one of this volume's contributors. He explores how culture, class and race interrelate in this community (*sector* in Ecuador), focusing on material culture and indigenous social economy from the field of consumption studies. Another example is Erdmute Alber's (1999 [1993]) exploration of the Peruvian community of Huayopampa[44] (Lima), where the author explains how local people changed completely traditional settlement patterns and economic activities, in order to become the exclusive producers of fruits for Lima's market. Alber focuses on local migration, which is characterised by its mobility between the community and urban centres, rejecting the Andean (1960s–80s long-termism) from a revisionist-influenced perspective.

---

44 Alber (1999 [1993], p. 91) explains that she chose Huayopampa because it had been the object of previous ethnographic studies, defining it as a 'classical community'. This revisiting strategy has been common, allowing the changes and contrastive theoretical approaches to be explored.

Community ethnographies with more or less long-termist approaches were also produced in the 1990s, following previous paradigms, or incorporating new and diverse theoretical references and thematic foci. An example of the former is the study by Inge Bolin (1998) of Chillihuani (Cuzco), a high-altitude herding community in Peru. The author examines local rituals, considering them as direct and practically unchanged survivals from Inca times. This book is beautifully written and offers fascinating ethnographic insights, but is also highly idealised and avoids the academic debates and polemics that were going on at the time. As examples of the former, other community ethnographies from the 1990s–2000s explored concepts such as history, memory and literacy. This resulted from a certain thematic and theoretical assimilation with wider anthropological trends, adapted to the Andean context. For example, outside the core Andean region, Joanne Rappaport's (1998 [1990]) ethnography of Colombian Andean communities of the Nasa ethnic group (Cauca), explores native concepts of history and its relationship with writing, comparing it with Eurocentric history, by tracing the intellectual past of this group. In a similar vein, the study by Thomas A. Abercrombie (1998) of the Bolivian community (and ayllu) of Kulta (Llallagua) explores Andean concepts of history and memory.

Some years later in Peru, Frank Salomon, another prestigious author linked to 1960s–80s long-termism and another contributor to this volume, follows similar lines of research in his excellent ethnographies of Tupicocha (Huarochirí, Lima). Owing to the fortuitous and extraordinary discovery of the conservation and ongoing ritual use of Inca-style *khipus* (ancient Andean skeins of knotted cords used to store information), Salomon undertook ethnohistorical research in this community leading to a tentative but highly complex and convincing interpretation of the meaning of these devices, whose codes have been long forgotten (Salomon, 2004). On the basis of this research, Salomon and Niño-Murcia (2011) explore, challenge and expand notions of literacy and orality among Andean peoples, by analysing the writings of this community throughout history. These are all examples of ethnographies that transcend the case studies on which they are based to reach much wider issues, challenging established concepts of history, memory, literacy and writing in the Andes.

Since the 2000s anthropology has been going though further diversification, theoretically, methodologically and thematically. Ethnography has been reevaluated, and the exploration of indigenous cultures has also regained importance and been renovated. However, community ethnographies have remained largely marginal within the discipline, at least in their most traditional form. In the field of Andean anthropology there have been new research foci (for example, urban-rural interconnections, Evangelism, Peruvian 'violence', international migration, Andean identity and indigeneity) and theoretical approaches (for example, environmental and gender studies), with the world of development studies and projects, and non-governmental organisations (NGOs) becoming increasingly important (see Ávila, 2000b). In this academic context, the anthropological study of Andean villages and community ethnographies has continued to lose ground compared with the situation in previous periods, mirroring the decreasing demographic importance of these areas, caused mainly by migration. As a contrast, other disciplines, such as cultural geography or even economics, have increasingly incorporated ethnography and fieldwork in Andean rural areas and communities (see Pajuelo, 2000, pp. 161-4).

Nevertheless, these ethnographies continue to be produced and play an important role in the study of Andean culture, partially because the latter continues to be mainly rural and community-based in highland regions; and also because these ethnographies have evolved, overcoming some previous limitations and gaining new approaches. For example, the distinction between long- and short-termism – and the subjacent dichotomy between social change and historical continuities – has lost most of its previous connotations to the point that it can be considered largely obsolete. Moreover, there has been further diversification, and an overall theoretical and thematic assimilation with anthropology elsewhere, such as the study of topics such as literacy, memory, violence and reconciliation.

As a result, community ethnographies' research foci have also changed, and some that were previously central have declined, often becoming marginal, due to the aforementioned process of revisionism and more recent developments in anthropology. This is, for example, the case with regard to ritual practices and religiosity, social organisation and other issues related mainly to traditional aspects of local culture. In this academic context, communities tend to be just another research setting used to study particular phenomena, and not much attention is paid to the actual community itself. Nevertheless, new perspectives of and hybrid approaches to these places have been introduced. For example, Henry Stobart's (2006) ethnomusical study of Kalankira, a high-altitude Quechua-speaking hamlet in Northern Potosí (Bolivia), combines influences of 1960s–80s long-termism and postmodern-influenced concerns with subjective and subtle aspects of life, such as the sensory dimensions of music and ritual; while Beatriz Pérez-Galán (2004) explores traditional authorities and their ritual activities in Pisac (Cuzco) district communities, located in one of the more tourist-frequented parts of the Andes, the 'sacred valley' of the Inca, exploring the impact of tourism and social change on these communities and authorities.

I believe that the general lack of continuity in the study of some topics, particularly Andean communities, is regrettable. They have undergone important transformations in recent years, in a context of wider social change that has been challenging for Andean countries, Latin America more generally, and beyond. Since the 2000s the region has been increasingly integrated into globalised international markets, through a dominant export-led economic model of growth. Politically, leftist governments of more radical or moderate nature have expanded, defined as a 'left turn' or 'turns' (for example, Ardite, 2008). In some Andean countries this left turn has been accompanied by a rise in indigenous movements, resulting in sympathetic governments in Ecuador (Rafael Correa since 2007) and particularly in Bolivia (Evo Morales since 2006), where an unprecedented and remarkable pro-indigenous constitution was promulgated in 2009 (see Postero, 2010). Meanwhile, Peruvian governments have followed orthodox neoliberal policies with remarkable macroeconomic success, although this has generally failed to reach the poorest sectors of national society to any significant extent. Generally in Andean countries, highland and jungle regions remain among the poorest, despite the fact that primary resources are mostly found there, contributing to the creation or worsening of social conflicts and environmental problems. Moreover, the ongoing Great Recession that started in the USA and Europe in the late 2000s threatens the social and economic advancements of previous years and decades in the whole region. Regrettably, apart from a few exceptions, Andean communities are not being studied as they previously were in this wider and challenging context of social change, nor with the in-depth attention and insight allowed by ethnographies.

Nevertheless, other examples of excellent community ethnographies have been produced in recent years in the Andes which continue to incorporate new thematic, theoretical and methodological approaches and concerns. One example of this is Olga M. González's (2012) study of Sarhua (Ayacucho), a community well-known for crafting painted wood panels which borders Taulli, the village in which I was based. Here, the author explores concepts of memory, secrecy and reconciliation in the context of the 1980s–90s armed conflict, focusing on some violent events that took place there in the 1980s, through local testimonies and a series of 24 paintings about the conflict made in the 1990s by local craftsmen. Another example is Andrew Canessa's (2012) excellent ethnography of the Aymara-speaking community of Wila Kjarka, in the Bolivian region of La Paz, in which he explores Andean concepts of indigenous identity and history, and intimate aspects of local life and social interactions, among other topics, based on decades of fieldwork in the community. These examples demonstrate the ongoing validity, importance and capacity to reinvent the ethnographies produced in the Andes, and how they can still play a key role in the study of Andean culture, despite having declined in number and academic status.

Regarding this academic evolution, I have argued that community ethnographies are still 'valid and necessary, and that their limitations do not eliminate their also remarkable advantages' (Ferreira, 2012, p. 40). In the particular case of Andean anthropology, I gave three main reasons to justify these statements: the centrality and fundamental importance that highland communities continue to have in Andean culture, despite their declining demographic – and also academic – weight; the scale and significance of the social transformations these communities are experiencing, in the current and wider context of change in Andean countries; and 'the existence of a very rich academic tradition of Andean community studies that serves as a key source of knowledge and comparison, deserving continuity' (ibid.). Nevertheless, my defence or vindication of these ethnographies is not uncritical, as I also recognised their many shortcomings and uneven quality. I particularly vindicate and use as a model those that somehow manage to transcend their intrinsic limitations, or even their particular academic perspectives, to help understand Andean communities, and illuminate key aspects of their culture (ibid.). I have also argued that beyond particular theoretical references, periods, or focus of study, these ethnographies can be seen as pieces of a fragmentary puzzle that allows for a partial reconstruction and understanding of the rich and diverse world of Andean communities and rural areas since the 20th century. Besides, and despite their limitations, they have also been fundamental to the study of key aspects of Andean culture that go well beyond the geographical boundaries of the settlements being explored (ibid., p. 91).

Authors and chapters

This edited volume brings together some of the authors of the community ethnographies that introduced me to Andean anthropology, and influenced my PhD research. Due to the particular circumstances of my research, these authors were mostly linked to 1960s–80s long-termism – so criticised in the context of 1990s revisionism – and their ethnographies were mainly conducted in the southern highlands of Peru. I wrote an earlier publishing proposal presenting the project to potential contributors, in which I suggested specific guidelines and themes with reference to achieving a certain thematic homogeneity, and overall coherence, across chapters. For example, I proposed that contributors explain how and why they ended up producing a community ethnography; how they chose the communities in which they worked; the kind of relationships they established with local peoples during and after fieldwork; and how these communities have altered over time. I also suggested that they outline their original theoretical and methodological approaches and findings, reassessing their validity and explaining how their views about these topics have evolved or changed since the original fieldwork and publication of their ethnographies. I encouraged them to analyse the impact of these studies and the influence they had on their later work and careers; and their views on the role, evolution and current validity of community ethnographies in the study of Andean culture. Of course contributors finally and freely chose different orientations in and approaches to their respective chapters. However, I think the book for the most part covers these original suggestions and guidelines.

With this early proposal I started contacting the authors that I had in mind for the project. A few of them were unable to participate for different reasons, among them being too busy with other enterprises or a reluctance to revisit their old work. However, the rest were highly positive from the outset, viewing the project as an opportunity to address and develop academic and personal concerns with which they had been preoccupied, often for a long time. Along the way, and following several debates and delays in the publishing process, we decided to widen the book's original geographical scope, to include other authors who could provide unique and privileged insights into community ethnographies and research in other Andean countries. The definitive list of contributors and chapters that follows is the result of that process, presented in the chronological order in which the authors conducted and published their studies.

In chapter 1, **Billie Jean Isbell** reassesses her community ethnography of Chuschi (Ayacucho, Peru), first published in 1978, based on fieldwork undertaken between the late 1960s and the first half of the 1970s. As I have already outlined, this is a classic ethnography that takes a structuralist approach, and focuses on the local sociopolitical organisation and ritual life. I have also explained that this community happened to be the place where Shining Path conducted its first armed action in 1980s; and, as a result, Isbell unwillingly became a protagonist in the heated academic debates and critical reactions that took place in the context of 1990s revisionism. Entitled 'Reflections on fieldwork in Chuschi', the chapter reveals how Isbell ended up undertaking this research, as part of a wider project directed by Zuidema, explaining how structuralism influenced her fieldwork, and describing several episodes that took place during her time in the community. Inevitably, much of the chapter is dedicated to the traumatic effects of violence on local people, and on her own work and life, addressing also the scholarly debates that came out of the armed conflict.

Catherine J. Allen, in chapter 2, reassesses her community ethnography of Sonqo (Cuzco, Peru), which was first published in 1988 and was based on fieldwork undertaken between the mid 1970s and mid 1980s. In her chapter, entitled 'Losing my heart', she recalls her earlier academic studies and theoretical development, and how she ended up turning to Andean anthropology. Allen explains how she originally went to Sonqo to undertake fieldwork for a research project related to material culture; and how her experiences there led her in an entirely different direction, the end result being a classic community ethnography and a key reference work for understanding the ritual and symbolic dimensions of coca in Andean culture. Allen also shows how this research influenced her later work, and how she interrelated this with periodical visits to the community across the years. She also discusses the profound changes – sometimes dramatic – that she witnessed there, and the effects they had on her in terms of human relationships and her views on the community. Her chapter puts special emphasis on the role of serendipity, fortune, and following one's instincts and feelings in fieldwork.

Chapter 3, by Peter Gose, is a reassessment of his community ethnography of Huaquirca (Apurímac, Peru), entitled *Deathly Waters and Hungry Mountains: Agrarian Ritual and Class Formation in an Andean Town*, which was first published in 1994 (with later Spanish editions in 2001 and 2004) and was based on fieldwork undertaken in the early 1980s. I have explained that this excellent study focuses on the internal socioeconomic organisation of the community, interpreted along class divisions, and on local agricultural rituals, while theoretically (and originally) combining 1960s–80s long-termism with Marxism. Entitled 'Deadly waters, decades later', the chapter explains how Gose's ethnographic work in the community and the Peruvian highlands was disrupted by the 1980s–90s armed conflict, forcing him to turn to historical research. He also states how, as a result, he did not return to Huaquirca until 2014, in order to write this chapter, offering a fascinating account of the effects on him personally that this return meant, and the far-reaching changes he found in the community after decades. His chapter also pays special attention to the theoretical background of his original work, offering illuminating insights into the problems and conflicts surrounding the application of theory to fieldwork, and differences of interpretation and perception between researchers and researched. Gose explains his later academic and theoretical evolution, and how this altered his views on his original ethnographic work in the Peruvian highlands. He also gives a critical assessment of the evolution of anthropology in recent decades following the pernicious effects of neoliberalism in the discipline – in relation to the study of indigenous cultures, for example.

In chapter 4, **Carmen Escalante** and **Ricardo Valderrama** reassess their community ethnography of Yanque Urinsaya, in the Colca Valley of Arequipa (Peru), based on fieldwork undertaken between 1985 and 1988. This pioneering anthropological work on irrigation in the Andes, entitled *Del Tata Mallku a la Mamapacha. Riego, sociedad y ritual en los Andes Peruanos* (1988), explored the practical, social and ritual dimensions of this activity. Their chapter, 'Yanque Urinsaya: ethnography of an Andean community', especially focuses on the exceptional context of their fieldwork, which originated during, and was conducted and concluded by, the Peruvian armed conflict. They explain how they originally combined ethnographic research in Yanque Urinsaya with development work for an NGO in the area. They pay special attention to their personal experiences during fieldwork, and the links they created and maintained over the years with local people. Escalante and Valderrama's work is particularly engaging since they are both Andeans whose first language is Quechua. As such, their project raises interesting issues that can be linked to the question posited by Kirin Narayan (1993) in the article, 'How native is a "native" anthropologist?'. The authors also elaborate on being native ethnographers, and offer a passionate defence and vindication of the legacy and ongoing validity and need for community ethnographies.

Chapter 5, by **Rudi Colloredo-Mansfeld**, is a review of his community ethnography of Ariasucu (Otavalo, Ecuador), entitled *The Native Leisure Class: Consumption and Cultural Creativity in the Andes* (1999), which was based on fieldwork undertaken in the early 1990s. His study, focusing on consumption and material culture in Ariasucu, addressed questions about indigenous social economy, the materiality of social connections and how culture, class and race interrelate. Entitled 'Recordkeeping: ethnography and the uncertainty of contemporary community studies', the chapter outlines the academic and theoretical context of Colloredo's introduction to Andean anthropology. He also describes how he ended up working in this particular community, his fieldwork experiences, and how they have continued to shape his research and writing, resulting in other community-based ethnographies (Colloredo-Mansfeld, 1999; Colloredo-Mansfeld and Antrosio, 2015). The chapter offers an interesting contrast to the others because his ethnography was conducted in Ecuador, in the context of 1990s revisionism, and took a scholarly approach that could be defined as short-termist, with its focus on cultural change. In fact, Colloredo recalls how mainstream anthropology was at the time hostile to ethnography as a methodology, and to rural communities as research settings, particularly in developing countries. He also explains how his fieldwork experiences finally led him to undertake a community ethnography within that hostile academic context, in which 'ethnicity, indigenous rights, postcolonial nationalism, peasants and the politics of resistance seemed both urgent and interesting in the way that older disciplinary work about social organisation, ritual, work, and ecology seemed dated' (this volume).

In chapter 6, **Frank Salomon** addresses several aspects of his fieldwork in Tupicocha (Lima, Peru), and other surrounding communities. The main output of this research was *The Cord Keepers: Khipus and Cultural Life in a Peruvian Village* (2004), based on research conducted in the 1990s and early 2000s. As I have pointed out, this resulted from the extraordinary discovery of Inca-style khipus in this community, where they are still used in ritual contexts, and led to his highly elaborated, although tentative, interpretation of their codes and uses. Moreover, this fieldwork also spawned another co-authored, community-based ethnography which, together with the original study, challenges past and present notions of literacy, orality and writing in the Andes (Salomon and Niño-Murcia, 2011). In 'Long lines of continuity: field ethnohistory and customary conservation in the Sierra de Lima', Salomon explains that his introduction to Andean ethnography and Quechua language, and his earlier work in the translation of the 17th-century Huarochirí manuscript, were landmarks in his academic formation. This early work also led him to his first fieldwork in the area where Tupicocha is located, and where he found local khipus many years later. Salomon focuses his chapter on the conservation and curatorial dimensions of his fieldwork in the area's settlements. He describes how he physically dealt with and managed local khipus, and discusses the politics involved in this process. More broadly, Salomon also offers insightful thoughts and reflections on the ethnohistorical study of Andean communities.

In chapter 7, entitled 'Avoiding "community studies": the historical turn in Bolivian and South Andean anthropology', **Tristan Platt** offers a particularly interesting contrast and critical counterpoint to the previous chapters, because he directly addresses the limitations of community ethnographies and settings. Platt, who is the only contributor here not to have produced a conventional community ethnography (a monograph based on a single community), has conducted most of his research in Bolivia. In his chapter, he emphasises the specific limitations of such studies in the highlands of this country. These shortcomings result from the survival of ancient wider ethnical and territorial entities, ayllus, which include several communities and ecological zones within large and varied territories, overlapping other administrative divisions. He gives a fascinating autobiographical account of his academic career and personal experiences in Andean countries and beyond, summarising his previous scholarly and theoretical background, his introduction to Andean anthropology in the early 1970s, and his earlier ethnographic fieldwork in the Potosí region of Bolivia. There, he avoided community studies by extending the parameters of his work to search for the traces of 'something bigger', fulfilling this goal in the Macha ayllu. As he argues (personal communication), 'to study it (the wider ayllu) meant leaving the "community ethnography" behind, and getting into ethnohistory as a pre-condition for understanding the ethnography.' Platt also outlines his later career, stressing the variety and complexity of Andean culture, communities and research, and criticising Peruvian-centred approaches to them.

Finally, in chapter 8, **Enrique Mayer** also offers a wider perspective on Andean community ethnographies and anthropology, this time with the main focus on the Peruvian highlands, where he was born into a family of German immigrants. Mayer's study of Tangor (Pasco, Peru), entitled *Reciprocity, Self-Sufficiency and Market Relations in a Contemporary Community in the Central Andes of Peru* (1974) was researched in the early 1970s. His chapter, 'In love with *communidades*', reviews several aspects of his early work, which explored reciprocal relations in this community as a holistic organising principle of local life. However, Mayer goes well beyond this ethnography to offer an autobiographical account of his later community-based fieldwork and research. These have resulted in seminal and fundamental studies of topics such as the effects of the 1969 Peruvian agrarian reform and post-1980s neoliberal policies, ecological adaptation, and environmental and social conflicts. Moreover, he combines and relates this personal account with insightful analyses of key academic debates and historical developments related to Andean communities and their study. His views and interpretations are especially interesting because Mayer is a major figure in Andean anthropology, who combines a national perspective as a Peruvian, with an unusual personal background and international projection.

All of these contributors are well-known and recognised authors with much longer academic trajectories than the community ethnographies and research they write about here. In most cases their studies served as an introduction to their scholarly careers. This earlier research was normally an important landmark in their professional and personal lives, so they tend to explain how it influenced – and sometimes conditioned – later work and trajectories, and how they have evolved and changed. In fact, community ethnographies have frequently played this role of paving the way to an academic career, as these types of research settings allow key research skills to be developed, and the later transition to wider studies and settings. Valderrama and Escalante are different, and so too is Salomon, as they were already well-known authors with solid trajectories when they conducted their community ethnographies. The last two chapters by Platt and Mayer therefore complement the previous ones but can also be contrasted with them, offering wider critical approaches to community ethnographies and research in the Andes, through the personal perspectives of two towering figures from the world of Andean anthropology, having specialised respectively in Bolivia and in Peru. In their chapters, they offer informed thinking and privileged insights into the academic issues covered in this volume, providing some final and highly personal overviews of the possibilities, and also limitations, of community-based fieldwork beyond the scope of more conventional ethnographies. As such they serve as an excellent culmination to the book.

Taken together, these chapters and their authors cover a large and significant part of the history of Andean anthropology. Geographically, the chapters cover a large proportion of the Andes, from coastal, central and southern highlands of Peru to northern Ecuador and southern Bolivia. As a result, this book can be seen as a kind of journey through the history and evolution of Andean anthropology, at least in this core region, undertaken through the work and experiences of some of its protagonists. The particular focus on Peru and some theoretical predilections limit the scope of this retrospective exercise, but key academic debates and polemics are also illuminated that have definitively influenced the evolution of Andean anthropology. Moreover, such evolution is directly linked and intimately interrelated with much wider anthropological debates, and the evolution of the discipline; offering telling examples of their manifestations in the context of the Andes. These chapters also illustrate more specific aspects of Andean anthropology, such as the impact of key institutions. For example the universities of Cornell and Illinois in the USA, San Marcos in Peru, projects (such as Vicos) and figures (like Murra and Zuidema), forming and inspiring generations of new scholars and influencing the evolution of the discipline. In the case of Peru, they also illustrate the impact of the 1980s–90s armed conflict in Andean anthropology.

Obviously, this volume will be particularly meaningful and interesting to those who have read the original community ethnographies that are reassessed here by their authors. These readers will have the opportunity to recall the original studies and gain new perspectives on them, their authors, and the circumstances in which they were produced. Nevertheless, I believe that this book will also be of interest to those who have not read the original works, as all the chapters can stand alone, and efforts made to provide enough context for each of them. I hope that those who have not read the original works will be spurred into searching them out and reading them, thus contributing towards giving them the new lease of life that they all deserve.

I also hope that this volume will stimulate thoughts and reflection on the contribution and evolution of community ethnographies within Andean anthropology, and even the wider discipline, and that it will be a helpful reference work which will increase understanding of such studies. As a result of its reflective and retrospective perspective, the book may be also relevant to wider scholarly circles, as it ultimately relates to the way academic disciplines evolve and change: theoretically, methodologically and also thematically. It can thus be attractive to a public beyond the academic and geographical boundaries of the Andes. This book mainly refers to research conducted in the past, going against a certain 'dictatorship of the present', meaning that scholarly literature is too often – from my point of view – bound to urgency and contingency; and sometimes to certain fashionability. Personally, I believe it can be helpful to look back in order to look forward with perspective. Whatever your view, I just hope that you will enjoy it.

1. Reflections on fieldwork in Chuschi*

Billie Jean Isbell (in collaboration with Marino Barrios Micuylla)

As a new student of anthropology, I arrived in Chuschi, Peru in 1967 after two years of Peace Corps service in Colombia (1963-5). I was thankful that I spoke Spanish, the official language of the state of Peru, but regretted that classes in Quechua had been unavailable. I knew that being unable to speak Quechua would be a disadvantage and hoped to learn as much of that language as possible in the seven months we planned to be in Chuschi. After an initial period in the city of Ayacucho, a gruelling eight-hour trip in the back of a truck brought us to Chuschi on a miserably cold, wet February day at the height of the rainy season. We were soaked, muddy, cold and looked like drowned rats. During the journey, the male passengers had been forced to use chains three times to haul the vehicle out of the mud. After a night in the truck, we pulled into Chuschi on Thursday, the day before market day and found lodgings in the so-called 'hotel' on the plaza. I say this because in reality the 'hotel' was comprised of only a row of tiny rooms with dirt floors and no windows in the back of a local *tienda* [shop]. When I asked about a bathroom I was led to an adjacent pig sty where a huge sow and her piglets provided sanitation disposal. The sow intimidated me until my mother suggested that I carry a stick and whack her on the snout if she came too close, which she often attempted to do. We spent three weeks in the 'hotel' and nothing in my Peace Corps experience prepared me for accommodating my bodily functions to the local conditions.

During those three weeks we took our meals with school teachers at a food station on the plaza. The woman who prepared the food decided that because we were white foreigners we should be served white rice – mounds of it. I commented one day that I would like not to eat so much rice but preferred the vegetable soup she prepared for other customers because I was always trying to *bajar el peso* [lose weight]. Later during a walk in the high *puna* above

---

* I dedicate this chapter to Guadelupe Ccallocunto, who 'was disappeared' on 10 June 1990, and to all the women and men of the National Organisation of Kidnapped and Disappeared Persons (ANASEP), the Catholic Church's Service of Peace and Justice (SERPAJ) and the social services organisation, Asociación pro Derechos Humanos (APRODEH). It is also dedicated to my mother, Mildred Richerson, a pioneer on the New Mexico frontier, and my companion in the Andes.

the village with a Quechua-speaking research assistant, he said: 'Excuse me señora, I'm going over there behind that boulder to *bajar el peso.*' Suddenly I understood why our meal-time conversations had focused on how to help me *bajar el peso* and why the cook insisted on serving me hot lemon water with my mounds of rice.[1]

I was most fortunate as an older, returning undergraduate (30 years old, married with a child), to have been selected to join a research seminar, the Rio Pampas Project, conducted by R. Tom Zuidema at the Universidad de Huamanga in Ayacucho. Its objective was to study the ethnography and sociopolitical history of seven villages in the River Pampas which constituted a colonial Curato de Chuschi. The small group of University of Illinois students, all graduates (except for me), were funded to conduct research for seven months. Because Bill Isbell and I had a small child, we were assigned to live and work in Chuschi, the district capital and market centre located at the end of the road that led into the River Pampas region. My mother, Mildred Richerson, accompanied us and became invaluable because she opened so many doors, even though she could not speak Spanish or Quechua. The Huamanga students were placed in remote villages only accessible via foot paths through the mountains. All were native Quechua speakers and, like me, were undergraduates in their early 30s. I was completing my BA at the University of Illinois and the first research I conducted in Chuschi in 1967 became my senior honour's thesis on the civil religious hierarchy which in a condensed form was later included in my 1973 PhD thesis: 'Andean structures and activities: towards a study of transformations of traditional concepts in a central highland peasant community'.[2]

The Rio Pampas research team members developed a special bond and I was accepted as part of the group even though I was the only woman. All of us felt privileged and excited to be included in a research project led by a European (Dutch) structuralist trained at Leiden University. We also felt a special camaraderie with Zuidema as he was only ten years older than we were, and he, his wife Louisette, and their three children lived in the city of Ayacucho.[3]

1   In all the editions of *To Defend Ourselves* (2005, 1985, 1978) readers will find a full description of our comic arrival and several desperate attempts to communicate with Chuschinos. One involved drinking kerosene instead of *trago* [cane alcohol].
2   The title reflects my growing awareness of the inadequacies of structuralism to capture transformations.
3   The Zuidema family formed a strong bond with Rio Pampas project members. Tom made regular visits to the villages we were studying, and when he stopped in Chuschi, my mother and I always made sure to prepare something special to serve him. They reciprocated in Ayacucho. We delivered many a live animal to the Zuidema household. Once, in 1969, Louisette gave Diana, our daughter, a birthday party and ingeniously prepared a 'cake' out of stacked pancakes with jam in between each layer and chocolate frosting. My mother followed her example and organised a baking party in the portal of the municipality for the

During our seminar meetings in 1967 at the University of Huamanga, Tom Zuidema told funny stories about having to be a strolling violinist in cafés in Cuzco because he had so little funding. He said he had ripped the crotch of his only pair of good pants, and had to keep his knees together when strolling and performing. At the time I wondered why he did not just sew up the pants, but as I got to know him better I learned that he never did any manual labour of any kind: his hands were reserved for the violin. As we studied Cuzco's ceque system,[4] we made jokes imagining this peculiar Dutch structuralist leading ritual processions along the ceque lines radiating out from the Qoricancha (the Temple of the Sun) in Cuzco's plaza, fiddling a tune on his violin like the Pied Piper with his knees clasped tightly together.

Even as we joked about our mentor, we were awed by his productivity and tenacity.[5] Zuidema's 1967 seminars were not embroiled in the political debates that were beginning to take place in the university: he kept our discussions rigorously focused on the history of the Inca empire and the local histories and ethnographies of the Rio Pampas villages. But Zuidema's seminars were often puzzling to me because he kept referring to places far from the Andes for structural comparisons. He had been trained to conduct research in Indonesia and after the Dutch were expelled from that country in 1957, he turned his focus to Peru and the Inca empire. Indonesian concepts of time and space figured in his comparisons. I grew to understand that the latter were made because Indonesia was situated five degrees south of the equator which was similar to the Inca empire's location on the other side of the world. Moreover, Indonesia had complex calendrical and astronomical systems that had become part of state structures and culture: these provided a starting point for his work on Inca astronomy and calendrics. However, I was especially puzzled by comparisons with lowland South American tribal cultures, especially the Bororo. With his heavy Dutch accent he pronounced it '*Bowowo*'. I and the Peruvian members of the Rio Pampas Project would mumble privately '*Quienes son los Bowowo?*' But once Zuidema introduced me to Claude Lévi-Strauss's *Le Cru et Le Cuit*, the first volume in his *Mythologiques* series (1964), I understood that, like Lévi-Strauss, Zuidema initially believed that the Americas should be treated as a single cultural complex with structures and myths reflecting the universal laws which make up the mind's unconscious activities. Demonstrating a major difference between Dutch and French structuralism, Zuidema in time abandoned the concept of the universal laws embedded in myths and turned to

---

entire village. One father dipped his finger in the frosting and declared: 'This cannot be good for you.'

4   We were reading his first publication, *The Ceque System of Cuzco* (Zuidema, 1964).

5   Zuidema's grand opus of 906 pages, on the Inca calendar, *El Calendario Inca: Tiempo y Espacio en la Organizacion Ritual del Cusco: la ideal del pasado* was published in 2011 and he continued to author a stream of publications until his death in 2016.

the ethnohistorical documents of the Inca empire and myths as narratives with actors and agency. However, Zuidema did continue to search for structural clues in art forms, but restricted his investigations to specific and relevant time periods.[6]

Falling in love with structuralism

While in Ayacucho, I read *A World on the Wane*, John Russell's 1961 translation of *Tristes Tropiques* (Lévi-Strauss, 1955)[7] in preparation for my first field experience. The translation has been rightly criticised for omitting four-and-a-half chapters and two-thirds of the original photographs. Discovering the Anglophile bias that prompted Russell's exclusions taught me an important lesson about translations. I had struggled to learn French in order to read the three volumes of *Mythologiques* and I was able to compare Russell's translation with the French edition. It was like reading two entirely different books. Lévi-Strauss's unambiguous criticism of colonialism (especially of the British in India) and his rejection of evolutionism at that time did not come through in the Russell translation. I think many contemporary students in anthropology are not aware that Lévi-Strauss wrote *Tristes Tropiques* while he was Secretary General of UNESCO's International Council of Social Sciences (1952–61). During those years he travelled extensively and found a disturbing harbinger of the world to come in India's high population concentrated in overcrowded urban centres where lack of adequate basic services, such as water and sanitation, was combined with crushing poverty and a deterioration of social structures. At the end of his life on 30 October 2009 aged 100, he declared that the world had become a place in which he no longer wished to live.

One aspect I found compelling in *Tristes Tropiques* was the *persona* (Narayan, 2007, p. 132; Gornick, 2001) that Lévi-Strauss presented to the reader. He openly expressed the difficulties and ambiguities of fieldwork, and that appealed to me as I began my first intense fieldwork experience. Moreover, I was also awed by his power of describing things he did not understand. In the oft-quoted beginning of *Tristes Tropiques*, he declares, 'I hate traveling and explorers. Yet here I am proposing to tell the story of my expeditions' (1973 [1955], p. 3). He continued that it had taken him 15 years to overcome the repugnance and shame that prevented him from writing the travelogue for so long, but at the same time he also thought he was following in the steps of 16th-century travellers and explorers. He acknowledges presenting the narrator-protagonist as hero but claims he was not duped by French society's adoration of (masculine) travellers. However, I agree with Sontag (1994, p. 74),

---

6   For example, see his latest publication, 'Hacer calendarios en quipus y tejidos' (2014).

7   I recommend the 1974 translation by John and Doreen Weightman (Penguin).

who points out that Lévi-Strauss paints himself as a new scientific masculine hero. In my current rereading of his work, it appears to me that he maintained that image to the end of his life. In a 1988 interview with biographer Didier Eribon (1994, p. 73), when asked about writing *Tristes Tropiques*, Lévi-Strauss responded: 'I suffered from a guilty conscience that I wasn't working on a second volume about the complex structures of kinship ... I thought I was committing a sin against science.'

I embraced the 'Science of the concrete' (*The Savage Mind*, 1969 [1962], chapter 1) with a vengeance during my first introduction to fieldwork in 1967 and I fell in love with structuralism, and with anthropology as science. I encountered structures everywhere in Chuschi and I thought I had died and gone to structuralist heaven. Residence in one of the moieties determined a community member's service in the complex, hierarchical system of civil-religious authorities responsible for the annual cycle of rituals. Structures literally marched up and down the village byways. *Hanay barrio* [upper moiety] was located below *uray barrio* [lower moiety] and confirmed that structures were symbolic as well as physical. Reciprocity was the fuel for the engine of the communal subsistence economy: agriculture and herding. All activities were maintained by a system based in kinship and *compadrazgo* [ritual bonds] with yet other complex account structures, a bookkeeping arrangement which seemed designed to keep a perpetual cycle of labour and goods exchanges. Moreover, allocation of land was based on service to the community, not on private ownership: all land was held communally. I had never seen a non-capitalistic economy at work and I was amazed at the level of communal labour, coordination and reciprocity required.

Structuralism was the first instrument in my anthropological toolkit and it allowed me to map, chart, describe, photograph and analyse a complex world that I had never experienced before. My first paper, given at the American Anthropological Association and followed by my first publication, was on children's acquisition of Quechua morphology (1972) using a series of exercises with nonsense words I had created based on the research of psycholinguist, Jean Berko. What stands out in my memory now is that the nonsense words were soon adopted into playful word games throughout Chuschi. The greetings of people passing me on the village pathways would be peppered with the made-up words as if we were sharing a private joke. I should have studied and documented the rapid diffusion of such fictional vocabulary, but I was too busy 'doing science'. This linguistic work was followed by articles on kinship and reciprocity (1974; 1977; 1978, chapters 5 and 7) that I also considered scientific. These were preceded by a series of symposia and it was thrilling to participate in gatherings of anthropological scientists to describe and analyse Andean kinship, marriage and reciprocity for the first time. As a newly minted anthropologist, I wrote my papers without the benefit of *The Elementary Structures of Kinship*, by Lévi-Strauss (1969 [1949]), because the kinship system I encountered in Chuschi did not conform to any of his models. I argued that Chuschi's kinship system was based on bilateral sibling-centred kindreds (siblings included terminologically equivalent sisters, brothers and first cousins). Furthermore, I did not conceptualise women as circulating in marital exchanges; rather, these exchanges consisted of brother/sister dyads between families to maintain reciprocal relationships. Moreover, I observed marriages between couples where either the man, or more usually the woman, changed their paternal surname in order to marry, not for love but for reciprocity. They invented their own kinship to establish reciprocal networks. I began to see kinship and marriage 'from a sister's point of view': but the early oral presentations of these arguments were not well received by many of my male colleagues. I will never forget a well-known Peruvian anthropologist blurting out loudly after my presentation at an international conference: 'Billie Jean! *No puedes decir esto!*' [Billie Jean, you can't say this!]. As a male member of upper-class intellectual elites, he appeared to feel it was his privilege to police and control me. My response was: 'I can say whatever I want'.[8]

Falling out of love with anthropology as a science

Having understood that the androcentric perspective of structural theories did not capture the dynamic and often inventive nature of kinship, marriage and reciprocity in Chuschi,[9] I began to doubt one of the other major tenets of structuralism: the universality of laws that govern the mind's unconscious activities. I remember debates with Tom Zuidema that would begin in our graduate seminar on Levi-Strauss's *Mythologiques*, and would usually continue out into the hallway and often up to Tom's office. On one occasion I followed Tom up the stairs, arguing against archetypal, universal structures in myths. He stopped, turned and asked with a quizzical expression: 'Was I going up or was I going down?' I responded: 'That's the problem with structuralism; you can't tell if you are going up or going down.' Our debates propelled me to search for theories and methodologies, not to replace structuralism but to augment it: to put flesh on the bones, so to speak. I became fascinated by Husserl's notion of the remembering, recollecting, visible subject who uses language to make sense of the continuous flow of occurrences in the world, and thus turned

8   I became acutely aware of my lack of agency, voice and subjectivity after I assumed my new appointment as a woman on a tenure track line in the anthropology department at Cornell University in 1977, which was about the same time I discovered the writings of Luce Irigaray (1977). Her essays spoke to my experiences in academia. I redoubled my efforts to focus on gender, voice and subjectivity (see the section on gender below).

9   Times have changed. For an example of innovative, award-winning research on kinship and marriage, see *Given to the Goddess* (Ramberg, 2014).

increasingly to linguistic analyses. I also embraced Maurice Merleau Ponty's emphasis on the body as the primary site of knowing the world (1945). Thus the door to phenomenology was opened and my next fieldwork project in 1969–70 focused on videotaping children's perceptions and representations of their cultural concepts as they 'communed with' (to use Merleau Ponty's phrase) miniature rag dolls and the paraphernalia needed to enact rituals. The idea was to divide the children into cognitive age groups, following Piaget's schema, and videotape their representations of rituals of birth, death, marriage and the cycle of agricultural celebrations. But before I could give the children any instructions, they undressed the dolls and inspected them, complaining that they were not 'complete' – I had copied the Chuschino dress styles for men and women with care to represent all the clothing symbolism I had observed, but I had not put genitalia on the dolls. As the tapes rolled on the huge reel-to-reel camera, the children manipulated the dolls and positioned them in coitus, often changing who was on top. They also made the dolls 'speak' in rhyming falsetto verses. I watched the copulatory chaos, baffled: my scientific research was confounded by the children's creativity. Later, I learned from adults who roared with laughter as they viewed the tapes exclaiming: 'Oh that's *Vida Michiy* – we used to do that when we were young.' They went on to explain that the children were representing adolescent competitive riddle games which also involved group sex. The game was known as *Vida Michiy* [to put life out to pasture], or *Pukllay* [to play].[10] My 'science' had been derailed, but I had stumbled upon one of the most interesting aspects of sex and gender in the Andes.

The arrival of Shining Path in Chuschi truncated my early research and I turned with urgency to the violent events of the war. As I became entangled in the war, I began to focus on memory, agency and representation. However, I did retain Lévi-Strauss's notion of *bricolage* [characteristic patterns of mythological thought] as I watched actors 'tinker with' the residue of their wartime experiences to create new structures and representations. The notion

---

10 The complete texts of the riddles and a description of the 'game' are available at http://isbellandes.library.cornell.edu. The resulting publication (Isbell and Roncalla, 1977) applies theories of cognitive development and is pretentiously entitled 'The ontogenesis of metaphor: riddle games among Quechua speakers seen as cognitive discovery procedures'. As a new PhD and faculty member, I was invited to give a presentation to the all-male board of trustees. I had been told that the board often helped new faculty members find funding for innovative research. That did not happen. I retreated back into 'scientific mode', hence the title above. Today, I would write a very different article with the title 'Quechua women win the riddle and sexual game, *Vida Michiy*'. Unfortunately, Catholic University lost all the tapes and I was never able to reanalyse them.

also proved helpful as I applied myself to the production of art and music as memory narratives during the war (1995; 1998; 2004).[11]

Most contemporary ethnographic research begins with some form of structuralism as the ethnographer attempts to make sense of an unfamiliar world, but generally ethnographers move on to other issues, methodologies and theories, often ignoring structuralism's legacy from the past. Nevertheless, it has survived in transformations that may mask its political functions. The most prominent example I can think of is the Musée du Quai Branly, announced in 1996 by Jacques Chirac and completed in 2006. The architect, Jean Nouvel, intentionally designed the museum to 'disappear' in an old neighbourhood on the banks of the Seine, one that opposed the museum's insertion into their surroundings. Nélia Dias (2008) writes that the museum is a double erasure that elides France's colonial history and the history of the collections. Celebrating cultural diversity, the collections comprise objects from the Museum of African and Oceanic Art (now closed) as well as objects from the ethnographic collections, famous for their exoticism and occasional bizarreness, such as the body of a Khoisan woman known as the Hottentot Venus that was displayed until 1974. The Musée de l'Homme was closed from 2009 to 2015 and has reopened primarily as a research museum that forms part of the national network of natural history museums. I wonder where all the 'politically incorrect' objects have gone as France reconfigures its representation of its colonial past?

Paul Kahn visited the Musée du Quai Branly shortly after the 100th birthday celebration of Lévi-Strauss on 28 November 2008. Lévi-Strauss did not attend the day-long event but Kahn argues the centenarian anthropologist's presence is palpable in the permanent collections on display. Kahn reflects on how the America exhibit was organised:

> an America that Lévi-Strauss unified in his imagination. There is no North, Central and South. There is no high and low culture, no empires, no rise and fall. Mexico is with Brazil, Peru with the Northern Plains, the Eastern Woodlands are beside the Andes. The objects in the cases are organized in visual pattern groups. Each object is placed and aligned to emphasize pattern similarities or variations. (2012, p. 3).

A video screen showing a series of images of stone and ceramic objects that morph into each other is explained by anthropologist, Emmanuel Désveaux: 'They make transformational groups, tokens of uniqueness of Amerindian artefacts: even before being instruments in themselves, they are regarded as instruments of meaning' (ibid.). Not only the exhibit itself but the video

---

11 In an excellent review of *Art from a Fractured Past: Memory and Truth Telling in Post-Shining Path Peru*, ed. Cynthia Milton (2014), Joseph Feldman (2015) raises critical issues. For example, he asks what are the implications of using art as a mode of truth-telling in post-conflict societies?

programme that accompanies it, the computer code that generates the video, and even the museum's architectural structure are all determined by patternology and combinatory logic eliminating the need for computational mathematics. Lévi-Strauss saw an analogy between the combinatory logic of structuralism and genetics 45 years ago and he believed such a logic created contingency and agency in the history of humankind. Structuralism is not the only example of its application for it is also found in Gregory Bateson's system theories and in architecture, perhaps the most striking contemporary example.[12] Kahn states that viewed from the outside the Musée du Quai Branly resembles an interlocking set of colourful cubes hoisted on legs over a grassy marsh that remind him of the drawings by anime master, Hayao Miyazaki (ibid.). The colourful cube motif is repeated in the 30 exhibition galleries visible from the outside in which the interplay of pattern variations is emphasised. Not everyone appreciates the museum. Michael Kimmelman, the architecture critic for the *New York Times* describes it as a 'Heart of Darkness in the City of Lights' and declares it to be a spooky jungle in which objects are arranged with hardly any discernible logic.[13] Furthermore, he asks, are the objects artistic or anthropological? The exhibits seem to alternate between the two but one message is clear: the Branly redefines France's colonial past.

First fieldwork: lessons in politics

Upon my return two years later in 1969–70, political debates swirled around the Rio Pampas research group at the University of Huamanga because another Pied Piper was attracting legions of followers to his weekly lectures in a boarding house that became known as El Kremlin.[14] Abimael Guzmán had been recruited in 1962 to teach philosophy by the university rector, Efrain Morote Best,[15] a brilliant anthropologist and folklorist who had conducted extensive fieldwork in the rural countryside of Ayacucho and knew the conditions peasants were enduring. A few years later when Zuidema arrived from Holland to teach anthropology and conduct research, Huamanga was beginning to

12 Müller-Wille (2010). I am grateful to Roberta Militello for referring me to patternology in architecture, specifically *The Architecture of Patterns* (Anderson and D. Salomon, 2010). For a concise definition of patternology and examples of urban architecture consult Roberta Militello's sites: http://robertamilitello.com/portfolio/patternology-2/ and http://robertamilitello.com/portfolio/fabrications/.

13 'Heart of Darkness in the City of Light', *New York Times*, 2 July 2006, www.nytimes.com/2006/07/02/arts/design/02kimm.html?_r=0.

14 The article, 'Maoism in the Andes: the Communist Party of Peru-Shining Path and the refusal of history' (Starn, 1995), see www.latinamericanstudies.org/peru/shining-path.pdf, is an excellent comparison and critique of Guzman's ideological writing alongside *Siete Ensayos de la Realidad Peruana* by Jose Carlos Mariátegui (2005 [1928]).

15 Who, along with his three sons, became members of Shining Path's central committee.

gain a reputation for its radical faculty and students who hotly debated Soviet versus Maoist interpretations of Marxism and what form of revolution should be carried out in Peru. Guzmán became a central figure in those debates. He visited China for the first time in 1965 and made additional trips before returning to Huamanga to become head of personnel at the university and to continue as a professor of philosophy. In the heady environment of radical debates in Ayacucho, Guzmán founded the Pro-Chinese Communist Party of Peru in 1970 that later split and became the Communist Party of Peru-Shining Path (commonly known as Sendero Luminoso). He continued to be a central figure in radical politics until he left the university in 1975 and went underground.

By my third fieldwork project in 1974–5 after completing the PhD, the presence of Sendero was palpable in the university, the city of Ayacucho, and in Chuschi. Revolution was in the air. Four major conflicts characterise that third field experience: 1) Chuschi's with the Catholic church; 2) Their dispute with a *hacendado* [landowner] whose lands bordered on Chuschi's pasturelands; 3) The village's dispute with the Chuschino migrant community in Lima; and 4) My conflict with the municipal mayor.

After repeated clashes between the Catholic church and Chuschi, the priest was expelled in 1972 and all the church's property and herds were seized by the community. In 1974–5, the church was still attempting to regain its property but did not succeed, and to my knowledge, the Catholic church has never opened again for 'business': the priest required payment for all funeral, baptismal and wedding services, and even ritual paraphernalia such as crosses and burial litters had to be rented.

In a communal meeting on 6 April 1975, *comuneros* voted to move the herds of the *cofradía* [Roman Catholic group responsible for ceremonies] on to the lands of the only hacienda on their borders in order to spur the agrarian reform officials into action. This tactic was indeed a success. On 28 May, a national land judge arrived to inspect the boundaries and litigate the dispute: the day before the hearing, 50 comuneros on horseback had driven the cofradía herds on to the hacendado's land and damaged his potato fields. One of the latter's men shot a dog owned by a Chuschino, the only violence to take place.

Each household in Chuschi had been required to provide one male representative and failure to do so meant a fine of 3,000 soles: about 30 dollars which was a considerable amount at the time. It was an impressive sight when at dawn on the morning of 28 May two hundred men arrived on horseback from the valley and crossed the puna to attend the hearing. This took place in Ninobamba adjacent to Chuschi's communal lands, known as Inga Wasi. In April, I had met with the national land judge and the SINAMOS officials in

Ayachucho.¹⁶ The land judge was enthusiastic about our proposal to create a public document of the agrarian reform at work. The officials from SINAMOS were reluctant but finally gave in and granted us permission to videotape the proceedings. I still remember laughing at the hacendado's lawyer when he argued that Chuschinos were capitalists attempting to grab the *minifundio* of a retired Guardia Civil sergeant and thus deprive him of his land and livelihood. The lawyer presented a bill of sale supporting his claim that the land had been sold to the hacendado's great grandfather.

The lawyer for the Chuschi community argued that the bill of sale was a forgery and the president of the Chuschi administration (also a *compadre* of mine) provided a copy of archival documents which included the record of the 1593 *visita* during which the communities' land and boundaries were established. The land judge ruled that the hacendado had to vacate and Chuschi's communal lands were to be restored. Watching the land judge hear testimonies from 7am until dusk accompanied by his 'scribe' pecking away on a tiny portable typewriter in the back of a truck made me think of the land judge as a modern *visitador*, the colonial official who was the King of Spain's agent sent to adjudicate similar disputes and report his findings to the colonial powers in Peru and to the King. Who received the land judge's reports that were being typed in the back of the truck? SINAMOS? Or other government officials in Ayacucho or Lima?

The cofradía herds were at the centre of another dispute between Chuschino migrants in Lima and comuneros in Chuschi. The migrants in Lima attempted to form a cooperative to profit from the 250 head of cattle and 1,500 head of sheep that made up the church's cofradía herds. Chuschinos organised and blocked the migrants' efforts and the cooperative was never formed. They were rightfully fearful that surrendering control of the herds to the migrants would mean the community losing possible income from the herds that had previously been under the church's dominion. I never learned the ultimate outcome of the conflict.

Finally, I became embroiled in a dispute with Chuschi's municipal mayor.¹⁷ I had travelled from Lima to Chuschi in 1974 to attend the Independence Day celebrations on 28 July, after teaching on a Fulbright at Catholic University and conducting research in the Squatter settlement called *7 de Octubre*. I returned to Chuschi in April 1975 without my family after I had secured funding from the Ford Foundation, and sponsorship from the Peruvian Ministry of Education, to develop a bilingual educational programme and to

---

16 The name SINAMOS was originally created to denote 'without masters' – *Sin Amos*. It is short for El Sistema Nacional de Apoyo a la Movilización (National Social Mobilisation System). For a discussion of the Agrarian Reform Law's impact, see chapter 2 of *The Village in the Context of a Changing Nation* (Isbell, 1978).

17 For fuller details see 'Written on my body', a memoir (Isbell, 2009b).

continue the video-taping of children's enactments of rituals that I had begun in 1969–70. I had discussed both projects with teachers in 1970 and they seemed enthusiastic. However, shortly after my return in 1975, the municipal mayor, who was also a teacher, stopped our filming and informed me that I did not have the licence required by the municipality (costing 100 soles – about one dollar) to videotape children, and moreover he said he would not approve the establishment of a bilingual school, even though I had letters and funding from Lima's ministry of education. I also had letters of approval from the prefect of the Ayacucho department and from the officials of the province capital in Cangallo. Moreover, I had never been told about a video tax.

The conflict with the municipal mayor erupted into minor drunken violence between him and a Peruvian member of my research team during the Corpus Christi celebration. Trying to alleviate tension, another research assistant, a young woman with an undergraduate Fulbright fellowship, asked a band member if she could play his trumpet. He gladly relinquished his battered instrument to her and she joined the band as it marched around the town plaza. The next day the trumpet's owner came to our house, walked up to the tall, beautiful, blonde '*gringa*' (the Fulbright student) and greeted her by simply cupping both of her breasts in his hands. He then turned to me and because my mother was not in Chuschi that year, he solemnly requested that I compose a letter to our father (he assumed my student was my sister) asking for her hand in marriage. In halting Spanish, he proceeded to enumerate all of his qualifications for becoming her husband: the number of herd animals he owned, the house he was building, and most importantly he vowed that he would never beat her. I had to explain that she was not my sister and that my father was dead. That news saddened him, but he and the Fulbright student continued to march with the band, sharing his trumpet. The episode certainly did relieve the tension.

In the days during Corpus Christi, a comical battle of telegrams ensued between the mayor and me to the authorities in Ayacucho and Cangallo, with the telegraph operator telling each of us what was in the other's telegrams. The mayor escalated the conflict by contacting the Peruvian Investigative Police (PIP) in Ayacucho, claiming that I and my research team were CIA spies. When the PIP investigator arrived in Chuschi, he questioned the whole team: he was especially interested to know whether I had encountered a foreign professor with an accent who taught at the University of Huamanga and was known to be travelling with a group of students to remote villages. The PIP suspected them of fomenting revolution in the Rio Pampas region. I told him that I not only knew them, but moreover had participated in the research group, the Rio Pampas Project. I explained that each student was assigned a particular village to research the archival history of the region's Inca resettlement as well as to conduct ethnographic research on the contemporary communities. I went on to clarify that I had been assigned Chuschi and I showed him the history of the community that I was preparing in Spanish for the schools. I also assured him that the 'foreign professor' (Tom Zuidema) was not fomenting revolution. 'Mr PIP' said that, nevertheless, they were under surveillance. He paused and smiled, adding cordially: 'You and your research team have been under surveillance for some time as well.' He also questioned me about the politics of the new school teachers but I said I didn't know of any specific actions that any of them had taken. Obviously, the various control agencies of the state were already engaging in surveillance in the Rio Pampas in 1974–5 and suspected the teachers of being Sendero members using the schools for recruitment. The reality of being under surveillance became apparent a short time later when I and members of my research team were required to travel to Cangallo to be finger-printed. The sequence of events has been described in other publications.[18]

In retrospect, one of the most significant aspects of the conflict with the municipal mayor was that my compadre (the *alcalde vara* [traditional staff holder]) and other comuneros devised a strategy for me to follow – they advised me not to engage in verbal exchanges with the mayor; rather, sponsor a musical group for the Corpus Christi festivities and join the sponsor of the celebrations, the *mayordomo*, as he displays his generosity to the community. I sponsored *waqrapuku* [curved cattle horn trumpet] players and by marching around the plaza with the musicians my research team was incorporated into the mayordomo's *kuyaq* [those who love him]. Sponsoring the musicians established a reciprocal relationship between me, my family and my research team with his extended kin. As we marched round and round the plaza, the new school teachers looked on sullenly from the municipal balcony. They were strongly opposed to such backward traditionalism.

As we stomped around the plaza with the *waqrapuku* players, the municipal mayor shouted drunkenly from the front of the church (padlocked by the community) that his people were going to kill us and burn not only our house but my compadres' homes as well. He did not burn any houses but he did destroy documents belonging to my compadre, the alcalde vara, and the birth certificate of his newborn son which would have had serious political consequences later as the war with Sendero developed, but I reported the action in one of my telegrams to the prefect and the documents were restored. The municipal mayor fled Chuschi when Sendero took full control of the village.

18 *Finding Cholita* (Isbell, 2009a) incorporates narratives from these conflicts including my house arrest and command attendance at the celebration to mark the 120th anniversary of Cangallo as province capital, and my rescue from sexual assault by the Chuschi *varayoq*. Full details are in Isbell (2005), chapters 10 and 11.

Sendero actions in Chuschi from 1980-6[19]

I believe that Sendero chose Chuschi not only as the site for announcing the beginning of the armed struggle by burning the ballots there in 1980, but also as the place to establish one of the earliest *escuelas populares* [popular schools] staffed by Sendero sympathisers. When the ballots were burned, only three of the 18 teachers in the Chuschi school system were from the region.[20] Many Chuschinos claimed in 1975 that the popular schools provided the best education they had ever experienced. In revisiting the events of 1974-5, I have come to the conclusion that during that time Sendero was laying the ground by placing cadre members among the new teachers in the school system. This allowed them to intensify their control immediately after the ballots were burned.

Sendero's moralisation campaign began in August 1981 with the public execution in the plaza of two well-known cattle thieves from the neighbouring village of Quispillaqta. Abuses within families were targeted next: a man who lived openly with two women was whipped publicly; another for beating his wife. In the open court established by Sendero several village women denounced their husbands for beating them. These actions received general approval. In September 1981, Senderistas arrived without hoods or masks and took up residence in Chuschi. In October, they closed the municipality and organised an alternative governance structure.[21] All functionaries renounced their positions in a general assembly held on 22 November 1981. However, to the outside world, Chuschi appeared to be governed by officials named by the prefect in Ayacucho. Sendero attempted to establish a 'people's army' but that failed; they also attempted to organise communal agriculture based on moiety residence; that also failed. Their efforts to resolve the long-standing boundary conflict over pasture lands between Chuschi and neighbouring Quispillaqta went nowhere. All of these failures reveal that none of the Senderistas had participated in, or even read, our research on the Rio Pampas produced in the 1960s-70s. Had they done so, they would have known that agricultural production was based on a complex network of reciprocity. Sendero also tried to abolish the Civil Religious Hierarchy, the cycle of annual rituals and ritualised drinking: all failures. Perhaps one of the most spectacular defeats was

---

19   Most of the information in this section is drawn from intensive interviews conducted in 1986 with Chuschinos who had fled from their district and were living in Lima. Carlos Iván Degregori also provided me with interview material. A longer and more complete discussion, including conflict analyses and historical background, can be found in Isbell (2005), chapter 11.

20   See Ricardo León report in *El Comercio*, 'Chuschi, hoy, a 30 años del nacimiento de la violencia terrorista', 17 May 2015, http://elcomercio.pe/peru/lima/chuschi-hoy-30-anos-nacimiento-violencia-terrorista-noticia-479840.

21   For details see Isbell (2005), pp. 292-3.

the attempt to close the weekly market. The outcry was: 'Where will we get our salt?', especially ironic because the region's first Spanish administrator had been sent to manage the colonial salt-mine near Chuschi. The final blow, which resulted in comunero withdrawal of support for Sendero, came on 1 July 1982 when they attempted to execute Bernardo Chipana, governor of Chuschi, publicly in the plaza as an informer. When they turned to the community for affirmation of their actions, the resounding response was: 'Do not kill him!'[22]

As anthropologist Sánchez Villagómez, who conducted research in the region during the years of violence has confirmed to me, brutal conflicts developed between communities during the six months from December 1982 to May 1983. Sánchez states that in the imaginations of comuneros from Chuschi, Cancha Cancha, Uchuyri and Pomabamba, Quispillaqta in the high puna had become a centre of Sendero support. That community paid the greatest price in loss of life when on 15 May 1983 a combined force of 70 military personnel dressed in civilian clothing and a hundred comuneros, all calling out Sendero slogans combed its annexes for Senderistas and sympathisers. As a survival tactic, comuneros were accustomed to greeting military and Sendero alike with shouts of welcome. Those who had gathered for a communal work day in the Yuraqcruz annex were tricked by the yells of the disguised military and responded with '*bien venidos, compa*'. Eight men were captured who subsequently 'disappeared': Narasmo Achallma Capcha, Antonio Carhuapoma Conde, Valentín Núñez Flores, Julián Mendoza, Pedro Núñez Pacotaype, Reynaldo Núñez Pacotaype, Hilario Núñez Quispe and Máximo Vilca Ccallocunto. Their bodies were excavated by the Truth and Reconciliation Commission (TRC) in 2003. The TRC documented 14 Quispillaqteño deaths, but through my own interviews I calculated 41 deaths or disappearances from that community compared with three to five fatalities for neighbouring ones. I believe that Quispillaqta was targeted because of long-standing boundary disputes with neighbouring communities, especially Chuschi.

Searching for a way to represent the voices of the war[23]

During much of the 1980s and 1990s, I worked with human rights organisations and victim associations to record the testimonials of refugees from the war in Lima but I struggled to find a way of representing their stories. Becoming disenchanted with the testimonial literature of the time, I began to experiment with new paradigms and practices that involved examining the representation of violence in Peru through art[24] and by writing fiction and drama using

22 Carlos Iván Degregori (1900–1), p. 14. He gave me access to his interview materials.
23 See 'Missing the revolution: anthropologists and the war in Peru' (Starn, 1991).
24 See my article, 'Violence in Peru: performances and dialogues' (1998). This was revised as 'Protest arts from Ayacucho, Peru: song and visual artworks as validation of experience' (2004).

interview materials from victims, perpetrators and human rights activists. My crisis of representation became especially acute in 1986–7 when I had two research fellowships: first at the Wilson Center in Washington DC, followed by a position as Chercheur Associé of the Centre national de la recherché scientifique (CNRS) at the Ecole des Hautes Etudes in Paris. My proposals to both institutions stated that I would write a book about the research on violence I had conducted in Peru. I successfully gave oral presentations at both institutions but I could not find a voice to represent the stories I had collected until I published *Finding Cholita* in 2009.

I turned my full attention to the revolution in 1985 when a hand-delivered letter arrived at Cornell from a compadre in Chuschi describing how the village had been burned and was almost totally abandoned. He and his family had fled to Lima and were living in a squatter settlement with relatives but they could not find work. 'What are we to do?', he asked.

With a small grant from Cornell's Peace Studies Program, I arrived in Lima in 1985 and reconnected with the Association of Families of the Assassinated, Kidnapped, Detained, and Disappeared (AFASEP), which had originated in Ayacucho in September 1983 in response to the violent human rights abuses perpetrated by the Peruvian armed forces. Made up of volunteers, mostly Quechua-speaking women relatives of victims, AFASEP quickly founded the Adolfo Perez Esquivil Comedor in 1985. Its volunteers, who still feed 300 orphaned and displaced children a day, formed a network of victims' relatives who petitioned the military and government officials on behalf of their loved ones. Amnesty International (AI) took up their cause and an international rapid response petition and letter-writing campaign was initiated.

An early volunteer in Ayacucho was Guadelupe Ccallocunto Olano, a 30-year-old mother of four, whom I had known since she was a child in Quispillaqta, Chuschi's neighbouring village. She became involved with AFASEP after her husband and brother were arrested and then 'disappeared' in 1983. She presented a petition to Ayacucho's military garrison demanding their release but the military denied any knowledge of their whereabouts and they were never seen again. From that time on, Guadelupe was probably under constant surveillance. I interviewed her in 1986 shortly after her return to Lima from Santiago, Chile. She had assumed her old role as AFASEP secretary and was living in a safe house in Lima, sponsored by the Catholic Church's Servicio Paz y Justicia (Peace and Justice Service, SERPAJ), which provided sanctuary for Peruvian women in danger. The Servicio scheduled them to be transported to Santiago, Chile in the hope that they would be able to escape surveillance and arrest. Against everyone's advice, Guadelupe returned to Lima because she was concerned about her four children who were living with relatives. She was detained for four days on 13 May 1986, questioned and released on 17 May. However, she was rearrested on 24 May, interrogated and water-boarded in the military anti-terrorism centre, DIRCOTE, after which she was transferred to El Fronton Prison and held there for three months. Only after a concerted campaign by AI, AFASEP, SERPAJ and the Peruvian human rights organisation, APRODEH, was she released. Guadelupe continued working tirelessly for AFASEP and SERPAJ for four years: petitioning for the release of the kidnapped and disappeared, creating an archive of the latter, and supervising the SERPAJ mothers' workshop that produced knapsacks and *arpilleras* [stitched stories of the war] in Lima.

I interviewed several of the workshop's 60 members as they stitched stories of kidnappings, attacks and repression into the arpilleras. European funding, especially from Germany, supported the production and sale of these works of art. I remember smuggling arpilleras into the US in my suitcase and European volunteers did the same. This political art form quickly became 'cloth telegrams', communicating the depictions of the abuses against victims to global audiences at a time when those abuses were being denied (Isbell, 1992; 1994).[25] Among other folk art forms that communicate victims' experiences are the *tablas* [painted wooden boards] of Sarhua.[26]

At the beginning of June 1990, Guadelupe travelled to the city of Ayacucho with her children in order to vote in the election. She said she would be safe because 5,000 police and military were patrolling the city streets to prevent the national election from being disrupted. But at 2.30am on 10 June, just hours before voting started, 15 *encapuchado* [hooded], armed men wearing army boots broke into her home on Calle Grau. The house was occupied by her mother, Silvia Olano, her widowed sister with her dependent children and Guadelupe herself with her four children. Guadelupe and her youngest daughter, Nora, aged ten, were sleeping in the same bed. After robbing and terrorising the other occupants, the men burst into Guadelupe's room and one of them held a gun to Nora's head while three others turned the bed on its side and pulled Guadelupe out of the house by her hair. Barefoot and wearing only her pyjamas, she was last seen by a guard on duty at the market being dragged up the street in the direction of the Los Cabito military base. One of her last actions was to telephone the SERPAJ president, Esteban Cuya, and report the kidnapping of another SERPAJ member the night before. Sadly, Guadelupe Ccallocunto joined the long list of the disappeared and in spite of concerted efforts made by the organisations she served, she was never seen again.

25 The articles, images of the art and some protest songs can be accessed and downloaded from http://isbellandes.library.cornell.edu. Also, see my article, 'Shining Path and peasant responses in rural Ayacucho' (1994).
26 *Unveiling Secrets of War in the Peruvian Andes* by Olga González (2011) is an important study of the tablas de Sarhua.

In 1993, I toured with a Quilt of the Disappeared that had been loaned to me by AFASEP to university campuses across the United States. The trip was arranged by AI and anthropologist Carole Nagengast, its former chair, joined me on the programme at the University of California, Riverside. The 12 x 20-foot quilt resembled a number of arpilleras, each depicting individual stories of disappearances, all stitched together. I spoke about my experiences after each exhibition and we usually gave students the opportunity to read dramatised excerpts from *Public Secrets from Peru*,[27] a play I had written based on my interviews. It allowed students to speak in the voices of victims, perpetrators and political actors from Peru as well as those of the US embassy staff members I had interviewed. At that time the war was said to have claimed 26,000 lives but by the time the final TRC report was released in August 2003, the death toll was placed at between 61,007 and 77,552 – which is probably a conservative estimate.

Chuschi revises the history of its ballot-burning clash after 35 years

On 17 May 2015, *El Comercio*, Peru's major daily newspaper, ran a story by Ricardo León under the headline, 'Chuschi, today, thirty years after the birth of terrorist violence' (translated from the Spanish). His report contradicts the official version of the events that occurred at dawn on 18 May 1980. Florencio Conde Núñez had maintained all this time that a group of hooded men, claiming to be from the military, broke into the municipal building on the plaza while he was guarding the ballots and stole them. Having recalled that Don Florencio was the municipal building's custodian at that time, I was intrigued to read how he and his sons, Julio César and Bernardo, subsequently came forward to reveal what actually happened. A cousin of Florencio's came to keep him company during his vigil, armed with a bottle of trago (120 proof alcohol cut with water). Florencio now believes that the cousin was involved with Shining Path and got him drunk intentionally. In the middle of the night, the cousin (they would not reveal his name) escorted Don Florencio home, helped Diodora Vilca, Florencio's wife, put him to bed, and left. Diodora sent their two sons who were aged 14 and 10 to the municipal building to guard the ballots. The boys grabbed animal skins to sleep on and ran to the electoral office that had been set up in the municipal building. At dawn they were awakened by angry voices and pounding on the door. The men identified themselves as military from the base in Cangallo and demanded that they open the door. Bernardo, the eldest, answered in Quechua: '*Manan kichamuykikumanchu*

---

27 I used Michael Taussig's (1999) notion of 'public secrets' to indicate what he calls the 'skilled revelation of skilled concealment' for the title of this play. The drama is posted on http://isbellandes.library.cornell.edu.

papaymi piñakuwanmanku' [I can't open the door – my father will be mad at me]. He added: 'The *cumpa* (companeros, Senderistas) kicked down the door and took everything.'

Bernardo ran home and told his father what had happened. Florencio, dazed and probably hungover, raced from the house to rescue Julio Cesar, the ten-year-old, before the military arrived. Bernardo said what hurt him most was seeing his father run out of the house without his hat – 'he never leaves without his hat'. After rescuing Julio Cesar, Florencio, accompanied by the governor, Alejandro Galindo, and several *varayoq* [local traditional authorities], found the burned ballots and trapped the principal suspect, Bernardo Azurzán, who later escaped. He was a new teacher in the high school and not from the region. After the high school was built in the early 1970s, new teachers were assigned to Chuschi under a national programme requiring them to serve in rural schools for one year before they could apply for positions in urban settings. Ricardo León in his *El Comercio* article reported that in 1980 when the ballots were burned, only three of the 19 teachers in the Chuschi school system were from the region. His article confirmed that Sendero had placed cadre members in local schools to infiltrate and indoctrinate and, by 1980, they were in full control. It has taken 35 years for the story of the burned ballots to be revised. According to León, Julio César Conde Vilca, now a 45-year-old school teacher, has written a book, *El Lunar Rojo del Mundo*,[28] describing the events surrounding the ballot burning in 1980.

Chuschi today

The story of my collaborator, Mariano Barrios Micuylia, who keeps me up to date via Facebook, illustrates the histories of so many whose lives were disrupted by the war. This is his personal narrative: born in 1965 in Cancha Cancha, he is the eldest of ten. At the age of 12 he enrolled in the new secondary school, Colegio National Ramón Castillo, in Chuschi and completed three years of study (1977–80). After Sendero took full control of Chuschi, he fled to Lima in 1981. Mariano escaped the mandatory celebration in Cancha Cancha in 1982 requiring comuneros to march in columns as the 'Popular Army' and sing Sendero slogans. Had he been in his home community, he might have been 'kidnapped' by Sendero and indoctrinated. Cancha Cancha denounced Sendero and the *Guardias* responded with a strong military presence in December 1982. In retaliation, Sendero attacked Cancha Cancha four times in as many months between December 1982 and April 1983. Mariano fled again and was able to find work in Lima and to finish the fourth and fifth years of his secondary education at night schools in 1983 and 1984. He

---

28 The *El Comercio* article does not cite publication information.

returned to Ayacucho in 1987 to study at La Universidad de Huamanga and completed two years (1988-9). However, he was again forced to abandon his studies because the university's political atmosphere was dire with the Peruvian military responsible for frequent forced student disappearances.

He fled the city of Ayacucho in 1990 and found work 125 miles away over the crest of the Andes in the coca-growing Valley of the Rivers Apurímac, Ene and Montaro (VRAEM). During the seven years he worked there, he became a leader of the coca growers, served as his community's president of the Committee of Counter-Subversive Civil Defense, and became the zonal coordinator of Mantaro combatting Sendero. He also met the mother of his children in VRAEM and returned to Ayacucho with his family. In 2001-2, he was president of the Federación Agraria Departamental de Ayacucho (Agrarian Federation of Ayacucho, FADA) and participated as a leader in the march of the *suyus* [Four Parts] that toppled Fujimori's government in July 2000.

Mariano spent the next decade involved with various organisations as an indigenous leader and expositor of Andean culture travelling throughout Latin America. From 2004-9, he worked for the International Agrarian Development fund in the Cuzco–Puno regions. In 2010 he returned to his natal homeland working as the sub-director of social and human development and coordinator of ten Quechua municipalities in the Rio Pampas region. Currently he is sub-director of social and economic development in the Sarhua municipality. He organised the celebration of Andean knowledge and technologies marked by the replacement of the suspension bridge over the Rio Pampas in February 2014. Salvador Palomino Flores,[29] an original member of the Rio Pampas research team, attended from Sweden to give a lecture.

Mariano ends his personal history by lamenting that extreme poverty remains high: over 50 per cent in the region; chronic infantile malnutrition is at 60.8 per cent, and illiteracy is estimated to be at 25 to 28 per cent. He also reports that state programmes for women are too often paternalistic converting them into dependent recipients of aid and disempowering them. I am surprised at how many Rio Pampas natives have returned home but am not surprised that the state programmes to eradicate poverty, and improve the status of women, have not made much headway in the postwar period. There have been advances in education with more schools being built, and local infrastructure has improved, especially the road system.

---

29 Palomino-Flores (1970) published *El Sistema de oposiciones en la comunidad de Sarhua* in 1984.

The place of art in the battle for memory and recognition

The volume, *Art from a Fractured Past: Memory and Truth-Telling in Post-Shining Path Peru*, edited by Cynthia Milton (2014), brought together scholars from diverse fields to examine the role of art in making sense of Peru's armed conflict. Its contributors ask what the implications are when using art as a mode of truth-telling. I turned to fiction as a means of conveying the stories that I collected from victims of the war. I believe that fictionalised narratives capture the affective worlds more accurately than the non-fiction explanatory ones common to cultural anthropology. The retablos, tablas and arpilleras which came out of the productive 'memory work' and record of the war, produced by Andean refugees in Lima during the 1980s and 1990s, are their visual testimonies. As Joseph Feldman points out, Milton's contributors ask critical questions: for example, 'what are the implications of using art as a mode of truth telling in post conflicts societies?' (2015, p. 500). I would ask 'Can art be used as historical resources in the current time of contested histories in Peru?'

Lima has become a battleground in terms of memory narratives as the nation struggles to represent the war and its aftermath. In 2005, Dutch-born artist, Lika Mutal completed a sculpture in the Campo de Marte of Jesus María, Lima. It commemorates 32,000 victims by means of inscriptions on river stones of their names and dates of death, the details of which had been provided by the TRC. Eighty artists and peace activists helped Mital to inscribe the stones, which form a spiral around a monolith from which water drips. Named "The Eye that Cries', the sculpture was inspired by the *Yuyanapaq* – the TRC's 'To Remember' photo exhibition held in 2003. The last name Mital inscribed was that of a three-year-old child. There was opposition to the sculpture from people who discovered that it included the names of 41 prisoners killed during the Castro Castro jail raid in 1992, all of whom had been organisers and militants of Sendero. The controversy that ensued was taken to the Inter-American Court in 2006 which ruled that the 41 names should remain. But on 29 September 2007, the night policeman who guarded the sculpture was beaten and tied up and red paint was poured over the monolith. When I visited the work in 2010, it was still closed and I had to ask APRODEH to arrange a visit for me and my students from Cornell. We saw that Mital and her colleagues had reinscribed the names and repaired the monolith. I, like others who visit the sculpture, walked round the spiral and looked for names of people killed in the conflict. I cried when I found them. Annual pilgrimages from Ayacucho continued throughout the period the artwork was closed. On one occasion, Ayacuchanos from AFASEP reported to me that the mayor of

Jesus Maria scheduled a dog show next to the sculpture on the day of their visit to disturb them as they honoured their dead.[30]

The other battle site for memorials and recognition is the Museo de Memoria,[31] planned for erection on the Avenue of Memory in Campo de Marte, Jesus María where the 'Eye that Cries' is located. Germany donated two million dollars for construction in 2009 but President Alan Garcia rejected that offer saying that Peru had more pressing matters to attend to. After a loud public protest by Vargas Llosa and international pressure, the donation was accepted but the plans languished in political turmoil for five years. The Avenue of Memory was scrapped and finally in 2014 a museum opened on the Costa Verde of Miraflores. Its new name is the Lugar de Memoria, Tolerancia y Inclusion Social (Museum of Memory, Tolerance and Social Inclusion), known as LUM, and it is run by a team of young, professional staff trained in Europe and the US. They see their mandate as educating generations who know nothing about the political violence that tore the social fabric of Peru. They are adept at the 'skilled revelation of skilled concealment' so aptly described by Taussig (1999).

What is being erased and what is being revealed about the war with Shining Path? Walter Benjamin (1969) has taught us that memories of events are not retold like the beads of a rosary. Chuschinos have just revealed a new version of the ballot-burning story from 1980. What other aspects of their 'times of trouble', as they currently call the war years, will they revise? As Olga Gonzalez (2011, p. 9) has argued, 'contentious and traumatic memories solidify and lurk, awaiting the transgressive moment of revelation.' While writing my own memories of those 'times of trouble' for this chapter (which has been most difficult and painful), I wondered what I may have concealed about that past and what other versions might contradict my own? I invite that dialogue. Benjamin has also taught us that remembering and forgetting are always intertwined. What have I silenced or erased? I can only invite others to provide the answer by presenting their versions of our shared history. I am absolutely delighted that I am engaging in conversations with Chuschinos on Facebook, because once I post this chapter, I hope to be flooded with responses. Is this a new form of ethnography? As I age and can no longer physically travel to Chuschi, I'm glad I can journey over the internet.

---

30   See Hite (2012) for further details.
31   See Feldman (2012), in which he concludes that 'memory museums' risk diverting attention away from the multilayered nature of such museums that must be understood as memorialisation discourses located in specific places and historical moments.

Return to Chuschi in 2001: rediscovering gender

In 2001 I had a revealing discussion with the Machaca sisters, from the neighbouring village of Quispillaqta, whom I had known since their childhood: playmates of my daughter, Diana, during our various return trips to Chuschi in the 1970s. Both were agronomists and directors of the non-governmental organisation, Asociacíon Bartolomé Arpepaylla Ayacucho. As we travelled to La Union in the high puna above Chuschi for a region-wide seed exchange, the Machaca sisters and two male agronomists asked how Diana was. Bumping along the rutted winding road I had to explain that my daughter, Diana, was now Cid, my son, transgender with a male identity. In the ensuing conversations, they all adamantly claimed there were no gays or transgender people in Andean communities. I had to remind the sisters of their cousin, born male who dressed as a woman, was known by a female name, and sold prepared meals every Friday in the market. The 'boy's' father took the 18-year-old to the national police garrison nearby and begged the officer in charge 'to make him a man' – a month later the officer returned the boy to the village claiming that all the kid did was cry. Thereafter, she was accepted back into the community and lived as a female continuing to sell prepared food every market day.

In my earlier research, I also found that, symbolically, both sexes were considered to be more male than female in old age. One old woman explained that the elderly were 'like *chuño*' [freeze-dried potatoes]. I interpreted this as meaning that the wrinkled, dried tubers were non-reproductive and asked myself if that meant the elderly were without gender identity at all or was it another category along life's gender path? I thought of this gender path as going from *imaduro a duro* [young and immature to freeze-dried and hard] (Isbell, 1997). Another early experience had taught me to be sensitive to gender. When I arrived in Chuschi in 1969, I still did not speak Quechua well, but my level of understanding was pretty good. I did not reveal that I understood Quechua because I wanted to 'listen in' on their conversations. At an all-night ritual, I overheard speculations about me being a *wari* [a being or animal with both male and female genitalia]. Fascinating! I later learned that among herd animals, especially sheep, a wari is considered to be the mother/father of the herd in spite of the fact that the experience of herders tells them that such animals are sterile. When I went out along the pitch-black pathway to urinate, adults would send children to try to determine if I was indeed a wari. The children returned and reported that they could not see well enough. That event launched an entirely new avenue of investigation on sex and gender that has proven most productive.[32]

32 As mentioned earlier, my first reflections on how children learn about and experiment with sex and gender were published with Fredy Roncalla (1977). The research was conducted

My final return to Peru in 2010: a new era of internet ethnography

As a Senior Fulbright Specialist at Catholic University in September 2010, I participated in a week-long workshop on diversity in which three students who had been awarded Ford Diversity Fellowships from Chuschi and Quispillaqta participated: two men and one woman. Through the auspices of Florencia Zapata and The Mountain Institute we were also able to include representatives from the community of Vicos in the discussions. The Ford fellowship students said they felt that all the minority students, regardless of their ethnic backgrounds or languages, were separated and isolated from the rest of Católica's student body. Moreover, a young man from Chuschi studying agronomy complained that the traditional knowledge he wanted to share in his classes was ignored and denigrated.

I was pleased to send the students back to the communities with two new books: *Para defendernos* (2005), which contains the two additional chapters on Sendero Luminoso in the Rio Pampas; and the edited collection, *50 Años de Antropología Aplicada en el Peru: Vicos y otras experiencias*, in which I have a chapter entitled 'El retorno de Cornell a Vicos, 2005' (2010). Internet conversations with both communities have begun. I am now participating in collaborative internet ethnography.

I have provided here a personal history of my fieldwork in Chuschi and outlined how I found sanctuary in art and fiction when I could not find a voice, a methodology or a paradigm for what I was experiencing as an anthropologist working in an area of the Andes torn by war. I found that voice in narrative and telling peoples' stories. I have provided synopses of Mariano's and Guadelupe's histories to illustrate, on the one hand the tragic disappearance of Guadelupe and, on the other, the story of Mariano's survival and return to the Rio Pampas. I claim ownership of the interpretation and translation of their stories. I could provide many more; rather, I refer readers to *Finding Cholita* (Isbell, 2009a).

---

with children in 1969–70 when we discovered the sexualised riddle competitions played between adolescent girls and boys. It was published as a study of metaphorical language but, in retrospect, the sex and gender dynamics among the adolescents are more interesting. Those materials are summarised in the second half of 'De inmaduro a duro', entitled: 'Tropos de género que recorren el curso de la vida: el proceso de diferenciación' (Isbell, 1997). These two publications demonstrate a major theoretical shift in my thinking about sex and gender from a static structural interpretation presented in 'La otra mitad esencial: un studio de complementariedad sexual andina' (1976) to a processual view of gender development. According to this view children begin life as symbolically male and develop gender identity through the life course, becoming once past child-bearing age more of a male symbolic figure, thereafter being thought of as dried, wrinkled, sterile *chuño* in old age. I argue further that maleness is marked in the semantics of gender.

2. Losing my heart*

Catherine J. Allen

One day in the mid 1970s I hiked into a small Quechua-speaking hamlet called Sonqo. I was in my mid 20s, a doctoral student, and in search of an Andean community that still used Inca drinking cups. That first visit went so well I went back and stayed for a long time. After a while I realised that it was the wrong place for my project but by then didn't really care. It was the right place in many other ways.

Here is the story of how I came to be looking for Inca cups in Sonqo and how that affected the rest of my life and work. From early childhood I had been fascinated by the archaeology of Greece and Egypt. When I began thinking about a career, I was drawn to writing and classical archaeology. I did my BA at St John's College in Annapolis, Maryland, the 'Great Books' school. The curriculum included plenty of classics but no archaeology, which didn't worry me because I planned all along to pursue graduate studies. After some research, I decided that anthropology would be a broader and more interesting field than classics. So it was that in 1970 I began graduate work in anthropology at the University of Illinois in Urbana, expecting to specialise in Old World archaeology. There was a possibility of participating in the excavation of a Bronze Age site in Sicily.

To my dismay I found myself crushingly bored by the basic nuts and bolts of archaeology – site reports, soil samples, stone tool types, endless potsherds. This discovery brought about a kind of existential crisis. I realised that I had been drawn to the classical world by its literature, art and landscape. I loved the

---

* This chapter spans some 50 years. I found it difficult to write, yet immensely useful. How can I properly thank all who supported and facilitated my life's work? My first fieldwork in Peru was supported by the Doherty Foundation; subsequently, small grants were awarded by the National Science Foundation, Wenner-Gren Foundation and George Washington University. Precious support for sustained periods of writing has been provided by the Dumbarton Oaks, the Centre for Advanced Study of the Visual Arts at the National Gallery, and the Guggenheim Foundation. I am deeply grateful to Sonqueños who opened their homes to me, and continue to share their lives with tolerance and good humour, and I am immensely appreciative of the stimulation and constructive criticism received from family members, teachers, students and colleagues in North America, Peru and Europe, some of whom are mentioned in these pages. Finally, I am grateful to Francisco Ferreira for conceiving this project and steering the volume to completion. Thanks to you all! Any memory lapses or other errors of fact and interpretation are my own.

way Greek and Latin connected me with the lives and thoughts of people who had lived thousands of years in the past. I began to think I would be better off in a comparative literature programme.

Eventually I confided these doubts to my adviser, Charlie Keller, an archaeologist who worked in the African Palaeolithic. 'You're really upset about this aren't you?', he observed as I poured out my heart. 'Let's get out of my office'. Off we went to Treno's, a local hangout where we could drink beer and just talk. Charlie listened to my doubts and helped sort through my still vague aspirations and motivations, from time to time noting comparisons with his own career and relationship to his chosen field. The upshot of that long afternoon was that I decided to stay on in the graduate programme; to change course in anthropology rather than leave the field altogether. I sometimes wonder how my life would have unfolded had that conversation never happened. I doubt that I would ever have gone to Sonqo.

Over the next year-and-a half I muddled on with a vague focus on linguistics and material culture. It was the early 1970s. Claude Lévi-Strauss was in his heyday (to the distaste of cultural ecologists, also at full bore); Victor Turner was getting big and Clifford Geertz was about to burst on to the scene. My first source of inspiration, however, was less contemporary. Donald Lathrap's class on the anthropology of art introduced me to Franz Boas, whose *Primitive Art* (1955 [1927]) remains one of my foundational texts. In Boas I found humanism combined with empirical rigour and, more specifically, I discovered style as a conceptual gateway to the study of culture. Franz Boas's concept of style, like Pierre Bourdieu's *habitus* (which I encountered later), compels one to focus on the material manifestations of human activity, externalised in artefacts and/or internalised in the body.

Lathrap also introduced me to the work of Gregory Bateson, whose emphasis on art as skilful communication about 'the interface between conscious and unconscious' resonated with Boas's stress on 'the formal element in art.' Both emphasised that (as in the music of Bach) extreme formalism is in no way incompatible with the expression of deep feeling. Other courses introduced me to Erving Goffman's symbolic interactionism (for example, Goffmann, 1967), an approach to style in performance that I saw as complementing Bateson's explorations of emergent *ethos* and *eidos* in small group interactions. A bit later I discovered semiotics. I read Charles Sanders Peirce, Roland Barthes, and was especially taken by the discussion of pragmatics in *Foundations of the Theory of Signs* by Charles Morris (1938).

None of this would have propelled me into the Peruvian highlands on the lookout for Inca cups. That came about because I signed up for Tom Zuidema's seminar on the iconography of Nasca ceramics. At that time I knew next to nothing about South America and had never studied Spanish. During the first weeks I felt overwhelmed by my lack of background knowledge, yet fascinated by the strange creatures of Nasca iconography. I was equally fascinated by Zuidema. Here, I felt, was a completely original mind drawing on an unfamiliar intellectual tradition (Dutch structuralism) in which I felt curiously at home. So I stuck with Zuidema and plunged into Nasca iconography. I wrote my MA paper on the killer whale motif and assisted Zuidema in organising his huge slide archive. During those many hours spent poring over pots and images of pots on slides and in books, I became well acquainted with the Nasca creatures in all their guises and phases. The Cosmic Deity, Masked Mythical Being, Bloody-Mouthed Killer Whale and endless Trophy Heads were companions of my waking hours and even populated my dreams at night. I began to feel like a little kid talking to imaginary friends and realised that it was time to stop. The questions that really interested me had to do with living context, with the functions and meanings of the ceramics in the lives of the people who made and used them. Inconveniently, these people were long dead and the pots themselves had little archaeological provenance. Once again, I hit a wall and considered dropping out of anthropology.

Tom Zuidema suggested that I simply transfer my interest to artefacts for which context was more accessible. He had an extensive slide collection of *qeros* [decorated wooden tumblers] that were used in Inca ritual consumption of *chicha* [maize beer]. Qeros bear a complex, lively iconography and are easy to locate in museum collections. Rather than petering out of use after the Spanish conquest, qeros underwent a remarkable florescence. They are well described by Spanish chroniclers and, finally, they are still to be found in parts of the Andean highlands today, providing a link between the Andean present and the Inca past. Thus, while my project would be carried out mainly in museums, archives and libraries, it would incorporate an element of ethnographic comparison as well. My study would also include other kinds of ritual drinking vessels that were reportedly still in use. *Pacchas* have two openings allowing chicha to pour in one end and out the other. *Qochas* are bowls containing figures of animals or people; some are composed of three concentric rings for three different kinds of beverage.

The project appealed to me. I was excited by the prospect of doing research in Peruvian museums and studying old Spanish texts. The ethnographic component appealed to me intellectually, yet I dreaded having to do it. I had never considered ethnography as an option, thinking myself too introverted for that kind of work. I thought I was suited temperamentally to work with objects and texts – but people? Not so much.

I finished my coursework. It was a golden age for South American anthropology at the University of Illinois. I was part of a lively and supportive cohort, students of R. Tom Zuidema, Don Lathrap, Joe Casagrande and

Norman Whitten. I took classes with Gary Urton, Jeanette Sherbondy, Ted MacDonald, Jorge Marcos and Regina Harrison (moonlighting from the comparative literature programme). Just ahead of us Billie Jean Isbell was writing her dissertation; Deborah Poole, Joanne Rappaport, Colin McEwan and Clark Erickson came along just behind us. Bruce Mannheim sometimes joined us from the University of Illinois Chicago Circle. We studied, shared ideas and partied together. I spent the summer of 1973 assisting Zuidema's research in Cuzco, and the summer of 1974 studying Quechua at Cornell.

I threw myself into learning Quechua and neglected to get any formal training in Spanish, operating on the boneheaded assumption that I could somehow pick it up on the fly. In hindsight this was the big lacuna in my preparation. Although with time I have picked up enough Spanish to converse, read and lecture, I have never become truly fluent in the language, nor have I developed ease in reading Colonial Spanish texts and documents. Weak Spanish doomed the project – as originally conceived – from the start. But I get ahead of myself.

Fieldwork

I wrote a grant proposal that got funded by the Doherty Foundation. Although ethnographic research was but a component of the larger project, I knew that I could not get away with just taking day trips from Cuzco to attend a few festivals. Zuidema was adamant that ritual drinking had to be understood in the context of people's lives, and that this would require immersion in routine activities. Many traditional practices, moreover, were closed to outsiders, and I would have to build trust and rapport before I could hope to witness and participate in them.

So it was that I sidled into fieldwork in spite of myself. I left for Peru expecting to spend six months in museums and a further six in a highland community. My husband Rick Wagner took a leave of absence from his graduate studies in English to accompany me. His companionship, support and active interest were a tremendous boon. In March 1975, after two months of museum research in Lima, Arequipa and Cuzco, it was time to head into the countryside. To locate a community where qeros, pacchas and qochas were in use, I turned for guidance to the anthropology faculty at the Universidad San Antonio Abad in Cuzco. Juan Nuñez del Prado, a professor there, had seen qeros in a community called Sonqo, located in the province of Paucartambo, north-east of Cuzco. In nearby P'isaq I had seen three-ring qochas for sale that were said to be from that region as well. So I decided to pay a visit to Sonqo. Juan's father, venerable Oscar Nuñez del Prado, helped me secure a letter of introduction from Cuzco's board of education. Armed with this letter and a credential from the Peruvian Ministry of Culture, Rick and I climbed aboard a truck to Colquepata, capital of the district where Sonqo was located. There, the teacher received us cordially and let us spend the night in a classroom. The next day we set off on the ten-kilometre walk to Sonqo with a fourth grade student as our guide.

After about two hours we rounded a curve on our hilly path and a new vista opened. 'There's Sonqo', announced our young guide. His mission completed, he said his goodbyes and scampered back toward Colquepata. There was nothing to distinguish the landscape ahead of us from what we had been passing through except for one building with a bright blue aluminium roof – the school. Otherwise the same treeless hills spread before us, scattered with fields of green potato plants and blooming *tarwi* (*Lupinus mutabilis*, similar to black-eyed peas). An unfinished dirt road disappeared around another curve far ahead. To our eyes, unschooled in reading this landscape, nothing visibly announced, 'You are entering Sonqo'. There was nothing to do but continue to huff and puff along the trail toward the blue roof, clearly visible yet still far away.

As we finally neared the school we saw two men on the path ahead of us. Both wore ponchos, one brightly patterned, the other a simple brown colour. On our approach we observed 'bright poncho man' carrying a small portable shrine containing a painting of crucified Christ as well as some bits of money. 'Brown poncho man' bowed to the shrine and placed a coin in it. Later we learned that 'bright poncho man' was collecting contributions for that year's pilgrimage to the mountain sanctuary of Qoyllur Rit'I, which is one of the most important in the Peruvian Andes. By this time we were face-to-face and I needed to do something. Employing that most basic ethnographic method, 'monkey-see, monkey-do', I bowed and placed a few coins in the box. '*Allinmi!*' [Very good!] said 'bright poncho man' seriously in thanks, betraying none of what I later learned was a mixture of surprise, pleasure and amusement. That was how we met Don Luis. He, as much as anything, was the reason we stayed in Sonqo.

'*Iskwelachu?*' [The school?] I asked, pointing to the path ahead, my six weeks of intensive Quechua rapidly deserting me. Don Luis turned round and led us towards it. Rick tried to start a conversation: '*Sonqo es "Corazon", no?*' [Sonqo means 'heart', doesn't it?]. '*Arí, corazoncito*' [Yes, little heart] was the answer. The word *sonqo* refers to the heart, the innermost part and the seat of emotional intelligence. I never learned a reason for the community's name. It is one of several places in the same river valley but is no more central geographically or politically than the others. 'It's just a name', people would answer when I asked about it.

The teacher received us cordially and sent us off with Luis to attend a community work party then underway. That was another stroke of luck for it introduced us to the people immediately and naturally. I have written about that, and the months that followed, in my ethnographic study, *The Hold Life Has*. Nevertheless, a brief overview of the neighbourhood is in order:

Sonqo is a rural *ayllu* [indigenous community] in the district of Colquepata, which is located in Paucartambo province in the southern Peruvian department of Cuzco. Its approximately 85 households are dispersed over about 1,825 hectares of almost treeless *puna* [tundra] spread out along one side of a small river valley between 3,200 and 3,600 metres in altitude. When I arrived there in 1975 Sonqo was a monolingual Quechua-speaking community with an agro-pastoral economy oriented more to subsistence than the market. The inhabitants raised over 40 varieties of potatoes, supplemented by *ullucus* and *ocas* (other Andean tubers) as well as beans, barley and tarwi. Although each household had hereditary usufruct rights to specific plots of land, all land was collectively owned by the ayllu, which had ultimate authority over its distribution. The inhabitants coordinated their crop rotation in a traditional system of sectorial fallowing. Herd animals grazed and left their manure on the fallow fields. Most households raised herds of llamas, alpacas and sheep, numbering from a few to upwards of 50 beasts. I was told that 20 years earlier herds had been larger, and that Sonqueños also tended animals from llama caravans that passed through their territory on the way to Cuzco. Many families also raised chickens, pigs, guinea pigs (for meat), and kept dogs for protection. A few owned a cow or one or two horses.

Sonqo is one of several *comunidades campesinas* [legally recognised peasant communities] in the district of Colquepata. The district capital, also called Colquepata, was founded in 1595 when the colonial Spanish administration forcibly resettled the previously dispersed population into a Spanish-style town to expedite administration and missionisation. It seems, however, that within a few decades many families managed to return to their old settlement pattern; apparently it was during this period between 1600–50 that Sonqo was founded as an ayllu with legal title to its territory.

It was a point of pride among Sonqueños that theirs was a free community which had never belonged to a hacienda. Nevertheless, they were economically subservient to the mestizo townspeople of Colquepata through ties of debt peonage and *compadrazgo* [ceremonial kinship], which limited their freedom to travel and market their own produce. When I arrived in 1975 the Agrarian reform of the Velasco Regime (1968–75) was beginning to undercut these local power relationships; haciendas had been expropriated and aid programmes initiated for comunidades campesinas. Sonqueños welcomed the reforms enthusiastically, although they came to resent the oppressive bureaucracy some of these programmes entailed.[1]

1   There is extensive literature on the Velasco Agrarian Reform. Among works by anthropologists see Seligmann (1995) and Mayer (2009).

In 1975 the community had a dual system of governance. A newly instituted system of civil authorities consisting of a president, vice-president, secretary, treasurer and guardian of civil order coexisted with the traditional system of *varayuq* [staff holders] consisting of an *alcalde* [mayor], *segundo* [vice-mayor] and four *regidores* [councilmen], serving mainly as town criers. There was also a rather fluid set of religious cargoes that involved sponsorship of religious celebrations. A division of labour had developed in which the president and his officers handled relations between the community and representatives of the state, while the alcalde and his officers presided over communal work parties as well as Carnival and other celebrations of the Sonqo ayllu, the community. The Velasco government's policy was to permit traditional authorities to function in mainly symbolic capacities with the expectation that they would eventually die out.

Why did I stay on in Sonqo instead of checking out other communities that, in hindsight, would have been better suited to my research? In part it was because we had a good reception and made friends there. That seemed promising, so I hunkered down, concentrated on improving my Quechua, and waited for ritual drinking vessels to emerge from hiding. In early May came the festival of Santa Cruz (Holy Cross) and indeed chicha was served in qeros, simple undecorated goblets of recent manufacture. I assumed that it was just a matter of time before pacchas and qochas would emerge as well. Yes, people denied having them but I thought this was simply a matter of building trust. Eventually some people did honour me with confidences and show me secret possessions – but pacchas and qochas were not among them.

I finally had to conclude that (like Saddam Hussein's weapons of mass destruction) they really weren't there. By that time I was committed. Rick and I had accompanied a delegation from Sonqo on the pilgrimage to Qoyllur Rit'i, a profound bonding experience. From then on my sphere of acquaintances widened, my Quechua improved and every day I learned something new and interesting. Yes, Sonqo was cold; living there was uncomfortable and exhausting, yet I loved it.

A sea change was taking place both in my work and my sense of self. Ethnographic curiosity became the driving motivation for my research rather than qero iconography. I rationalised the shift by focusing on drinking practices rather than drinking vessels. In Sonqo, which is too high for corn cultivation, the usual alcoholic beverage was not chicha but a kind of rot-gut rum called *trago*. It was served in shot glasses, not qeros, yet its consumption occurred within a ritual frame and followed protocols close to those described by Spanish sources of the 16th and 17th centuries. I learned to drink the way that Sonqueños drank. This was a demanding kind of participant observation; I paid a heavy price in hangovers but learned a tremendous amount. Although my facility with Quechua was still limited, I was nevertheless able to pay close attention to non-verbal behaviour and to the minutiae of serving and drinking etiquette. My reading in Goffman led me to question what each interaction expressed about group members' relationships. As I sorted out participants and roles I came to appreciate the parts played in the interactions by the witnessing earth and places (which I expand upon below). Because there were no pacchas, I learned to follow the flow of liquid as it dribbled out in libations and was poured down people's throats. Eventually I realised that the body itself is a kind of paccha, a passage for the flow of substances.

Before I left for Peru, Joseph Casagrande suggested that I take drawings of qeros to the field with me to draw out conversations about the iconography. During my initial period of museum research Rick made good rollout drawings which sparked interesting conversations about the Incas, whom Sonqueños considered as their ancestors. I also took Sonqueños to the archaeological museum in Cuzco. Although they found it strange to see the objects ensconced in glass cases, my friends enjoyed the visits immensely. They had little to say about qero iconography per se but got into lively conversations about weddings and animal fertility rites, occasions at which they thought the items must have been used. Their responses to other items were enlightening in unexpected ways – Dona Basilia was delighted with a stone penis – '*Kawsaq kikin*!' [The living one itself!]; Don Luis was intensely interested in a large adobe brick – back in Sonqo he described to friends its size, shape and composition. I stored up these disparate items of interest in my mind and field notes; some of them only percolated to the surface many years later when I finally wrote up a paper about pacchas.

All along, from my first hours in Sonqo, I was being instructed in *hallpay* [coca chewing]. Before beginning fieldwork I knew that coca leaf had ritual importance but I had not thought about studying its uses, much less consuming it myself. It was clear, however, that our acceptance in the community hinged on our chewing coca. Unlike trago, which was drunk only occasionally, coca leaf was shared and consumed several times a day, always according to a specific etiquette. People paid attention to my command of this protocol, correcting my mistakes and reminding me that to chew coca was to communicate with the animate earth and mountains. Here too Goffman served me well, for I had to recognise places (hills, springs, rock outcrops) as participants in these highly stylised and deeply meaningful interactions. In this way coca opened a window on to the Sonqueños' way of life.

This window would never have opened had I stayed mainly in museums and archives with brief forays into the countryside at fiesta time. Zuidema had advised me against asking leading questions; his counsel amounted to: be patient, pay attention to what happens and be ready to follow up. I did not mind 'going with the flow', especially as at day's end there was always something interesting to write up. The best guide to fieldwork still seems to me to be Malinowski's introduction to *Argonauts*: record what concrete data you can, pay heed to the imponderabilia of actual life – and carpe diem! Be ready to seize unexpected opportunities.

Writing up

After 15 months in Peru, about 11 of which were spent in Sonqo, I returned to Urbana. The downside of my laidback approach to fieldwork was that I had a lot of disparate data but no clear idea what I was going to do with it. The different components of my research project no longer meshed. Inca drinking vessels – the starting point for the whole project – had fallen by the wayside. I had studied and photographed dozens of qeros but my mind and heart were invested in Sonqo. I asked myself what I had actually learned, and the answer was – I learned how to chew coca. I reviewed my data and my memories of that activity, and began to see that regular daily coca chewing provided a template for social and ritual practice in general. I recalled the attention that Sonqueños had paid to my invocations over coca leaves, and the frustration that led Luis finally to sit me down and explain how they needed to be done. Here I had concrete examples of something that was deeply significant. I realised that, with Luis's instructions in mind, I could unpack the various strands of meaning that came together in these brief poetic phrases and the gestures that accompanied them.

Coca chewing took priority over drinking; my dissertation became 'Coca, chicha and trago: private and communal rituals in a Quechua community' (under my then-married name, Catherine Allen Wagner). The goblet-shaped qeros of Sonqo did make their way into the dissertation as elements of public ceremony, but were far from being the centrepiece. Nevertheless, my fascination with drinking vessels as vehicles for social relations and expressions of cultural values – an interest that originated in my one-sided conversations with Nasca pots – did inform my research from start to finish. Sonqo simply shifted the focus of my analysis from drinking cups to coca leaves and the human body.

I was fortunate that Tom Zuidema did not insist that my dissertation stick to the original museum-based project, and that he and the rest of my committee were open to my writing in a personal 'literary' style. This was before 'reflexivity' and 'thick description' became popular buzz words. Writing the dissertation meant not only making sense of a rather disparate body of data, but also with an experience that had changed my relationship to anthropology. My marriage with Rick was ending, moreover, which gave poignancy to the writing process.

The 'coca problem'

Other reasons for writing about coca were ethical and political. Although my research was not politically motivated it was impossible to ignore the 'disconnect' between the profound significance of coca leaf in the lives of Sonqueños and the low esteem in which it was held by much of the rest of the world. I knew from my own experience that masticating coca leaf was mildly stimulating, but no more so than drinking coffee or smoking cigarettes. At this time the illegal use of coca's highly refined derivative, cocaine, was widespread mainly as an expensive party drug among the urban upper classes. Crack cocaine was virtually unknown when I wrote my dissertation in the mid 1970s. I was amazed to learn that coca leaf was included along with cocaine and heroin in the United Nation Single Convention on Narcotic Drugs. This classification was based on the conclusions of a 1950 Commission of Inquiry into the status of coca leaf, the final report of which concluded that coca chewing 1) contributed to malnutrition; 2) induced 'undesirable changes of a moral and intellectual character'; and 3) reduced 'the economic yield of productive work'.[2] I felt that it was important to counter these conclusions and to distinguish indigenous coca use from cocaine consumption. In the mid 1970s there was not much empirical information addressing the physiological effects of masticating coca leaf. Happily several studies emerged in the next few years; I was able to incorporate them in my 1981 article in the *American Ethnologist* and in my book, *The Hold Life Has: Coca and Cultural Identity in an Andean Community* (1988).

The position on coca articulated in my dissertation and 1981 article – that suppression of coca chewing would have dire consequences for Andeans' health – now seems overstated. Coca chewing has some health benefits but people can survive quite well at high altitudes without it. By 1988 I had reached a more nuanced position which I continue to maintain: 'The passionate focus on health issues has obscured a more fundamental problem: the heart of the debate is not coca itself but the cultural separateness of the people who chew it' (2002, p. 192).

In 1978 I moved to Washington DC to take up a teaching position at George Washington University. For a few years I tried to communicate to policymakers my insights about indigenous coca use, and the need to distinguish it from cocaine. I did reach a few sympathetic ears but all in all it was like trying to empty the ocean with a teaspoon. In hindsight it is impossible to tell whether my work has had, or will have, any effect on US policy. In *The Hold Life Has* I tried to convey coca's centrality to a coherent way of life and to present its users

---

2   *Report of the Commission of Enquiry on the Coca Leaf*, United Nations Social and Economic Council (ECOSOC) Official Record. Twelfth Year: Fifth Session, Special Supplement no. 1, May 1950, p. 93.

as fully realised human beings. Though it was not my intention, the book has been much used in undergraduate teaching; it had a second edition in 2002 and remains in print. A Spanish translation came out in 2008. I hope that some of the book's many readers have come away with a better understanding of coca and its role in Andean culture, and that this helps to counter the widespread tendency to demonise the plant.

The Hold Life Has

In 1979 I made some revisions to my dissertation and submitted it to a university press for publication. It was not accepted and, needless to say, I was disappointed. In hindsight, I am grateful for the rejection. Though it took me ten more years, I eventually produced a much better book. Realising that I could not – indeed, did not want to – publish the dissertation as it was, I took several more unsatisfying stabs at revision during breaks in my teaching schedule but did not hit my stride until my first sabbatical in 1984–5. At that point I recognised that, although I would keep coca at the book's centre, I needed to rethink and rewrite virtually every part of the manuscript.

During the decade between writing the dissertation and publishing *The Hold Life Has* I was reading new authors (Pierre Bourdieu, Mikhail Bakhtin, Michael Taussig, Dennis Tedlock) and encountering fresh ideas. At the same time I was adjusting to the intellectual milieu of Washington DC. Although I felt (and still feel) like a fish out of water in this context, participating in discussions of policy and 'international affairs' broadened my perspectives considerably. For several years George Washington (GW) University's Division of Experimental Programs supported an interdisciplinary seminar called 'Modes of domination in the Andes' that I taught with Cynthia McClintock (political science) and Peter Klaren (history). We also initiated a monthly seminar on Andean culture and politics that drew in colleagues from around the Washington DC area. Both these ventures helped fill considerable gaps in my background knowledge about Andean nations' histories and politics, especially after Independence, and they kept me abreast of current events unfolding in the region. I was motivated to interrogate my rather myopic vision of Sonqo and to pay more attention to internal differences in power and wealth within the community.

In a different vein, I had the great good fortune to join Colin Turnbull (then of GW's anthropology department) and Nate Garner (theatre and dance) in another experimental teaching project. Their course explored the interface between anthropology and theatre by using actor-training techniques to explore ethnographic material. After Colin left GW in 1983, Nate and I continued our work together; our collaboration is described in the introduction to our ethnographic drama, *Condor Qatay: Anthropology in Performance* (Allen and

Garner, 1996). The collaboration lasted another 15 years and transformed my understanding of 'culture'.

Steeped in Lévi-Strauss (whose work I still love), I had come out of the 1970s thinking of culture as a coherent model of reality that somehow resided in people's minds. I liked Edmund Leach's analogy to a symphonic score (1976). At the same time, Geertz's hermeneutic approach appealed to my literary inclinations and bolstered hopes of finding my niche in the discipline of anthropology. It also challenged my understanding of 'culture'. Some of the subsequent criticisms of Geertz did not occur to me then, and still seem to me to miss the point. I never literally took culture to be an 'acted document'. The phrase was a useful heuristic and suggested an analytical approach I found congenial.

Geertz's idea of culture as existing in evanescent moments of mutual interpretation dovetailed with my experience of teaching the anthropology/drama class. Our students read Andean ethnographies and (after various other kinds of preparation) were assigned roles in a peasant household. Then we had them improvise non-verbally in fairly routine situations (like a family eating dinner or getting up in the morning), using what they had learned in order to behave convincingly and respond to the behaviour of others. Most of the time they floundered, but on rare occasions there were moments that 'worked' – in which I had a fleeting and almost eerie sense of déjà vu. I was amazed to realise that American university students, thrown into a featureless black box theatre space, could produce an 'Andean moment'. I began to think of 'culture' as less like a symphonic score and more like a jazz jam session.

I returned to Peru in 1978, 1980, 1984 and 1985. Although I intended to start a new research project in a different community, I always found myself back in Sonqo or spending time with Sonqueños in Cuzco. In Sonqo, where I had good relationships and felt comfortable, I could hit the ground running; could pick up loose ends left hanging in my previous visits. I was acquainted with places as well as people in Sonqo, with the temperaments and abilities of its hills, ravines, springs and rock outcrops. Returning to Sonqo, and renewing my acquaintances with its people and places, I felt confirmed in my interpretation of coca as a crucial facilitator of these relationships. With my new reading of Bourdieu in mind, I developed a much better understanding of the ayllu, a flexible mode of group coherence that was articulated at the most intimate and transitory level in the routine etiquette of coca chewing. These visits also confirmed my enduring interest in the ontological status of the living landforms that formed part of local society.

During my initial fieldwork in 1975–6 I became interested in the way Sonqueños talked about their history; time was patterned in terms of stable eras, each with a trio of leaders, punctuated with periods of chaos. The most recent of these eras was dominated by three men bearing the same name – Anton Quispe. In 1985 I received funding from the Wenner-Gren Foundation to search for the Anton Quispes in archival records with the aim of comparing the oral tradition with the historical record. Alas! I never did find them. I did, however, develop a better understanding of Sonqo's early (16th–18th centuries) and recent (20th century) history, some of which I incorporated into *The Hold Life Has*. While doing that research, I had opportunities to spend more time than previously with Sonqueños living in Cuzco, which broadened my perspectives on regional relationships as well as the role of temporary urban migration in their life cycle.

In 1984 I returned to Sonqo proposing to study 'cognitive patterns' that were expressed in textiles and carried over into other media like dance and narrative. It was the beginning of a project that took shape really slowly and was not fully realised until the publication of *Foxboy* in 2011. During that field season – a happy period mostly spent listening to stories – I found Sonqo much changed. The road had been completed, setting off a shift in settlement patterns. Cash crops and chemical fertilisers were changing the old system of crop rotation and severing the traditional interdependence of the agricultural and pastoral economies. This material went into the book as well. I did not, however, appreciate the extent and rapidity of the changes that were taking place.

I finally finished the book in 1987, the year I turned 40. It was published in 1988 as *The Hold Life Has: Coca and Cultural Identity in an Andean Community*. By that time I had married Andras Sandor, a Hungarian poet I met at American Anthropological Association meetings; our daughter was born in 1987 shortly after I finished the manuscript. I did not return to Sonqo again until 1995. Raising my daughter took priority, and I did not want to take her to a country descending into civil war. I continued my work on anthropology in performance with Nate Garner and began to turn my mind back to questions about style and aesthetics.

Heading into the New Millennium

The collapse of the Berlin Wall changed the course of our lives; Andras could again think about living and publishing his work in Hungary. We spent a year there in 1991–2 and returned for several summers thereafter. It made sense to reorient my research in that direction too. I seriously considered changing my professional focus to Hungary and was surprised by the emotional turmoil this caused me. I had recurring dreams about Sonqo and don Luis. Our trans-Atlantic family life took other tolls as well; eventually we separated and I turned my focus entirely back to the Andes.

When I finally returned to Sonqo for a few weeks in March 1995, and again in the year 2000, I found the community changing in ways I did not expect. Some families had converted to evangelical Protestantism, alcoholism had become a serious problem and the systems of sectorial fallowing and communal pasturage had collapsed decisively. I wrote about this complex of interrelated changes in a long 'afterword' to a second edition of *The Hold Life Has* (2002), suggesting possible causes and reflecting on my relationship to them. I will briefly summarise them here, with the caveat that a few paragraphs cannot do justice to their complexity.

I will begin with the sectorial fallowing system. Ironically, after investigating the collapse I had a much better understanding of how the system had functioned previously. Ayllu lands were divided into *hawa hallpa* [outer] and *uray hallpa* [inner] zones. Each of these was divided into eight parallel sections called *surt'is* (known elsewhere as *laymi*). Households had usufruct rights to fields scattered throughout all 16 sections.

The outer zone consisted of high potato fields where a single year of cultivation had to be followed with seven years of fallow. Therefore, in any given year, only one *hawa surt'i* was under cultivation; the other seven 'rested' and served as pastureland. The inner zone extended down the slopes to the valley bottom and permitted more intense cultivation of several crops, including beans and tarwi. Most fields in this uray hallpa followed a three- or four-year crop rotation followed by four or five years of fallow (for example, potatoes – ullucus – beans – tarwi – fallow – fallow – fallow – fallow) (see figure 2.1). Because not all lower fields followed the same cycle, rotation in this zone was not as neatly coordinated as in the upper one; nevertheless, in any given year, cultivated land was concentrated in four sectors with the other four lying fallow. This year-by-year movement of crops across the ayllu was called *muyuy* [circulating around]. Sibling groups usually collaborated and moved as a unit through the eight-year cycle. The figure below shows one muyuy for both upper and lower zones by projecting the eight-year rotation cycle on to a grid. (I find it intriguing that this grid produces diagonal patterns strikingly reminiscent of the layout of some Inca tunics. I have no evidence, however, that Sonqueños ever represented it in this grid form).

This communal system coordinated the agricultural cycles with the demands of pastoralism for open grazing land. Because Sonqo's territory was large it could take an hour to walk from one end to the other, and many families preferred to shift their residences frequently to stay close to their fields; thus the distribution of household residences 'circulated' somewhat in coordination with crop rotation. It was easy enough to move. Houses were small, thatched, one-room adobe structures; a new house could be built in a matter of weeks and the old one left to the elements.

LOSING MY HEART

		Surt'i 1	Surt'i 2	Surt'i 3	Surt'i 4	Surt'i 5	Surt'i 6	Surt'i 7	Surt'i 8
Year 1	h	P	F	F	F	F	F	F	F
	u	P	F	F	F	F	B	T	U
Year 2	h	F	P	F	F	F	F	F	F
	u	U	P	F	F	F	F	B	T
Year 3	h	F	F	P	F	F	F	F	F
	u	T	U	P	F	F	F	F	B
Year 4	h	F	F	F	P	F	F	F	F
	u	B	T	U	P	F	F	F	F
Year 5	h	F	F	F	F	P	F	F	F
	u	F	B	T	U	P	F	F	F
Year 6	h	F	F	F	F	F	P	F	F
	u	F	F	B	T	U	P	F	F
Year 7	h	F	F	F	F	F	F	P	F
	u	F	F	F	B	T	U	P	F
Year 8	h	F	F	F	F	F	F	F	P
	u	F	F	F	F	B	T	U	F
Year 1a	h	P	F	F	F	F	F	F	F
	u	P	F	F	F	F	B	T	U

Sectorial fallowing in Sonqo

P (red) = potatoes   h = hawa hallpa (upper zone)
U (orange) = Ullucus   u = uray hallpa (lower zone)
T (yellow) = Tarwi
B (green) = Beans
F (brown) = Fallow

Figure 2.1. Sectorial fallowing in Sonqo. Created by C.J. Allen

Why did this ancient system collapse within a few years?[3] There were a number of factors, among them the chemical fertilisers that were introduced in the late 1970s and early 1980s by agricultural extension agents. Peru's agrarian bank offered rural farmers low interest loans to buy chemical fertilisers in order to cultivate fields more intensely and decrease the number of fallow years. At the same time a brewery, Cerveza Cuzqueña, offered loans of barley seed to be repaid when the first crop was harvested. Needless to say, farmers were obligated to sell to the brewery. The completion of a wide dirt road through the community facilitated this process.

Offers were made to individuals rather than to the ayllu as a collective, so it was up to individual households to decide whether to accept the loans. Not everyone wanted to risk going into debt so some enterprising individuals struck out on their own, 'varying' from the communal rotation schedule. *'Ñawpata kuska muyupun; kunan variapushayku'* [Previously it circulated around together; now we're varying], said don Luis. The lower uray hallpa, which was never as coordinated as the hawa hallpa, quickly lost its coherence. By 1984 barley and oat fields were scattered across the entire lower zone. The upper zone kept its traditional rotation schedule longer, mostly because those fields were too high for growing cash crops. The hawa hallpa was devoted to many traditional varieties of potatoes, most of them good for making *ch'unu* [freeze-drying] but of little commercial value. In the early 2000s some older Sonqueños were still adhering to the traditional rotation cycle in the upper zone but the younger generation had, for the most part, lost interest in following a communal schedule.

By 1984 the road was completed and passable during most of the year. I noticed that the settlement patterns were changing as families opted to live as close to the road as possible. They also preferred to live above the road, which cut horizontally along the mountainside, explaining that it dirtied the water supply below it. Grazing, moreover, was becoming problematic because fields were no longer concentrated in one part of the territory. The agricultural and pastoral economies were no longer bound together in a complementary relationship in which animals grazed and left their manure in fallow fields. To avoid damaging the growing crops, families were obliged to take their animals far into the hawa hallpa. Camelids need a lot of open pasture and raising them became increasingly onerous as the years passed. The llama and alpaca herds dwindled and by 2011 were completely gone. Their demise was hastened by a

---

3   Sonqo's surt'i system is typical of the indigenous adaptation to the Andean environment. I do not know its history but I think it probably dates back, in some form, to the formation of Sonqo ayllu in the early 1600s.

parasite, the liver fluke, which became endemic during the same period.⁴ Most families continue to raise sheep and a few pigs.

Within a few years the social fabric of the community changed significantly. Wire fences enclosed many of the fields. The solidarity of the sibling ground was weakened as family members made different decisions about whether and when to 'vary' in their crop rotations. Traditional relations of *ayni* and *mink'a* [reciprocal labour exchange] diminished in value as individuals aspired to live primarily from money.

When I returned to Sonqo in 1995 there seemed to be a general consensus that the new fertilisers had degraded the soil. The barley initiative, moreover, had fizzled due to the killing frosts typical at high altitudes. Repeated crop failures had propelled once-hopeful farmers into a spiral of debt to the brewery and banks. The excitement and high expectations of the early 1980s had given way to a kind of resigned disappointment. Peru was just emerging from a violent decade of instability and economic collapse. The central highlands had experienced outright civil war as Sendero Luminoso, a Maoist-inspired guerrilla movement, attempted to topple the government. The department of Cuzco was spared the worst of this violence and, fortunately, Sonqo was not a site of armed conflict. Sonqueños did, however, suffer great economic hardship that dashed their hopes of a better life. The end of market subsidies and a steep rise in the cost of transportation made marketing counterproductive; they were thrown back on their old subsistence strategies. Although it was fortunate that they could still do this, they experienced it as a demoralising setback.

The only upside of their dire straits was that they qualified to receive various kinds of aid, especially after the *Mapa de Pobreza* [Poverty Map] (1999)⁵ placed Sonqo in a zone of *extrema pobreza* [extreme poverty]. This brought various development projects to Sonqo and its neighbouring communities. Plan Internacional, an affiliate of Save the Children, provided materials for larger two-storey houses, promoted small animal husbandry and introduced an 'adopt a child' programme in which North American and European sponsors established long-distance bonds of 'friendship' with specific children. With the assistance of the Instituto de Manejo de Agua y Medio-Ambiente (Institute for Water and Environmental Management, IMA), a Peruvian-Dutch collaboration, Sonqueños constructed an impressive system of *agua potable* that piped clean water from a mountain lake to spigots outside individual homes.

---

4   I have heard it suggested that the invasion of liver flukes was related to the use of chemical fertiliser because the fluke spends part of its life cycle in tough scrubby grass, such as grows when chemically fertilised fields are left fallow. This seems plausible but I have no confirmation that this is the case.

5   Published by the Peruvian National Institute of Statistics and Information (INEI), https://www.inei.gob.pe.

Two volunteers were trained in maintenance, and when I visited in 2011 the system was still functioning well.

Once a family has constructed a fine two-storey house with running water, they will naturally be disinclined to abandon it for a new location closer to their fields; in any case, the fields are no longer localised in one sector of the community. Thus the old pattern of multiple shifting residences is giving way to one of more permanent homes strung along the road. When I visited in 2011, people living along the road mentioned visits from agents of a land-titling programme proposing that they receive individual title to their house plots.[6] I do not know, at the time of writing, whether anything came of this initiative.

The once highly popular 'closed corporate community' model of Latin American peasantries (Wolf, 1955; 1957) has been practically criticised to death – with some reason, since no community is completely closed and corporate solidarity is almost always challenged by countervailing tendencies. Describing Andean highland communities as 'closed' and corporate obscures the ayllu's essential flexibility as well as its complex historical relationship with colonialism and the Peruvian state. It ignores the necessary networks of relationships that connect individuals and families with kinsmen, *compadres* and traders in other similar communities. Nevertheless, the model does approximate a certain reality that characterised Sonqo ayllu up to about 1980. Until the agrarian reform was implemented, Sonqo was a free community in a region historically dominated by haciendas and the mestizos in the district capital. Sonqueños had ties of kinship with families in haciendas, and sometimes worked as temporary peons under demeaning conditions. After the reform they continued to be exploited by mestizo shop owners in Colquepata. In contrast, within the ayllu one could develop a sense of self-worth, maintain one's dignity and be respected by one's fellows. This was not so much closure as an intensely inward focus, a defensive posture necessary to live even a moderately satisfying life in an oppressive and often predatory social environment. As the community 'opened' many Sonqueños welcomed what seemed like a brave new world of opportunities to travel, market one's own produce, try new farming methods and, in general, expand one's horizons. The tragedy of this 'opening' is that the brave new world (such as it was) collapsed, and by that time cooperative structures internal to the community had irrevocably disintegrated.

Blind-sided by religious conversion

Between 1995 and 2000 another major change took place: close to half of the community converted to a Pentecostal Protestant sect called Maranata. Its

---

6   Programa Especial para la Titulación de Tierras (PETT).

members embraced projects with short-term benefits, like better houses and animal husbandry, but were generally not interested in projects with long-term communal benefits like the piped drinking water and a reforestation project (also sponsored by IMA). The extension agent who supervised the building of the water system told me that he found Sonqo so fraught with dissension over religion that it was impossible to work with the community as a whole. Fourteen families, all traditionalists, volunteered to participate in the project. In the process they coalesced as a community in the eastern part of Sonqo's territory while the Maranatas clustered more to the west. The ayllu, which had seemed a bastion of solidarity, divided into distinct neighbourhoods of Maranatas and traditionalists. By 2000 the traditionalists had gained legal recognition for their sector, which they called Mama Samana. Although not independent of Sonqo, Mama Samana functions like an autonomous entity with its own *casa communal* [meeting house]. The Maranatas, for their part, are also a close-knit group with a separate ritual life. The community-wide celebrations I describe in *The Hold Life Has* – carnival, saints' days, the pilgrimage to Qoyllur Rit'i – are no longer observed by Sonqo ayllu, although some traditionalists participate with kinsmen in other communities. Keeping in mind that ayllu is essentially a flexible and situationally based mode of social cohesion – manifested even in an event as temporary and fleeting as a coca-chewing session – it is unsurprising that in times of national instability the ayllu fragments and, in the process, gives birth to new social entities like Mama Samana and the Maranata fellowship. The same or similar fissioning processes were evident in ayllus throughout Colquepata district.

Why did religious conversion appeal to Sonqueños? Needless to say, the reasons are complex. In the second edition of *The Hold Life Has* I provide a more extended discussion of Protestant conversion and other changes, including alcoholism, coca scarcity, new gender roles and a changing relationship to money. To make a long story short, I think that, when confronted by the hopelessness of the 1990s, conversion presented an opportunity to change one's life. It was also a response to a marked rise in alcoholism that Sonqo experienced during the same period. Maranata, like other evangelical Protestant sects, forbids alcohol consumption. Conversion thus provides a kind of home-grown Alcoholics Anonymous.[7]

My perspective changed during the ten years that I worked on *The Hold Life Has*. I relaxed my focus on cultural continuities with Inca society and came to appreciate discontinuities as well. In 1975, I was dismayed when Don Luis proudly performed his *llama chuyay* [libation for the llamas] with a pair of yellow plastic teacups rather than the eagerly awaited qocha. Ten years later I had come to see the teacups as equally interesting. I could appreciate and

---

7   Converts do continue to chew coca.

enjoy the way material culture revealed disparate currents of history flowing against and into each other. I was delighted to find, among the ingredients of a pre-prepared *dispachu* [offering bundle for the Earth], a communion wafer carefully wrapped in a page torn from *Mademoiselle Magazine*. Nevertheless I felt blindsided by the conversion of Sonqueños to evangelical Protestantism. Probably I underestimated the extent to which younger Sonqueños would feel driven to desperation by their economic and political marginalisation – or, better said, I did not expect religious conversion as a response to this condition.

Did I also overestimate the tenacity of bonds with the landscape due to my own fascination with them? Because I was drawn to interlocutors who were intensely involved with this relationship, I may have minimised inevitable elements of ambivalence and scepticism. Sonqo's Maranatas maintain relationships with their landscape that, while transformed, appear to be complex and interesting. I would like to know more about them – but someone else should do that study. I find it hard to go back.

'You can't go home again'[8]

My extended 'afterword' to the second edition of *The Hold Life Has* ends in a farewell to Sonqo. Although I returned for short visits in 2003, 2008 and 2011, I do not expect to carry out more sustained fieldwork there. With great sadness I miss Luis and others who have passed away; in fact most of the people I wrote about in *The Hold Life Has* are dead, including those in my own generation. On the other hand, it is good to see the people I knew as children and babies, now grown up with their own families. They welcome me warmly – in fact they try to outdo each other in feasting me, which becomes greatly tiring. I feel immensely grateful for their affection and consideration, yet I am constantly on guard for requests and expectations I cannot meet.

To give just one example – I am particularly fond of Esteban, whom I have known since he was seven years old. As a boy he liked to accompany me when I visited other households. These were often distant from each other so as a teenager he took to transporting me on the back of his bicycle. I called him my *taxista*. We reminisced jokingly over this in 1995 and I somehow left him with the expectation that I would buy him a taxicab! He was deeply disappointed and I was mortified when, on my return in 2000, we recognised the misunderstanding.

A Spanish translation of *The Hold Life Has* was published in 2008 by the Centro Bartolome de Las Casas in Cuzco and I was relieved to finally see it available in Peru. The English title was deemed untranslatable, so the Spanish edition is called *La Coca Sabe* (*Coca Knows*). Because I knew the book would

---

8   The reference is to Thomas Wolfe's novel, *You Can't Go Home Again*.

be available (and hopefully read) in Cuzco, I made a dubious decision to use pseudonyms in the Spanish translation. I opted for these because in 1995 Luis had complained about *sunsukuna* [stupid people] who came looking for him by name; apparently they had read about him in my book. He found this frightening and hid out in the puna until they were gone. In 2008, however, when I delivered *La Coca Sabe* to Sonqo, my friends were deeply disappointed not to find their own names in print, and I regretted my decision. This is the only feedback I have received so far, other than from Don Luis's granddaughter Madeleine, who was born and educated in Cuzco city. She was shocked to learn from the book that her grandmother had died in her 13th childbirth (only four of those children survive today). Although most Sonqueños now speak Spanish, they have less fluency with sustained reading. It would be fascinating to read the book with them.

After *The Hold Life Has*

As time passes I find myself turning back to a kind of comparative literature. By far my favourite part of fieldwork was sitting by the fire with Erasmo Hualla, a master storyteller and healer, especially when he told tales in Quechua for his appreciative family (and my tape recorder). '*It felt remembered even then, an old / rightness half-imagined or foretold.*'[9] Listening to Quechua stories – transcribing, translating and thinking about them – simply and positively fills me with happiness. It gets tedious and tiring, but that doesn't bother me.

In the 1980s I began to explore 'cognitive patterns' common to Andean stories and other expressive activities like weaving, music-making and dancing. I am not sure what I meant by 'cognitive patterns', a term I have long ceased to use. What these activities have in common are compositional strategies grounded in a habitus of the mindful body. In other words, weavers organise cloth in ways that parallel the organisation of verbal compositions.

I had to develop some new habits of listening as I worked at making sense of how the narratives were structured. Pondering over my recordings from Sonqo, as well as collections of Quechua and Aymara tales, published by others, I noticed that many of them were composed episodically; that is, the tellers drew on a store of short traditional accounts and put them together in original ways; stories in different combinations draw out different aspects of each other. Moreover, tellers build a narrative symmetry (also evident in textiles) in which the story's end brings listeners back to the beginning; they express an idea that *contrast is mutual containment*; opposed elements enfold one another so that each is implicit in its antagonist.

---

9   From Seamus Heaney's 'Scrabble', in *New Selected Poems 1988–2013* (2014, p. 15).

One of Erasmo's stories provides a particularly good example of this creative strategy and became the nucleus of a new book. *Foxboy: Intimacy and Aesthetics in Andean Stories* took shape slowly over several years as I experimented with adapting these Andean expressive strategies to my own voice in a written medium. Julia Meyerson contributed beautiful illustrations, drawing on her own experience living in the Andean countryside. Towards the end of the book I commented:

> Writing the book this way has been an act of appreciation, and also of cultural preservation – preserving the tradition by using it, making it part of my own – which means, of course, transforming and in a sense destroying it. (2011, p. 177).

With *Foxboy* completed, I am turning to another long-standing interest, one that also goes back to my first days in Sonqo when participant-observation forced me to suspend disbelief and operate on an 'animistic' premise that all things – earth, mountains, houses, weavings – are subjects with their own viewpoints. According to this orientation all activity is embedded within a communicative context including non-human participants. 'Rethinking animism' as a valid orientation to the world has many aspects that I am beginning to explore: it dovetails with the current 'ontological turn' but draws on a rather different context from other studies of that stripe (for example, Viveiros de Castro, 2004; Willerslev, 2007); it engages with 'indigenous cosmopolitics' in Andean nations (de la Cadena, 2010) that brings non-human actors like mountains into the political arena (in opposition to mining, for example); it explores the possibility of dialogue across profound cultural differences (Ricard-Lanata, 2005). And finally I find myself coming back to a version of my old doctoral project, in dialogue with archaeologists on ways in which ethnographic understanding and the archaeological record may illuminate each other.

Conclusion

While I was revising my manuscript of *The Hold Life Has* some colleagues warned me that I would never get published unless I changed my writing style and 'took myself out' of the manuscript. Writing differently, however, was not an option for me. I derived a deep satisfaction from writing well and finding my own voice in the process; more to the point, 'taking myself out' felt intellectually dishonest. It was obvious that my understanding of life in Sonqo was only that – my understanding. Why pretend otherwise? To justify my stance (since it seemed to need justification) I turned to the 'intersubjectivity' of Edmund Husserl and Alfred Schütz, as well as to Geertz's arguments for the interpretive nature of ethnographic description. I articulated this position at the beginning of *The Hold Life Has* but did not dwell on it; theoretical discussion was relegated to a footnote.

Fortunately my colleagues' well-meaning advice proved to be wrong. By the time I submitted the manuscript for publication 'reflexivity' was becoming not only respectable but fashionable. By the time the second edition of *Hold* was published, reflexivity had become a central and much debated issue in anthropology. I was not inclined, however, to rewrite my introduction to address postmodern debates, nor to bring my footnote into the main text. Certainly, the nature of our subjectivity, its relationship to the world and to the subjectivities of others, raises fascinating philosophical and practical issues. Though these learned discussions interest me, they have not affected my basic stance, which seems to me (dare I say it?) obvious and simple.

My book's title, *The Hold Life Has*, alludes to Bronislaw Malinowski's comment in *Argonauts* that anthropologists must 'study what concerns man most intimately, that is, the hold life has on him' (1922, p. 25). A colleague warned me against using that title – not because it was hard to understand (which it is), or because Malinowski was sexist (which he was), but because aligning myself with him would lay me open to charges of exoticism. I did not take the colleague's advice and remain unrepentant. Certainly there is plenty to criticise in Malinowski's work but I prefer not to throw out the baby with the bathwater. 'The hold life has' sums up what I was trying to get at. To recognise difference and find it interesting, even enlightening, is not in itself exoticism. Exoticism voyeuristically exaggerates difference as an end in itself; is egocentric and perceives the 'other' as completely foreign. But to recognise difference and extend oneself to meet it is not exoticism – it's just life. My work in Sonqo was simply a special case of what we do all the time, just to get along in the world.

3. Deadly waters, decades later

Peter Gose

I welcome this opportunity to reflect on the ethnographic research I conducted during 1981-3 in Huaquirca, an agricultural village of 800 people in Apurímac, Peru. It is a particular honour to do so in the company of the other contributors to this volume, whose work has always been a guide and point of reference for me. While I am some years younger than most of them, events have conspired to make me, for most practical purposes, part of the same intellectual generation, which I gladly accept. My research resulted in a 1986 PhD thesis that I revised into a book called *Deathly Waters and Hungry Mountains: Agrarian Ritual and Class Formation in an Andean Town*, published in English in 1994 and Spanish in 2002 and 2004. To reflect on my ethnographic project is a complicated matter now, over 30 years after the fieldwork that generated it and 20 since the book was first published. A full natural history of the book, starting with the world it emerged from and following through to its last reading and repercussion, is impossible and unnecessary. It is enough to say that like all books do, this one has outlived the time of its emergence, and in the process has partially escaped my own intentions and the conversations from which it arose.

I begin by briefly restating the main arguments, partly as an introduction or reminder to the reader, but also to suggest how I see them now. Since I am largely unrepentant, however, it makes little sense to pretend that I can or should usurp the rightful role of others in assessing my own work. Instead, I will connect my ethnography to my subsequent historical research, and use it to comment on changes that have occurred in Huaquirca and anthropology in the intervening years. This seems the most productive way to remain faithful to my ethnographic project and show the formative effect it had on me, while also acknowledging that it was an unrepeatable experiment whose intellectual moment and Andean setting have since altered, sometimes to the point of straining recognition. Rather than try to smooth over the differences involved, I prefer to let them stand out in all their starkness, while also noting when others (in their own way, of course) affirm now some of what I affirmed then.

The arguments: context and retrospect

Deathly Waters used the village study genre to ask the broader question of how class and indigeneity overlap and interact in the Andean countryside. Nowadays, the notion of intersectionality designates these relationships and makes them much easier to discuss but back then no such covering concept existed. I argued that the differentiation of Huaquirca's inhabitants into *comuneros* [indigenous commoners] and *vecinos notables* [non-indigenous notables] was not simply 'ethnic' as most commentators held at the time, that is, a matter of differing cultural orientations, but was also very class-like. Whereas notables did not do manual labour for others and systematically monopolised local political office, salaried work and (to a lesser extent) commerce, commoners acted as the town's labour force, lived in undistinguished or impoverished material conditions, and discharged their civic obligation through labour tribute instead of holding political office. Andean relations of cooperative production such as *ayni* and *mink'a* were key in this differentiation, as were the amounts of property held and strategies for claiming it. To be sure, this differentiation implied diverging cultural orientations, but ones that were primarily oriented towards social distinction, and only 'indigenous' or 'Spanish' to that extent, not in any holistic way. In short, I argued that class was at work inside of ethnoracial differentiation, colouring it or overtly providing its main criteria and to that extent, merging with it.

Most of the book explored the annual cycle of agrarian work and ritual through which commoner praxis establishes and reflects upon relations of production, property and political power in a class-inflected version of indigenous Andean culture. Briefly, two seasonal regimes comprise the yearly cycle: the growing season and the dry season. The former involves a collective productive effort that spans the sowing of the crops to their maturation, in which labour circulates against food and drink across household boundaries through the egalitarian relation of ayni. Ritual imagery derives the rains from the dead during this season, but also uses death as a model for the expenditure of energy and depletion of the body in agricultural labour. An equalisation of the large and small souls that define personhood is one expression of this depletion, and it links to the emphasis on symmetry in ayni, the exchange of like for like across household boundaries. In short, this circulation orchestrates a collectivising but depleting expenditure, of which death is the model. By contrast, the dry season reverses this expenditure and restores people's depleted bodies once the crops become consumable and subject to private appropriation by individual households. This change begins during Carnival when the notables, as quintessential proprietors, perform a first fruits ceremony that initiates a season of consumption. Here, the emphasis is on hierarchy, both in the restoration of asymmetry in the relationship between souls in building up the depleted body, but also in the sacrificial restitution to the mountains of fluids and precious metals they expend during the growing season. These sacrifices become a tribute that recognises the mountains as ultimate owners and rulers of their territories and allow households to legitimate their acts of private appropriation in relation to them. Thus, the dry season foregrounds consumption, corporeal asymmetry, political hierarchy and property, very much in contrast to the growing season's emphasis on egalitarian collective production.

Seasonal differentiation thus turns on differentiating collective labour from private appropriation. Transition between these regimes in the yearly cycle is abrupt and highlights their contradictory relationship, itself a symptom of class in that (private) appropriation violates the (collective) principles established in production. That notables should initiate the transition to private appropriation is no accident. It indicates that this regime of activity is subject to class-ethnic coding, just as the phase of collective production is commoner in its subordinate and depleted egalitarianism under the signs of death and ayni. The point, then, is that the rich and florid symbolism of Huaquirca's annual cycle rituals is articulated through and ultimately converges with and reflects upon practices that embody the town's class relations. Of course this is not the only thing this symbolism does, nor, to the extent that it addresses class, does it do so as an explicit or doctrinaire 'class consciousness'. Yet when one follows through those symbolic references thematically and seeks their relevance in the practical context from which they spring, there is no denying that they reflect and refract questions of production, property and political power and, to that extent, constitute a close experiential awareness of class. That sense of class is largely implicit and does not necessarily commit people to any articulate position on the issues involved, but by providing an experiential baseline in which they are already elaborated, it nonetheless pushes them forward. Thus, the book argues that a large swathe of ritual and practical activity that is central to people's lives is 'about' class. By extension, the version of indigenous Andean culture that arises from it is similarly class-inflected.

An understanding of the state and Andean commoners' relation to it also emerges from this complex. Mountains emerge not only as owners, recipients of sacrificial offerings, and mediators in the circulation of life across the landscape, but as lawyers who act on commoners' behalf with the judicial system or political authorities who directly embody state power in their own right. Their typical human form of appearance at the time of my research and earlier was as white, blond-haired, blue-eyed men wearing the apparel of an *hacendado*, but they nonetheless spoke Quechua and were at least receptive to the interests of commoners. Recent research suggests that they may no longer appear as white and may even adopt indigenous guises, but they continue to personify state power (Salas Carreño, 2012). Either way, they render the state susceptible to Andean sociability and ritual practice, particularly sacrifice, through which they receive and direct the substance of life-forms under their management, including human beings. As sovereign powers that are nonetheless consubstantial with the subordinate beings they rule, mountains link political authority to a broader circulation of life best described by Catherine Allen (1988). By virtue of sacrifice, humans gain some latitude to negotiate their relations with the mountains' power and the state, leveraging the material connections they have established to maintain or extend their own claims, primarily to the land. Thus, this system converts lost human life and that of voluntarily relinquished animals into political economic claims. It uses consubstantiality to demand recognition, and to that extent, is a crafty hegemonic bid from below. This strategy registers and tries to overcome a history of racialised exclusion from power, valiantly recuperating the otherwise senseless loss of life that has followed from it. I consider it to be one of the most important things I learned in Huaquirca, and note its contrast to the anarchism that has become normative in anglophone intellectual circles and social movements since neoliberalism.

As an outgrowth of 1970s Marxism, my ethnography was unusual in combining both the political economy and the praxis strands of that tradition. Most Marxist work at the time recognised only the critique of exploitation and either ignored questions of culture and world construction entirely or reduced them to ideology. Antonio Gramsci (1971) and E.P. Thompson (1963) were great inspirations in aiming for something more satisfactory, but did not provide models I could readily apply to ethnographic work. The symbolic and interpretive anthropology of the 1970s, particularly Clifford Geertz (1973), was extremely useful for the kind of cultural analysis I needed to do, but often hostile to the Marxist underpinnings of my work (for example Sahlins, 1976). I felt a need for something more than a marriage of convenience between these contending approaches (Gose, 1988), but quickly realised I was out of my depth, and have intermittently read hermeneutic philosophy ever since on the increasingly confirmed hunch that it shares with Marxism a fundamental concern with praxis, the objectification and appropriation of human life and meaning in the making of a world. If I were to pitch the theoretical basis of my ethnographic project today, it would be along those lines, and in the future I still hope to write about the deep compatibility between these oft-opposed traditions.

Within my ethnography, I resolved these issues practically by showing a reciprocal interdependence between ritual and political economic practices in the annual cycle. On the one hand, agrarian observances generate a regulative framework through which people make claims on each other, the land and the state. On the other, these same political economic facts give practical grounding and motivation to these rituals and so shape their meaning. Indeed, without that practical implementation, the rites offer only a diffuse imagery that falls well short of any symbolic or predicative meaning. Conversely, without their accompanying observances, the political economic practices of the annual cycle exist merely 'in themselves' without the cultural expansiveness that enables them as active dispositions. In short, I argued that ritual and political-economic practice each mediated and referred to the other in the annual cycle and therefore needed to be described together ethnographically and taken together interpretively in order to do justice to either. Although anthropological holism and philosophical pragmatism both informed this argument, its fundamental concern was with the matter at hand, finding a unit of analysis whose internal relations were sufficiently dense and systemic to stand on its own credibly. That unit was the annual cycle of ritual and political economic activity. Most of the exposition was necessarily village-specific and inward looking, but by systematically citing other studies, I also suggested that my findings could be generalised to at least some extent across the southern Peruvian and Bolivian Andes, and that these same Andean understandings of production, property and power informed such historic events as the peasant land occupation movements of mid 20th century Peru that brought the hacienda system to its knees. In short, my book was simultaneously something less and something more than a village study: it took aim at the relations between ritual and political economic practice within Huaquirca's annual cycle but argued that they held more generally across the southern Andes.

My principal anxiety about this method was and continues to be its potential to generate propositions that people do not actually hold. On the one hand, this is a false problem since I was not making a simple expressivist argument, rather one located at an experiential level somewhat below conscious intention. By deriving a cosmology containing a sense of class from the interplay between agrarian labour and ritual, I was dealing in already objectified and institutionalised forms. The well-worn grooves that knit these components of the annual cycle together are, I would argue, the sedimented outcome of centuries of practice, not a set of ideas that someone believes in or not. That they so clearly arise from a pragmatic interpretation which I performed appropriately distances my claims from anyone's intentions. On the other hand, such arguments are only effective and plausible to the extent that people do reflect and act in ways that are consistent with them. For my interpretation to be valid, people do have to take up the objectified forms I discuss and use them more or less as I suggest. An analysis pitched at the level of pre-reflective orientation must eventually make good at the level of volition. Otherwise, I might produce, greatly against my own intentions, another variant of the

Marxist tradition's problematic imputation of class consciousness on objectivist and more or less determinist grounds (for example Lukács, 1971). It is all well and good to trace and compound the layers of localised class experience in the annual cycle, but some of its observances, for example the Christmas ritual dance *wayliya*, are arguably accumulating the imprint of returning migrants and the experience of trans-locality. These rites afford other uses than the ones I discussed, some of which have undoubtedly been actualised to some degree and left their marks. It is therefore inevitable that my analysis will not resonate with all uses or all users of these rituals. So I supplemented my account wherever possible with snippets of verbal reflection and concerted action that confirmed it. But those supplements were just that, and my sense of unease over this issue has never entirely dissipated.

At the time, I tried to channel these misgivings as productively as possible into an engagement with Pierre Bourdieu (1977; 1990). My ethnography argues against a monolithic notion of *habitus* and treats the structuring effect of these rituals as localised and ephemeral, which is why there are many of them, each defining a specific moment in the annual cycle. But this issue spilled over into others where Bourdieu was harder to deny. As my analysis of the annual cycle became more and more elaborate, I became acutely aware how much work would be involved and that my studious attitude was far out of line with the natural attitude of the practitioners I knew. When people came together to make each one of those moments, only occasionally did they verbally reflect on them in the deeply 'Andean' terms my analysis was assembling. My less than adequate Quechua was sufficient enough to grasp that most talk going on in the fields was about the details of the work, relations between the participants, or anything that might be entertaining. People regularly take part in these activities without conscious reflection on their ritual details, let alone giving them the kind of weight my analysis did. From time to time, however, they would also speak to me from within that ritual framework, using its terms without any hesitation or doubt, taking their applicability, viability and truth for granted. More rarely still they might put these terms forward in political action, using them to stake claims to the land and recognition from the state. These instances encouraged me that I was on the right track, that the observances really did define a durable disposition despite their intermittent presence. Yet people clearly pass into and out of the mode these rites define: some go further in and stay longer than others, and some barely enter it at all. This is not a contrast between ritual and everyday life, since these observances clearly operate within mundane workaday realities, but it does indicate that people have more than one way of doing the everyday, more than one practical mode. I would argue now that these available alternatives allow rituals to drift out of meaning and even out of use, as they are known to do, and explain why they must undergo periodic revivals that rearticulate their meaning (Tambiah, 1985, pp. 165–6). Outside of those moments, rituals may not actively define people's understandings or their politics, but lurk somewhere on the continuum between disposition and dead letter, where they cannot be overtly meaningful without some labour of explication and interpretation. Such labours can come from organic intellectuals firmly immersed and implicated in the context or others who are less so, including anthropologists like me. The risk of outsider interpretations is obviously that insiders may wholly or partially reject them so it is not surprising that nowadays fewer and fewer anthropologists are willing to take it, even when their host communities allow them to.

I felt compelled to assume the risks of an ambitious interpretation not simply because of my project's immanent logic, how anthropology was at that time, or to prove my own ability, but above all because I felt that what I had encountered in Huaquirca addressed me and demanded a response. Initially, this feeling arose through the thematic concern with outsiders in the rituals I studied, particularly the figure of the *qatay* [son-in-law] that people regularly applied to me. They had a systematic interest in bringing outsiders in, domesticating them through relations of give and take, and establishing long-term relations of productivity and solidarity with them. It affected me personally and was meant to do so. Only much later did I come to understand this sense of being addressed as something more than a personal or anthropological madness, but inherent to interpretation. Perhaps the most fundamental point of Hans-Georg Gadamer's philosophical hermeneutics is that interpretation pre-supposes, creates and reaffirms a bond with what it addresses, so that it is not detached research but an intervention in and extension of the life of that upon which it comments (1975, pp. 284–5, 295). Those who interpret do so because their object has already addressed and interpolated them (ibid., pp. 282, 360–1), because they are already in a relation of solidarity with it (1981, pp. 80, 86–7). That connection does not annul historical or cultural distance or prevent the interference of the prejudices they involve, but means a commitment to monitoring them, putting them to productive use, illuminating the horizons of both interpreter and interpreted, and working through their differences (1975, pp. 290, 296–7). In very much this spirit, my interpretive efforts strove not just to be right in some flat objectivist sense but to valorise and even enlarge the practices I wrote about, to help them advance their claims on the world. I can only hope the successes of this affirmative stance will ultimately outweigh whatever excesses or mistakes have also resulted.

From ethnography to history

When I left Huaquirca in April, 1983, I would not have believed that 31 years would pass before I returned. My relations with people there were solid and

I hoped to return to discuss and improve on my thesis and maybe work with herders in the *puna*, building on a trip to the regionally important mountain of Supayco I had taken in November 1982. To say that things did not go as planned would be an understatement. I did not finish my thesis in the one year of funding that remained to me at the London School of Economics and during that year, I sensed the beginning of what would later emerge as the 'Marx was wrong' current of academic neoliberalism within the larger rightward lurch of those times. When my funding ran out, I returned to Vancouver in the summer of 1984, lived in my parents' basement, and divided my time between various temporary labouring jobs, writing my thesis, and doing human rights solidarity work with and for Peruvians caught in the worsening conflict between Sendero Luminoso [Shining Path] and government counterinsurgency forces. My life improved dramatically when I got together with Frances Slaney, an old friend who later became my wife: I moved to Ottawa in June 1985 and, slightly over a year later, finished my thesis while working in a grocery store. Shortly before defending my thesis in December 1986, I was interviewed at the University of Lethbridge and got the job, which started in January 1987.

During my early years as an academic, the situation in Peru deteriorated further and I came to accept that more fieldwork there was impossible for the time being. So I eagerly accompanied my wife when she carried out doctoral fieldwork in the Sierra Tarahumara of northern Mexico during 1989–90, my role being to do the economic component of a larger joint research project. Although we searched diligently for a place free of drug cultivation, our research site eventually proved to be no exception to that rule and my economic investigations quickly imperilled the whole project, so I shut them down and withdrew into being my wife's research assistant and looking after our daughter. There was no hiding from how the drug trade had factionalised the region politically, however. People were either involved or they were not, and sincere proclamations of our disagreement with the 'war on drugs' made absolutely no difference. After ten months of greatly productive fieldwork, a shooting war broke out in town, I was threatened, and we decided to leave, and within months so did many of our closest friends there. To watch a second field site blow up into violent conflict was more than I could bear. I concluded that I was bad luck for the places I studied and decided at age 35 that I was finished as an ethnographer. Upon our return from Mexico, I continued revisions to *Deathly Waters* and again took up research on the Andes, now focusing on the history of the Incas.

As someone who was greatly influenced by E.P. Thompson, I was already predisposed to history as an ethnographer, read Andean history as systematically as I could, and did small stints of archival research in Cuzco during breaks from the field, one of which led to the discovery of a document I later published

(1995). Even then, I imagined taking up historical research at some point in the future, perhaps when I was too old for ethnographic work. When that moment came far sooner than expected, I was not entirely unprepared but had to learn palaeography and what various archives had to offer. Turning to historical research entailed continuity with my earlier ethnographic work as much as it did disruption, since it allowed me to remain focused on the Andes intellectually, even though Lima, Sevilla and Madrid became my main research sites. Inevitably, however, this displacement also had overtones of exile, and meant that my historical pursuit of the Andes involved the recapitulation of some of my ethnographic themes. This is particularly clear in my study of death and hydraulic cycles under the Incas (1993), and to a lesser extent in my article on gender and mink'a in the Inca labour-tribute system (2000). In both cases, however, I was careful to reconstruct these phenomena in their own right and in their own historical context, which prevented any simple collapse into ethnographic patterns and raised, I hope, some genuine historical questions about discontinuity in addition to continuity. My best work on the Incas was a study of oracles and had little to no ethnographic resonance (1996). Thus, even my transitional work on the Incas resisted the construction of an idealised, trans-historical Andean culture of the sort one might expect from an ethnographer in exile as a historian, and which did characterise some Andean historical anthropology. My main difference from others in that milieu was that I never accepted structuralism, a tool they used to posit such continuities. Rather, I learned from hermeneutics to expect and exploit key non-identities between the ethnographic horizon and those of the past as the disjunctive foundation for discovering and reconstructing temporally different orders.

This approach permeates my second book on colonial ancestor worship (2008) which, among other things, is a genealogy of the mountain spirits, mortuary and seasonal rituals that the ethnographic literature describes. The book moves forward in time through successive articulations and transformations of localised divine kingship, all more or less committed to mediating with foreign powers. Yet my familiarity with the ethnographic culmination of this sequence inevitably sensitised me to its differences with earlier iterations, and highlighted their significance. To this extent, a developed retrospective awareness informs the book, without hijacking its organisation or arguments. Thus, I specifically took aim at how the ethnographic phenomenon of mountain spirits with tutelary and territorial relations to Andean people arose from the breakdown of earlier descent groups represented by *kurakas* [hereditary indigenous rulers] and the worship of mummified ancestors. Those mummies had the same titles as modern mountains (such as *apu*, *mallku*, *wamani*), and were similarly conceived around notions of divine kingship that combined political authority with ritual regulation of circulating vitality. Mummies received seasonal sacrifices and libations comparable to those described in the ethnographic record and, like mountain spirits, served as mediators with larger states that incorporated localities defined by these entities. However, they differed crucially in that they underwrote the power of kurakas, who brokered Inca and Spanish indirect colonial rule. That role had an uneasy relationship with the notions of kinship, hierarchical solidarity and nurture that defined mummy-worshipping *ayllus* [descent groups] internally, and took form most concretely during seasonal rituals in which the living took the ancestral dead from their mortuary caves to feed, libate and dance with them. During the 16th and 17th centuries, indigenous descent groups were torn between being units of colonial extraction and communities that commanded their members' sociopolitical loyalty. By the mid 18th century this tension was no longer containable and indigenous commoners began to revolt against hereditary kurakas for violating ayllu values of solidarity and identifying exclusively with Spanish colonial power. In the process, they abandoned the cult of mummified ancestors that underwrote kurakas' authority, asserting new, more egalitarian and territory-centred notions of community and fresh notions of ancestral tutelage that cohered around mountain spirits, and were no longer corrupted by colonialism. My second book showed that these developments were linked to Tupac Amaru and the surrounding age of insurrection that spread across the southern Andes in the late 18th century. They changed how people there now view death, and are responsible for the predominantly negative view they now hold of the mummies (variously known as *gentiles*, *machukuna*, *ñawpakuna* and so on) that persist on their territories. In short, my colonial research dates the ethnographic horizon of Andean social, political and ritual life to the mid to late 18th century, and argues for its revolutionary and republican character. Although these arguments have not made all commentators happy, they have yet to be rebutted.

Inevitably, these historical arguments have changed how I look back on my ethnographic fieldwork, and they make me wish I had been more attentive to matters that now seem relevant. For example, during my research in Huaquirca, people mentioned gentiles as mummies who exist in specific caves or springs, and although I jotted their observations down, I never pursued the matter systematically and the gentiles are at best a minor theme in my ethnography. Others (Casaverde, 1970; Allen, 1988; Platt, 1997; Abercrombie, 1998; and, above all, Salomon, 2002), however, saw their significance better than I did. Eventually their work led me to understand that Andean peoples' own reflections on the past and my archival research intersected over these mummies and the epochal break that their rejection articulated. Before that historical break, these mummies were objects of deep ancestral devotion but, during what might be called the ethnographic horizon, they have since been ridiculed for their pagan backwardness and marginality. This is most clearly expressed in the notion that the rising of a Christian sun drove them into caves and springs where they linger, hoping one day to reclaim their dominant position on the earth's surface. These ambitions make them dangerous to contemporary Andean people, whose bodies they are liable to invade through unboiled water, malevolent winds or nocturnal sex, making them sicken or die. Such mummies are, in short, anti-ancestors with whom contemporary Andean people frequently deny any kinship: they belong to an earlier epoch and are adversaries. In a different cultural register, my historical research converges with these contemporary Andean convictions about the gentiles, and explains what was and is at stake in them, including why their rejection defined a new order, the ethnographic horizon, that is Christian, egalitarian and republican. By way of a different encounter between history and contemporary understandings of the gentiles, Frank Salomon (2002) had earlier arrived at the same fundamental conclusions. Whether the notion of memory is used or some other process is posited to connect contemporary Andean views of the gentiles to revolutionary historical events of the 18th century, that connection exists. Acknowledging it allows history to give horizontal, even collegial, validation to contemporary Andean peoples' understandings of their own past, and helps us incorporate their epochal thinking into our own appreciation of what the ethnographic horizon of Andean culture represents, throwing it into temporal relief.

The implication is that the past is largely malevolent but not entirely over, that Andean peoples' consciousness of it alternates between attitudes of vigilance and humorous reflection, which in turn reinforce the epochal break on which they are predicated. This may help to explain a puzzling and seemingly-unrelated fact from my ethnographic research: in Huaquirca, the 1960s land occupation movement was directed not at the notables, who were arguably a more deserving target, but the descendants of Huaquirca's hereditary indigenous rulers. Apparently, it was more important to continue the struggle against hierarchy and hereditary distinction within the indigenous population than it was to challenge external *gamonal* [local strongman] domination which at that time was still an issue. In Huaquirca, the historical break of the 18th century was therefore in some sense still playing itself out in the 1960s, perhaps as part of the vigilance that Andean people maintain against the remnants of that earlier order, which there include not only mummies but a once aristocratic clan that remembers its former glory. Whatever the case, contemporary vigilance against the gentiles underlines the internal dimension of the revolt against indirect colonial rule that occurred in the 18th century. It was not just against Spaniards but also, even primarily, against the indigenous lords who facilitated their rule, and without whom colonialism was lost. Nor did this revolt just occur and then fade into the past: instead, it constituted a more durable disposition that has carried forward for more than two centuries.

The ethnographic horizon's emergence out of the 18th-century Andean age of revolution underscores *Deathly Waters*' basic arguments about how class and indigenousness overlap. Andean culture's ethnographic horizon is the product of a deeply egalitarian revision of an earlier, more hierarchical version articulated around the power of hereditary kurakas. That colonial version of Andean culture attempted but ultimately failed to encompass what became a pronounced class antagonism between hereditary lords and peasant commoners. When that antagonism erupted and commoners rebelled against indirect colonial rule through their indigenous overlords, they not only overthrew their political leadership, but the forms of community and ritual that supported them. From that point onwards, Andean culture has become a primarily subaltern affair, one that is massively grounded in the class position and class experience of commoner peasants. To be sure, that culture extends into other popular strata including miners, merchants and urban labouring classes (Platt, 1983), and still partly includes notables, who arguably replaced kurakas in rural Andean class relations. But the hegemonic core or centre of gravity of that formation is unmistakably commoner, and the emergence of its defining features, such as the cult of mountains, dates to the kurakas' overthrow. Particularly in Peru, this intersection between lower class positions and indigenousness means that class mobility continues to imply ethnoracial mobility, even when the latter is more complex than a simple rejection of indigenousness. By showing that the concatenation of class and indigeneity resulted not only from colonialism but the manner in which it was overthrown, my historical research reveals some of the layered depth of the class-indigenous relationship present in my ethnography and those of others, and underlines my claim that they are better viewed together than in analytical separation.

At another level, however, this historical perspective strengthens the contention, also present in *Deathly Waters*, that Andean people simply do not accept that they are 'indians' and are ambivalent or evasive about related notions that their culture is primordial or somehow indigenous (Salomon, 2002). If one takes seriously the Andean view, supplemented by document-based history, that gentile mummies had been indigenous pagans who lived immorally until they were driven underground by the rising of a Christian sun that populated the earth's surface with contemporary Andean people, then the latter cannot be primordial or indigenous, and they continue to prove it when heaping scorn on the gentiles. Analytically, one can observe that even this repudiation conserved large parts of an indigenous tradition of localised divine kingship and that Andean people maintain many practices of indigenous origin, but what if they do not recognise them as indigenous and identify them instead as Christian?

Are we to tell them that they are wrong and that they are really indians? This is a real dilemma for the strategic essentialist politics that has become globally normative since it arose in the USA during the 1960s and subsequently became an integral part of neoliberalism. Although I accept that there may be countertendencies that lead people to self-identify as indigenous, as is clearly the case in Bolivia and Ecuador, it is important to identify what they consist of and how they interact with this opposing tendency to disidentify with the indigenous. In Huaquirca at the time of my fieldwork, that repudiation was paramount and though my ethnography records that fact, it did not ground it in Andean epochal thinking, as I now think fitting after doing the historical work that vindicates ethnographic gentil narratives. I would now argue that the term '*comunero*' prevails in Huaquirca's social vocabulary not simply out of politeness to avoid 'indian', and related insults, but because the people so designated have more systematically extricated themselves from the framework of indigeneity in their self-conception.

Some ethnographies embody more than others this understanding of Andean culture's ethnographic horizon as Christian, egalitarian, republican and not necessarily indigenous. That is not surprising since this characterisation requires looking at Andean ethnography through a peculiar merger of contemporary Andean epochal thinking with document-based history. It should go without saying that this essentially temporal perspective should not dictate or constrain the direction of ethnographic research. It does, however, identify the ethnographic horizon's specific shape, as seen both externally (documentary history) and internally (gentil narratives). Ethnographers who really want to understand the practices they study will care about this, and realise that they are not dealing with a blank slate but a received assemblage that has already been worked on, lived through, and which contains its own fault lines, points of reference, sensibilities and orientations. When ethnographers take up elements of that assemblage for study, we are engaging with that legacy whether we know it or not. In this case, it includes an egalitarian overhaul of earlier versions of Andean culture, a repudiation of indirect colonial rule and its affective grounding in mummy worship, and the creation of new, republican forms of community. We may approach this reality with erroneous assumptions about unbroken continuities with an indigenous past or a host of other issues but that does not change the fact that we are dealing with a cultural formation that has demonstrably and self-consciously undergone revolutionary changes. To engage in Andean village studies, then, is not to retreat into a world of timeless indigenous tradition, what Orin Starn called 'Andeanism' (1991) with its putative Orientalism, spatial incarceration, denial of history and politics. Far from epitomising such defects, community and ritual turn out to be the most significant and sensitive indicators of revolutionary change in the Andean world. Even more than those they criticise, postmodern critics are guilty of consigning community and ritual to the savage slot, treating them as exotic indigenous markers, evacuated of the histories of struggle that give them meaning and command people's attachment.

That the ethnographic horizon's revolutionary underpinnings have been largely invisible to most observers is understandable enough. After all, the revisions in question lay some 200 to 250 years in the past, and require historical research to demonstrate. Over that time, what began as an articulate political project became a bequeathed ritual legacy. People worked through, assimilated and integrated developments that were initially revolutionary, so that they are no longer a conscious project but rather a received point of departure, an established baseline, or part of an environment. As people continue to rework this ritual complex in piecemeal ways, more or less purposively in relation to their current circumstance, the disposition founded on republican changes largely becomes implicit, and could disappear entirely into subsequent developments. If all rituals exist between revitalisation and falling out of meaning, even more so, I would add, do those that made revolutionary changes. Yet fading into oblivion and into a pre-reflective disposition are not at all the same thing, since the latter entails the continuing or even enhanced efficacy of an established orientation, not its extinction. The evidence for conservation through disposition includes contemporary attitudes towards gentiles, the dogged but successful struggle to win back the land during the republican period, and throwbacks to the earlier critique of indigenous aristocracies in places like Huaquirca during the 1960s. I take these as sufficient to show that indigenous republicanism is an ongoing project, not a dead letter.

Huaquirca since 1983

As mentioned above, my relationship with the people and place of Huaquirca was broken during the Sendero Luminoso years and has yet to recover fully. Nonetheless, two important reunions since the passing of that crisis have given me the basis for what I write in this section and, more importantly, reason to resume those relationships despite all the time and trouble that have intervened.

In 1995, I visited the notable family with whom I lived during the majority of my time in Huaquirca. They had moved to Cuzco shortly after my departure in 1983 and liquidated all of their land holdings in Huaquirca in the process. Unlike many others who fled Huaquirca subsequently, their departure was planned in advance and not entirely in reaction to the immediate danger of Sendero's presence. During that visit, they told me some of what had happened during those years, including who had died and who still lived. They sensed that it was safe to live in Huaquirca again, and mentioned that some people were moving back, but at that time nobody could yet gauge the more permanent changes that the Sendero years had effected in the town.

In 2014, accompanied by my wife and very much at her urging, I returned to Huaquirca for a few days at the end of an archival research trip to Lima. It was an emotional return, all the more so because I did not know what sort of reception to expect, and saw myself as the bad fieldworker who had not returned when people had been through so much. So it was overwhelming when so many people remembered me, and with evident fondness and warmth. I had gone there expecting to deliver the Spanish translation of my book at last and perhaps declare closure on the entire experience but found instead that I had been missed and that many people were eager not just to reminisce but to resume old relations and forge new ones. Although I do not see myself seriously resuming work as an ethnographer in Huaquirca, I kick myself for not having returned earlier, and am devising other reasons to go back soon. What follows in this section, then, is what my not-yet fully resumed relationship with the people and place of Huaquirca allows me to say.

Let us start with the Sendero years that lie at the root of so many changes in Huaquirca, and my interrupted relationship with the community. In fact Sendero's actions in the upper Antabamba Valley preceded my arrival there: in July 1981, a Sendero contingent including one local recruit passed through the region talking up their cause, and blew the eucalyptus wood door off the Banco de la Nación in Antabamba. I entered the area shortly afterwards and, on my first trip in, encountered a militarised police unit that had gone in to investigate. No further incidents occurred until after my departure in April 1983. Some people suggested that later that year, Sendero briefly entered Huaquirca for the first time, whereas others held that it was not until 1985 that they did so. In any event, there is consensus that after 1985, Sendero became a regular presence in town, coming and going at will, preventing any institutionalised political processes from occurring, taking young people away, and for the most part keeping the army at bay in the towns of Antabamba and Matara on the other side of the Antabamba Valley.

Several incidents stand out in people's minds about those early years of Sendero's presence in Huaquirca. First was the night that they finally arrived in town, after much rumour and speculation, with a hit list to execute. Most of the town's notables were assembled at a social event that evening when word of Sendero's arrival came from the street. Some remained at the event, whereas others tried to sneak home or into the fields to avoid detection. Only a few were specifically targeted, however, and of these one narrowly escaped by slipping into the shadows between buildings and lying low all night. Some commoners who occupied political office were also on the hit list, and they were not so lucky. One United Left alderman was captured, bound and battered to death with a large stone. A similar fate would have befallen the then president of the *comunidad campesina* de Huaquirca, but he somehow managed to find a knife, sever his bonds, stab the Senderista guarding him, and flee into the fields dodging machine gun fire. Although hit in the leg, he managed to escape and got to Lima, where he now lives. Sendero's actions were not confined to the town of Huaquirca but also occurred in its puna hinterlands, which were part of the strategic corridor between the regions of Puno and Ayacucho they wished to control. One notable described how they indiscriminately machine-gunned people's flocks there in order to make themselves feared and obeyed. While this person never articulated, to me at least, Andean ideas about the nurturing and circulation of life, his disgust at this nihilistic violation of herders' commitments in this regard was evident, and I take this incident as a shorthand for Sendero's larger discrediting of itself within the community.

The most obvious consequence of Sendero's occupation of Huaquirca was that many families, primarily but not exclusively notables, left town and took refuge with relatives in safer places including Lima, Cuzco, Abancay and Arequipa. As one person recounted, the Sendero years were tumultuous and confusing: people did not know who to trust and life became extremely difficult in Huaquirca. Nonetheless, the town never became completely depopulated as comparable settlements in Ayacucho did. At some point, seemingly more due to the larger contours of insurgency-counterinsurgency than any local struggle against Sendero, the latter withdrew from the area. Some mentioned 1990 as the year in which this occurred, whereas others were not so precise, and opined that it was not until Abimael Guzman's capture in 1992 that Sendero ceased to occupy the area. That such memories are disparate is hardly surprising, particularly for those, mostly notables, who had fled town after the incidents described above, and were trying to assess if it was safe to go back. By the time of my 1995 family visit to Cuzco, people had clearly concluded that it was, but had only recently done so, and not all who intended to return had yet managed to do so. For notables, the matter was not as simple as picking up and returning home. As schoolteachers, most had requested and received transfers from Huaquirca to other jurisdictions, most commonly Abancay and Cuzco. Once ensconced in their new positions, transferring back to Huaquirca was not always possible immediately, nor was it necessarily what these people unambiguously wanted, given their more urban orientation. During my 1995 visit, I was sobered to see how much harder the family I lived with in Huaquirca was having to work in Cuzco to maintain a diminished version of the livelihood they had enjoyed in the country, but their commitment to the project was such that they did not look back. Other notable families were not so resolute and tried to retain some of the old economic advantages by cultivating their fields in Huaquirca while living in nearby cities. Some still continue this arrangement. Today, over 20 years since people began to return to Huaquirca, the town's notable population is approximately half of what it was previously, and this seems to be the most consequential change to result from the Sendero years.

The decline of the notables is not merely demographic, but a much more systemic phenomenon. With the most powerful members of the most powerful families either dead or gone, those who returned or remained no longer have the same esprit de corps as before, and their basic distinction from commoners is more tenuous now than previously. Economically, notables lost their local monopoly on salaried work, such that only a small minority of the town's teachers now come from their ranks, and the rest are commoners or outsiders. Whereas, previously, notable economic power consisted of a fusion between salaried work and privileged access to agrarian property in both the valley and the puna, now these elements have largely been broken apart. Notables still have their land holdings for the most part but these distinguish them from commoners only quantitatively, at best, and not in all cases. Schoolteachers from the outside have their salaries, but most of them lack the more refined dwellings and local land base with which the area's notables complemented their incomes back when they monopolised these positions. The result is a disarticulation of a previously unified form of local class power and, with it, the breakdown of a previous continuity from notables' agrarian dominance into a professional educative relationship with commoners.

One important expression of this breakdown is physical: Ñapaña, the notables' neighbourhood in Huaquirca, is remarkably dilapidated compared to 30 years ago. On several streets, including the one on which I lived, the fortress-like adobe walls that separated house compounds from public streets have crumbled and collapsed, as in some cases have the inner buildings these walls protected. Members of the once-powerful notable families who lived in such compounds are now domiciled in less impressive quarters as their ancestral homes collapse under lack of upkeep. The sense of abandonment and decay is palpable, and speaks not only to the notables' loss of numbers and economic clout, but to how this decline has resulted in the material embodiment of forms of distinction breaking down that once seemed entrenched and formidable. A second major symptom of notables' decline is their loss of political power at the district level. Whereas notables had previously always held the position of mayor and only at the time I was conducting my fieldwork had commoners begun to occupy alderman positions, they now hold every elected position. This dramatic reversal of fortunes would have been inconceivable at the time I was carrying out my research, and speaks to the comprehensiveness of the changes that have occurred since.

Not surprisingly, those notables who remain in Huaquirca are not entirely happy about these changes. Even the most progressive among them, those who were and remain the most trenchant critics of *gamonalismo* [rule by local strongmen] as it once existed in Huaquirca, and who created a United Left alternative that included both notables and commoners, now regret that commoners have 'lost respect' and consider themselves equal to notables. Such sentiments were only expressed by the gamonal old guard during my fieldwork. Contradictory as such sentiments might seem, they are consistent with the implicit hierarchy in the progressive, educative project around which notable rule was reconstructed in the last third of the 20th century, and which Sendero disrupted so dramatically. Given that some 'abusive' notables remain in place, it is not entirely impossible that such sentiments could spawn a gamonal reaction of sorts. The prospects seem slim, however, given the massive loss of class power experienced by notables and a second complex of changes (to be described below) associated with mining. The latter have further strengthened commoners politically and economically while diminishing the region's geopolitical encapsulation that was historically the condition of gamonal rule. At this stage, it seems that epochal changes have occurred in Huaquirca's class-ethnic relations. Differences that once seemed so solid have melted into air as their real foundations crumbled. In that regard, as in several others, my ethnography has become a historical document.

Another major set of changes in Huaquirca began around the year 2000 with the revival of mining in the region. This is part of a larger extractivist boom to sweep the country (Hoetmer et al., 2013) and the continent, in which the predominant structural arrangement has been joint venture partnerships between Peruvian and foreign (usually Canadian) companies. The government of Alberto Fujimori laid the foundations of this extractivist model and every subsequent government has followed it, such that it has come to define Peru's insertion in the global neoliberal order. At another level, however, as many commentators have observed, contemporary extractivism simply continues older colonial patterns, as is particularly clear with mining. Indeed, many of the new venture partnerships have reopened older colonial mines in the 21st century, a case in point being the mine on Mount Utupara in the upper Antabamba Valley. Nonetheless, the recent neoliberal mining boom is dramatically more intensive, extensive and capitalised than any previous iteration, such that the colonial comparison somewhat downplays contemporary extractivism's magnitude.

Mining has had a substantial impact on livelihood possibilities in the villages of the upper Antabamba Valley by making labouring jobs available. For the first time in over half a century, populations have grown in the region, with people who had previously migrated to urban centres returning to reap the combined benefits of subsistence production and a wage. Previously, only notables had enjoyed this combination through their monopolisation of schoolteaching positions but now wages have become more broadly available to commoners who have enthusiastically taken them up, further levelling the economic score with notables, and in some cases surpassing them. A further consequence is that notables and richer commoners now have to compete with the mines for the labour of their poorer compatriots, which has led to a relative decline in the agrarian deployment of such relations as the previously described mink'a, *jornal* [daily wage] and *yanapa* [collaboration] that pre-supposed significant wealth differentials. The overall result has been a relative prosperity that is relatively equally shared, further accentuating the decline in notable power and the egalitarian trend in the town's social life.

Yet for all these obvious benefits, mining has proved controversial in Huaquirca and not just among notables. Even the most enthusiastic commoners realise that the prosperity it has brought is temporary and has the potential, already realised in certain instances, to degrade the land and its ability to sustain agrarian livelihoods. Moreover, some compare the relative prosperity of new-found wages unfavourably to the quantity of extracted wealth from the mines, and ask uncomfortable questions about the difference. Sometimes this results in more or less ecosocialist critiques of extractivism, whereas at others it has involved allegations of corruption (whose validity I am in no position to assess) against elected officials for collusion with the mining consortia. The latter deny such charges and counter that those who question mining lack sufficient intellectual formation to comprehend its workings and benefits. Yet of course even the educated disagree about such matters. Increasingly, everyone acknowledges and regrets that Huaquirca is politically divided over mining, but these divisions seem truly political in nature, and difficult to read off from the old notable-commoner divide or any other social cleavages. What appears to be at stake is whether people's primary orientation remains with agrarian activities or whether they are willing to commit to extractivist modernisation. That this difference cuts down the middle of the hybrid economic strategies responsible for Huaquirca's recent relative prosperity suggests that people themselves recognise an incompatibility at their core and hence a need to choose (or at least privilege) one element over the other. As of this writing, anti-mining sentiment appears to be gaining the upper hand. The comunidad campesina decided to demand higher royalties from the Alturas explorations on Mount Utupara, to which the latter responded by laying off the local workforce and all but closing down operations. Far from folding under this retaliation, people were pushing to make similar demands of another company operating in Huaquirca's territory. On 24 May 2014, the day I left town, the comunidad campesina again assembled to formulate, debate, and either approve or reject those demands.

Clearly, the politics surrounding mining in contemporary Huaquirca deserves much more extensive study than I was able to undertake in a short visit. Yet neither is the current reaction against mining any great mystery given the extent to which it has superimposed itself on agrarian activities and materially changed the landscape of the upper Antabamba Valley in the process. Road construction is the single most obvious example. Most new roads go to exploration sites and mines, departing from previous roads that were never intended to bear the traffic of heavy vehicles. Whereas 30 years ago, an average of two trucks per month arrived in Huaquirca, it is now common for 20 large trucks to pass through town per day. They frequently have to back up and manoeuvre to make right angle turns in town, occasionally hitting the sides of adobe buildings, and shaking houses to their foundations as they labour up the main street from Ñapaña to Huachacayllo. From there, the mining consortium has slashed a new road into the hillside going towards Utupara and beyond into the puna. Several other new routes depart from the Caraybamba-Antabamba road, the majority leading directly to exploration sites or mines. Other new roads, however serve as transportation arteries to move extracted ore from the mines of Antabamba and adjacent provinces through the puna and across the continental divide to Cotahuasi and the Pacific coast. To access this artery, a new route passes from the town of Antabamba up the Antabamba River and into the puna by the splendid and previously remote Mount Supayco, the most important mountain in the region. Previously only paths traversed this vast area and only herders lived and worked in it with their animals. Not all of the area's new roads were expressly constructed for mining, for example the new route up the Antabamba River from its confluence with the Pachachaca and the Pan-American Highway was government-driven, pre-dates the recent mining boom, and spawned connector roads to Antilla and Sabayno which were previously inaccessible by car. Other towns like Vito have recently been connected to the road system, but as a part of extended high-voltage power lines into the region to service mines. Those lines themselves have required the construction of new roads and innumerable spurs of existing ones. The cumulative impact of all this road construction has been the visual transformation of a landscape that was once dominated by terraces and subsistence agriculture into one in which these activities are increasingly subordinate.

My earlier research (1994, chapter 7; 1986) documented escalating sacrificial demands on the landscape in the progression from agriculture through herding to mining: to what extent has this framework informed Huaquirquinos' responses to extractivist mining outlined above? The question is an empirical one, and deserves treatment as such through ethnographic investigation, but elsewhere it is being answered in the affirmative (de la Cadena, 2010; Salas-Carreño, 2012), so I offer some observations by way of hypothesis. First of all, Huaquirquinos' initial (and in some cases, continuing) receptivity to mining, and their integration of it into an economic strategy that also includes subsistence agriculture and herding, suggests that they do not view these activities as inherently or necessarily incompatible. My previous research supports such an inference by showing how agriculture, herding and mining are linked in a single sacrificial nexus in which vitality, life-forms and precious metals circulate more or less freely among these different practices, linking them together in the process. Mountains are the main mediators in this circulation, the ultimate owners of the energies, substances, life-forms and landscapes involved, and therefore the primary addressees in sacrificial rituals, which seek to discharge debts to them created through productive activity, and to intensify productive collaborations with them. Thus, only one economic system is at work here, and Andean principles encompass practices such as mining that might well, in other traditions of reflection, be treated as separate enclaves along the lines of capitalism *v.* non-capitalism, market *v.* subsistence production and so on. The unity in principle of these activities, then, is arguably why Huaquirquinos and other Andean people can hope to pursue them all without encountering irresolvable contradictions.

The relationships among these activities easily become strained, however, because of mining's intense demands on the mountain spirits, which threaten to monopolise claims on substances that need to circulate for the less intensive demands of agriculture and herding to be met, and thus destabilise the overall system. Mountains become depleted and voracious when any productive activity is not properly managed with sacrificial restitution, but particularly so with mining, which makes the most intense demands on them. These are localised in their core manifestation: the mountain's interior, often taken as the abode of its spirit or the inside of its body where its testicles or other regenerative organs may be vulnerable to extraction. When subject to such invasions, consummate ritual skill is required to maintain the mountain's equilibrium, a skill which people in the upper Antabamba Valley readily attributed to miners during my original research, when no mining was in fact going on. Any failure to provide for the mountain's needs was thought to result in its direct seizure of what would make it whole, typically the lives of animals taken through lightning-strike, the organs of humans taken through wasting sicknesses or violent deaths, or human lives taken in apparent accidents in or around the mines. A particularly troubling culmination of this trend is the de-ritualised slaughtering of people by the *ñakaq*, a shadowy outsider figure whose predatory extraction of fat from human bodies accompanies the predatory extraction of metals from the landscape. This practice helps consolidate them in forms which no longer circulate and which threaten to form a separate and alien system, even if it never quite manages to escape Andean sacrificial principles (Gose, 1986).

For the purposes of this chapter, it is particularly significant that even public works such as road construction that disturb the landscape's generative surfaces have been said to 'bother' mountain spirits and cause them to take human lives in 'accidents' in recompense for the damage involved (Favre, 1967, pp. 131–2; Vallée and Palomino, 1973, p. 14; Velasco de Tord, 1978, p. 197; Ortiz, 1980, p. 85). In combination with the more fundamental invasion of mining, such assaults on the productive surfaces of the land are now ubiquitous in the upper Antabamba Valley, and it is hard not to suspect that they are turning people against the mines, even if they do not articulate opposition through the notion that these activities are causing the mountains to take people's lives in 'accidents'. Whether or not one is dealing with explicit 'beliefs' to this effect is an interesting question. No less important, however, may be a pre-objective, gnawingly environmental and inexplicit sense, still informed by the same sacrificial complex, that the cumulative impact of the current extractivist scarring of the landscape is deleterious to agrarian lifeways. It should therefore be rejected on practical grounds even if in principle it ought to be reconcilable with them. The sense that something was not quite right was palpable during my May 2014 visit, when the rains continued sporadically two months later than they normally should have, preventing the corn from drying fully for the harvest, and obliging people to take extraordinary measures to prevent it from rotting. Global warming and its disturbed hydrological cycles are certainly affecting the Andes (Bolin, 2009; Carey, 2010), are something that people there are acutely aware of, and are easily assimilable into the sacrificial/circulatory understanding of life just discussed. None of this is to insist a priori that Huaquirquinos or any other Andean people must understand current environmental issues in these terms, or these terms only, but merely to point out how impressively adequate that sacrificial framework is to addressing such issues. This question needs to be studied in far greater depth than has been attempted to date.

I suspect that the agrarian rituals I studied may be informing people's responses to mining in Huaquirca because those observances remain an intense source of pride for them, something they foreground in how they present themselves to their community and to outsiders, and which they eagerly wanted to discuss with me in 2014. Although I was moved that upon my return people associated me so strongly with those rituals, and in several cases even extended me honorary Huaquirquino status because of it, I make no such claim myself, but instead attribute this remarkably charitable response to a larger collective affirmation of these rites. Their reaction is one that greatly exceeds but will hopefully subsume my own efforts once people have read and evaluated the ethnography I wrote. For during the last decade, local forms of documentation and commentary on the same phenomena I researched have accumulated, creating a broader and more diversified record that relieves my book of the burden of being a sole or privileged account, and places its claims amid those of others who can evaluate and/or appropriate it as they see fit. That local intellectual ferment includes a book on the Huaquirca customs by the retired schoolteacher Atilio Motta, an old friend whom I met in the mayor's office upon my return, where we each had gone to deposit a copy of our respective works. Photo essays and blogs on the internet liberally supplement such published writing, and similarly gravitate towards ritual and folklore, although several essays focus on history and the remarkable terraced landscape of the upper Antabamba Valley towns. Video, however, is the medium that has attracted by far the greatest participation in documenting Huaquirca's ritual life. YouTube, for example, has many clips capturing the Christmas wayliya dances from recent years, and several of the dry season *t'inka* observances as well. Videos of these and other rituals circulate in less public venues such as migrants' clubs, familial and personal networks, and comprise an extremely rich documentary record, not only for what the videos portray but for the themes people find worthy of documentation. Once again, it is worth noting that these rites enjoy pride of place in this constellation of cultural production and commentary. To make sense of that recurrent fact, I echo the basic point made by Gadamer (1975) that acts of interpretation and documentation do not stand apart from the objects they address, but form instead part of their extended reproduction in time and space. This does not mean that the documents and commentaries somehow replace the rites themselves, but rather that they prepare an audience for them, amplify and extend their influence through other media or representational practices that nonetheless subordinate themselves to the rituals and valorise their claims on the world.

The growth of this peri-documentary, peri-constitutive penumbra around Huaquirca's agrarian rituals is, of course, related to displacement and migration, which create both the felt need to connect with the original and sometimes an interpretive need to address the lived differences involved. Mining, as I suggest above, may well provide a similar affirmative motive in its extractivist disregard for the land with which these observances are so strongly embroiled. In these cases, people may valorise rituals as a way of dignifying the places to which they are connected without necessarily proclaiming that they are 'indigenous'. Folkloric takes on ritual are noteworthy for their studious ambiguity (or principled silence) on that point, and their focused affirmation of locality. Village-study ethnographies, to the extent that they have done more than call people 'indians', share in this project. A significant feature of this growing documentary record is that it partially overcomes the ephemerality of the rites themselves by objectifying them in ways that persist over time, and so facilitate historical reflection. For example, during my discussions of video with Huaquirca's mayor, he mentioned that the Christmas wayliya changed when the police prohibited the wild general melées that used to occur and insisted on more orderly one-on-one fights between consenting and equally matched combatants. We did not get around to discussing how women in standardised dress became a part of the Christmas dance troupes, but this too is demonstrable from the documentary record that has accumulated over the decades. But even the reflective function of commentary and documentary, including that which indicates historical change and so seems most disjunctive, ultimately plays into the extended reproduction of the basic ritual phenomena by reiterating their importance and making them the register of continuity across whatever changes they also record. That documentation and interpretation reaffirm their object helps explain why local people respond to ethnography in predominantly Gadamerian terms, as an act of solidarity with the practices addressed, and seldom with the Foucauldian suspicion that it is a power/knowledge operation or a hostile form of subjectification (Foucault, 1982).

That contemporary anthropology has so firmly insisted on this second dystopian view, usually as a theoretical maxim without any compelling empirical arguments for doing so, is a matter that requires separate discussion below. Here, it is enough to observe that Huaquirca's rituals are alive and well, not always in exactly the same form as I documented them more than 30 years ago, but not in a radically different form either. Exactly what they involve now, and how they relate to parallel forms of agrarian labour and mining, would of course require a new study. A Japanese ethnographer recently completed two years of fieldwork in Huaquirca, which I hope will illuminate how such matters stand nowadays. What is not in doubt is that these observances continue to be practised and are points of considerable affective attachment and elaboration. The very fact that they have encompassed ethnographic and other kinds of writing, blogging and video documentation shows if anything that their claim on the world and other forms of expression is expanding, not shrinking. Recent studies of Andean cattle rites (Rivera-Andía, 2014) similarly suggest the ongoing vitality elsewhere in the Andes of the kinds of rituals I looked at. Although I take comfort in this, not all is well: despite the fact that these observances continue to thrive in the Andes, they do not as objects of anthropological study, notwithstanding the publication just cited. This is a matter of concern if, as I argued above, anthropological research is part of the penumbra of practices that prepares the ground for and extends the influence of these basic practices themselves. When anthropologists refuse to valorise these rituals as objects of study, they deny them a needed avenue of solidarity to assert their extended claims on the world, and so condemn them to a more marginal existence than they would have if they engaged with them. It is therefore necessary to turn to why this abandonment has occurred specifically within anthropology, when it has not elsewhere in the extended reproduction of these phenomena.

Meanwhile, back in anthropology

Anthropology has changed massively since my ethnographic project was conceived and executed. Then, differences of culture and livelihood defined anthropology as a comparative field of study and oriented most research done in it. Now, neoliberal notions of identity, modernity and globalisation have displaced those earlier concepts, which many continue to pre-suppose but few are willing to defend publicly. The most obvious watershed was the so-called 'crisis of representation' and the rise of postcolonial theory in the 1980s, which institutionalised suspicion of the culture concept and ethnography's geopolitical conditions of possibility. Some of these interventions were more sophisticated than bald assertions that anthropology was predicated on colonialism or that the culture concept was racist, but the kinds of discourse analysis that spawned them moved inexorably towards those conclusions. Power-knowledge analyses confidently derived the political effects of the culture concept and ethnographic practice from their colonial pre-conditions, seldom considering recalcitrant evidence such as the expressed politics of those so impugned or how their interventions challenged the more or less colonial contexts in which they worked. These critiques implied that ethnography's subjects would be better off without it, which was hard to square with the quasi-genocidal violence that disabled ethnography in Peru during the Sendero years. Anthropology's glib Foucauldian flaying nonetheless proceeded apace, consolidating cultural studies and 'poststructuralism' in their specifically American form within the academy. Their scrupulous concern with power somehow overlooked the discipline of economics (Sangren, 1988) and its central role in the neoliberal counter-revolution that continues to impoverish billions and destroy our planet. As the 1990s wore on, this critique's novelty faded and it became clear that ethnography would remain anthropology's core research practice. What stuck, however, was a newfound but visceral moral aversion to 'exoticism' in defining anthropology's subject matter. Henceforth, with a few inconsistent exceptions for Amazonia and hunters and gatherers, nobody was allowed to be even partially outside the system. Anthropology became the comparative study of modernities, identities and transnational flows, in short, the handmaid of neoliberalism.

In such an intellectual context, anything that smacks of a village study or treats culture as something more substantive and political economic than ethnicity will fare badly. Nowadays, few do fieldwork in the Peruvian Andes and nobody in their right mind would attempt anything like my ethnographic project for an anthropological audience. Over the last ten years, the discipline has become mesmerised with neoliberalism as the contents table of any anthropological journal will show. *Cultural Anthropology* has even institutionalised this reality sense by dedicating a number every year to 'neoliberal futures' (Allison and Piot, 2014). Much of this work is ostensibly critical yet its exclusive focus on neoliberalism only reinforces the sense that nothing else exists. After the 'end of history', the ethnographic present insidiously colludes with the ever-expanding neoliberal present. Anthropology no longer believes that another world is possible, let alone that many might already partially exist. At a time when social movements across the planet are struggling desperately for alternatives, anthropology repudiates its rich ethnographic record of human possibility as an irresponsible exoticism. Of course the work that anthropologists now do on displaced and urban populations is necessary, and is bound to entail a different sensibility than work on peasantries, particularly those that are indigenous or exercise significant control over their conditions of existence. That such people are becoming invisible anthropologically when they remain such a large proportion of humanity, however, suggests that this shift in research focus does not simply reflect the world as it is today. Rather, an active erasure is involved, one that rejects lives taken to be pre-modern for their lesser involvement with capitalism and the carbon economy, foreclosing the possibilities they contain. Here is the thinking involved:

> People don't want to hear about victims. Many people benefit from resource booms. And why privilege indigenous residents over migrants? Cultures never sit still; it is nostalgia to speak for what is being lost. Anthropologists have been especially cautious to avoid stories of 'disappearing cultures': those stories seem too caught up in a discredited connoisseurship of culture. (Tsing, 2005, pp. 25–6)

Refusing to know about such people disturbingly echoes the racism of the societies in which they are enmeshed, and makes the chauvinism of 1950s modernisation theory seem mild by comparison. Anthropology cured of 'exoticism' smells like genocide. It may pretend to recognise indigenous 'political identities' but lacks their anger or grief over destroyed ways of living, and ignores their ongoing or revived practice.

Against this dreary horizon, it has been encouraging to see the beings formerly known as mountain spirits reemerge in anthropological discussions under the aegis of the 'ontological turn'. Ignored or rejected until recently as an exoticising Andeanist preoccupation, they emerge as mobilising presences in new ethnographies of anti-mining struggles in Peru (de la Cadena, 2010; Salas-Carreño, 2012; Li, 2013) that confirm and update the work that many of us did in earlier decades. Particularly important is Marisol de la Cadena's major new study of a father and son, Mariano and Nazario Turpo, that traces their relationship with apus over the period 1945–2007 (2015). An important leader in the struggle against the Hacienda Lauramarca in the mid 20th century, Mariano Turpo was also a *yachaq* who mediated with the Apu Ausangate during those events, and remained active through to the hacienda's expropriation in 1969 and ultimate return to ayllu control in the 1980s. Parts of this story had entered the academic literature previously, but de la Cadena's account is far more satisfying and comprehensive. It continues with Nazario Turpo's life in the aftermath of these events, how he eked a precarious living from the lands reclaimed from Lauramarca and ultimately used his abilities as a yachaq to become an 'Andean shaman' for the tourist industry around Cuzco, a development whose complexity the study handles well. A final chapter on *rondas campesinas* [autonomous peasant patrols] shows that ayllu-based claims on the local state and administration of justice, often conflict-ridden, continue into the present. I am delighted to see central themes from my own work reemerge in these newer ethnographies but underlying theoretical differences complicate any simple picture of continuity and are worthy of discussion in a reflection such as this.

Newer studies have insisted that mountain spirits are more than a 'cultural belief' about an invariant nature but instead constitute a distinct but partially connected world to the one modernity has made (de la Cadena, 2010; 2015, pp. 31–4). In effect, they are a product of a distinctive ontological order, one that is generated by practices in which human and other forms of being co-arise (2015, p. 101). Following Latour (1993), the argument is that earth beings are a nature-culture that defies this binary. Thus, there is some derision for previous work on the topic for failing to displace culture as a conceptual framework (de la Cadena, 2010, pp. 350–2), and in this regard ontological scholarship continues the postmodern critique instead of providing an alternative direction. I strongly support the attempt to reground Andean earth beings as realities and not beliefs but doubt that posing them as a distinct world as opposed to part of a distinct culture is much of an advance. For one thing, this move only heightens the sense of encapsulation already present (and problematic) in some notions of culture, and arguably turns worlds into purely idealised spaces abstracted from the rough and tumble of hegemonic struggle over common (but not homogeneous) ground. Citing Viveiros de Castro (1998) on multinaturalism does not make the mines go away or the glaciers stop melting. Moreover, to the extent that both worlds and cultures derive from practices, any contrast between them is merely verbal. Do epistemic introspections accomplish anything conceptually when they police language, substituting ontology for culture or earth being for mountain spirit? If what de la Cadena (2010, p. 337) calls 'earth practices' are the heart of the matter, then these studies are noteworthy for the thinness of their descriptions and their tendency to defer to earlier ethnographies conducted under the culture concept, which is curious given their antipathy towards it. This is a missed opportunity since actor network theory (with which these works are loosely aligned) does have a distinctive approach to practices that might well contribute new insights into the apus. But if de la Cadena hesitates to treat Andean mountains like the *actants* in Latour's laboratory studies (2015, p. 149) there must be a reason. Again, this is unfortunate because there is plenty of room to improve existing ethnographic work on mountains, mine most definitely included, but so far Andean ontological scholarship has not really addressed their practical grounding.

Arguably the foregoing comments are beside the point because de la Cadena's goal is not so much to improve the ethnography of Andean world-making projects as it is to explore the 'controlled equivocations' that result from their partial connection to the modern world. Such a reflexive effort is certainly worthwhile, and contributes to her aim of 'slowing down' our own interpretive processes so that they do not merely make sense of an Andean world but also explore the issues that arise from its partial incommensurability with our own (2010, p. 336). But of course this pre-supposes a viable understanding of that Andean world derived from ethnography that reveals how its practices generate a landscape endowed with specific kinds of agency. Marisol de la Cadena mostly accepts this point and thus implicitly depends upon an earlier ethnographic record. Sometimes, however, she explicitly accepts and even makes an analytical virtue of the fact that parts of the Andean world escape modernist understanding. This is refreshingly honest and accurately indicates the limits of what Andean ethnography has accomplished to date. But it does not change the fact that controlled equivocation and hermeneutic understanding are joined at the hip and break down at exactly the same point: we cannot map or compare that which eludes us.

On the other side of this reflexive coin is an overly-robust conviction that a nature-politics binary defines 'modernity' and has necessarily blinded previous ethnographers of the Andes:

> However, although some of these authors discuss the participation of earth-beings in local politics, and human negotiations with them (e.g., Nash, 1993; Platt, 1997; Taussig, 1988 [1980]), none of these studies consider these beings potential actors in national politics, let alone their different ontology disrupting the conceptual field of politics. Other-than-human beings belong in the ethnographic record as 'indigenous culture' not as a potential disagreement to take place in the field of what Mario Blaser (2009) calls political ontology. (ibid., 2010, p. 365)

By my reading, many ethnographers have recognised mountains as political protagonists (Favre, 1967, p. 140; Earls, 1969; Núñez del Prado, 1970, p. 105; Isbell, 1978, pp. 59, 151; D. Gow, 1980, p. 287; R. Gow, 1982, pp. 200-1; Gose, 1986; 1994, chapter 8) so this claim is not only wrong but unfair. Whatever we might have supposed 'the conceptual field of politics' to be, the apus intruded upon it, and in so doing, brought ontological import to 'indigenous culture' even if we did not label it as such. Discourse analysis discredits itself when it wilfully misreads arguments to subsume them under a putatively compulsory episteme. None of this is to deny that Andean ethnographers struggle with a nature-culture split, which is institutionalised in capital's expanded self-valorisation (Burkett, 1999; Foster, 2000; Foster et al., 2010) that overwhelmingly shapes the world we come from. The point is simply that it does so through a practical horizon that distorts our senses and cripples our ability to attune to other ways of being (Marx, 1844), not as a matter of 'belief', categorical blockage or a free-floating 'modern constitution'.

From this perspective, a phenomenological rethinking of mountain lords remains a relatively unexplored and potentially fruitful option. Pre-objective or non-representational relations to the land (or anything else) are notoriously difficult to reconstruct in an objectifying or representational mode but close attention to orienting practices remains a good strategic bet. In my case, extensive traversing of the land and participation in work/ritual were extremely helpful but ultimately insufficient to dissolve the limits of my world in the Andes. It did not entirely remake my previous life or anticipated future, did not commit me to the precariousness of an agrarian livelihood in the Andes, or subjugate me to the whims of gamonal power there, to name only the most obvious differences I can imagine. Undoubtedly there are many more that I cannot. But I do note that Huaquirca's *pongo*, the man who acted as a medium for the local mountains during my years there, was among the village's poorest and most vulnerable members. These attributes seem central to the experiential horizon from which mountain rulers emerge. Thus, I continue to hold that a large dose of class resides inside of being indigenous in the Andes, and am glad to have worked in a place like Huaquirca where that was obvious, as opposed to the ayllus of Cuzco or Bolivia where it is less so. With that said, one of de la Cadena's great achievements is to have mobilised a sense (much better than I did) of what it is to be subject to a *munayniyuq* or owner of a capricious alien will, a term equally applicable to gamonales and apus (2015, pp. 243-7). When the time is ripe for a proper ethnographic phenomenology of Andean mountain lords, this will be an important piece of the puzzle.

In the meantime, those eager to challenge any nature-culture split with regard to Andean earth beings could do worse than to build on the pioneering rejection by Olivia Harris (1980) of that framework, which recent studies have scandalously ignored. Without ignoring the issue's theoretical and epistemic dimensions, Harris nonetheless managed to transform it into an ethnographic inquiry. The salutary conclusion is that although the Laymi do not live by a nature-culture opposition, they do significantly order their world around a distinction between the wild and the domestic, one that affiliates mountain lords with the wild. To an important extent the distinction is relative because wild animals are said to be the counterparts of the domestic animals that humans keep and the mountain's interior may be a luxurious dwelling, and to that extent a domestic space in its own right. Indeed, there is no small degree of perspectivism (Viveiros de Castro, 1998) in this parallel organisation of worlds. That they nonetheless remain distinct along wild-domestic lines becomes evident in how humans experience the mountains, and their metonyms such as water and *ichu* grass, as unruly, and how people use strategies of feeding and marriage to tame and socialise the mountains' disruptive power. The sociality that connects people and mountains is tenuous and consists not only of nurturing the relations of *uyway* (de la Cadena, 2015, p. 103) but also the predatory relations of *ñakay* (Gose, 1986). Again, this is not an opposition between nature and culture but neither is it a static or univocally benign condition. Exploring such tensions might yield more insight than continuing to insist that Andean mountains are a nature-culture, correct as this essentially negative assertion may be.

Conclusion

As an artefact undergoing displacement in space and time, *Deathly Waters* has embarked on multiple journeys and is being read by multiple audiences in unpredictable ways. Two decades after its publication, its fate as an anthropological study has probably been sealed. After a ten-year run in which it was taught and around 1,000 copies were sold, the book went out of print in English and there is little prospect of a future reprinting. Yet even as its career as an anglophone academic commodity winds down, new avenues open up. Its life as a historical document has only just begun, and I am glad to have initiated its historical appropriation, along with other works that comprise the ethnographic horizon, in my second book. Meanwhile, it is still in print, being taught in Latin America, and even cited by Bolivian Vice-President Álvaro García Linea thanks to Alison Spedding's translation, for which I am immensely grateful. People in Huaquirca are just beginning to read it and several conversations are underway. At a time when the Peruvian government is trying to revoke Huaquirca's status as an indigenous community to deny them the right of prior consultation over mines, commoners themselves invoke their rituals as proof of their indigenousness. I hope that my book will prove useful in such a context even though it was written for a completely different one.

Eventually, the individuality of its arguments will recede into the collective legacy left by a generation of Andean ethnographers of whom I am a younger member. Like all successful interpretations, the ones we provided have largely disappeared into their object, whose enhanced intelligibility consolidates and ultimately erases our labour. Our collective work created an even more important good, namely a larger public space of visibility, recognition and contestation for Andean earth beings and the people who sustain them. This is solidarity, even if it was not intended as such, and even when it has made us unwilling accomplices to the creation of a tourist market for 'Andean culture' or other mixed blessings. The result has been new resources and possibilities of struggle for those communities and that, to my mind, is a good thing, unquestionably better than mining.

4. Yanque Urinsaya: ethnography of an Andean community (a tribute to Billie Jean Isbell)*

Carmen Escalante and Ricardo Valderrama

We have studied the Andes and Andean culture together for more than 40 years, conducting a great deal of in-depth fieldwork and undertaking numerous ethnographic studies in Quechua-speaking highland communities in Peru, both for academic research purposes and as part of development projects. Between 1985 and the early part of 1989, we focused our entire attention on the Colca Valley in the Arequipa region, carrying out the research described here.[1] The chief outcome was the ethnography which we produced on the Yanque Urinsaya community (1988), and a study of the systems and routes which local herders use to trade their products (Valderrama and Escalante, 2012; Valderrama, 2012). Our ethnographic account pioneered the study of irrigation in Andean societies, highlighting irrigation water management in the locality in relation to its culture, technology, rituals and worldview, and examining the complex levels of social organisation which such management requires. The publication of the resulting book had a significant bearing on later studies of other communities in the Colca Valley and other parts of Peru.

The book also had a significant impact on local population members, helping raise both awareness of the importance of their culture and pride in their own identity. This detailed ethnography stressed the importance of their rituals and their worldview of respect for nature, which, while keenly embracing it, they feared might prompt criticism or censure from urban society or the authorities. It also drew attention to aspects of local culture of which not even they had

---

* Chapter translated from Spanish to English by Eliot Jones.
1 Our previous work together began in 1972 when we documented oral traditions related to the mountain shrine of Quyllur Rit'i (Cuzco) and the annual pilgrimage there from the nearby communities of Paqchanta, Lauramarca, Tinki and Ocongate. From 1974 to 1977, we conducted fieldwork in Fuerabamba and Pumamarca in Cotabambas province (Apurímac) (1992). From 1978 to 1979, we worked in Poques, in the province of Calca (Cuzco), to which we returned in 1980, 1981, 2004 and 2007. This became our lengthiest fieldwork project and gave rise to several publications, including a compilation of oral traditions (1992). From 1981 to 1984, we studied four communities in the Huancavelica region, which led to Carmen's doctoral dissertation (2010) and several articles on local customs and myths (e.g. Valderrama and Escalante, 1983).

been aware. The community members, for instance, believed that the irrigation-related rituals which they performed as a matter of custom and tradition had existed since 'time immemorial', but they did not know that accounts of some of these practices featured in chronicles from the 16th and 17th centuries, and that similar practices also existed in other parts of the Andes.

When the book was published, the local people realised they could perform their rituals and be open about them without fear of censure or persecution. They could also actually touch this description of their culture and rituals. The older women would lay their hands on the book and say '*ch'iqakmi kay*' [this is true]. The book is now highly prized in the village, where it is kept on display in the local Uyu Uyu Museum. Over the last few years, the community's main water-related ritual celebration, an annual event held in an area annexed to Yanque called Challhuanca, where the River Chili rises before irrigating the fields of the Arequipa region, has even been injected with new life as part of an environmental initiative and as a tourist attraction in its own right.

Since we concluded our work there in 1989, we have continued to do research and fieldwork in many other Andean communities of Peru, chiefly in the Cuzco region, but also in Lima, Junín, Cerro de Pasco, Huánuco and Cajamarca.[2] Our work and experiences lead us to believe in the importance of further ethnographic studies in Andean communities; firstly, in order to add to the corpus of ethnographies, which is small and needs to be augmented; and secondly, because we still have much to research and these ethnographies can help us discover new social forms, economic structures, technologies, specific

---

2   In 1989, we worked in several communities situated in the Cuzco provinces of Acomayo, Anta, Espinar and Paruro, evaluating part of the development project Proyecto de Desarrollo Rural en Microrregiones (Project for Rural Development in Microregions, PRODERM). In 1990, we were in Q'ero, conducting research for the Food and Agriculture Organization of the United Nations (FAO)/Netherlands. In 1996, we did fieldwork in another five provinces in the Cuzco region (Acomayo, Canas, Camchis, Chumbivilcas and Paruro) to implement the Swiss Agency for Development and Cooperation's (COSUDE) project Saneamiento Ambiental Básico en la Sierra Sur (Basic Environmental Sanitation in the Southern Highlands, SANBASUR). We also did specific studies in Alcca Victoria, Wama, Coyabamba, Ccapi, Maskha and Inkakona (Cuzco) for COSUDE. We undertook consulting assignments for the Deutsche Gesellschaft für Internationale Zusammenarbeit GmbH (German Corporation for International Cooperation, GIZ) in Cuzco in the communities of Cachora, Ilanya, Huancarama, Limatambo, Curahuasi and Wiracochán in 1998, and in Ccalla in 1999. In 2001, we worked on the resolution of natural resource conflicts in Tintaya Marquiri, Yauri, Espinar, Umana, Huaynapata, and Ccapana (Cuzco), and Ahawaqollayniyuq (Ica). We worked in rural areas of Cajamarca, Lima and Cuzco in 2002, and organised workshops on child labour in the Ocongate and Huanoquite districts (Cuzco) between 2002 and 2003. From 2004 to 2007, we performed further fieldwork in Poques, where we had previously worked in 1978 and 1979, on this occasion to study how children learned their mother tongue before starting school aged six. Ricardo also worked in highland communities of Junín, Cerro de Pasco and Huánuco regions in 2005, and in others of the Lima highlands, such as Yauyos and Azángaro, in 2011, conducting fieldwork in Coropuna, Pampacolca and Tuhualqui (Arequipa) in 2012.

elements of worldviews and even linguistic terms, some of which may belong to extinct languages, but are still used in certain Quechua- and Aymara-speaking areas. In this chapter, we aim to explain some of the fundamental aspects of our fieldwork in Yanque Urinsaya and the ethnography we produced, reflecting on the role and validity of studies of this kind.

The peasant community of Yanque Urinsaya and the Colca Valley

Yanque Urinsaya belongs to the Arequipa region in the southern highlands of Peru and is located in the central section of the Colca Valley at about 3,500 metres above sea level (masl), between two major mountains in the western Andes, Ampato (6,288 masl) and Coropuna (6,425 masl). Its territory lies in the gorge formed by the River Colca, which lends its name to the entire valley. The fields which the people work are on the slopes of the right-hand river bank and were transformed hundreds of years ago into agricultural terraces, complete with irrigation canals and reservoirs. Another feature of this part of the valley is the pre-Hispanic archaeological site of Uyu Uyu, where the community originally lived before it was relocated to the current village as a result of Viceroy Francisco de Toledo's forced resettlements of the 1570s. Its origins date back to pre-Inca times as part of the Yanque Collaguas. Although this ethnic group was conquered by the Incas, the local oral tradition retains a remarkably positive memory of their rule.[3] Lots of other peasant communities, traceable back to the 1570s relocation programme, inhabit the length of the Colca Valley, their villages home to stunning colonial churches, each unique in its own way, and the area is awash with architectural remains from Inca and pre-Inca times. All within a manageable distance from the beautiful city of Arequipa, a popular destination in itself, the beauty of the valley's scenery and the charm of its communities have helped turn the Colca Valley into one of the Peruvian highlands' leading tourist hotspots over recent decades.

We began our research in the Colca Valley with the Centro de Estudios de Promoción y Desarrollo (Promotion and Development Study Centre, DESCO)[4] and its Programa Rural Valle del Colca (Colca Valley Rural Programme), which got under way at the end of 1984. As part of this programme, our job consisted of a preliminary study of the entire Caylloma province and a few neighbouring districts in order to make an initial diagnosis for a development project to be implemented by DESCO throughout the area (which had been declared a microregion). When we started, we decided to combine this work with an

---

3   Some local myths, for instance, claim that it was the Incas – and specifically the Inca king, Mayta Qhapaq – who first brought them maize seeds.

4   See www.desco.org.pe.

academic study to pinpoint the specificities of the inhabitants of the Colca Valley and their culture, focusing on irrigation water and its cultural and ritual dimensions, which are particularly sophisticated in the area. We realised that each community was, and still is, extremely interesting, but, being unable to cover them all, we decided to choose just one for an in-depth study. By that time, we had completed our Master's degrees in anthropology at the Pontificia Universidad Católica del Perú (Pontifical Catholic University of Peru, PUCP) in Lima. As part of the course, we had studied Billie Jean Isbell's book *To Defend Ourselves* (1978), which we consider a benchmark when it comes to approaching ethnography in the Andes, and her work influenced our decision to centre on a single community.

Geographical reasons ultimately swayed our decision to choose Yanque Urinsaya: an agricultural community in the middle of a valley in the western Andes, the side most prone to drought and where agriculture relies most heavily on irrigation. We wanted to work in a place that could be representative of the valley, where almost all the communities had been formed in pre-Hispanic or pre-Inca times and were then affected by Viceroy Toledo's colonial resettlement plans, so history and local identity also entered the equation. Yanque Urinsaya met all our requirements: its members identified as Collaguas, the current village had come into being as a result of resettlement and the area was peppered with archaeological sites, such as Uyu Uyu. Furthermore, the community had been both the local administrative centre in colonial times and the capital of the Caylloma province, to which it still belongs, in the Republic's early days.

Internally divided into the Hanan and Urin sectors, the community also had the bipartite sociospatial structure typical of most of the settlements in the valley. Each sector occupied one side of the river and had its own independent water system and forms of social organisation to manage irrigation water and keep its canals and reservoirs in good repair through communal work. Both these water systems are considered age-old, as is the 'mother canal' which supplies them and is in turn fed by Nevado Mismi, on whose eastern slopes lies the source of the River Amazon. As in most of the area's communities, the management of irrigation water in Yanque was not free from conflict, both internal (between community members) and external (with other communities), particularly with the neighbouring one, Coporaque. Finally, Yanque's members had a strong collective identity, which found expression not only in their language, Quechua, but also in ritual celebrations and practices, kept alive in traditional festivities such as the Carnival and religious celebrations like Holy Week,[5] which now attract a growing number of tourists.

5   The documentary *Cuando el mundo oscureció* (*When the World Turned Dark*) (1987), in the credits of which we appear as anthropological consultants, is about Holy Week in the Colca Valley and Yanque Urinsaya. Directed by José Carlos Huayhuac and produced by María Lobo, it won the Margaret Mead Filmmaker Award.

When we started work in the Colca Valley, the area and its local communities had not been subject to much study. The 'Denevan Mission', a team of biologists, archaeologists, anthropologists, historians, geographers and geologists led by Professor William M. Denevan, had previously worked in the area, issuing a final report when it completed its studies (Denevan (ed.), 1986).[6] Save the odd exception, such as Anne-Marie Brougère's study of herders in Sibayo (1980), practically no specifically anthropological research had ever been conducted. Not much research from a historical perspective had been undertaken either, the most prominent historical study being Franklin Pease's work on the Collaguas (1977a and b).[7] The Yanque Urinsaya church is home to an archive containing colonial documents from the entire Colca Valley and this had drawn the attention of a few historians, including Franklin Pease and Noble David Cook (Cook, 1975; 1982). It was there that we met the historian María Benavides (1986), who had to look through the documents by candlelight because there was no electric light anywhere in the valley, apart from in the capital, Chivay. The area had been studied by Alejandro Málaga (1977) and other historians from Arequipa and the university based there but, with the faculty still in its fledgling years, local anthropologists had yet to come. Regarding archaeological studies, the most notable of the area were produced by Pablo de la Vera Cruz (1987).

When we arrived in Yanque Urinsaya in the mid 1980s, we ran into a number of foreign anthropologists working in other communities and villages in the valley, and we ended up becoming a 'community' with shared interests where we could support one another. John Treacy, for instance, was working in Coporaque (Treacy, 1994) and always dropped in on us for a cup of Cusqueño coffee when passing through Chivay, before going back to his country, where sadly he died in 1989. Karsten Paerregaard, whom we had met before when he was studying change and continuity in the Junín region, was working in Tapay (Paerregaard, 1991), and Paul Gelles, whom we had met in the PUCP, was working in the community of Cabanaconde (Gelles, 1990). Paul and his wife used to visit us in Chivay and we would go to see them in Cabanaconde, and we always had many anecdotes to share. That was at the height of Sendero Luminoso's (Shining Path) reign of terror, which we shall return to later, and so we always insisted that these friends kept in touch to let us know that all was well.

---

6   Importantly, these studies dated the local agricultural terraces to around AD 700, confirming their pre-Inca origins. An earlier National Geographic Society expedition had also studied the depth of the Colca Canyon in 1972; and in 1982, Jacques Cousteau led an expedition to the summit of Mismi to study the source of the River Amazon and bring it to the world's attention.

7   Several volumes of colonial documents from and about the area have since been published (e.g. Robinson, 2006; 2009; 2012).

Fieldwork, theoretical approach and methodology

Our work in the Colca Valley lasted four years, from 1985–8, because we felt that in-depth ethnographic studies call for long-term fieldwork. As mentioned earlier, we were also members of the first DESCO team in the area and, as such, lived and worked there determined to develop the local population's standard of living. So we coupled our academic research with a 'philosophy of commitment' to achieve short- and medium-term development objectives. When we arrived, we set up home in Chivay, the provincial capital, and made an initial tour of the entire valley in order to produce a diagnosis to serve as a starting point for the Programa Rural Valle del Colca, making first contact with the inhabitants of Yanque Urinsaya. After that first visit, we went back at weekends to take part in farming work, festivals and rituals alongside local families, and soon started to develop ties of friendship and *compadrazgo* [co-parenthood] with several of them, always trying to ensure that such relationships were as two-sided as possible. The community's nuclear families formed part of large, extended, but close-knit, families whose members helped each other out with farming and handiwork. This made being accepted easier for us and helped us get to know the people.

The fact that we were a family consisting of a mother, father and two small children allowed us to forge deeper personal relationships because it provided a source of affinity between us and the local families, making stronger bonds with some of them possible.[8] As father and head of the family, the husband could take part in 'male activities', and the wife could engage in 'female activities'. Meanwhile the children could join in and make friends with other young people. Besides, being parents was well looked upon socially because it was associated with the productive and not the *qollo* [barren]. Being a non-local mestizo couple also played to our advantage because the local families were interested in getting to know us and in forging ties of kinship – as godparents, co-parents or co-sponsors – through religious celebrations and ritual practices. As a result, we served as sponsors for weddings, baptisms, first communions and first haircuts both in Yanque and other communities in the valley, and, as a couple, took part in rituals to do with irrigation water, Pachamama (Mother Earth), the *apus* [mountain spirits] and the sowing of maize. Speaking Quechua also aided our integration a great deal because it meant we shared the same mother tongue and cultural codes as the local families, who opened the doors of their homes and culture to us.

---

8   For us, it was quite normal to conduct fieldwork as a family, as we had seen others do in the 1970s: Billie Jean Isbell in the community of Chuschi (Ayacucho) with her husband, daughter and mother, or John Earls in Cuzco with his wife, who was also an anthropologist. We also knew Norman Long, who had taken his wife and two small children with him to do fieldwork in Africa.

In terms of methodology, our fieldwork in Yanque Urinsaya was based on living with the community members in order to gain their confidence, sharing many of the activities they performed, dangers they faced and endeavours they undertook. The rapport so established paved the way for a year of participant observation tracking the local farming cycle, including journeys to trade products and livestock. At the same time, we observed the cycle of rituals, focusing principally on water-related rites. We managed to complete our observation of the annual cycle in the second year. The third year consisted of writing up our results and filling in gaps with additional interviews and further research. When interviewing community members, we took a range of criteria, such as gender, age and level of education, into account. Other factors we bore in mind, in order to discover and collect data on the richness of their society, included the interviewees' economic situation, the degree of consolidation of both the household unit and the unit of production to which they belonged, and their knowledge of and opinions concerning local culture and history. In the fourth year, we concluded our research.

Agricultural cycles differ according to climatic factors such as El Niño and La Niña, which occur every eight years or so and vary in terms of intensity, including periods of heavy rainfall and drought, in which complex rituals are performed. So one advantage of long-term fieldwork of this kind in the highlands is that it makes studying such longer cycles possible.

From the outset, we recognised the great importance of comprehending the kinship ties which united families in order to understand the alliances and agreements between them. We learnt, for example, that it was possible to differentiate between three social groups in the community on the basis of the amount of land and livestock owned: the comparatively rich, those of average wealth and the poor. We also tried to identify the history of each family group and its own particular customs and traditions within the general framework of the broader community's customs and traditions. Regarding irrigation practices, for instance, we discovered that the members of the Checca family were in charge of performing all the rituals related to the spring known as Mama Umahala. It was a family tradition for its members to organise and cover the costs of these rituals. A male member of the family acted as the officiant, or *yana*, while another made the ritual offerings, the family in its entirety taking part in all the other activities involved. This earned them the respect of the other families in the community. And so we realised that ritual responsibilities of this kind had a bearing on the status of the families in that village and the esteem in which they were held, which depended not only on the quantity of land or money they possessed, but also on the traditions they upheld and the roles they played in them.

The case of the descendants of the old hereditary aristocracy, the *kurakas*, was also unique. Although they were no longer called kurakas and did not enjoy any particular privileges as a result of their lineage, they continued to hold certain civic-religious posts and positions of authority. They also performed specific duties, such as putting up and feeding the community's guests, there being no restaurants or places for visitors to stay at the time.

We studied the annual cycle of irrigation and water-related ritual practices performed by the *comuneros* of Yanque as participant observers for three years, from 1985–7, interviewing key community members so they could explain them to us. We also searched for written information on these practices in colonial documents and studies already conducted on similar rites. We asked the interviewees what they knew about the history of the rituals they performed, which aspects of them were the oldest and what had changed and why. Experts on the subject gave us specific explanations, also providing us with other more general information on their worldview, local myths and oral traditions: legends about supernatural beings and mythical stories about mountains and irrigation canals, or the origin of maize and its ties with the Incas.[9]

Between 1985 and 1988, we also studied the trade circuits used by herders from the area.[10] We examined how the journeys made by herders from Sibayo, Tisco, Callalli and other pastoralist societies in Caylloma province worked. They transported fresh meat, jerky, rope and sacks to the Colca Valley's maize-producing communities to trade them for maize, beans and oats. They also went on other trading journeys to get dried figs, chilli peppers and salt, venturing as far as the Quispicanchis province, in the Cuzco region, for potatoes and *ch'uño* [dried potatoes].

We also carried out other research and work in the area for development and cooperation purposes, meaning that our relationship with the local comuneros encompassed research, action and participation. As part of the DESCO advocacy team, we ran workshops to identify the chief problems in the area, analyse them in depth and seek or suggest solutions. These workshops were coordinated through communal assemblies, at which we reached agreements on how they should be performed and found out how widespread

9   We later published some of this information in a book on the mythology of the Colca Valley (1997).

10 In the Colca Valley, as in other places in the Andes, circuits pre-dating the advent of colonisation exist for the non-monetary exchange of products. These routes of economic organisation are used by herders who trade products from different ecological zones, transporting them on llamas from the *puna* [higher-altitude Andean areas] to the valleys, particularly maize-producing parts. Here they exchange them for local commodities and take them back to the puna, using ancient tracks which join up all the different ecological zones and niches of production. These routes of trade and territorial articulation are not only economic and geographical, but also entail social, political, cultural, environmental and ritual aspects, including the exchange of knowledge and ways of thinking as well as the coordination of a variety of common interests.

interest was regarding certain proposals. We also came up with outlines for development projects on subjects like irrigation and education, mainly with the aid of communal authorities and using resources such as brainstorming, and strength and weakness analysis. A multidisciplinary team would then write up the outlines and the projects themselves, bearing in mind national and international policies and organisations which could fund them or collaborate in their implementation and management. We used gender-based, generational and ecological approaches for these projects, and then applied the same foci to our ethnographic research and fieldwork in the community.

One of DESCO's main strands of work centred on training and instructing the communities' members in technical matters and regulations, offering, for example, specific courses for crop farmers (for instance on pest control) and herders (such as herd and pasture management and care, the training of veterinary advocates, how to improve and market fibre), and continuous training for peasant promoters. This advocacy and training work proved extremely useful for our research as it allowed us to get to know – and work with – the local herders, who opened their culture up to us.

Our fieldwork experiences in Yanque and the Colca Valley also affected us a great deal on a personal level. The people there taught us to appreciate nature and live in it distinctly. We learnt to take delight in the rain, when water gushed along the main irrigation canal filling the reservoir to the brim; or when the shoots of maize ruptured the soil, creating a contrast of green on brown which filled our hearts with joy; or the mere fact that we had two healthy children, laughing and playing with the local youngsters.

Theoretical references, conclusions, results and contribution

Our work in the Colca Valley was influenced by a range of theoretical approaches and references, one of the most significant being the historical ecology practised by such authors as John Murra, Billie Jean Isbell, Enrique Mayer and Cesar Fonseca, who focused on exploring how Andean peasants adapted the surroundings to make their land more efficient and allow them to cope with the adverse geography and climate of the environment they lived in. On the basis of this approach, which was specifically reflected in the resulting book's first and second parts, we defended the dynamic, creative and ever-changing nature of the relationship between the comuneros of Yanque and their environment. Studying the local water and terracing systems, we established that the ancient Yanque Collaguas modified three geographical and climatic features of their environment: steep ground by means of agricultural terraces; long dry seasons and drought – typical of the western Andes – through irrigation; and low temperatures and wind by creating microenvironments on their terraces, sculpting them to form amphitheatres against the wind. We therefore concluded that the local agricultural system based on canals and terraces was in balance with nature.

Historical ecology also proved important when it came to addressing the community's past as part of the Collagua ethnic group. It had inherited its terraces, irrigation systems and infrastructures (for example paths, retaining walls) from its Collagua forebears and that material heritage had brought cultural heritage along with it. We focused on different historical features of the community and its family groups (for example knowledge of the past, oral traditions, myths and legends), and explored the system of local knowledge through which not only had they been able to conserve and continue using these infrastructures, but also knew how to maintain and improve them. We discovered how the comuneros used past experience to construct their present and future, and how that meant that they needed to preserve and maintain ancestral knowledge, and reconcile it with the acquisition of newer knowledge and techniques. We observed, for instance, that local authorities called meetings with the community's most experienced elders when faced with technical problems concerning the water system to ask them how they had solved such dilemmas, or to quiz them about oral traditions centring on similar problems so they could ponder and decide how best to address the matter.

Our ethnographic study also centred on the community's worldview and rituals related to irrigation and the water system. As a theoretical basis from which to tackle the subject, we relied on historical-structuralism, which we had learned from Nathan Wachtel and R. Tom Zuidema through their publications and lengthy conversations held with them in the cafés of Cuzco, and from Juan Ossio Acuña and Alejandro Ortiz Rescaniere from the PUCP in Lima. As a result, we tried to decode the sequence of the rituals we studied as part of our fieldwork in order to identify their dualistic, tripartite and quadripartite features, and interpret each sign, signifier and signified in the elements involved in an attempt to discover the continuities and changes intrinsic to them.

As for the findings and conclusions of our research, our ethnography of Yanque Urinsaya highlighted the fact that the community's water system was pre-Hispanic and one of the many which had been kept in operation uninterruptedly in the Colca Valley; and that the social organisation of the local families was fundamental to the system's functioning, ensuring its good management and maintenance, which in turn required a substantial system of values through which to exercise the rights and perform the duties associated with the undertaking. We also showed how knowledge and experience of the water system was passed down from generation to generation, both orally and through practice; and how the right to use irrigation water and take part in the related decision-making processes was tied in with meeting community obligations at assemblies and in the form of communal work. Our ethnography, therefore, provided a detailed picture of the locality's irrigation system, the forms of social organisation and ritual practices related to it, and the ideological universe underlying these usages and activities.

We also demonstrated that the community members were fully aware of their history and were proud to have descended from the Incas and the Collaguas, from whom they had inherited the water system. The comuneros see themselves as temporary guardians of the waters which descend from the snow caps, which their predecessors handed down to them and which they must pass on to their children, and this is key to the sustainability and continuity of both the irrigation system and the community itself. Irrigation water, therefore, gives power to those who administer it and entails a whole array of interests and values. We concluded that the water system, together with the system of knowledge and beliefs associated with its use, was crucial to the locality's ability to conserve its environment in a sustainable manner, allowing its members to survive the hostile, dry terrain of the western Andes. On the basis of our case study, we also arrived at the conclusion that the viability of these Andean communities and their productive capacity depended to a large extent on their ability to adapt efficiently to the environment, not only technologically but also culturally.

We believe that this focus on sustainability is one of the most significant contributions made by our ethnography because it can teach lessons of great relevance to these times. We are convinced that knowledge and attitudes of this kind could benefit humanity and that ethnographical studies of Andean communities can help salvage and promote them. We pointed out, for example, how the Incas, and the Collaguas before them, made reservoirs to collect rainwater to prevent it from going to waste and use in drier seasons, and how they built retaining walls on the appropriate hills in order to achieve their aim. These reservoirs fell into disuse during the colonial era, but rainwater is now being harvested all over the Andes for a similar purpose. We hold that lessons like this are one of the main reasons why community ethnographies are still both useful and necessary. There are now more and better theoretical and methodological tools with which to carry out studies of this kind, combining, for instance, gender-based, environmental, ecological and intercultural approaches. Nor should we overlook, of course, the socioeconomic and political interests which drive people and groups, or analysis of the development of the phenomena under study over time.

Our ethnography of Yanque Urinsaya was a pioneering study of Andean irrigation systems and helped open up not only new possibilities and opportunities for studies of this type, but also debate on the very importance of studying the water systems of indigenous rural communities in America. Consequently, it encouraged other researchers to conduct similar studies both there and in other regions, attracting students working on their theses and also foreign researchers. When we did our research, in the 1980s, no-one placed as much importance on ecology, let alone water and irrigation, as they do now. Nobody could foresee how important they would become in the future. So our ethnography of the water systems of Yanque Urinsaya was groundbreaking in this regard as well.

Numerous studies now exist on the irrigation and water systems of communities in Peru, Ecuador, Colombia, Bolivia, Chile and Argentina. They highlight significant historical and cultural continuities not only in the management of key natural resources like land and water, but also in the cultural and ritual aspects of irrigation, including recurring features which, on occasions, have not varied by much in hundreds of years, such as the offerings made to mountains considered sacred. These studies provide clues which open the way to retrospective interpretations of the ritual aspects of recurring historical phenomena. Our work in Yanque Urinsaya also drove home the importance of taking a long-term approach to ethnography, particularly as far as fieldwork and data collection are concerned. As previously mentioned, being able to study in the area for four years proved most constructive, but some subjects, such as specific astronomical cycles or periods of rainfall and drought, or exceptional temperature extremes, require even longer periods. We realised this when we observed certain special rituals, like those in which community members travelled to the coast to collect seawater in bottles to pour into the 'eye' of a specific spring or into the mountaintop ponds from which their irrigation canals emanated. This was not a routine ritual, but rather one performed when the stars said that it was necessary to summon the waters of *la mar qocha* [great mother pond], in order to stave off serious drought. We believe, therefore, that state institutions should take charge of promoting long-term studies of this kind.

Our work was original from a methodological perspective, in that it combined academic research based on participant observation, development work and also support work in specific areas of the community. Part of our ethnographic study's originality also lay in the fact that we shared the same collective Quechua identity as the people we were studying, whom we regarded as our brothers, spoke the same language as they did and, in many ways, shared the same culture. Methodologically speaking, this is none too common, but in Yanque Urinsaya it proved very important because it paved the way for particularly symmetrical relationships with the comuneros, meaning that they trusted us and were more willing to reveal the secrets of their rituals and worldview to us. At a more personal level, we believe that the study helped make us better qualified, more perceptive investigators, allowing us to train new researchers better by holding up an example of how to conduct ethnographic studies properly. Academically, the study prepared us for further research of this kind, but, more specifically, it taught us to see irrigation and the multiple manifestations of water in a different light, aware and respectful as we now are of how our brothers from Yanque Urinsaya perceive them.

Ethnography and armed conflict: Shining Path

As pointed out earlier, our fieldwork in the Colca Valley coincided with the most violent years of Shining Path, the worst of which lasted from 1980-93. Some refer to this period as one of internal or civil war, though we believe that 'internal armed conflict' is a more suitable term. The conflict might conceivably have developed into true civil war had the Land Reform of 1969 not been implemented. Of that we cannot be sure, but we do believe that the violence would have reached a greater scale and proved more catastrophic had the comuneros not owned their land by the 1980s. The fact that they did led them to defend it and stand up against the savagery of Shining Path. When the conflict first started, guerrilla members began to enter Andean communities and, after the initial months of confusion had passed, local comuneros tended to offer the guerrillas their support, providing them, for instance, with food and accommodation. However, as Shining Path's demands of them grew, for example, by supplying combatants and taking part in killing and pillaging, the people of the communities held their ground and ultimately withdrew the support. Providing visitors with food and a place to stay was part of these societies' culture of solidarity and their idea of hospitality, but they would have nothing to do with such levels of violence. As a result, Shining Path started to sow terror among those communities which refused to support them, executing their leaders, kidnapping their children, ransacking and burning down their homes, preventing them from taking products to market to get money for basic supplies and even prohibiting crop sowing and the possession of large herds of livestock.[11] Given the situation, the comuneros began to organise themselves into self-defence committees and peasant patrols to defend their lives and their land, engaging in bloody skirmishes with the guerrillas (Degregori et al., 1996). And so, from an armed group which had put the very government in check, Shining Path turned into an organisation which preyed on the weakest groups

---

11 In April 1983, for example, Shining Path killed 69 comuneros from the Lucanamarca community (Ayacucho). The survivors of this and other similar massacres suffered severe physical injuries, such as having lost limbs to machete blows, but, above all, they suffered from their country's indifference to their plight. Cases of this kind are included in the *Final Report of the Truth and Reconciliation Commission* (1994).

in the country, such as the Andean comuneros who lived in areas beyond the immediate control of the Peruvian state.

In 1984, before we went to the Colca Valley, we had worked in other highland communities in the Huancavelica region, where the climate of violence was mounting. The communal authorities could no longer ensure our safety, they themselves being those most at risk, the guerrillas constantly hunting them down.[12] Professionals like ourselves, anthropologists who lived within the communities, were considered a nuisance by Shining Path, which wanted to bring the comuneros round to its way of thinking. Meanwhile, the anti-insurgent forces also looked upon us with suspicion. Our credentials were enough to get us off the hook with the security forces, but provided no guarantee when it came to the guerrillas, so we decided to leave. In Huancavelica, we met DESCO workers who were also leaving the region due to the increasingly unstable security situation and they suggested we work in the Colca Valley as part of a development project they were about to begin. So our time in Arequipa came about by chance, from the need to find a safer area than Huancavelica. In the Colca Valley, we were no longer alone; we formed part of a team which included an agricultural engineer, a vet, a zoo-technician, a sociologist, an economist, two drivers and a secretary, as well as other professionals who made the journey from Lima whenever necessary to support our development work.

Violence in the Colca Valley had not reached the scale it had in other Andean regions like Ayacucho, Huancavelica or Apurímac. As DESCO anthropologists, we evaluated and analysed the local inhabitants' socioeconomic situation and discovered that they did not endure the kind of extreme poverty we had witnessed firsthand in Huancavelica and other Andean regions, this possibly accounting for the relatively peaceful situation. The area is riddled with livestock tracks leading to mountainous areas in the neighbouring regions of Puno, Cuzco and Apurímac, and to other locations in the highlands and on the coast. The local comuneros told us that Shining Path used these routes in the Colca Valley as a 'corridor' between Puno and the coast, and so were disinclined towards violent action in the area in order to avoid drawing the attention of the State's counter-insurgency forces, thereby ensuring free passage for themselves through the valley. Only afterwards, thanks to the *Final Report of the Truth and Reconciliation Commission* (1994), did we find out what was happening in Peru while we were there between 1985–90. At the time, however, the information that reached us was limited, based on what we heard on the radio in Chivay and what we learnt from the newspapers and magazines

---

12 When doing fieldwork, initial contact with a community consists of introducing yourself to the local authorities, showing them your credentials, explaining the objectives of your research and asking them for permission to work there. The authorities then explain the situation to the other community members, usually at general assemblies, ensuring their collaboration and the safety of the researchers for the duration of their stay.

we bought in Arequipa. These only reported the higher-profile and bloodier events, such as the prison massacres and the bombing of electricity pylons. We started to pick up television signals during the last couple of years we were in Chivay, but the channels we received did not speak about the troubles in the country.

A few years after our arrival, the situation in the Chivay area grew dangerous as well. At first, the comuneros from the communities we were working in told us that they sometimes saw suspicious groups of people, neither farmers nor herders, walking remote paths in order to avoid detection. The comuneros distrusted these people and hid from them, thinking they might belong to Shining Path. Suspicion and mistrust came to form part of our everyday lives and work, and we started to take precautions, like not travelling at night or picking up strangers on the roadside. During the workshops we held in the communities, we were careful to elude specifically political questions, particularly when asked about Shining Path, believing both the guerrillas and the army more than capable of planting informers amongst the participants. Sometimes when travelling, we came across people we did not know who tried to flag us down, albeit to no avail, and once a suspicious group of strangers came to visit the DESCO office in Chivay and broached subjects related to Shining Path but, as always, we did not voice our opinions.

We trusted neither the army nor the police and when we travelled to Arequipa or Lima for work reasons, we did so in groups. On one occasion, we were stopped at an army checkpoint and when they saw that one of our engineers had a Quechua surname and was from Ayacucho, the soldiers detained him for interrogation and thoroughly searched his belongings. Out of solidarity and to ensure he was not harmed, we all decided to stay behind with him until he was released. On another occasion, a friend who had come to Chivay to study Quechua went to the local market to practise his reading skills with our book on Gregorio Condori Mamani (1977). He started reading the book out loud so people could correct his pronunciation and soon attracted quite a crowd. This drew the attention of the police, who, on seeing the book was in Quechua – a language they did not speak – took him into custody. When we found out, we went to the police station to try to secure his release. One of us stayed outside to be on the safe side, while the other went in to try and explain that the book was a biography of a porter from Cuzco and the detainee was the son of a well-known right-wing congressman. In the end, the problem was cleared up with a simple phone call to Lima.

Later on, the presence of guerrilla forces was confirmed in the puna on the border between the Caylloma province and the regions of Cuzco and Puno, and that brought the army to the area. Around that time, explosives were also stolen from local mines and the presence of Shining Path was confirmed in the

Madrigal district, some parts of which are practically inaccessible. In 2011, a mass grave dating from the period was discovered in some pre-Inca ruins in the area; all the skulls had bullet holes through them. With the passage of time, the situation got even worse and, in 1988, DESCO felt that the presence of Shining Path combatants made it too dangerous for its workers to stay there, so it arranged for them to live in Arequipa and only visit the area when necessary and safe to do so. We were the only ones who opted to stay on in Chivay because, as a family, life was more comfortable there and, besides, we felt safe. We trusted the members of the local population, with whom we shared bonds of friendship and ritual kinship – by that time we had many god- and co-children as a result of baptisms, weddings, first communions and high-school graduations – so we felt we would be protected in the event of danger. Moreover, we were convinced that we were doing a worthwhile job and doing it well, and so had nothing to fear from Shining Path, believing they only executed rustlers and criminals. The situation turned from bad to worse, however. First of all, threats against the local authorities started to circulate and some of them decided to move to Arequipa and only visit the area when they had to. It was then that we began to feel we were in increasing danger ourselves, from both army and guerrillas alike.

Early one morning in Chivay, our dog started barking like mad. When we looked out to see what was going on, we found our street had been taken by troops. They knocked at our door and said they wanted to search the house. We were not particularly worried because we had nothing to hide and let them in. We saw that some of the soldiers were shaking. We did not know whether it was from the cold – it was chilly that early in the morning – or fear. While they looked through our things, we heated up water to make them coffee, which the soldiers drank with trembling hands. They took all morning, examining the walls, ceilings and floors in search of hiding places and false bottoms. Two superior officers went page by page through each and every one of our books, journals, magazines and newspaper supplements, which were mainly on anthropology and included numerous community ethnographies from Peru, Bolivia and Ecuador. They seemed particularly interested in the books with red covers, which included our Latin American Bible and the complete works of Shakespeare. They found a literary journal from the University of Huamanga (Ayacucho), where Shining Path had been founded, and asked us about it, but in the end they left.

A few months later, we heard a knock at the door one night. It was four young men who introduced themselves as anthropology students from the PUCP. We believed them initially and invited them into our living room, where they too started thumbing through our books. When we asked after members of the PUCP's academic staff, we realised they did not know any of them and were not students from the university at all; whoever they were, they had made their way into our house by deception. We did our best to hide our distress and they asked us about our research. On hearing our explanations, they told us it sounded interesting, but that the time was not right for such studies and they warned us not to stay in the area. Eventually they departed, but their visit left us most uneasy and the next day we found out they had vanished without leaving a trace, even though Chivay is a really small place.

We finally decided to abandon the area in December 1988 when we heard that Shining Path had killed two French and three Peruvian aid workers in the community of Haquira (Apurímac). Over the previous months, there had been no end of threats against international non-governmental organisations (INGOs) and aid workers providing support and services in rural areas beyond the state's reach. Shining Path wanted to bring an end to everything that might alleviate poverty and that was enough to view aid workers as their enemies. We had met the two French aid workers a few months earlier in Arequipa and had chatted with them about Apurímac and shared our ideas about development projects like the ones we were applying in the Colca Valley. We were not only deeply grieved to hear of their deaths, but also extremely shaken. We realised that the threat was real and you did not need to do anything 'wrong' in order to die a bloody death at the hands of the guerrillas. To fall victim to that violence, all you had to do was support the peasants, live among them in their rural communities and try to build a fairer society. So, in March 1989 we left DESCO and the Colca Valley, and went back home to Cuzco, where our families lived and we could at last feel safe.

The truth is that throughout all those years, the peasants from the communities affected by the conflict saw even the most basic pleasures of life slip through their fingers, like the joy of sitting around a bowl of food or having a roof over their heads and a bed to sleep in, even if it was only a couple of hides and a few blankets laid out on the ground. It was not just a case of extreme poverty, but also one of extreme hunger, cold, fear, pain, inhumanity, violence, sexual abuse and silence. Given the situation, the Quechua comuneros often demonstrated great bravery, although this has barely ever been recognised or studied. The peasants only had themselves to rely on, countering the Shining Path slogan of 'the party has a thousand eyes and a thousand ears' with their own Quechua maxim: '*huq umalla, huq makilla, huq sunqulla*' [with one head, with one hand, with a single heart]. Applying that principle was the only way to get through such difficult times.

Personal relationships over time and going back

We believe that the social and human relationships which anthropologists forge with the populations of the areas in which they conduct their ethnographic studies are different to those established by any other kind of professional or academic, and that this is particularly notable in the case of community ethnographies. Anthropologists live with the members of these societies and take part not only in their work and rituals, but also in their life cycles, remaining at their side as new families are formed, children are born and loved ones die. In the Andes, we are exposed to the same risks and inconveniences as the local population, sheltering ourselves from storms and lightning bolts, crossing rivers, climbing mountains and withstanding the cold. And when our fieldwork is done and we leave a community, we do not forget them and they do not forget us. We find ways to keep in touch and visit one another whenever possible, helping and supporting each other as best we can.

It is possible to hold an entire community dear, but true affection, respect, esteem, camaraderie and sentiment only exist between specific people. Our relationships with the families of our friends and ritual kinsmen in Yanque Urinsaya are ongoing. When these families' children come to Cuzco on the trip they take to Machu Picchu to celebrate graduation from high school, they stay with us and once we put up an entire form, complete with their three teachers.[13] As is the custom, we also invited our co-parents from the community to Cuzco for the *cargos* [traditional offices] we have held there and we have visited them on special occasions, such as relatives' weddings.

We have a particularly close relationship with one pair of co-parents and an anecdote from some time back should suffice to illustrate the bond between us. When one of us was ill with cancer, a sociologist friend who was visiting Yanque Urinsaya broke the news to them. When she returned, she described the extent to which the news had alarmed the mother and how she had cried. Months later, our daughter told us that the father had rung to inform us of the death of a woman from his family, but she could not remember her name. Deeply saddened, we supposed it had to be his wife and broke down in tears. When we finally managed to contact them, we found out that it was one of their daughters who had died, in an accident. Quite some time later, we visited them and together we recalled the sadness and confusion of those dark days.

The last time we went back to Yanque Urinsaya was in 2012, for the wedding of one of this couple's nieces. We saw that the community had changed a great deal, mainly due to tourism. A number of families had teamed up to offer 'participatory tourism' activities and take part in experience-based and adventure holiday packages. They did things to attract tourists, like dressing their llamas up in the same decorative garb they would adorn them in for long trading journeys, and parading them round the village square; the tourists then

---

13 For the last decade the students from Yanque Urinsaya have made this journey on completing their studies. In order to pay for it, they dress up in traditional costume and dance the *wititi* [a traditional local dance] in the village square to collect money from tourists.

paid to have their photos taken with them. They also trained eagles and falcons to perch on tourists' arms and shoulders for photographs.

The local craft market had grown greatly thanks to the increase in demand from tourists. Embroidery, which had previously only been used on articles like blouses, bodices, skirts and blankets, could now be seen on new items like wallets, belts, purses, bracelets and bags of different shapes and sizes. The designs used in craftwork of this kind are quite distinctive and engaging, with highly characteristic figures and motifs (such as eight-pointed stars, representations of birds, vicuñas and, above all, flowers, plants and fruit). Married and engaged women, for example, wear capes embroidered with mermaids, while single women's clothes are decorated with flowers, stars and animals, particularly small birds, a symbol of freedom. Unfortunately, this iconography has not been studied in detail, unlike in Cuzco, where a number of studies have given a real boost to regional craftwork.

On that trip, we also observed other significant changes which had nothing to do with tourism. In the field of political organisation, for example, the provincial mayor had assigned representatives to the community for the last decade and women and young people now played a more significant role in local and provincial government as a result of laws and initiatives to enhance representative democracy. The area also had better communications thanks, among other things, to new tracks extending to highland farming compounds and areas a great distance from the village. Certain local traditions and customs had also changed. We attended several weddings, for example, and saw that the outfits worn by both bride and groom, and the gifts they received had changed considerably. The latter used to include cloth and dough mermaid dolls, which symbolise love, but these had now been replaced by Barbie-like plastic dolls with mermaids' tails stuck on to them. The music was also more uproarious. A band from Arequipa, complete with sound system, was invited to play at one of the celebrations and the music could be heard from most of the village.

Perhaps nothing exemplifies these changes better than the fact that when we arrived, we discovered our co-parents had set up a small museum in their house and built and furnished two rooms to rent out to tourists on one side of the yard, alongside a washroom with outdoor shower; we decided to live in these rooms for the length of our stay. Our co-parents and a number of other families were taking part in an experience-based tourism programme which had recently been started in the community. Our co-mother still only spoke Quechua and her children were unskilled workers, but some of her grandchildren were now studying in Arequipa's university and one of her daughters was in politics, standing as a candidate for the post of municipal representative.

We also found, however, that certain important things had not changed too much. The community still farmed in much the same way as it always had, although there were fewer pack animals than before as a result of the increased use of motor vehicles; the farmers and herders also continued to exchange their products with one another, albeit less than before. The people, particularly the women, continued to wear traditional dress, with embroidery and iconography specific to each village. This was encouraged by the influx of tourists and so the stallholders, particularly the young girls, wore such attire at the local market to attract custom. Quechua was still the mother tongue, but had been enriched with words borrowed from Spanish and English (for example *quway wan dólar* = give me one dollar). Traditional customs and celebrations were still observed, such as Holy Week or the Carnival. Local rituals actually seemed more entrenched and now served as an attraction for tourists, who were invited to take part. You could say, therefore, that the community members had learned to place greater value on their local culture. No better example of this than the Uyu Uyu museum, created on the initiative of a comunero family, the descendants of the old notables of Yanque Urinsaya, and displaying family heirlooms in pride of place.

Community ethnographies in the Andes

Community studies have proved key to the discovery and investigation not only of Andean culture in general, but also of many of its more specific fundamental features. Not least, they provide us with insight into local social and political organisation, show us how land and natural resources are managed (land, water, pastures, woodland, underground resources), explore rituals which help open up these peoples' ideological and symbolic universes, and highlight the multiple interrelationships which exist between all these different cultural features. Studies of this kind have also allowed us to discover extremely peculiar systems of organisation among peasant communities, unclassifiable in political, social, economic and ritual terms, revealing the specificities of each area, the interrelationships between them and the existence of social phenomena of great interest.

The advantage of these societies is that they are small social units which share the same territory, language, history, customs and traditions, making the community ethnography an extremely useful unit of analysis. Ethnographies of this kind also offer specific case studies through which to review, verify or refute broader studies and generalisations. This methodology – almost a literary genre within anthropology – has made a decisive contribution towards 'ethnographic research (achieving) a high degree of recognition within the academic social science community thanks to its ability to respond when it comes to studying problems which traditional research fails to address' (Bernal, 2010, p. 64).

Highland communities, both peasant ones and others in the rural environment, are still fundamental components of the countries to which they belong and their Andean cultures. They exhibit significant changes and continuities, and cannot be lumped together or boiled down into sweeping generalisations because they embrace a wide range of complex realities. Meanwhile, major gaps still exist in our knowledge of them. For all these reasons, we strongly encourage further study of these communities, not only through anthropology and ethnographies, but also through other methodologies and disciplines, such as archaeology, linguistics, history and geography. To a large extent, however, their realities defy academic categorisation and so multidisciplinary approaches, capable of pinpointing what makes these peoples' outlook so different and so remarkable, could well be the answer.

We place particular importance on studies conducted from within these communities which reflect the viewpoints and visions of their inhabitants. While we should continue to study their 'classic' features, such as language, social organisation, kinship systems, water and land management, and power structures, other increasingly important aspects are also emerging, such as those related to climate change and global warming. This last field of study is especially relevant in the Andes, because, as scientists are ready to acknowledge, Andean societies have, ecologically speaking, managed for millennia to adapt quite remarkably to change in the particularly hostile environment of the highland ecosystem. The knowledge they have developed and built up, on the conservation of their environment and how to adapt to it, is particularly relevant to the present day. This knowledge should be retrieved and studied so that we can learn as much as we can from societies of this kind. Peru has only been the subject of a scattering of ethnographic studies, so we think it especially necessary that more be conducted in those regions which have been studied less, particularly jungle areas. We would then know more about these places and be able to carry out comparative studies not only of different highland regions, but also drawing comparisons between these and other types of area in the country.

In short, community ethnographies allow us to discover stores of learning, forms of social relations, knowledge on how to manage natural resources and other features of Andean culture which would otherwise be unavailable and unknown to us. Our ethnography of the peasant village of Yanque Urinsaya has contributed to this knowledge, enabling us to learn more about and improve our understanding of an axial characteristic of the Andean world, namely irrigation water management, its cultural dimensions and ritual manifestations. As the Peruvian economist Adolfo Figueroa once said (1984), Peru is still a reality without a theory, and we are absolutely convinced that community ethnographies are key to exploring that reality and developing that theory.

Conclusion

Now, many years after completing our ethnography of Yanque Urinsaya and looking back on our work in the community, both as ethnographers and in other capacities, the first thing we realise is that we chose a high-risk profession. We recall the long distances we covered on foot along ancient tracks, skirting sheer drops as we went; the rope bridges we crossed, the River Colca twisting and turning way beneath our feet; the nights we slept on the slopes of Nevado Mismi, just below the snowline; and the threat posed by Shining Path and the army. During those years, we faced mortal, and often constant, dangers but we did so with great joy and relish, thrilled at the idea of living with local people on equal terms and eager not to miss out on anything. The community members shared their food and drink, the hides they slept on and their hardships and dangers with us, and we felt part of the Quechua culture. Youth, health and fortitude, now wistful memories, were all on our side. But the same passion and dedication has enabled us to produce some worthy ethnographies; thorough, detailed, reliable studies based on first-hand information. We have never been committed to any political party, but we are committed to the Quechua culture and improving the living standards and quality of life of Quechua-speakers, a group to which we are proud to belong. We are still moved when we hear a potato- or maize-sowing song, or the melody of a *toril*, a *santiago* or a *llama taki*; it is like a physical reaction which runs through us from head to toe. It is our culture, our people, our language, our Andean sensibility. In a nutshell, it belongs to us.

The social sciences have come on a great deal since we conducted this ethnographic study in the 1980s and new fields and perspectives for research have been developed. The question of identity, for example, has become an important subject of study, addressing topics and issues which caught our attention when we were in the Colca Valley. We saw how the children of local comuneros then living in cities, in places like Arequipa and Lima, used to return to the community for important festivities like the Carnival, during which they donned traditional costume and took a lively part in the celebrations, proud to be Yanque Collaguas. Back then, we were not sure how to characterise and define those city-dwelling emigrants, who were nonetheless still Yanque comuneros. They would now be classified as an instance of 'multiple identities', a concept which Arguedas bordered on when he announced: 'I am not acculturated; I am a Peruvian who is proud, like a happy demon, to speak Christian and Indian, Spanish and Quechua' (1971, p. 297).

So there now exist new theoretical frameworks to help us analyse and define contemporary Andean communities and their core features, such as the multiple identities of the Yanqueños as Quechua-speaking comuneros, maize and irrigation farmers, and Spanish-speaking workers (such as carpenters and drivers) in cities like Arequipa and Lima. Following the example of multiple identities, we should continue to develop new theoretical frameworks and concepts with which to study and define Andean societies, and how they change and develop, particularly those aspects which have still not been clearly identified or defined, and those currently developing of which we know little or have not studied in any depth. In order to do all this, community ethnographies have proved and will continue to prove both useful and necessary.

It is important to bear very much in mind that no society or culture is in possession of an absolute truth and that we should respect and study smaller and less prevalent societies and cultures, because their knowledge, experience and epistemological systems are just as interesting and maybe just as or even more valid than those of any other. Unlike in its western counterpart, for example, in the Andean culture people are not considered *runa kay* [human beings] by simple birthright, but become human as a result of their actions, particularly through services to their community, which make them human and integrate them in society. Among many other things, community ethnographies reveal beliefs and knowledge of this kind to us, and we are all the better for it.

5. Recordkeeping: ethnography and the uncertainty of contemporary community studies

Rudi Colloredo-Mansfeld

My goal in this chapter is to understand why I have been constantly sceptical about the reality of community in the northern Ecuadorian region of Otavalo but also how, despite my doubts, I became remotivated and rediscovered purpose in practising my own ethnographic methods. At first my concerns were empirical. Confronted with rural regions losing population to migration, the reorganisation of development projects' infrastructure, and the stripping down of their subsistence practices, communities seemed to be on the ropes. They were places where, to use James Scott's memorable phrase, 'the big battalions of the state, of capitalist relations in agriculture and of demography itself are arrayed against them' (1985, p. 27) Professionally, training to be an anthropologist in the anti-colonial, postmodern, world-system-savvy 1990s required a sophisticated stance towards local culture. Rejecting a rural community study seemed an easy way to obtain credibility. Ethnographically, articles by Ecuadorian anthropologists described a diverse Otavaleño countryside of parish seats and dispersed settlements, integrated by means of a busy weekly market (Buitrón, 1962; Collier and Buitrón, 1949; Buitrón 1947; 1945). In this account, communities seemed little more than nodes of artisanal specialisation. Theoretically, ethnicity, indigenous rights, postcolonial nationalism, peasants and the politics of resistance seemed both urgent and interesting in the way that older disciplinary work about social organisation, ritual, work and ecology seemed dated and fusty.

Yet, for all the scepticism, I could not overlook community. The state, in its neoliberal turn, promoted it as a unit of decentralised economic development. For its part, the national indigenous movement elevated community as a primordial and sufficient symbol of indigenous life and authority. And, key concepts used to guide my inquiry into Andean politics and society – reciprocity, production zones, rural-urban linkages and so on – were drawn from community studies, especially those authored by my fellow contributors to this volume.

Working under these circumstances, I ended up crafting the research that would be published principally in my first book *The Native Leisure Class:*

Consumption and Cultural Creativity in the Andes (1999) but that would also form part of two subsequent volumes, *Fighting Like a Community: Andean Civil Society in an Era of Indian Uprisings* (2009) and *Fast Easy and In Cash: Artisan Hardship and Hope in the Global Economy*, written with Jason Antrosio (2015). My research in the early 1990s focused on the materiality of social relationships in Ariasucu, comprising approximately 130 households located on the physical and economic fringes of the booming Otavalo handicraft market. The fieldwork resulted in a diverse set of records: spreadsheets of time-allocation observations; lists of household inventories; maps of house locations; numbers of looms; records of belt styles; photographs of market days and *mingas* [Quichua[1] for official community work parties]; videotapes of new house parties and baptismal fiestas; neighbourhood kinship charts; sketches of tools and furnishings; transcripts and extensive field notes about the events that patterned the days of those who lived in Ariasucu. In all of this, I pursued social relations on almost every scale but a community one: households, *compadre* and kinship networks, a shared textile trade, a multisector water project and an indigenous ethnic group.

Over the year of my fieldwork, though, I experienced moments of convergence between my recordkeeping and the interest of the community council. Where my images, lists and maps crossed over with the sector leaders' projects my education in community purpose began. This knowledge ultimately induced me to write what was essentially a community study, *The Native Leisure Class*. In the spirit of such studies at that time, it was a detailed account of cultural change within a particular place – this north Andean setting due to the transition to commercial livelihoods within a self-confident indigenous group. If the processes of ethnic boundary-making, agrarian transition and small commodity production had been theorised at a broad level, my work, like other studies of this nature, offered advanced knowledge on how these changes actually worked. It was community research as 'case study' as described by Flyvbjerg (2006) – one that moves the observer from general theory to some competence in how it is to be applied. But, having the fieldwork come together in this way then caused me to revert to scepticism about just what could actually be said to be the lesson of my particular research community.

I chronicle in this chapter how this project evolved and how the writing that followed is for me an ongoing lesson in witnessing community life. In part, I show the durability of community and thus the value in its study. I also share the uncertainties of trying to apply the knowledge of this collectivity more widely. I begin with undergraduate experiences that oriented me towards the Andes and the kind of materially-grounded ethnography to which I still aspire. I then pick up the story of how I became linked to families in Ariasucu and

---

1   Ecuadorian spelling of 'Quechua'.

endeavoured to make the crossover between what I learned during my initial stay there and the anthropological debates of the early 1990s that I witnessed at the University of California, Los Angeles (UCLA). I finish with how the year spent in Ariasucu has continued to shape my research and writing to the present.

Undergraduate orientations

The spare tyre is on top of the *colectivo* shown in the slide projected on the screen – this is what Bruce Winterhalder wanted us to notice. Having introduced our undergraduate course, 'Human evolution and adaptation', in terms of the ecology of Andean farming communities, Winterhalder was taking time in class to share pictures and stories from his own fieldwork. He had taken that tyre as a good sign of a well-prepared driver, savvy about the road that lay ahead. Winterhalder then laughed and said that the tyre instead turned out to be a sign of there being four bald tyres on their vehicle. It was not a matter of if they would get a flat, but when. This was my first anthropology class, taken in 1985, and I still remember such details. Taxis were not really our concern. Winterhalder was leading us through the adaptive advantages of coca chewing. Explaining to us how Peruvian officials and development agencies had condemned coca chewing, he showed that the claims farmers made about coca had held up in a series of experiments – coca allowed them to work longer, stay warmer, and it also forestalled hunger. It was a simple and powerful lesson about anthropology: the claims a group made about their lives and actions should be respected and a sign of that respect was the care one took in observing, recording and assessing those claims.

A year later, a friend and I obtained funding for summer research and, with Winterhalder's help, we got connected to a project in the Colca Valley, Peru, working for a geographer named Charles Mahaffey. When we joined him, Mahaffey sent us off to investigate a high-altitude, wide drainage system constructed for long-abandoned terraces which used to be part of present-day Achoma's ancient agricultural landscape. How did the old irrigation system work? Where did the water come from? What state were the terraces and ditches in? Off we went. For three weeks, we hiked up out of Achoma each morning, crossed over a ridge into the drainage area, and got to work with our compass, altimeter, map and notebook. Eventually, we realised that the terraces here divided into two parts. The lower section had well-defined water channels, tightly built walls, and flat surfaces for cultivation. The upper levels were rougher in every way. Perhaps they were only just coming into service when the population collapsed. Or maybe the ancestral community was cultivating something different on their highest land. We could only guess. The uncertainty did not diminish our sense of accomplishment in detecting the basic split in the agricultural landscape, a reality revealed gradually through days of scaling terrace walls and scanning the sparse vegetation for stone-lined water courses.

Returning for my senior year, I completed my anthropology major. The classes began to frustrate me. Too often we seemed to finish an ethnographic case with a disclaimer that the people no longer live that way – pursuing bride-wealth, worshipping cargo cults, passing through lengthy initiations or whatever cultural issue we had just learned about. It seemed that rather than exploring cultural diversity, anthropology was becoming another kind of history. I kept wondering, 'But what are they doing now?' I graduated, went to study German in Vienna, worked briefly in Europe, and then returned to Massachusetts where I was employed as a salesman for a radiator factory for two years. It was not until 1990 when I enrolled at graduate school at UCLA that I started working on a way to answer that question.

Launching fieldwork in Ariasucu

I returned to fieldwork in the Ecuadorian Andes in June 1991. After a year of graduate seminars – a mixed bag of social theory and ethnography – I had devised a project to research ethnicity, economy and material culture inspired by the book, *Food, Gender, and Poverty in the Ecuadorian Andes* by Mary Weismantel (1988). I wanted to do with homes and furnishings what she had done with food to see how Andean families brought together urban cash economies and rural subsistence practices in their methods of consumption. To establish some contacts in Ecuador, I had written to the Instituto Nacional de Patrimonia Cultural for any material they had on rural vernacular architecture and received a pamphlet detailing different techniques of constructing earth walls and straw roofs.

Casting about for a place to work, I figured I would start in Otavalo. In 1990, it was a market town of about 40,000 residents located a two-hour bus ride north of Quito on the Pan American Highway. In the wider canton of Otavalo, a dense network of about 60 rural communities spread across the slopes of Mount Imbabura and were home to tens of thousands of Quichua-speaking residents. These were the famed indigenous Otavaleños, described extensively by both Ecuadorian and foreign scholars for the way they had developed artisanal manufacturing and pursued trade opportunities in Peru, Colombia and Venezuela. The chapter, 'The weavers of Otavalo', by Frank Salomon (1981), Anibal Buitrón's articles mentioned above, and other writings (Rubio Orbe, 1956) suggested a people whose distinctive native identity emerged from the aggressive methods they used to take advantage of economic opportunities. Yet even as they prospered through commercial acumen, they reproduced agrarian traditions in their home province of Imbabura. My first-year proposal focused on the utility of Otavalo as a case of economic change and was puffed up with claims of my prior Andean research experience. The department granted funds to get me to Quito.

Once I arrived, my initial preparation seemed to desert me, or I it. My first morning in Quito, I shelved the idea of going to Otavalo and set off for the Instituto Nacional de Patrimonia Cultural offices in central Quito to consult with someone about my project. I talked my way in to see the staff architect who had mailed me the pamphlet. When she finally understood how I came to be standing in front of her desk, she was alarmed. Explaining that her job was to oversee conservation projects at Quito's colonial churches, she said she knew nothing of rural architecture. She was, however, resourceful. The next thing I knew we were striding off across the old city centre to visit a university classmate of hers who directed Fundación Ecuatoriana del Habitat (FUNHABIT), a non-governmental organisation (NGO) supporting rural construction projects using improved adobe techniques.

For the next six days, I would live at the FUNHABIT field headquarters in a straw-roofed, adobe-walled demonstration house on the outskirts of Pujili in the province of Cotopaxi. Each day I rode with a young engineer on his supply runs and to his community meetings. The foundation was supporting three projects: a *huahuahuasi* [pre-school/childcare centre] in Salasaca; a casa communal in a sector just outside of Pujili; and 40 private houses for families in Quiloa in the Tigua region. In the cab of our sturdy little Toyota pick-up, he tutored me in proper etiquette for our community meetings. 'Don't call them communities', he said, 'up here they call them "sectors"' and 'it is always "comrade" (Quichua: "*mashi*" or Spanish: "*compañero*") not "uncle" or "aunt", "mother" or "father"'. He was intent on stripping me of any romanticised notions of native Andean communities. Here in Cotopaxi he insisted that one found an assertive peasantry that was stepping up to manage its own development.

The Quiloa supply runs, in particular, quickly showed me how difficult this development could be. To begin with, three houses were going up outside the community boundaries in other jurisdictions. Kinship ties and an intercouncil debt of some kind shifted them from Quiloan recipients. It was clear this spreading of the project across sector boundaries irritated the engineer. It complicated the programme and suggested some corruption in the community president's commitment to the plans that had been developed. Second, even the simplest tasks had to be negotiated.

For example, the distribution of bags of cement and rafters involved a time-consuming reconciliation between the engineer's list (the reflection of a construction schedule) and the community council's list (the reflection of each household's labour contribution to the project). As dedicated as the engineer was to getting materials to specific houses at the right stage to make the most effective use of the supplies, he gave ground to the community leaders. They repeatedly directed portions of our cargo to those who had diligently 'paid their minga', that is, had shown up for officially organised community work days and been registered by the council for the work they had done. Even I could see that allocating our supplies along these lines would mean that the material would sit unused in a storage room while progress on a neighbour's half-built house stalled. Thus within a week of my arrival in Ecuador, the anthropological readings had been pushed from my mind. Instead I was being oriented by what I had experienced in Quiloa and its house-building endeavours: NGOs were integral to the changes that were taking place; indigenousness might not be the overarching frame of encounter; and residents set the terms for what outsiders did in their sector.

After nearly a week, I left the FUNHABIT projects to return to Quito and then continue up the Pan American Highway to Otavalo. As most do, I began that visit in the Saturday market among the handicraft vendors and purveyors of household items, but soon set off down the railroad tracks towards Peguche. An hour out of town and now heading up Mount Imbabura's less-travelled lanes, I was hailed by a man who had also left the cobbled bus road to proceed uphill. He asked me the usual, question: 'Where are you going?' In response I mentioned my status as a graduate student in anthropology, my research plans, my recent trip to Quiloa, my interest in the different houses this far from town, my stay in Ecuador, my university in California, my photographs, and my walk up from Otavalo. (Later I would learn to answer this common question with 'up' or 'down'). Antonio Castañeda Camuendo took all of this in and smiled. This stranger, who was to soon become my guide, then host, then later a compadre, and eventually, years later, the companion of quiet Sunday afternoons after Parkinson's disease had robbed him of his ability to weave, gestured for me to accompany him up the hill.

He mentioned that an anthropologist had recently lived in the adjoining sector. Later he let me know that this researcher's host family had a new roof and a cement-paved driveway to show for the association. Antonio did not know what anthropologists did, but he saw potential benefits in being connected to one. He offered to be my guide for the rest of the day. As we followed the footpaths on Imbabura, he met my queries – about new two-storey houses or weathered straw huts or sturdy, rammed earth houses – with speculation about a migrant who worked in Colombia or a widow or a distant cousin. Where I was seeing buildings, he was seeing individuals or types of people.

I hired him for the next day and spent a long afternoon meeting both Antonio and his wife Elena Chiza by the end of which we had worked out how I could move in with his family to pursue my project. To help me navigate the parish buses, Antonio informed me his house was located in Ariasucu. He also warned me that some bus drivers would not know the sector's name because they saw it as merely a neighbourhood of the much larger and better known communities on either side of it. I too had read about those two communities and consequently took 'Ariasucu' to be a neighbourhood and bus stop known to insiders – a distinct zone of houses perhaps, but not a real community. Much of the remaining summer entailed correcting this misperception.

I returned to Quito. There, I picked up topographic maps, developed photographs of houses from all the places I had visited up to that point, organised my sketches, and assembled a pictorial account of my project in my large sketch book. It would be both an aid for explaining my work and a base for a simple survey about respondents' preferred houses. Upon my return to Ariasucu, the sketch book was the instrument that connected me to a second resident of the sector, a man who was to become a crucial ally in my work for years to come. He was Pedro Vasquez and over that period he took on roles ranging from being my Quichua instructor and research assistant to serving as a weaving tutor and mentor on community work days. As with Antonio, I met Pedro quite by chance. After I moved to the sector, I took up the habit of finding a spot along a pathway in the afternoons to draw houses or landscape views. People often stopped by to see what I was rendering. Sometimes adults lingered and chatted about the drawing. Usually kids mobbed me. One afternoon, Pedro came along to rescue me from being crushed, shooing the children away and sitting beside me to find out what I was doing.

After leafing through my drawings and especially my maps where I had plotted different house types, he invited me up to see a map he had recently made of houses and footpaths. It was my first look at Ariasucu's physical extent from the community's perspective. We compared our efforts side by side matching up his inventory of paths to the incomplete but more topographically accurate map that I had created. A few days later I returned to Pedro's to get his reaction to a new map I had drawn which incorporated information from both our previous creations. This version had given me a tangible feel for the place.

As I approached Pedro's house with the new map, I saw he had a visitor and left without speaking to him. When we next met, Pedro was troubled. He explained that the visitor was from the Federación Indígenas y Campesina de Imbabura (FICI) the largest peasant organisation in the province and a powerful unit within the national indigenous movement. Pedro reported that the FICI representative was suspicious of me and my project and had told Pedro to avoid me. I was not sure how to respond. I pledged to leave Pedro full copies of my mapping work. For his part, Pedro was ready to shrug off the warning. He had recently served on the community council, a role that motivated him to draw the map and was the reason he was connected to the FICI representative.

Pedro was not enthusiastic about outsiders telling him what to do, even if they were indigenous. He remained a willing consultant throughout that summer when I participated in ever more activity in Ariasucu. As I joined in a work party on a new house, then later a community minga for a water project, I matched my tasks to his in an effort to blend in with the flow of work. When I needed a basic lesson in belt weaving, I watched him at his loom. If I was living with Antonio and Elena and learning the labours and rhythms of a household there, I was apprenticed to Pedro to see how work and community came together in Ariasucu.

Pulling together a doctoral project

These were the materials out of which my study would grow:
- a mobilised provincial indigenous society; uneven but real economic progress
- development projects and the local administration to realise them
- politicised assertion of indigenous identity
- politicised downplaying of indigenousness
- a rich scholarly literature on the industriousness and commercial heritage of Otavaleños
- Weismantel's model of capitalism and subsistence clashing within the bounds of a household
- my research commitment to methodical observation of material world
- personal ties to two greatly different households within Ariasucu.

How all this intersected the anthropology of the early 1990s would preoccupy me for the next two years. The politics of international ethnographic fieldwork had become fraught at UCLA. During my first year, flyers signed by the Radical Anthropology Graduate Students (RAGS) attacked one senior faculty member for his entanglement with the Central Intelligence Agency (CIA); another for his purported racism. The professor of one of my first theory seminars had such stature that graduate students from across Los Angeles signed up. One participant then used the seminar to share information from ACT UP, the AIDS activist organisation; another student wanted to refocus our discussion and pleaded with us to talk about how we could be both politically correct and an anthropologist. When I approached one of the two advisers assigned to me in my first year for a letter of support for my research, I was not just turned down; the professor repudiated my project as dated and imperialist. Simply going abroad for fieldwork was cast by some as a colonising venture. My doctoral adviser, Timothy Earle, was not deterred by all this. Perhaps because he was an archaeologist, he did not feel the need to take sides and kept encouraging me to take seminars in everything from poststructural theory to quantification in cultural anthropology. I found my way through by, in effect, 'scaling up' the focus of my analysis and bringing together literatures on ethnicity, peasants and emerging work on consumption.

Most of the writing available on the Otavaleños dwelt on their ethnic distinctiveness, an identity rooted in a history of trading and artisanal production. While race and racism would return to be central to problems of difference and inequality in the Andes by the late 1990s, class and ethnicity were the starting point for discussions of the early 1990s – an orthodoxy inherited from *Inequality in the Peruvian Andes: Class and Ethnicity in Cuzco* by Pierre van den Berghe and George Primov (1978). 'Ethnicity' rang especially true to me as a way to grapple with the case of the Otavaleños, a group that seemed vested in the cultural boundaries that not only divided them from mestizos but also from other indigenous groups. In theoretical terms, thinking of the object of my study as an 'ethnic group' situated my work in contemporary political and cultural currents and not just a long sequence of Andean community studies. Vincent's phrase a 'mask of confrontation' (1974) gave the topic its edge. Practically, it felt a good fit to me. It was a label that could be applied across residents in provincial market towns, scores of rural communities and a growing international diaspora; it focused usefully on language, clothing, hairstyle, distinctive commercial traditions and the cultural apparatus of boundaries.

If ethnicity offered a cultural vocabulary, peasant studies raised the issue of power. Wolf was foundational here. The Closed Corporate Peasant Community (CCPC) (Wolf, 1957; 1986) was itself a theoretical model moving across scales of analysis from national political economy to local community. His *Europe and the Peoples without History* (1982) was required reading in two of my early seminars and situated peasants more clearly in a history of capitalist expansion. However, *Weapons of the Weak* by James Scott (1985) had succeeded in making agrarian studies fashionable – relevant for anyone concerned with inequality, exploitation and tactics of self-preservation pursued by the poor. For me, Scott served as a guide to get through the thicket of postmodern discourse-centred theory. With his ideas about public and hidden transcripts, Scott's formulation of discourse was imaginable in the examples I was already gathering from an engineer, peasant political organiser and an Ariasucu resident. Beyond Scott, the task of reading a lot of the peasant literature felt like eating lukewarm, unseasoned oatmeal. Fortifying, but dull. Weismantel was different. Her focus on the increasing mismatch between the praxis of men and women tackled the structural categories – male and female, semi-proletariats and subsistence farmers, mestizo and indigenous – at work in daily life. She helped me think through Bourdieu's theory of practice, which had been assigned reading in multiple graduate seminars. Showing how the routines of rural life could speak to bigger social forces at work, *Food Gender and Poverty* delivered on the theoretical promise of agency.

In all of this, though, it was the literature on consumption that felt really new. This scholarship was an answer to postmodernism's hard textual turn. Daniel Miller's work was especially useful in setting out a theoretical pathway that underscored the importance of materiality for understanding subjectivity. He also promoted consumption studies as central to the transformation of anthropology: 'a final expunging of latent primitivism' in his words (1995, p. 269). Economic anthropologists had also begun writing about consumption linking up that topic with production and power, Sidney Mintz (1985) famously so in his masterwork *Sweetness and Power: The Place of Sugar in Modern History*. But creative work was also being done in the Andes, as represented in the writings of Weismantel, Benjamin Orlove, Cathy Costin and Timothy Earle (Weismantel, 1988; 1989; Orlove and Rutz, 1989; Costin and Earle, 1989).

Of course, doctoral preparation entails both theory and method and it was seminars in research design and method that shaped the character of the books I wrote about Ariasucu. Allen Johnson's research design class championed the importance of quantification for cultural anthropologists (Johnson, 1978). The message I took from this was not that ethnography depended on statistical significance to be persuasive. Rather, it was that an ethnographer had an obligation to undertake close, systematic observation of culture and behaviour. I saw in his approach a kind of ethics: the importance of the random sample was fairness and everyone having the chance to be included. Moreover, choosing a sample size meant trying to ensure diversity and inclusivity; and the development of a full data set entailed perseverance – a kind of respect for what people within these Andean communities themselves toiled to accomplish.

If Johnson offered design, it was the linguists at UCLA, especially Alessandro Duranti and Eleanor Ochs, who shaped my method. In an introductory seminar on sociolinguistics, I got my first graduate-level discussion of community, in this case a speech community. I learned the lesson not to look through language as some transparent medium, but rather as an expressive form, accomplished jointly during an interaction and richly informative about people's identities, knowledge and purposes. Attending to events in Ariasucu as a beginner sociolinguist offered a powerful way to track how people 'cued' their economic accomplishments through acts of consumption and made them relevant to their social aspirations (Duranti and Goodwin, 1992). I went on to sign up for back-to-back seminars in videotaping, recording, transcribing and presenting natural speech acts. In the course of my doctoral research I shot over 40 hours of tape in weaving workshops, at new house parties, during wedding fiestas, and on people's patios at the end of a farm workday. I logged every minute of those Hi-8 tapes, transcribed portions of many of them, and included dialogue and descriptions from them in each chapter of *The Native Leisure Class*.

Had I been asked to describe my project in 1993, 'a community ethnography' would likely have been the last way I would have done so. Rather, this was an investigation of cultural and economic change in an indigenous ethnic group, a study that tracked individual and household behaviour to reveal the force of subsistence practices amid commercial livelihoods. Yet, just as the Colca Valley's abandoned irrigation system emerged through weeks of walking, observing and photographing the terraces in Achoma, so did the channels of community life start to cut across the stories, surveys, transcripts and reflections that I accumulated as the months passed in 1994.

A year in Ariasucu

Restarting fieldwork in Ariasucu in December 1993 involved two shifts in practice from the methods I had used for my master's. At first, I was accompanied by my wife Chesca, who had secured a year's leave of absence from work. As a married couple, we were able to convince our hosts Elena and Antonio to let us build a new room attached to their house. For four weeks we lived in their storeroom, ate with their family and worked with a maestro to dig the foundations, mix cement, carry cement blocks and frame the roof. In the final stage of construction, a neighbour and Elena's father arrived to help nail down the tile runners and finish the roof. I discovered that there is no more gossipy moment for men than when they are up on top of a house. Ostensibly working, they instead track the comings and goings of their neighbours with whispered commentary. The arrival of a private car, a rare event in Ariasucu, would spark half an hour of speculation as to who might be visiting whom and why. It was an early lesson in how closely people attended to each other's fortunes. I eventually learned I would have plenty of partners with whom to share my speculation about what was going on in the sector.

The second change involved my commitment to learning Quichua and conducting as much of my research in the language as I could. At UCLA, I had taken a two-month immersion course in Quechua from Jaime Luis Diaz, a Bolivian anthropologist and skilled language teacher. It was useful to understand the structure of Quechua, and I got a jump on learning vocabulary. Of course, speaking fragments of Bolivian Quechua in Imbabura got me mostly laughs and looks of incomprehension. To adapt, I had picked up a slim book of Quichua exercises in Quito. I soon realised it was for missionaries and traders in the *oriente*, with practice sentences such as 'I will only pay X for that jaguar pelt. It has five holes in it.' I then got my hands on photocopies of Chuquin's and Salomon's pedagogical grammar of Imbabura Quichua. This was a lifesaver. I spent each morning working through its exercises and then an hour midday with my map-making companion Pedro Vásquez to practise what I had read. (Towards the end of my research, I crossed paths with Salomon in

Peguche at his compadre's house. We all spoke almost entirely in Quichua – I was so self-conscious about how rudimentary my Spanish had remained over the course of the year, I thought it best to stick with Runa Shimi).

While Chesca and I settled in, I launched the formal tasks of my research. In reality, as I began my work, I was both overcommitted to and under-appreciative of the idea of Ariasucu's community-ness. My 'over-commitment' was built into my research plan. I took the boundaries that Pedro and I had come up with on our joint map as proof of Ariasucu's physical existence and the minga lists for the water project as evidence of the bounded set of community members. With these, I established the samples I would use for an 11-month time allocation study as well as the paired comparisons of 34 households that I used to document the belt-weaving enterprise.

Yet, even as I operationalised the community as a research site, I did not give much thought to Ariasucu as a place of meaning and belonging. The engineer's term 'sector' had stuck in my head. I thought of Ariasucu as a slice of Otavaleños' broader ethnic group. On the bus ride from Otavalo out to Ariasucu, one passed across the sloping fields of Imbabura, by houses, and through many indistinguishable neighbourhoods. They all seemed interchangeable. Moreover, the market, churches, health clinics and schools in Otavalo and the parish seats united and blended residents from all these places.

Further, my research began to confirm the non-localised lives led by Ariasucu families. Spread out amid subsistence plots, houses were still set up as instruments of agrarian production. Ploughs hung in rafters; grain mills and grinding stones could be found by the hearths. Yet, they were worked at a fraction of their capacity. It was not long before the spot observations in my time study showed how little attention subsistence agriculture received. The final one I carried out revealed seven per cent of total observations for women, five per cent for men were spent in farming. Commerce, not cultivation, paced the tasks of residents' days.

Other observations reinforced this fact. For instance, I inventoried at a later stage the possessions that families had accumulated. The blankets, stereos, televisions, blenders and other items often traced travels through the Otavaleños' commercial diaspora: Quito, Cuenca, Bogota, Cartagena and beyond. They were mementoes earned elsewhere, not surpluses built up in Ariasucu. Although my informants now resided in the community, they continued to reach beyond it. After videotaping baptisms, confirmations and new house parties, I and the hosts would review the tapes together. These couples would pay close attention to the guests' arrivals, explaining for my benefit where they lived: down in Otavalo, over in Ibarra or up in Tulcan. Of course, there were modest events involving a small circle of local family. Yet, the all-Ariasucu nature of these celebrations mostly confirmed the poverty of the hosts, not the importance of place.

Community, though, began to reappear elsewhere in my transcriptions and notebooks. It could show up as a telling detail. Early in our year-long stay, for example, Elena and Antonio purchased a refrigerator. I admired it, saying there were not many in Ariasucu. Elena noted, 'There are only three others' among the sector's 131 households. Months later, after I had completed my inventories, work survey and time allocation observations, I realised she was exactly right. However aloof she often seemed from her neighbours up the mountain, she tracked her accomplishments most carefully in relation to them.

Throughout 1994, the water project became my appointment for recording the community's preoccupations. When I could, I joined the work and videotaped the meetings that closed the day, sessions that entailed a roll call of workers, planning for the next minga, and discussions of potential new projects. Towards the end of our stay, the Canton of Otavalo unveiled a plan for building a sewer system throughout the parish. Community members debated the costs of participation and one man spoke eloquently against joining the project, noting that the people of Ariasucu barely had enough money to buy 'salt and fat' each week. Later, when writing up the sewer project, I searched my laptop field notes for details of that meeting and speaker, typing the words 'salt and fat' into the query to retrieve the moment he spoke. To my surprise, 11 instances of the phrase were returned and reading through them I found the rhetorical use of it was similar in every circumstance. Speakers rose to protest demands placed upon them by provincial authorities or neighbouring communities, contrasting Ariasucu's lean country lives with the cash-flush handicraft-selling communities on their borders. I began to get an idea of Ariasucu's sense of difference – its identity in relation to its rivals.

When the council vice-president realised the scope of my field documents, he enlisted me directly in the cause of elevating Ariasucu's formal status as a community. He had me print out copies of my map and then the two of us walked around its upper boundaries. For lack of information, I had left them unmarked. He wanted to fix the boundaries and include the revised map in a petition for recognition from the Ministry of Agriculture. The council secretary also came for some material. Anticipating the commissioning of the new water system and the need to issue monthly bills, he wanted an example of how to keep a spreadsheet to track community members and their contributions.

If I came to see the importance of community in all this, I also saw how tentative it was. The boundaries and lists were less fixed political objects than flashpoints in a long debate about the wisdom of actually registering a jurisdiction with the government. My records joined theirs as devices that the council put to service to project and affirm Ariasucu. Many of its residents, though, stood at meetings to argue against joining in projects or formalising their council.

I was beginning to see that 'local community' was a phrase that paired quite different ideas. It would take work to join them, to actually make a 'community' become 'local'. Certainly, the notion of locality was not in doubt. It was palpable in the shared lives of the extended families whose homes stretched up along the shallow, slant-wise gully and whose lives folded together in layers of meaning. Among them, an angry word could cue a bad relationship between brothers-in-law that had begun a generation ago; a gift at a fiesta could signal a friendship from 1970s Quito. Within this world, the arrival of a new television in one home could affect social story-lines across four others. This closeness made them local, a group living amid a rich context of shared history. But it did not make them a community.

Rather, a 'community' was an abstract unit of administration, an instrument of material development. Residents of Ariasucu needed to be this kind of community if they wanted a share of the electric grid or a partnership with an NGO. However, in Otavalo in the 1990s the political and cultural pressures to be such a community became even greater. Indigenous authority at a deeper level was at stake. The handicraft boom was entering into its third decade and the wealth of successful entrepreneurs transformed neighbourhoods, not just in the town of Otavalo but in well-known indigenous communities such as Peguche and Agato. As Pedro Vasquez told me once, 'In Peguche, they live almost like lords'. Politics now favoured these richer, stronger communities over marginal ones such as Ariasucu. When mobilising indigenous peoples, the national leadership of La Confederación de Nacionalidades Indígenas del Ecuador (Confederation of Indigenous Nationalities of Ecuador, CONIAE) turned to the community councils of officially recognised peasant communities. Those without jurisdictions registered with the Ministry of Agriculture could be ignored, not just by the state, but by the charismatic leaders of indigenous uprisings. In places such as Ariasucu, there was a growing sense of collective decline in status. By becoming official, Ariasucu could restore that 'horizontal comradeship' (Anderson, 1991) with both the most assertive indigenous sectors and the rising middle-class Otavaleños. To some inhabitants of Ariasucu becoming a real community promised to uphold a distinctive sense of political parity and respect that money and activism were eroding in the 1990s.

My records offered an image of Ariasucu as it flickered into official life. Conceptually, the more carefully I attended to meetings and mingas, the more I shifted my sight from Otavaleños as an ethnic group to Otavalo as a township of segmented and competing jurisdictions. And I became more aware of becoming 'community-bound' in my research. Throughout 1994, Otavalo was home to quite a group of doctoral researchers. Lynn Meisch lived in town, generously hosting pot-luck parties when luminaries such as Frank Salomon or Norman Whitten came through the area. Linda D'Amico lived in Peguche with her two children and, at least once a month, Chesca and I walked the 45 minutes or so down from our home, past the waterfall, and across the fields to have dinner with them, then hike back up the mountain in the dark. Mark Rogers and Elizabeth Marberrry Rogers also had an apartment in Otavalo. All of these peers and friends were pushing their projects in creative translocal and transnational ways (Meisch, 2002; D'Amico, 2011). Chesca, too, had found work with CARE, an international NGO that was experimenting with new ways for communities to diagnose their own development goals. Her job often required her to travel across the province. By the end of my fieldwork, I had the most circumscribed working life of us all.

Chesca and I wound our lives in Ariasucu down in November 1994. In taking our leave, our focus was on the core families of my project. In February, I had selected 18 households for their weaving occupation and another 18 because a random number function on an Excel spreadsheet had picked them up as matches from a community census. Two families dropped out, but the others graciously continued. Over time, the character of the visits changed, and control over their meanings emerged from the hospitality of the visited, not the data needs of the observer. Their warm greetings marked my visits in the register of a social call. Where a household undertook preparations for a baptism, wedding or confirmation, I would try to arrive with a small contribution of beer or soft drinks. Thereafter, householders would react to my spot observing as to a hurried compadre's visit – a material instance of socially meaningful exchange. What began as abstract research design was melting into human connection and being reformed by rural etiquette. So as we prepared to leave, Chesca and I tried to honour these sentiments, parcelling our possessions among the 34 households. Blankets, kitchen utensils, clothes, basins and bins – useful items of little value. Amid emotional goodbyes, we handed each item over, marking the debts that we continue to carry.

Making something of Ariasucu

How much community can actually be taken up in an ethnography before it loses its relevance to the discipline? The conventional answer has been 'not much'. The idea, as Geertz puts it, is that 'the locus of study is not the object of study. Anthropologists do not study villages (tribes, towns, neighborhoods...) they study in villages' (1973). That had been my plan, too. I would set up in Ariasucu to study the economic transformations of an ethnic group. In the end, though, I was studying the village. Once back in Los Angeles, I had to work my way back to my 'object of study', a more thematic contribution to the growing literature on consumption. It took two drafts of the dissertation and another two of the book manuscript to settle on a narrative that accounted for uneven mixing of subsistence values, entrepreneurship and the global handicraft economy that I saw in Ariasucu. Along the way, I discarded the starkest act of community solidarity that I had witnessed. The tense episode of capturing thieves, punishing them and justifying the act to a rival community that epitomised Ariasucu's drive for collective respect (Colloredo-Mansfeld, 2002). I set it all aside. It was not just that I wanted to focus on the social world of consumption. I was having a hard time making sense of how community justice worked and I did not want to linger on the problem. I trimmed my material with the hope of getting approval for a book about consumption.

In the event, *The Native Leisure Class* found some favour in the United States as a teachable ethnography. Reviewed in the *Times Literary Supplement* and tapped as a case of culture and consumption in a popular text book, it gained enough notice in its English version to build an audience. At the time of writing it is still available on Amazon. (In fact, the online retailer advertises used copies for as little as one cent – an appropriate price for a book with a chapter that touts the value of worthless things). My efforts to bring it out in Spanish have stalled. While I have a translated manuscript and a publisher, we agree on the need for a new chapter to bring the story up to the present. I have sufficient material to do so. Yet, other projects in Otavalo have intervened and completion keeps getting pushed off. Thus, one finds in Ariasucu a handful of English copies of the original book scattered among the households, gathering dust if not actually growing mould. People sometimes bring them out upon my return so that children can be shown the photos inside the book.

The shock that dollarisation brought to the Otavalo economy fundamentally redirected my project. In 2000, prices for wool, acrylic yarn and electricity were rising quickly and denominated in dollars. Knitters and weavers were at a loss to know how to price their goods and found all money earned from a sale would then go towards buying their next supply of raw materials. Craft production was costing them dearly. That year, I observed a summit between owners of seven factories which produced woollen yarn and the leaders of La Union de Artesanos Indígenas del Mercado Centenario-Otavalo (The Union of Indigenous Artisans for the Centenario Market of Otavalo, UNAIMCO), witnessing how they negotiated a price freeze and other concessions to try to preserve the textile economy. For the next seven years, I developed my own work in partnership with UNAIMCO supporting their efforts to rekindle 'an economy with identity'.

In its own way, the shift in topic, location and interlocutors became a practical test of the validity of community-gained knowledge. In the centre of Otavalo, and especially at UNAIMCO, affairs were directed by a university-educated indigenous elite, including mayor Lic. Mario Conejo, Lic. José

Quimbo, Arq. Humberto Lema, Lic. Segundo Maldonado and others. My collaboration with the union often had tangible goals, including using a set of new marketplace studies to develop proposals for artisan training workshops. We would take our survey results and seek financial backing from various agencies and ministries. In the case of FICI, in particular, the union wanted to show that their projects reached to rural constituencies, and they counted on me to reinforce that message. Following a meeting at FICI this led to a remarkable conversation when an official with the federation came over to continue speaking with me in Quichua after others had switched to Spanish. He said he knew me – he had been the man visiting Pedro Vasquez 13 years previously, in 1991. That is, he had been the one who warned Pedro not to speak with me. He quizzed me about Pedro and the situation in Ariasucu. Without smiling or much of a reaction, he ended our conversation but said he would like to talk more soon.

Generally, though, union leaders paid little attention to initiatives that would bring material benefits to the craft resellers who lived up in Ariasucu. While many in that rural sector held UNAIMCO identification cards, few at the union sought to improve residents' work. For example, rather than seek the physical expansion in the plaza or rules that would preserve rural, part-time craft sellers' access, the union focused more on production issues. For union leaders, it was not my community study that mattered, but rather a parallel textile study that Jason Antrosio and I were pursuing in Atuntaqui ten kilometres north on the Pan American Highway. Union leaders were keen to learn details of partnerships among Atuntaqui's casual sportswear manufacturers, the business services department at the Catholic University and international quality control consultants.

As for consumption studies, the topic evolved into diverging sets of concerns. Moving away from economically oriented analysis, many anthropologists shifted from commodities and consuming to the topic of materiality. Latour and others from science studies provided creative frameworks to pursue linkages among people, objects, agency and identity. These kinds of projects, though, rarely touched upon agrarian change. Other studies continued to pursue the meaning of commodities, but the research had again divided the world of production from that of consumption. Thus, ethnographers would note the meaning of an object, whether artisan goods (Chibnik, 2003) or fair-trade coffee (Jaffee, 2007) as they passed along a supply chain. Rarely was people's consumption united with an analysis of individuals' roles as workers or producers. The issue has reemerged, though, especially in new works on how people pursue 'the good life', the costs of achieving it and the price paid for falling short. In Latin America, Edward Fischer's studies in Guatemala provide especially rich examples of this (Fischer and Benson, 2006).

The unfinished business of community studies

In a review essay written a generation ago, Partridge offered from a North American perspective three phases of community studies in Latin America. In the 1940s and 1950s, ethnographers pursued a typological project, identifying the 'major human settlement forms of the Latin American hinterlands, their characteristic subsistence ecologies, the social and ideological structures that transmitted these from generation to generation, and something of the political economy to which they adapted' (1982, p. 130). Here a kind of old school structural functionalism prevailed, showing the integration of customs, belief and ecology. Then, in the 1960s, process and change came to dominate. Now, 'community traditions of Latin America were understood not only as adaptations to local conditions, but increasingly as responses to national and international political economies directed by powerful public and private corporate groups' (ibid.).

By the late 1970s, community studies had begun to swing back, bearing witness to the long durée of the local. Even in the face of agrarian reform, the spread of agri-business, the surge in migration, and institutionalisation of rural development programmes, so much seemed to endure: 'the cards have been reshuffled only to fall once again into the same old piles' (Stearman, 1973, p. 33). It is a telling observation. Not so much for whether the piles were really the same. Rather, in Partridge's eyes at least, this new set of ethnographers still had the chops to tackle the old problems of subsistence ecologies, social organisation and ideological structures in order to demonstrate the continuity of local history, the success of local adaptation. In anthropological accounts, the continuities of local culture testified to the regularity of ethnographic training.

These days that would be unlikely. To be sure, community studies not only abound but feature in research designs confronting the most urgent contemporary questions in the Andes. The use of geographically indicated trademarks in protecting artisan economies (Chan, 2011); the human response to climate change (Rasmussen, 2015); and the transformation of agrarian society through global exports of specialty crops (Laguna, 2011) have all been explored in such studies. But these investigations still suffer from the dilemma I faced when I began my work: we can take community as frame, but not as existence. We can lay out our research problem within the population and landscape of a specific place, yet the way people carry the history of that place into their aspirations for the future remains a shadow topic. Our robust and well-conceived methods for examining the forces unleashed by global capitalism do not have a similar counterpart for explaining the conversations, rituals and expressive life that carry today's Andean communities into the future. Of course, ethnographers still track local customs and social dramas and skilfully lay out aesthetic practices that endow them with a transcendent meaning. Since the 1990s, though, such efforts have no clear theoretical ligaments, no obvious way to exert themselves in disciplinary discussions. The crowd's interest has moved on.

It is tempting to suggest the short-termist perspective in Olivia Harris's conception has won out. For too long, ethnographers have focused on social change and development issues, neglecting historical continuities, especially those to be found in ritual practices. But I think this would be a misreading. It underplays just how burdened with meaning the institutions of community economic development have become. For an ethnographer, the instruments and acts of today's communities – even the newest sectors such as Ariasucu – need the same sensitivity with which a sociolinguist approaches language. One cannot simply 'look through' the words and events of work parties and village assemblies to access the reality of national development programmes. The timing, places and acts of meetings and mingas are themselves expressive forms, mutually accomplished, historically coded and richly informative about the work of a community. Taking an investigation seriously as a community study – in addition to being explicitly a project on commodities and consumption, development, or community organisation – an ethnographer must attend to the forms of encounter that link a sewer project meeting into much older ways by which individuals come to create themselves as the rightful people of a place.

As I pulled together my doctoral work, my committee member Alessandro Duranti published his book *From Grammar to Politics* (1994) and I remember him saying that one never really writes a new book, but just keeps writing the same one repeatedly. I do not know if that is actually true of Duranti, but I feel it could be fairly said of me. The fieldwork we did in 1994 has been tapped for three books. Together, they offer a time-lapse view of the lessons I have been learning from that year-long, immersive community study. For whatever Geertz says, anthropologists do study villages. In my case, I kept the faith with my research plan, recording what I could of a changing agrarian economy. But as boundaries between economic facts and social facts blurred, my quest for the facts meant 'getting Ariasucu right'. Ever since 1994, the multilayered, multipeopled world that I brought back in my records has felt like unfinished business.

Now and again a new research project goes down a path that reopens an issue that I first encountered in Ariasucu. I then tackle neglected examples from that time and this in turn helps me shed light on my current preoccupation. The meaning of my stay in Ariasucu has been unfolding across 20 years of writing. It is still not played out.

6. Long lines of continuity: field ethnohistory and customary conservation in the Sierra de Lima

Frank Salomon

> *– Say it, no ideas but in things –*
> *nothing but the blank faces of the houses*
> *and cylindrical trees*
> *bent, forked by preconception and accident –*
> *split, furrowed, creased, mottled, stained –*
> *secret – into the body of the light!*
> William Carlos Williams, *Book 1, Paterson* (1995 [1946], p. 6)

In 1966, when I was still an undergraduate, travels on Andean roads and the sound of the Ecuadorian Quichua[1] language fixed my southward orientation for good. It was an unformed inclination. Under a mistaken idea about social sciences, I became a bored graduate student in Michigan's sociology department. But there was a silver lining: I enrolled in Eric Wolf's course across the street at Angell Hall. Wolf was at that time researching what would become *Europe and the Peoples without History* (1982), and he was voracious for information about the less-documented edges of colonial empires. In a basement office under padded steam pipes, he soaked up what I had learned about Ecuadorian Quichua populations. Listening in was Wolf's junior colleague, the economic anthropologist Daniel Gross, who later became the National Science Foundation's (NSF) cultural anthropology programme director. Gross said, 'Well, if that's what you need to do, you might as well get paid for it. Go to grad school with John Murra at Cornell – he's the one who can teach what you want to learn.' I was attracted to Wolf, Gross and Murra because of their knowledge of South American societies, not their materialism. But much later, problems about the materiality of Andean culture would pull me back towards their insistence on society as lived with and through things.

---

1   Ecuadorian spelling of 'Quechua'.

Ethnography as the fieldwork of history and myth

At Cornell, Andean language meant southern Quechua. Following up on Antonio Cusihuaman's delightful Cuzco Quechua grammar courses, a few of us went on to study with the Bolivian ex-Jesuit and native Quechua speaker George Urioste, who was then Donald Solá's PhD candidate in linguistics. Solá wangled for Urioste a chance to teach a whole-semester seminar exclusively for reading, in the original language, the Quechua Manuscript of Huarochirí, the subject of his dissertation. This untitled, unsigned book is the only known early source that explains a South American body of myth and ritual in an indigenous language. Then thought to date back to 1598, it is now usually dated 1608. That seminar was academic bliss.

It had only been a few years since Murra had collaborated with José María Arguedas and Pierre Duviols (1966) to bring out the first published Spanish translation as *Dioses y hombres de Huarochirí*. Yet Huarochirí remained for Cornellians more a *locus classicus* than a research site; none of our peers or instructors had actually been there. Murra esteemed María Rostworowski's (1972) and Pierre Duviols' (1973) emerging works on the Yauyo/Yunca or Huari/Llacuaz social constellation. The early work of Karen Spalding (1970), just arriving from Berkeley via Lima, showed us how power in Huarochirí worked and changed on the ground. Like these authors we glossed the *llactacuna* in the manuscript as 'communities'. We perceived that the miracles of Paria Caca, Chaupi Ñamca and their fellow *huacas* [sacred beings] were pinned to a dense constellation of geographic knowledge and economic interests.

A decade after my doctorate, soon after I had been tenured at Madison, George Urioste called me saying 'I'm interested in publishing an English version of the Huarochirí text, but I need a co-author because I'm not a native English speaker.' It was easy for George to pull me back to our shared train of thought. We enjoyed our obsession hugely and made of it the 1991 University of Texas Press edition.

As we worked, the contrast between our textual knowledge of the source and my poverty of ethnographic knowledge bothered me. It became ever clearer that, irrespective of the persecutory trap Father Francisco de Ávila was building by collecting 'idolatrous' information, both the local tellers of legends and the Quechua writer who put the work together had purposes of their own. The probable author, Cristóbal Choque Casa, was synthesising internal conversations among 'the people called Indians', conversations that closely parsed in mythic and ritual idiom what sociologists and anthropologists had lumpingly come to call community. This was a hard book, challenging for reasons opposite to those usually found in colonial sources. Usually, Spanish administrators or clerics digest 'Indian' information into generic language, easy for Spaniards to follow. In Huarochirí the reverse happened. The book is difficult for us because the writer took for granted a lot of culturally specific indigenous knowledge about an Andean model of *llacta*, only partly translatable as community: nested, descent-based or clan-like corporate groups of originally dissimilar ethnicity, which saw themselves as integrated by sacred practices and politically coordinated resource claims.

Like other participants Choque Casa had partisan interests, and he was not above using his access to Father Avila as a chance to defame local rivals. At the same time, however, he meant to do more than incriminate his enemies. Exceeding his apparent mission as Avila's catspaw, he set about to use the resources of transatlantic bookish culture for a new purpose. He began to integrate 'Indian' ideas in a synthesis that he dared to call a *fe*: that is, a religion, rather than just a tangle of diabolic superstitions. Although the Huarochiri author was himself a strong Christian and an enemy of the old gods, he believed he could find in their myths a coherent system of thinking about how llactacuna came into being – a mythology, yes, but one that allegorised local social facts and added up to a local sense of historicity, though not exactly a history.

That is, I came to see, he was constructing an ethnographic sort of truth. Like an ethnographer, he was trying to reproduce expressions of the 'native point of view', and at the same time to synthesise them as a sociocultural whole not previously visible, not even to its own members. Where travel and theory provide critical distance for anthropologists, Christian theology and some degree of biculturalism provided it for him. He used colonial words for 'faith' and 'law' somewhat as we would use 'culture'. It fascinated me that this man, who was moved by political animus and anti-traditional doctrine, nonetheless thought that gathering huaca knowledge would improve the life of the llactas as ongoing collectivities. To compose the book the pre-Columbian ancestors would have written 'had they known writing' was a kind of ethnohistory in the subjunctive, encysted within the machinery of repression.

What I wanted to do by studying Huarochirí was to practice ethnohistory and ethnography in a way both historians and archaeologists could use. Colleagues warned that ethnographic analogy between ancient and modern societies would always be a controverted method. Archaeologists have never stopped thrashing each other about it. But with the ethnohistoric record rapidly expanding, I foresaw chances to define better 'grounded analogies'. That is, rather than using ethnographic facts from late dates to find or explain archaeological facts, we might concentrate on Andean features whose continuity or alteration could be demonstrated by document chains and material inheritances. For me, finding those long lines of continuity and alteration became the end and not the means. Or to put it another way, ethnohistory meant less the project of reconstructing a remote world 'without us', and more the project of seeing how Amerindia, reworking its pre-Columbian legacies, generated a part of our modernity. Studying the material things of culture was an appealing method, because things form both an independent testimony about past culture and a stimulus to cultural memory in the present. I did not guess, though, that such ventures would involve me in communities' ways of curating and using the material legacy. This chapter is concerned with how it happened.

In communities of letters and of cords

In 1989 and 1990, with help from the National Endowment for the Humanities, I set out up the jolting roads of the Mala River Valley to find the scenes of Paria Caca and Tutay Quiri. It was a bad time to start fieldwork because Sendero Luminoso (Shining Path) was forming its 'iron ring' around Lima in the headwaters of the Rímac, Lurín and Mala valleys with the purpose of strangling the capital's traffic. My excursions were anxious and short, but stirring. How astonishing it was to see on battered highway signs the very names of huacas from the Huarochirí myths! Transportes Asunción's exhausted bus trundled up the abyss, zigzagging through endless switchbacks. The dashboard had a built-in funnel through which the driver's boy sluiced cooling water into the engine. At every reversal of view I asked fellow passengers about landmarks, thrilled to hear names like Cerro Shiucaña (Sihua Caña, 'the most beautiful huaca' in the myths) or Chauti and Huangre (hamlets named for old ayllus, otherwise unheralded in anthropology). About many of them they remembered tales.

But in those times I found few interlocutors. Peru's economy was nose-diving and the state was losing its political war. Bombs and gunfire woke Limeños up at night even in the wealthy neighbourhood of Miraflores. In the Huarochirí sierra, a poor and neglected region despite its closeness to the capital, a pall of discouragement and fear descended. I was discreetly warned that Sendero watched people who befriended foreigners: 'Believe me, we'd welcome you. But your presence here is more dangerous to us than it is to you'. Police and military roadblocks detained fellow passengers and, once, me.

Bad field conditions meant that for the time being I would have to give first priority to archive work. I thought I should start by finding texts about the llactas in local archives, few of which scholars had seen. I hoped to complement Spalding's already unusually detailed historiography with even more ground-hugging documentation which might connect with the old Quechua vernacular record. (For example, intra-village records about land use and water rights tend to conserve older microtoponyms absent or replaced in higher-level records). For fieldwork, I decided on a census of letters. By including graffiti, epigraphy and ephemera, as well as document deposits I could view an angle on the nature of graphic community, without the kind of ethnographic kibbitzing that would be taken for spying. Although I could not do much fieldwork, at least I went back to Lima knowing that nearly all the places mentioned in the Huarochirí Quechua text had historiographic resources of their own, and that consciousness of the old sacred topography was still vivid.

In 1994–6 and then again in 1996–7 a Wisconsin sabbatical, together with funds from the NSF and the Wenner Gren Foundation, made possible the Huarochirí research that underlay *The Cord Keepers* (2004). I returned to the place where the Quechua manuscript was written, the large village of San Damián at the top of the Lurín drainage system. Unlike most villages, it housed two ancient ayllus as separate *comunidades campesinas*: San Damián de Checa and San Cristóbal de Concha. Checa's viewpoint dominates the central chapters of the Quechua source, and Concha is prominent too. Traces of the old mythology were thick on the ground in the form of pre-Hispanic *chaucallas* or *chulpas* [tomb-houses], flagstone paths connecting huaca-linked places, terraces and waterworks. Traces were frequent in the culture, too, in *bailes sociales* [costume dances] that reenacted ancient themes, and in provincial élite lore that edited them in the direction of 'Inca' indigenism for schooling purposes.

Since what I wanted to study was ongoing 'conversation' about the province's legacy of myth, symbolism and script, I sought out readers and writers. At that time, about 90 per cent of Huarochiranos were literate according to the census, and some were enthusiastic readers whenever fresh print arrived. Roberto Sacramento was the sacristan at the church of San Cosme and San Damián, where Father Francisco de Ávila had begun lashing out at 'idolators' 387 years earlier. He became my interlocutor. Due to his tuberculosis he could not do a full share on *faenas* [communal work days], but he was warmly appreciated as San Damián's *sacha cura* ('wild priest', as in 'wild onions') – a home-grown liturgical expert who performed masses in the absence of clergy. We conversed while he sprang about from the altar to planting terraces to the stall where he ran the bus agency. He had developed cosmopolitan and bookish interests while working in a Lima noodle factory and later while studying briefly in a seminary.

I brought an extra copy of Gerald Taylor's *Ritos y tradiciones de Huarochirí* (1987) for Roberto and hired him to read it and comment. Our chapter-by-chapter sessions, conducted on sunny boulders overlooking the Lurín River chasm, proved as absorbing as Urioste's Huarochirí seminar had been. Sometimes from the very rock where we sat Roberto could point out the huaca sites we were reading about. It was also from him that I learned an important fact about the constitution of community – one that escaped sociological and legalistic usages: the *huaranga de checa,* or Incaic 'Thousand of Checa' preserved in the 16th century as a colonial administrative term, still counted as a political model. Roberto pointed to the jagged northerly horizon, explaining that the comunidades campesinas, parishes and municipalities of the Lurín basin and parts of the middle Rímac were fragments of the Checa Thousand, unfortunately broken up by inner conflict and by imposed administrative divisions. Huarochiranos still considered it a 'natural' and valuable political unit. Tupicocha calls its most treasured historic manuscript the Book of the Huaranga, that is, the charter of a multi-llacta confederation much like the one implicit in the Huarochirí mythology. From these talks I came to see that I would have to get to know more comunidades campesinas – Sunicancha, Tupicocha, Tuna and so forth – to get an idea of the bigger orbit that Checa mythology sought to allegorise. I was sad to hear from a later ethnographic visitor, Sarah Bennison, that Roberto died in 2012, but happy to know that he always enjoyed remembering our mountainside seminar. His townsman Jhon Belén Matos mounted a homage to him on YouTube – one that notes Roberto's influence on academics from Peruvian and foreign institutions.

In San Damián Milton Rojas, a schoolteacher who grew up in a Huarochirí comunero home, kept a tiny part-time store. I liked to kill a twilight half-hour there because he had made a cheerful little museum of it. He painted the walls glossy green, and decorated them with a changing array of oddments gathered from magazines and non-governmental organisation (NGO) brochures. Because of his university training he understood my interests. In *The Cord Keepers* I remembered how he pointed me towards what would become the core of my ethnography:

> One evening, Milton said, 'You know, Salomon, you should visit my home village, Tupicocha. I think you'd be interested in the *equipos*.'
>
> Equipo means a team, usually a soccer team. I said, 'Well, I like soccer too, but I guess I can watch it at the field right here.'
>
> Milton half smiled and said, 'No, I really think you'd be interested in my village's equipos.'
>
> …I arrived [in Tupicocha] one morning just as the Tupicochans made their daily vertical exodus, up to the pastures and potato plots, or down to the orchards and cactus-fruit patches. My heart sank as distant couples with burros disappeared over the ridge. The tips of their steel tools glinted and were gone. But luck was on my side: I met a kinsman of Milton's, Sebastián Alberco. He was running an errand in connection with his duties as secretary of the Peasant Community, so he'd be in town for an hour or so. That gave him time to listen to my question, 'Why are Tupicocha's equipos important?'
>
> Sebastián shared the streak of dry wit for which their family is known. He guessed at Milton's sly way of educating me. 'Ah, the equipos. Sure, stick around, I'll show you something.'
>
> Along his errand, he said, 'We'll stop at my cousin's store. Our equipo is there, our equipocamayo.' Suddenly I realised important information had arrived,

in the humble form of a pun or folk etymology. Equipo had nothing to do with soccer. Equipocamayo would be a monolingually Spanish-speaking village's way of pronouncing the Inca word for a master of the knot-cord art, khipukamayuq. But could this rather ordinary-looking village retain a legacy that the classic places of Andean ethnography had lost?

As he briskly walked his errand Sebastián explained that Tupicocha consists of ten *parcialidades* ('sectors'), informally known by the ancient term *ayllus*, and that all but the newest of them were symbolised in political ritual by quipocamayos. Now the rest of that punning folk-etymology fell into place: each ayllu really is a 'team', not in the sports sense (though ayllus do in fact sponsor soccer teams), but in the sense of furnishing one 'team' in the complex relay of crews who, in friendly rivalry, do the village's basic infrastructural work.

When we got to Sebastián's cousin's store, the owner had not quite finished locking up to head for the fields. Sebastián rapped on the shutters and shouted 'Cousin! There's a foreigner who needs to talk to you!' Feet scuffed on a creaky stair and the door opened. In the store it was deep twilight, the shutters open just a crack to discourage disruptive last-minute buyers. The brass of a balance scale showed through the murk with a Rembrandtian burnished gleam. Sebastián's cousin pulled a plastic bag from a locked chest and upended it over the counter. Out flopped a multicolored tangle of heavy yarn. A few wine-red and yellow ornaments glowed amid a mound of tawny, dark, and mottled cordage.

Sebastián lifted the skein, demonstrating the first steps in handling a quipocamayo: how one picks up the extremes of the main cord, shakes the pendants down to a hanging position, and calls on a peer to 'comb' the tangled pendants out by separating them with the fingers. As the cords began to hang parallel, it became clear that this was nothing like the eccentric 'ethnographic' khipus documented elsewhere. It was a khipu right in the mainstream of the canonical Inca design tradition. In fact it looked quite a lot like some of the grander museum specimens, except that, as my fingers soon told me, it was made of wool and not cotton.

Sebastián then demonstrated how one displays the object to the village in its annual ceremonial array. He held the main cord diagonally from his left shoulder to his right hip, while his friend caught the long 'tail' up behind and tied it over his shoulder blade, so that the whole object formed a 'sash of office' – the metaphor he used in explaining this motion. We stepped out into the brightening morning and took a photo.

The survival of this complex put the matter of Huarochirí's lettered past into a different and more exciting light. The ayllus that owned the cords had, for the most part, the same names as the ones that made up the confederacy which the Inka regime called the 'thousand' of Checa. And these were also the same ayllus which figured as protagonists of Huarochirí 400-year old Quechua book of gods and heroes (Salomon and Urioste, 1991, pp. 1–38). Could it be that the cords held content related to that legacy? (2004, p. 5)

Figure 6.1. In Tupicocha, newly invested presidents of parcialidades (ayllus) visit the community office in 2010 to form the new directorate. Photo: F. Salomon.

This moment promised a novel approach to the long lines of continuity. Two important points were becoming clear. First, it would be possible to study the Andes' notorious 'lost script' problem from a new angle: no longer as objects retrieved by looters or archaeologists from tombs, but as patrimony of a living community whose organisations and regimens formed their original context. And second, that in practice this would mean seeing the Huarochirí manuscript within a larger sequence of communal inscriptive practices including both khipu and the alphabet.

The following two decades' researches and results are available in various articles and a pair of books, so there is no need to summarise them. However one aspect of research into patrimonial khipus and their successor medium, village manuscript books, never found its way into print: the way people handled and saved the material patrimonies which symbolised community and in a sense called it into being. The inheritors of community khipus today cannot read them. They think of them as in principle bearers of a text that can never be known literally. Because the literal meaning has become opaque, every tiny attribute of cords seems equally meaningful; their meaning is that they are detailed concretions of many generations' actions. This attitude runs over into the handling of intra-village paper records and is manifest in the disposition to transcribe attributes that are sublinguistic in the Saussurean sense, such as curlicues and traces left by seals.

The varieties of popular conservationism – or its opposite, a willingness to let objects suffer attrition – came to interest me as an ethnohistorian for two main reasons. First, being an ethnographer-historian who thinks our best hope for a multi-'quadrant' anthropology is to follow the material traces of people through time, I perceive the study of informal conservation as a methodological matter. Knowing about traditional curation or its opposite will help us know why some parts of material culture survive and others do not. This kind of knowledge might be useful for making sense of presences and absences in the archaeological record.

Second, there is a matter of being helpful. When a village grants access to its legacies, that entails a debt. But what sort of debt? An ethnographer is not a curatorial missionary. Respectful support has to be given 'with the grain' of a community's habits about its legacies, even if they are not practices a museum curator would endorse. In this regard, my first experience with inscribed legacies (Tupicocha) and my second (Rapaz) took diverse courses. Different conservation habits reflect different views of what inheritance contributes to community.

As I watched people do dissimilar things to similarly valued legacies, I wondered what purposeful continuity actually consists of. When people consciously decide to preserve, what is being preserved? Is it original design – the 'genotypic' ideal of a past culture, what Williams (1995 [1946])? calls 'preconception'? That is the preoccupation that justifies restoration work. For inheritors, visitors and some kinds of researchers, restoration has irresistible appeal as an aid to imagining a past. Yet it is in one sense an anti-historicist venture, because it upholds one moment's form as deserving exemption from the work of time. Restoration is compatible with an idealist notion of culture.

Or, on the other hand, is the object of preservation a culture's 'phenotype?' Is the important thing about an object the way it makes visible a culture's action, emergence and disappearance? If so, its 'creased' and 'stained' body is the very record of what Williams (ibid.) calls 'accident'. That would justify conservation rather than restoration. Conservationism is compatible with historicism. It is the attitude I tried to embody in the researches sketched below. But beyond curatorial ideas about restoration and conservation there are Andean components to the customary care of sacred legacies.

Loving the khipus to pieces in Tupicocha

Patrimonial khipus are venerable. Tupicochans often express respect for them as the 'magna carta' of each parcialidad or ayllu. They take pride in the fact that this unusual legacy attracts scholars and tourists. Yet they only minimally protect khipu as physical objects. In fact they stress them in ways that would give any textile curator chills.

To keep the quipocamayos (as they are called) safe, each person in his or her turn as president of the parcialidad (see figure 6.1) must protect his group's cords in a secure location. Usually this is a box that also contains the manuscript books of acts as well as group insignia, such as altar clothes, the *báculo* [standard] hung at meetings, figurines and chromos used as pledge tokens, the small work cross, and ornaments for the group's chapel. By moving the boxes around and keeping them scattered among many well-guarded spaces, officers maintain reasonable security. To my knowledge only one quipocamayo got lost, and that was not by theft, but because a certain president left it behind while drinking. When it was recovered, the finder so feared being involved in scandal that he or she tucked it in the eaves of an outhouse. From there a random finder could return it without incurring suspicion.

Measuring and documenting the details of khipus required borrowing them, obviously a challenge to traditional curation. When I began asking for loans in 1997, I was not a stranger. I had spent months in the village, donated to festival funds, brought along family and friends, and reported my doings to the *directiva* [board of officers]. I had attended the New Year Huayronas [community plenary assemblies] as faithfully as possible. At the Huayronas and ayllu meetings I learned the proprieties about the quipocamayos. Nonetheless, borrowing the crown jewels, so to speak, was hardly a routine request. Not one parcialidad denied me. In each consultation with the respective presidents, their faces showed hesitation. They waved off my offer to let them hold my passport as pledge, but they said they would be sending messengers to check up on my use of the cords. 'So much the better', I agreed, hoping frequent inspection would damp down any rumours about what I might be doing with the legacy. One by one over a year I borrowed and studied them. A few ayllus required me to return the specimen between working sessions but others wanted me to be responsible for their protection during various days and nights. Having a quipocamayo in my lodgings at night caused me anxiety, not about theft, but because children or animals might mess them up when I was not looking, or the roof might leak, or… My rented donkey nosed around a quipocamayo with

Figure 6.2. Tupicocha comuneros examining the author's work table. Photo: F. Salomon.

his muzzle, investigating the delicious salt with which many years of sweaty handling had infused it. What would I do if he chomped one?

My rustic study table had to be pieced together from furniture at hand because I never thought to stock up on portable scientific gear as an archaeologist would. I had the ethnographer's habit of thinking my backpack should be my lab. It had to be outdoors, because no building was well enough lit; that meant limiting work to the dry season (see figure 6.2). My tool kit amounted to a few metres of undyed muslin, rulers, coloured pencils, a pocket knife, lots of thumbtacks, pins, coloured paper to make temporary labels, a tape measure and film.

A quipocamayo spread out in radial array is a big object, sometimes three metres in diameter if it has long pendants, so I needed a big table. The grade school had some blue-painted wooden tables not in use and loaned them to me. When the school was out of session, I grouped them together near the school patio and pinned clean muslin over them. I made my work table alongside one of the main trails by which people enter and leave the village as they commute to pastures and fields, so that many of them would see me daily at work and get a correct idea of what the work was.

This turned out to have an unintended ethnographic payoff because most had never managed to get a good look at any khipu other than their own ayllu's insignia. As they looked and conversed, their comparisons helped me learn terminology about parts and colours. There did not seem to be any scruples about reserving the patrimony from profane viewing. But Tupicochans were puzzled and a little shocked to see me handling khipus alone, with the cords laid out horizontally on a tablecloth. It seemed oddly cold-blooded to them, since ritual khipu handling is always done using vertical or hanging deployment, and always between at least two people close together. But people approved of the care and close attention I gave the cords.

These were days of happy, solitary absorption. In the morning I concentrated on spreading and pinning cords so as to make all features visible. In early afternoon I concentrated on measuring each cord and drawing it individually, noting knots, twist, ply, damages and so forth in my elementary school spiral notebooks. The time for photography had to be midday, because at other hours the extremely sharp light of the dry-season Andes would make cords overshadow each other. To get a photo of a whole spread khipu one has to get quite high up. The only way to do that was to stack tables and chairs into a tower and climb on top of it. At midday every able-bodied person was far away in the countryside, so I usually had no spotter as I clambered up my tottering tower. Extending stiff arms I shifted my camera this way and that. The furniture creaked. One time the tower collapsed. Leaping as far as I could, I prayed in mid-air not to land on top of the quipocamayo. I caught a table edge with my arm as I went down, broke the fall, and landed with nothing worse than bruises. I got the khipu and the camera back to safe storage by sundown. The next day, asked about the bruises, I dared not tell what had happened.

Curators will read this with no great admiration. But they could also find fault with Tupicochans' own habits in handling the patrimony.

Like Inca users of khipus, Tupicochans retain the practice of coiling khipus into spiral fascicles. But they do this only as preparation for display at the annual plenum, not for storage as Incas did. The rest of the time they store khipus loose in bags. As a quipocamayo comes out of its bag, it is a tangled mess. Untangling it takes patience, as one should be careful not to tug on the often frayed pendants. Quipocamayo work is always done four-handed: one person holds the ends of the main cord while another arranges the pendant cords. When all pendants hang parallel from the horizontally extended main cord, the quipocamayo is said to be *peinado* [combed]. Again in four-handed partnership, the handlers now coil the main cord into a spiral from which all the pendants hang parallel in a column. The main cord's long 'tail' is helically wound downwards about the outside of the columnar bundle, so as to make a sort of floppy fasces. The main cord's end is then tucked into itself on the last turn, so as to stabilise the whole.

From this point on, handling deviates from Inca precedent. The two handlers, each holding one end of the rolled quipocamayo fascicle, twist the whole thing so that the pendants become a single thick cable (see figure 6.3). When the cable writhes from excess torque, handlers say 'It's fighting back, it has plenty of life'. Finally they tie the entire 'snake' into a single giant overhand knot, making a show of wrestling with its force. The preparation is said to have

Figure 6.3. One stress factor that causes damage to the Tupicocha quipocamayos is the practice of twisting them into a single cable prior to transport and display. Photo: F. Salomon.

Figure 6.4. The 'simulacrum' or replacement quipocamayo displayed by parcialidad Centro Guangre in Tupicocha, 2007. Photo: F. Salomon.

come out well if the large end knob of the main cord protrudes upwards atop the bundle. Now the quipocamayo is ready for display. The handlers lay it on a colourful cushion or pad of decorated folded cloth, often a woman's carrying cloth or a mantle embroidered by a woman; these supports are viewed as signs of female allegiance. It rides in a place of high honour as the ayllu troops off to the civic meeting. On entering the consecrated square, each ayllu places its quipocamayo where it belongs in the fixed array of precedence, each marked with a grass X.

As Huayrona day draws to an end, presidents of the ayllus don their groups' quipocamayos as their regalia of office. The outgoing president lifts the displayed quipocamayo, unknots and uncoils it with a co-handler's help, then drapes it over the new president from right shoulder to left hip with the knob end at the shoulder. He then ties the other end up the back to the knob end. As of this moment, the new political cycle begins.

Tupicochans view the quipocamayos with respect verging on reverence, speaking of them as the community's 'constitution'. To quipocamayos they attribute not just historical importance but occult knowledge; there is even a divinatory technique for eliciting information about the future or about secrets and mysteries by watching the patterns made by randomly dropped cords. 'The quipocamayos know', is the saying. Said to be of 'Inca' antiquity, they contain the very legitimacy of the parcialidades, the more so in recent times as media publicity has come to uphold them as an emblem of dignified self-government. Because nobody today claims the ability to 'read' or inscribe legitimate quipocamayos, it is taboo to alter them.

Reverence, however, has nothing to do with a hands-off, curatorial attitude. On the contrary, in engaging with the sacred legacy closely and physically they give it a lot of rough handling. I wanted to protest the pulling, twisting and crumpling of old cords whose integrity could never be restored once damaged. I kept my mouth shut, waiting for an occasion when the topic might come up on its own, and kept as close an eye on the quipocamayos as I could. It became evident that some maintenance was being done behind the scenes because, over the years of study, I noticed knots made to mend breaks and a few transpositions of perhaps-fallen cords. One main cord section from a quipocamayo that had become too decrepit for use was tied onto another main cord so as to conserve the broken specimen's end knob, which seemed to be a distinctive ayllu insignia.

One youngster made a surprisingly plausible likeness of his parcialidad's khipu during his father's term as president, and he possessed fragments of knowledge about how the old medium worked. In 2007 I was surprised to see a quipucamayo new to my acquaintance (see figure 6.4) draped on the president of a parcialidad that had previously lacked one. This group had felt shamed because, as a segment formed by relatively recent secession from an old ayllu, it had petitioned to receive a specimen from its parent-parcialidad and was denied. The new specimen was an impressively correct reproduction, made of genuine camelid fibres in the proper way. Everyone who mentioned it was careful to call it *el simulacro* [the replica] rather than quipocamayo.

Were these practices transgressions? I never heard any of them criticised. As an ethnohistorian and ally of archaeologists, that is, a devotee of material traces and codes, I was uneasy about destructive usage. But on reflection it was clear that the only reason Tupicocha still had its khipus, while most other villages had lost them (or perhaps just lost track of them), was that its intricate ritual-political regimen required the handling of khipus. In other words, the same practices that eroded the material patrimony were the ones that motivated people to keep it.

During the Huayrona seasons of several years I asked senior members of the parcialidades whether they thought anything should be done to prevent the quipocamayos from wearing out. I found there was a general reluctance to discuss damage. But in off-the-record discussions three ayllu presidents acknowledged that within memory certain khipus had either fallen to pieces or become so deteriorated that they were being reserved as unused relics – I saw and studied two such.

Some modernist-minded men wanted to convert from dispersed khipu storage, a symbol of the ancient confederated-ayllu constitution, to a centralised system more congruent with Peru's highly centralised state. A man who had become active in local politics and served as mayor of the municipality took the position that the municipality or the community should collect all the khipus in a central permanent place and showcase them as a cultural attraction. That would let tourists see them in any season, not just the Huayrona assembly. This position attracted a little support, chiefly among people who had become strongly assimilated to the customs of urban Lima and thereby distanced from what they saw as 'folkloric' customs. Tupicocha has a minority of Protestant converts (Pentecostal or Evangelical) and some of these also said they could support 'museification', because to them the tradition of the khipus had pagan connotations and they would rather not take part in it. Still others remarked that since khipus are 'Inca' they should receive support from the government entity charged with safeguarding archaeological 'patrimony of the nation.'

During my fieldwork the museum-centralising project never gained momentum. One argument I heard was that a museum would not help reconcile tourist needs with civic ones unless someone received a salary for curating and displaying it (because normally nobody with fields and animals can afford to stay in the village all day). Besides, up to then, the state had

Figure 6.5. In 2016 a display case inside the community meeting hall held a quipocamayo of ayllu Segunda Allauca. Photo: F. Salomon.

not been very forthcoming in financing guardianship except when there was to be a site museum. Looking to the state would create a new dependency on outside political forces. And if there were a salary from Lima, who should get it? Assigning the salary to anyone would inevitably be contentious. What's more, a central khipu deposit would be more vulnerable to theft, earthquake, fire or insects than dispersed storage is.

The most interesting criticism was that 'museification' would remove the khipus from the annual round of practices such as safeguarding, transfer, display and inventorying. These continually reinsert the community's things into strong norms of customary law. If khipus were taken out of those routines people would cease to learn how to handle them. They would stop feeling individually responsible for the regimen if they didn't see their parents held answerable to it.

Returning in 2016, I found, to my surprise, glass-fronted display cases installed inside the community meeting hall. The 'museum' project had apparently gathered some support. Nonetheless, all but two of the cases remained empty, suggesting that each ayllu or parcialidad considered conservation its own to decide as the old federated order might imply (see figure 6.5).

How khipu legacies endure: the smoke of the oracle in Rapaz

Arturo Ruíz Estrada, an archaeologist at San Marcos University, reached the lofty village of Rapaz in Oyón province on horseback in the later 1970s. He published a remarkable report (1981) on its 'khipu house' Kaha Wayi [Treasury House]. Ruíz Estrada observed a large collection of apparent community khipus preserved in the very house where they were said to have originally functioned. Ruíz Estrada commanded my respect all the more for being a speaker of the Quechua I language peculiar to central Peru, one rarely learned by non-linguists. He assured me that the strange tangle of thick cords in Kaha Wayi, the house of traditional governance, really were called khipus in Quechua I, and that the Rapaz patrimony had no other name.

He said that when he was first shown the precinct, it was jealously guarded, and its interior almost secret. People were concerned lest visitors profane the place where their officers invoked the mountains. Yet, Ruíz Estrada said, the khipu collection itself was neglected and 'untouched', and its protectors only reluctantly carried it into daylight to allow a photo. It would be all right with him, Ruíz said, if I attempted a fuller description. But would my bid find any welcome in this reputedly inward-looking village?

In August 2003, a twice-weekly *combi* brought me up a dizzying cliffside road to Rapaz, a small, tightly built-up adobe village on the brim of the Checras River canyon. Rapaz considers itself a unitary society with (now inactive) ritual moieties, so its leadership is simpler than Tupicocha's. One man, the vice-president of the legal comunidad campesina, holds the keys to the khipu house as well as the colonial (or possibly Inca) title of *kamachikuq*. Having made contact with 'vice' Toribio Gallardo's uncle in Lima, I met a generous welcome. I arrived in the chill of twilight. Don Toribio led me shivering into the walled precinct of inner governance.

Rapaz is a singularly conservative community. Its comunidad campesina, which has the usual legal apparatus, is housed in a hall on the main square. But the comunidad has within it a sort of inner cabinet consisting of *balternos* or *vara* officers, chaired by the vice. Its stronghold is a separate walled, locked precinct a few yards from the rear of the church. Within the walls stand two buildings: the old community storehouse called Pasa Qulqa, a three-storey stone structure, and Kaha Wayi, the seat of inner governance. When Don Toribio opened the latter, the last ruddy rays of day fell upon a matted tangle of woollen cords suspended from the ceiling. Little could be seen. In the shadows a mountain of coca leaves covered a table of small gourd vessels. Suspended bottles and dessicated birds swayed under the rafters. The little chamber smelled of wool, dry leaves, smoke and mildew. 'Don't touch anything', said Toribio.

In the course of explaining Kaha Wayi's double role as the seat of governance and as the altar of devotions to the mountains and lakes who 'own' the weather, Don Toribio pointed out problems of conservation. At one end of the chamber, a battered steel showcase of the sort used in rural stores lay upended. That, he said, had been intended as a protective display case for the khipus more than a decade before, but it had not worked out because the khipu set wouldn't fit. A neighbour had without permission let his sheep sleep in the Kahi Wayi attic, and urine dripped through; moth larvae chewed up the cords, which were almost entirely woollen; fungus and mildew grew on moist surfaces; the smoke of candles and of smouldering llama fat, an essential sacrifice, smudged everything. Later, I would learn that the attempted installation of a case had marked one moment in a complicated history of fluctuating attitudes about conservation. For the moment, however, I just took Toribio's point: if I wanted to learn more about Rapaz, I should consider making myself useful in the matter of khipu protection.

In principle I liked the idea of a partnership pairing conservationism with ethnography; the pairing promised intellectual symbiosis and a good ethical solution. But it was intimidating. I was untrained in conservation, and the request for an intervention went against my long-standing belief that ethnography should be done with a light touch. Should a community ethnographer at the same time be the boss of a complex group project, involving responsibility for sacred things as well as hiring and politicking? I decided I'd settle all that later; the thing was just irresistible. I wanted to find out if Rapaz's khipu house carried on something like Huarochirí's Huayrona complex, and what cord-keeping might have to do with ancient or colonial legacies.

Four months later, as 2003 ended, I rushed away from final exams at Wisconsin to reach Rapaz in time for the New Year cycle of plenary meetings. As in Tupicocha the Huayrona climax would be a gathering of the inner cabinet in the presence of the khipus. This was the only meeting of the year authoritative enough to make any decisions about them. I presented an ambitious proposal involving the hiring of conservation specialists. Together with the archaeologist Víctor Falcón Huayta, I also requested permission for scientific study of the khipus, for ethnographic and linguistic inquiries, and for a limited amount of archaeological survey and excavation. If granted preliminary approval I would raise funds, secure permission from the Instituto Nacional de Cultura, hire specialists, and have the project underway in 2005. Once a few doubts about whether the project would involve spending from the community's treasury were resolved, Victor and I got the nod.

Soon I went to consult the renowned mummy conservator Sonia Guillén to seek advice on assembling a conservation crew. She received me in her stylish new Lima house with coffee and a philosophical sigh. '*Todo vuelve*', she said: everything returns to dust. Not just khipus, everything. It would not be useful to concentrate on protecting the khipus because what damaged them was the whole of their microenvironment. She told me I would have to reach agreement to eliminate insect habitats, to reroof Kaha Wayi, to fix broken walls, and to clean every bit of the sacred jumble that existed around the khipus – and all of this cleaning would have to be done only by delicate mechanical methods, no fumigation or chemical treatments. Microclimate would have to be monitored, moisture flows regulated, pests excluded. She warned me that a conservator's assessment would result in advice the community wasn't going to like. To my everlasting gratitude, Sonia provided what would turn out to be the crucial help. Two textile experts at Centro Mallki, her mummy-rescue workshop, would soon be taking work leave. Perhaps, she said, they would be willing to do a stint in Rapaz.

Thus I came to meet the Choque Gonsales sisters: Rosa and Rosalía, comuneras from the Aymara-speaking highlands over Hilo, and expert textile conservators. Sonia had noticed their meticulous stitching when they worked mending hotel sheets, and trained them up to repair the clothing of Paracas mummies. Rapaz was no culture shock for them. On the contrary, they said they were delighted to be back in the cool heights and the small-town ambience. Rosalía's son was soon enrolled in the local school, and Rosalía became a star in the moms' network. In our first days together the Choque sisters and I rambled around visiting the houses of women who sold wool or worked it, and buying small samples so we would have a match for any fibre we might find damaged in the khipus. The Rapacinas loved these deft and kindly fellow fibre experts. Thanks to them, our crew became welcome.

Sonia Guillén also helped me meet the Brazilian museologist Renata Peters, who was then a PhD candidate at the University of London's Institute of Archaeology. Renata took a different view of conservation than most museums' professionals did: she thought museums should go to wherever patrimonies lived and help conserve objects within the bounds of local usage, instead of trying to remove and collect them under ideal but alien conditions. Richard Burger connected us with the young archaeologist Víctor Falcón Huayta, who designed our temporary field lab in the Kaha Wayi precinct, hired several young Rapacinos and carried out the delicate job of studying the floors of the two revered buildings as well as excavating a few squares within the precinct. Gino de las Casas joined us as an architect with specialisation in conserving traditional building techniques. Gino brought in Edgar Centeno, an architectural technician whose daily bread was kitchen remodelling in urban Lima, but whose vocation was for handling ancient materials. Carrie Brezine, then a PhD candidate at Gary Urton's Harvard-based khipu lab, lent her services for the technical description and analysis of the khipus.

The crucial thing was fitting study and conservation into the politics and ritual regimen of a community that had become sensitive about outside interventions, for good reason. Rapacinos had lived through several recent cycles of reform, revolutionism, violence, and administrative or financial intervention. Unlike most recent incarnations of the 'recognised community' structure Rapaz forbade all private property in land and maintained a demanding discipline of collective work on infrastructure. Yet that is not to suggest a steady state. Several successive institutional vessels for this policy had been broken and replaced over time. Rapaz's successful fight to win back usurped land from the neighbouring Algolán hacienda in the 1960s had doubled collective holdings and given rise to a new cooperative corporation. (One founder was still around, a grizzled, loquacious cowpoke named Nery Racacha. To my surprise, he greeted me in English – he had taken cooperative management courses on my own campus, Madison, 40 years earlier under a United States Aid for International Development grant, and even remembered some of my fellow-professors!) Only five years after the agrarian reform breakthroughs of President Belaúnde Terry's first term, President Juan Velasco Alvarado's nationalist 'revolution from above' sent personnel from the agrarian reform authority called Sistema Nacional de Apoyo a la Movilización Social (SINAMOS) to break up the cooperative and impose a very different state-centred agroindustrial model.

This was 'the time when they shouted against the customs', as Nery put it. Lima-oriented modernists saw Kaha Wayi as 'folklore'. At one point, the comunidad came close to allotting the precinct as a site for a member's new house. When Ruíz peered into Kaha Wayi in 1978 it had been neglected badly. Ruíz made a speech recommending conservation measures. Martín Falcón, a local schoolteacher and friend of Ruíz, brought in the steel showcase in an attempt at conservation in 1982.

Again, in less than a decade, political coercion endangered the venture as Sendero Luminoso began to send in armed *cumpas* (a euphemism for guerrillas). Because they found the pasture commons in unequal use by families with greater or lesser herds, they denounced bourgeois contamination and forced a sell-off. Army bases in the region and an armed village *ronda* [patrol] pushed back Sendero. After Sendero's defeat in 1992 the village adapted to the Fujimori era by availing itself of NGO connections, stabilised cash markets and new ministerial programmes. The resulting 'communal enterprise'

Figure 6.6. In Rapaz, the late Moisés Flores attends night-time balternos ceremonial inside Kaha Wayi, and in the presence of suspended khipu collection, New Year, 2004. He wears the formal dress of a balterno. Photo: F. Salomon.

involved a modus vivendi between livestock-oriented agropastoralists and 'deterritorialised' households with double domicile in Lima, Cerro de Pasco or Huacho, most families having members in both ways of life.

At the Huayrona season of New Year 2004, Víctor Falcón accompanied me to the assembly. Thanks to him we drew up a signed agreement with the plenum. That evening the balternos let us attend the nocturnal rituals inside Kaha Wayi (see figure 6.6). These included the installation of new balternos and rites to support *raywana*, that is, food considered as a divinity.

Freezing in the murk of the tiny chamber, breathing the smoke of llama fat and divinatory embers, we sat through the long and stirring series of Quechua invocations to the lakes and snowcaps. Víctor and I took pictures. Whether it was right to take photographs with flash bothers me to this day – not that I could possibly have abstained. Since 2005, two of the people present have died, and at least to their surviving relatives the images taken of them are valuable. I hope that these, like so many other intrusive photographs, will justify themselves eventually.

In successive weeks the balternos ruled that our work was to be supervised at all times by a balterno, that they would hold the keys, and that we would suspend work at any time when Kaha Wayi was needed for ritual work. The

Figure 6.7. Museologist Renata Peters (right, seated) in a 2005 working meeting inside the precinct with some balterno officers. Photo: F. Salomon.

Figure 6.8. Vendelhombre [ceremonialist] Melecio Montes (left) lifts the upper altar-cloth of Kaha Wayi's mountain altar, revealing a lower altar-cloth severely damaged by fungus. The lower cloth remains were repaired in 2005 by interweaving them with a fungus-proof synthetic fibre. Photo: F. Salomon.

balternos rotated supervisory turns and were paid. For technical meetings we gathered with the balternos on folding chairs in the precinct, with Renata and the vice presiding by turns (see figure 6.7). We would open our site lab to any villager who wanted to see what was happening. We would train younger women in the basics of textile repair. We would offer paid work to a master thatcher, and to others who had abilities needed by Víctor, Gino or Edgar. We were forbidden to introduce lights or use anything electrical inside Kaha Wayi, which turned out to be a difficult work rule. We were to respect the established schedule: the precinct was reserved for ritual and *rimanakuy* [political discussions] at night. It would continue to be open to visitors only in the day and only when the vice was present. After the field season the temporary lab would be removed and reassembled near the plaza as part of the comunidad's offices.

One icy night a crew of mine-shelter specialists finished building the laboratory. One by one our sub-projects came to life. In finding the levels of previous floors, Víctor discovered that the now-empty Pasa Qulqa was the older of the two buildings, a stylistic continuation of Late Intermediate construction. As soon as he mentioned this to the balternos, they invited him to see similar walls at the nearby Late Intermediate Pinchulín ruins. When the Choque sisters and Renate built a transfer 'bed' to carry the khipu mass into the lab, people gathered to watch; many, especially women, said that never before had they laid eyes on the famous relic. As the textile people cleaned the cords and the dismounted offerings with the tiniest of artists' brushes, they passed the time talking with villagers who thought they could recognise the little cloth figurines tied onto some cords. Thatching master Melanio Falcón required me to come to the site half an hour before startup every day to enjoy the meditative coca break. I found him a congenially serious man, and I learned much from his chronicle of the precinct's ups and downs. When I wasn't around the precinct, I walked around interviewing people who had long memories of Kaha Wayi and its rituals, or who had held important balterno offices.

Our work plan was designed around the fact that, ideally, the rains should arrive in October, and usually begin in November. The onset of rain was our deadline, because architectural repairs and roofing had to be finished and the patrimonial objects restored safely to their homes in Kaha Wayi before the rain. Time got tighter. Melanio required long clean roofing thatch from the high puna, but collaborators said they didn't have time or pack animals enough to make the ascent. We were still unloading thatch when the early sprinkles came.

Waiting for rain was an even more tense matter for Rapacinos. As the year advanced and the puna grasses yellowed, people began to scan the mountaintops for 'weather'. The contracted ritualist of the balternos at that time was Melecio Montes (see figure 6.8). The ritualist carries the title of *Vendelhombre*, that is, *bien del hombre* or 'human welfare', because his influence with the 'owners of rain' is the only defence against drought. In October the balternos called on him to spend the night sacrificing in Kaha Wayi and collect the debt of rain the powers owe to their devotees. In preparation Melecio was dispatched to the augury spring of Tukapia, considered a centre of superhuman communications. He brought back only vague promises.

A balterno quietly warned me: 'People are nervous about rain. You need to step back a little. Kaha Wayi is taken seriously by most of us. They're saying, "How can it rain when gringos are messing with Kaha Wayi?" You know, we get along well with your crew, but people can get angry suddenly. Be careful.'

A second balterno let me know that a rumour about the khipus was spreading, 'Some people say that you guys have been taking away the real khipus and substituting fakes, and that's why it can't rain. It's offensive to the owners of water that foreigners always want their things.' I was floored. 'No, that's a misunderstanding', I said. 'When you saw us making khipu cords, we were just practising. The Choque sisters tried out spinning and plying some of the wool we bought here so they could get a feel for the fibre structures in the real ones. We made simulacrum cords as a way of getting ready. They're still in the lab. Take a look at the simulacra and the real ones – they're different.'

October was advancing. Some days, as I walked to the site in the morning, a neighbour would greet me with a certain sly look, 'Another beautiful sunny morning, hmm, Dr Salomon?' The Vendelhombre Melecio Montes warned me that he was being put on the spot. 'They're talking about me all over, [saying] "can't he finish the job up now, quickly so it can rain?" [and] "Why doesn't the doctor speed it up?"' [and] "Have they thrown away the altar table?" The noise [of roofing] might bother the "owners". Even the people in [the neighbouring village of] Puñún ask me, because they trust me. And it's true, the climate is just so-so. It's not as it should be.' Yet another villager confronted me saying that the sacred mountains are losing their snowcaps, which are vital water reserves, because foreigners always make people do things that cause global warming.

A month later, most of the work was finished and our crew had gone home. I was living on alone in our lodging house and winding down the project. Dense fog muffled the village. Snow gathered on the heights. One afternoon hail came hammering down on the corrugated roof and then at last it turned into a generous rain. After a few more days, when we were sloshing through mud, Melecio Montes began to greet me civilly again; he was off the hook.

I have visited several times over subsequent years and inspected Kaha Wayi. I was happy to see that the balternos had carefully kept up the security measures Renata prescribed: foam cushions had replaced moth-infested sheepskins in the sanctum, and the recording microclimate sensor we had left in the eaves confirmed favourable conditions. The elaborate tempered glass case we built for the khipus remained dry and free of bugs. I asked the ritualist and the new vice whether they thought Kaha Wayi was in good shape. 'Yes', they said, 'everything is in place, we're comfortable in the rimanakuy, it works well.' There had been years of good rain.

Reflections on patrimony, transitoriness and on-site conservation

During the period of Rapaz research the idea of 'intangible patrimony' came into UNESCO vogue as a term for cultural practices (as distinct from things) considered worthy of preservation. It was as if various groups' habits were to be treated as monuments rather than projects. The more I got involved in the presentation of meaningful objects, the less this seemed to me a tenable idea. When one gets close up, one sees that what UNESCO calls intangible patrimony actually consists of tangibles: bodily practices, techniques, inherited or temporary objects. The ideal-typical tradition has no presence in the world except as people mobilise 'ideas in things'. The way things come into play is inseparable from contingencies and current purposes, and it has unprogrammed consequences. Ethnographic conservators have to reconcile themselves to this fact.

The very activities that constitute cultural patrimonies are the ones that relocate traditional objects, or alter them, or wear them out and replace them. Even when people treasure legacies, and we historians or archaeologists want to support them, what always happens is not conservation, but repair, replacement and reinterpretion. Participant observation in this sense means willingness to take part in these normal erosive processes; understanding these processes and the conversation around them is what makes conservation ethnographic.

This mindset might make us uneasy about prescribing technical interventions to serve a group's patrimony. Yet that is inevitably our part in the conversation, once we are invited. Some people who love the Andean tradition say they are sorry not to see the Rapaz khipus as they were in the 2000s. Visitors and balternos enjoyed the khipus' woolly smell and their gentle swaying. One felt close to the ancestors. But the balternos were right: without a strong protective case the khipus would soon become shreds – we did in fact find a pile of decomposing shreds under the extant collection. Participating in local conservation means taking positions about who will enjoy the evocation of the past and for how long.

In Tupicocha and Rapaz researches, I found no 'general will' about the care of the past. In Tupicocha, the assumption seemed to be that the illegible patrimony represented an ideal beyond corruption. Since khipus were originally the information infrastructures of each ancient corporate descent group, the

Figure 6.9. Vice-president and Kamachikuq Víctor Gallardo examines khipu cords during conservation work inside the temporary site lab. Photo: F. Salomon.

Figure 6.10. Comunidad Rapaz allows visits inside Kaha Wayi in the daytime, but on rare occasions crowding can be a problem. This mass visit was organised by an NGO in 2005. Photo: F. Salomon.

suite of khipus formed the material correlate of Tupicocha's federated-ayllu constitution. To be in close, corporeal, strenuous contact with the set, in choreographed action across all parcialidades, was to remember what mattered, even if it materially eroded the patrimony. Taking part in this anything-but-conservative conservationism is a core matter of identity and political legitimacy. Moreover, it has brought the village a degree of public honour and some tourist revenue, so any criticism sounds like arguing against success.

On the few occasions when anybody asked my opinion, I suggested that the village should seek a grant from one of the country's private or semi-governmental foundations to contract a textile conservationist and submit the khipus, one by one, to a round of cleaning and repair. Additionally, each parcialidad should acquire a stronger and more pest-proof, but still portable, storage box so as to continue rotating storage while minimising damage. I still think this was a good idea, but it did not find much favour. Perhaps that was because (at that time, around 2003) few felt confident that the village could contract with outsiders and still retain control. Should I have asserted the idea more insistently? Maybe I erred on the side of 'light touch'. Maybe I will try again.

The Rapaz situation was more complex than I had guessed, based on Tupicochan experience. When the conservation project was blamed for dry weather I was caught off guard. I realised only afterwards why this happened: the 'conversation' about ancient things had been a muffled dissensus. A minority of Rapacinos are used to talking with technocrats and good at dealing with outsiders. The plenary assembly lets these men (today, also some women) take the lead in negotiating with outsiders (see figure 6.9). Such people are generally modernist-minded; for example, they are the ones who decided to allow outsiders to visit Kaha Wayi (see figure 6.10). They feel loyalty to the customs of Kaha Wayi, and credit Kaha Wayi with a vital relationship to the landscape, but have no trouble adopting the outsider's viewpoint. They regard outsiders' visits to the Kaha Wayi precinct as a good thing because they validate Rapaz's past as 'Inca' and therefore important. Visitors furnish a modest income stream and raise the village's prestige.

But when these few spoke, a larger number remained silent. For them, Kaha Wayi was not relativised by the independent cognitive claims of technology, nationalism, or 'green' ideology. An older habit of mind ruled. Kaha Wayi was the fulcrum of a delicate balance between human claims and inhuman powers. This was not a fact one felt free to talk about. It had somewhat of a confidential character. There were in 2005 at least four living residents who were true experts on what Ruíz Estrada called the 'temple' functions of Kaha Wayi. One was the widow of a great Vendelhombre; the second was her son the current Vendelhombre. A third was a retired Vendelhombre. A fourth was the youngish heir-apparent to the Vendelhombre post. But in 2003–4, none of these ever spoke up in public on the matter of conservation.

Martín Falcón, the teacher who first proposed conservation measures, found out as we did that one does not drag the tokens of delicate, vital negotiations into profane settings. In 1982 Rapaz was to be the seat of a local soccer championship. Martín wanted to bring out the khipu collection to show the guests because it was little-known and special. 'The comuneros almost lynched me', he recalled. 'Nobody was allowed to see it. It was a sacred thing of the Inca. Rain would cease, landslides would fall. There would be sicknesses and mass death.'

One does not disturb the merit of centuries for cosmetic purposes. If things inside Kaha Wayi crumble, some felt, it is safer to let that happen. The very mess that Kaha Wayi was in, the soot and bugs and the bags of used-and-saved coca leaves, were the 'phenotype' of good practices. When we asked if we might move several gunny sacks of old, used coca, Vendelhombre Melecio Montes said they could never become garbage because they were the 'work' of Kaha Wayi. The distance between this traditionalist frame of mind and the conservationist platform was, at first, too deep to talk about. No matter how clearly we promised to be technologically conservative and comply with customary law, we looked to the old-timers like triflers without a real stake in the underlying relationships. In time, some old devotees did come to enjoy seeing the scene of their devotions repaired, and we became friends. But the many traditionalists who were not so much in on the project held on to their suspicions.

Hence the anger about rain. And a third discord was roiling under the surface: some Rapacinos are Pentecostal converts, and there was also a small Evangelical church. Some Protestants, urged by fiery circuit preachers, felt that Kaha Wayi was an idolatrous or satanic institution. For the sake of a modus vivendi some were willing to enter Kaha Wayi, briefly and without coca leaf or obeisances, when their offices required it. But more committed converts nursed anger that the 'diabolic' rites of pre-Columbian times continued to form part of the official culture in their community. Certain converts joined in conservation work, not out of traditionalism, but because (as I later learned) they saw foreign intervention as a step towards 'museification' and eventual decommissioning of Kaha Wayi. By 2016 this tension seemed to lessen as a generation born rather than converted into Protestantism began to assume civic duties. For them, religious integrity no longer depended on rupture.

Preservation turns out to be anything but a steady state. The khipus have had their ups and downs, their periods of neglect and of exaltation. What people do with the legacy of the past depends on what they think has been happening in history, and on this Andean communities of our time are no closer to consensus than other people. In community ethnohistory and on-site conservation one notices that correlations between local 'historicities' and local habits in stewardship of patrimony are not always the ones that would seem obvious. Of course, the tide of utilitarian modernism everywhere undercuts such traditional forms as the khipu. Amid this tide, reverent traditionalists become a minority in retirement. The interesting thing is why some untraditional people nonetheless want to speak for preservationist options. In the 1980s, the 2000s, and perhaps in prior times the assertive conservers have not been traditionalists, but rather locally rooted people with innovative, relativising or historicistic views. From 2014 on Rapaz has been receiving some in-kind subsidies from a mining company but Kaha Wayi has been kept aside from this relationship.

There is more to tradition-conserving activity than we have been led to believe by the ethnography of neoindigenism with its emphasis on invented tradition. Without 'inventing' anything, comuneros use historical khipus to demonstrate autonomous rather than state-sponsored continuity and proper relationships with the environment. The practice exemplifies what Gose, in chapter 3, characterises as the 'Christian, egalitarian and republican' recasting of the Andean legacy.

Having been bred to scepticism about continuity, and credulity about innovation, recent ethnographers in the Andes (and everywhere) tend to underestimate the weight of inheritances. Community life, and good community studies, depend on those who travel the long lines whether scientifically or otherwise. It is always worthwhile meeting the people who don't throw things away.

7. Avoiding 'community studies': the historical turn in Bolivian and South Andean anthropology

Tristan Platt

The word 'community' has different implications in different societies, and in different political and intellectual traditions. Is there a Quechua, Aymara or other Andean linguistic equivalent to the Latin word '*communitas*'? The word I came up against in the 1960s, while wondering where to do fieldwork in highland Bolivia, was '*ayllu*'. In the Andean south there was nothing quite like the debate on 'Peruvian peasant communities' described in the introduction by Francisco Ferreira. But there had been much discussion about what an ayllu is, even before Bautista Saavedra's book *El ayllu*, an evolutionist text published in 1903 during the aftermath of the Bolivian Civil War in 1899. This war was itself in part provoked by the 1874 Law of Disentailment, which aimed (unsuccessfully) at dissolving the ayllus as collective land-holding groups and privatising the lands of individual peasants to create a land-market.

The word '*comunidad*' in America derives from 16th-century Spain. The nub of the Latin root has been deconstructed by Espósito (2010 [1998]) as *munus*, signifying 'service, gift, obligation'. I have much time for this etymology (Platt, 2014), but in 1970, coming from British social anthropology, I deliberately avoided the road of US 'community studies' and sought ethnographic traces of 'Andean' forms of social organisation.[1] This allowed me to draw attention through field and archive work to the region of Northern Potosí and its *jatun ayllu* [great ayllus], which lies well to the south-east of Lake Titicaca and the Lupaqa where John V. Murra had concentrated some of his best efforts in the 1960s and early 1970s. This chapter, written in semi-autobiographical vein, tells how I found those ethnographic traces, and in doing so was led to historicise my anthropology.

---

1 The word 'Andean' with reference to pre- and post-invasion native American society has been proscribed as 'essentialist' by several writers. But 'Andean' does not deny historical change, as some nationalist historians have implied. On the contrary, it can refer to Andean societies which have been conquered by the Incas, invaded by the Spanish and incorporated into nation-states, combining threads of continuity and change in their actions and reactions to a constantly transforming context.

In the 1960s there was very little anthropological interest in the Andes in the UK, although John Hemming's *Conquest of the Incas* was published in 1970, coming long after Sir Clements Markham's pioneering efforts in the 19th century; both were from the Royal Geographical Society. I myself ended up in the Bolivian Andes by accident. I give here a few background influences. My maternal grandfather was a librarian, historian and antiquary, whose classic editions of *Early Yorkshire Charters* have just been republished (Clay, 2013 [1914–65]). I have often thought how his genealogical interests foreshadowed the time I have spent on early colonial Aymara family trees. My father was a singer with a passionate love of music who later founded a pioneering opera company, Kent Opera (N. Platt, 2001). He left me with his love of music and an appreciation of performance, with tips for achieving it in talks and lectures. My mother defended her PhD on the sociology of literature at the London School of Economics in 1961. She was a cultured adventurous rebel, who was always reading a new novel, loved poetry, music, travel and politics, and her hospitable house in London was littered with the latest books on sociology and social psychology; she taught at the Polytechnic of North London until her death in 1977 (Laurenson (ed.), 1978). My paternal grandfather was from Salford (near Manchester), lived in Bury (Lancashire) and was a member of the Liberal Club. When I knew him in the 1940s and 50s he was a tea and coffee merchant, selling a special blend of tea (the Platt blend). A kind, thoughtful and humorous man, he used to sing warmly between making brave jokes to take his mind off his excruciating arthritis. Before losing all mobility, he took me to an iron foundry and down a coal mine, as though in anticipation of my later interests in silver mining and metallurgy.

New questions arose while doing classical studies at school in London, with teenage trips to Greece, Rome and the Mediterranean, and then a pre-university visit to Bolivia, South America, where I spent nine months in 1963 as an 18-year-old volunteer teacher. That visit shook things up. Among other questions, I began to wonder whether it was possible to talk of the survival of 'Incas' through more than four centuries of colonialism. Though badly formulated, the question raised issues (of which I was unaware at the time) about the nature of historical process. Through many rephrasings, in which Quechua-speakers who had until recently spoken Aymara (and perhaps previously Puquina) replaced the idealised 'Incas' of my earlier imaginings, this pre-anthropological question lay behind my decision to do fieldwork in the southern Andes. Later, history and anthropology merged in a multisecular and interdisciplinary study of South Andean societies; silver production and circulation; speaking, writing and archives; and the subjects of agency in colonial and internal colonial situations.

First inklings

My arrival in Bolivia was the result of chance. In 1963 I was told I would be sent to do voluntary work in Cyprus, until I admitted I did not know how to drive. This confession meant I was sent to Oruro, Bolivia, and I spent nine months there teaching English, music and geography in the Anglo-American School; learning to dance with my novia, Marta González, whose family supported Walter Guevara and the Partido Revolucionario Auténtico (PRA), and who later introduced me to a circle of good friends in La Paz; helping to form the Oruro Fencing Club with Carlos Ferrari, owner of the Ferrari-Ghezzi biscuits factory; training the Anglo-American school choir to perform the 'Pilgrims' Chorus' from Wagner's *Tannhäuser*; and studying Spanish and trying to read pages by Cervantes, Lope de Vega, Calderón, Becquer and Lorca, as well as by the Bolivian poet Gregorio Reynolds. I saw the devil-dancing Carnival in the streets, and the enactment of the confrontation between the Inca and Pizarro up by the Virgin of the Socavon statue, at the main adit to Oruro's great tin mine. I watched the black-suited señores drinking cocktails and eating *salteñas* under the glare of the Altiplanic sun on the *pampa* outside the town, close by the armadillo-haunted sand-dunes; and the seated tall-hatted 'indian' women, chatting with them and selling them food, where commercial, ethnic and gender considerations mingled intriguingly. I was taken to see President Víctor Paz Estenssoro entering Achacachi near La Paz in a jeep, surrounded by *milicias campesinas* and showing his two-fingers-for-victory, the symbol of the Movimiento Nacionalista Revolucionario (MNR) (a little over a year later he was thrown out by his vice-president René Barrientos Ortuño). And I visited Cochabamba and its Archaeological Museum, whose director Geraldine Byrne de Caballero was also the British Consul. When I left Bolivia, I realised I had understood very little about the country, and took it as a challenge to find out more.

In September 1963 I returned through the space-time warp to four years of studying classics and philosophy at New College, Oxford: Latin and Greek languages, literatures, philosophy and historiography, as well as 'modern' philosophy (Descartes, Locke and Berkeley, Hume and Kant). I remember language tutorials on verse and prose style with E.C. Yorke, and Geoffrey Owen's classes on the pre-Socratic philosophers, as we read all of Homer and Virgil, some Plato and Aristotle, a few tragedians and key historians, in the original languages. Among many later readings for which this prepared me, I will only mention here Jorge Luis Borges' *El hacedor*, *El inmortal* and *La busca de Averroes*, which I took with me, among other things, to read during fieldwork.

I remember Alasdair MacIntyre's classes on virtues and morality in history and society; and I listened enthralled to the torrential flow of Isaiah Berlin's lectures on intellectual history. I also took copious notes at Herbert Hart's course on the philosophy of law. My ancient history tutors were the meticulous Geoffrey de Ste Croix at New College for Greece (the Peloponnesian War) and the convivial 'Tom Brown' Stevens at Magdalen for Rome (Cicero and the Catiline Conspiracy). I remember that, even then, some of us wondered at the near-absence from the curriculum of post-Kantian continental thought, in place of which we were asked to read the linguistic and analytical philosophy for which Oxford was famous.

So after graduating in 1967 I changed tack and undertook postgraduate studies in social anthropology at the London School of Economics (LSE), with the intention of returning to Bolivia and seeking answers to those youthful questions I had left on the shelf. Anthropology at the LSE began with Bronislaw Malinowski and Alfred Radcliffe-Brown, Marcel Mauss, Ambrose Evans-Pritchard, Gregory Bateson, Raymond Firth and Fred Nadel, with backward glances to Henry Maine, Edward Burnett Tylor, William Robertson Smith and W.H.R. Rivers. It continued forward through Max Gluckman on African law, Fredrik Barth on ethnicity and spheres of exchange, Mary Douglas on taboo and classification, Rodney Needham and David Maybury-Lewis on dualism, and Edmund Leach, the iconoclast who formalised political change as oscillation between anarchy and aristocracy (later systematised in structural-Marxist style by Jonathan Friedman). Together with Max Gluckman, Firth, Douglas and Evans-Pritchard, Leach remained with me; also Sutti Ortiz's reflections on perceptions of risk among Colombian peasants, which prepared me to understand South Andean productive strategies. Not least I still recall talks on anthropology and music with my contemporary and friend Alfred Gell (he was moving towards phenomenology when I was leaning towards Marx), and with Anthony Forge, the genial New Guinea specialist and anthropologist of art who supervised us both.

Another mentor was the sinologist Maurice Freedman, and I recall lectures and seminars by Firth (social organisation and Tikopia), Lucy Mair (witchcraft and Africa), James Woodburn (hunters and gatherers), Jean La Fontaine (gender and kinship), and sociolinguistics with Jean Aitchison. Also clear in my mind are the 1968 demonstrations outside the US Embassy in Grosvenor Square against the Vietnam War, including a students' boycott of LSE classes in which our classmates John and Jean Comaroff were active (they had come to study South Africa with Isaac Shapera). The major intellectual event among anthropologists at that time was probably the publication in 1966 of the (much criticised) English translation of *The Savage Mind* by Claude Lévi-Strauss, to which I promptly applied Oxford analytical methods in order to show it was strictly meaningless. It was not till I returned to Bolivia from 1970 to 1971 that the Andean peasants of Potosí taught me otherwise.

Meanwhile I prepared a research project, which was to be a linguistic analysis of decision-making processes among Andean peasants that might unite Oxford analytics with LSE anthropology; and this meant I had to study an Andean language. So in June 1969 I crossed the Atlantic to Ithaca, Upper New York State, to attend a Quechua summer school at Cornell University with Donald Solá and Demetrio Roca. And there I made contact with a flourishing multistranded Andean studies tradition, entirely absent from British social anthropology at the time. Solá's teaching methods, using materials from his fieldwork in Chinchero, were seductive and effective (he had us improvising sketches after a couple of months of classes); and I admired the slow, thoughtful precision with which he introduced key grammatical points. Of course, he and Roca taught Cuzco Quechua, not Cochabamba or any other Bolivian Quechua. But they gave me a base I have always been grateful for.

It was at Cornell that, through Solá and John Murra, I came across the idea of the ayllu. Recently arrived in Ithaca, John was sniffing around Solá's class to seek out possible recruits for his grand vision of Andean studies as an interdisciplinary scholarly community in close synergy with Andean intellectuals: peasants, poets, politicians and professionals, as well as academics. His knowledge and appreciation of the British social anthropologists of Africa and Oceania was gratifying, and he talked of Andean ecological verticality with minute attention to administrative sources and the middle- and lower-ranking echelons of local bureaucracies. He also talked of the Spanish Civil War, during which he had been an interpreter at Albacete and an Abraham Lincoln brigade member; and his disgust with the US Communist Party for its logistical failures was palpable. John was interested in people as emotional, political and social actors – what they did as expressions of who they were. He took a political economic approach with which I sympathised, and the materialist dimension of his famous 1955 thesis became evident when in 1972 I read Maurice Godelier's classic articles on the 'Asiatic mode of production' among the Incas.

Murra gave me his offprints, including the famous volume I of *Cuadernos de Investigación* (Murra et al., 1966, with articles by Cesar Fonseca, Enrique Mayer and Donald Thompson), and two graphics from his soon-to-be-famous article on the Andean ideal of 'vertical control of a maximum of ecological levels' (1972). So it was that I took away with me in 1969 pre-publication sketches of the Chupaychu and Lupaqa transformations of this powerful key to Andean understanding. They alerted me to a central feature of the people among whom I would end up doing fieldwork from 1970 to 1971.

In Cornell I learned of Andeanists such as Heinrich Cunow, Julio C. Tello, John Rowe, Tom Zuidema, Franklin Pease, Tom Lynch, Craig Morris and Murra's first student Heather Lechtman. I also met the Bolivian ex-Jesuit and linguist George Urioste, a doctoral student of Solá's, who gave me a copy of his transcription and English translation of the Quechua-language Huarochiri manuscript, as well as students such as Freda Wolf, Philip Blair, and of course Frank Salomon, a brilliant student of John's who later became a good friend and colleague. Other researchers (such as Jürgen Riester) I met in the hospitable house of Enrique Mayer in Miraflores, Lima, in those days a welcome stop-off point for Amerindianists en route from London to La Paz.

In short, meeting Murra at Cornell was a piece of great good fortune, and gave me a range of contacts and questions that served me well when I finally returned to Bolivia for the period 1970 to 1971, with support from the Social Science Research Council (SSRC-UK), the Ford Foundation and the London University Research Fund.

First fieldwork

I landed again in El Alto airport on the last day of 1969, my choice of a place to 'do fieldwork' still constrained by my pre-anthropological question. In La Paz I stayed with Edgar and Rosemarie Dick, friends from Oruro in 1963. Murra had advised me not to choose a place too quickly, and I took a while searching for ayllus in the warm valleys round Sucre. But so strong were the attractions of the exotic Other that I started trying to find a place which the Spanish hadn't got to, without realising that, in the Andes, none such existed. I am grateful to the Bolivian anthropologist and linguist Mario Montaño, whom I met in Oruro, and who listened to me before kindly saying that he did not know if such a place existed, but that, if it did, it would probably be in the north of Potosí.

By now I could drive, so I got into my Nissan Patrol, generously provided by the SSRC-UK (this was before Thatcher had ruled that societies did not exist, only economies; I was required at the end of fieldwork to sell the vehicle, which I called Sancho, and return the proceeds). I then travelled from the high *puna* via the tin mines of Llallagua, then Colloma and Chiru, down to the warm river valleys of San Pedro de Buena Vista (capital of Provincia Charcas), arriving just in time for the fiesta of the town's patron saint (29 June 1970). While dancing in the streets and drinking quantities of chicha, singani and alcohol, I began to ask people where the most distant, remote, inaccessible place in provincia Charcas might be; and there seemed to be a consensus (supported by my good friend in San Pedro, Serafín Taborga) that the right goal for me would probably be Canton San Marcos. I later found that, since 1882, San Marcos had been cut off from the old Chayanta province and placed with other valley lands into the new Charcas province; but San Marcos was too distant to be effectively administered from the Charcas capital of San Pedro and continued to be closely linked to its traditional puna counterpart in Chayanta. When I was there the influence of the distant *sindicato* [peasant trade union] leaders

Figure 7.1. San Marcos, 1970. Photo: T. Platt.

based in Banduriri, near San Pedro, was in tension with that of the equally distant ayllu leaders in the highlands of Chayanta and Macha.

Thanks to the availability of don Isidoro, an experienced muleteer who had actually been there, I set off a few days later – after a few postponements – for San Marcos. At first, I tried to ride a mule, but it was painfully uncomfortable, and I ended up leading it while walking beside don Isidoro as he directed the pack-mules. The journey took two wonderful, if exhausting, days plodding for hours along the hot, stony river-beds, following a route I later realised had been taken by Gonzalo and Hernando Pizarro in 1538 on their way from Cochabamba to Chuquisaca (Sucre today) in search of the Inca's silver mines at Porco. I made attempts to talk to local Quechua-speakers at the Alacruz pass where we spent the night. Many lived in ayllus whose names – as I later learned – were generally those of the component segments of the ancient federations of Qaraqara and Charka, which had been incorporated into the Inca and then the Spanish empires in the early 16th century. When, later, I read Juan Rulfo's novel, *Pedro Páramo* (1955), it reminded me of my journeys in the time-laden valleys of Charcas.

It was the evening of the second day when we finally climbed up the steep path to San Marcos (see figure 7.1). As we got higher, the network of mountains and river valleys opened beneath us like a gigantic fan. Though dusk was falling, the local *dirigente* in San Marcos at once called an open-air meeting; and, after I had explained in halting Quechua that I wanted to come and learn the local ways of life and language, they agreed to my staying.

Those were the days when General Alfredo Ovando, followed in October 1970 by General J.J. Torres, presided in Bolivia, and I had armed myself with a sheaf of credentials before leaving La Paz. I added to them at each descending rung of national and sindicato administration. The art lay in deciding which credential to show to whom. But the credentials did not spare me the usual suspicious accusations of being a communist guerrillero, an agent from the Central Intelligence Agency (CIA), or a *llik'ichiri* (= *pishtaco*; a fat-sucking murderer). This was the time of the Teoponte guerrilla, and Che Guevara had only recently been killed by the Bolivian army and the CIA in 1967. One day I came back to find a dead coral snake draped over the latch of my house.

The crumbling ruins of San Marcos were perched high up on the hillside. The town had been founded (as I later learned) at the behest of Viceroy Francisco de Toledo's inspectors in the 1570s. Close by its dilapidated church there lived three or four '*moso*' (mestizo) families, who were keen for me to come and join them; but I avoided being assimilated into the town, guessing this would place class and ethnic barriers between me and the 'indians' in the countryside. It was better to be available to my preferred hosts as a foreign object of curiosity; and I had brought a big *cesto* of coca-leaves with me to encourage conversation. So I chose to take up an offer from the dirigente, a cheery monolingual Quechua-speaker called Víctor Gómez, whose family became my neighbours. This took the form of an abandoned thatched, one-room adobe hut, built to serve as a school, which had a fabulous view over the valleys and was on a main footpath 20 minutes' walk from 'town'. The rent was symbolic; there was no door, or even *q'uncha* [mud-stove]; and the straw roof was tatty. I got the first two installed, and then sprayed the roof with Baygon, which brought down a shower of dead and dying vinchuca beetles, vectors of Chagas disease, that infest thatched roofs in the Andean rural valleys, drop on sleeping people's faces and then bite near the eyes, shitting into the wound.

I learned that my home was built on a patch of land belonging to an ayllu called Yuqhuna. This was potentially interesting, but I did not realise that these were just the valley lands of a large *cabildo* called Yuqhuna whose main lands were situated on the distant puna of the great ayllu of Macha, and were part of minor ayllu Majacollana and moiety Majasaya. But I am leaping ahead, because I still did not know the difference between the great ayllus, the moieties (or major ayllus), the minor ayllus (of which I found there were five in each moiety) and the cabildos (or minimal ayllus, subdivisions of the minor ayllus); only that the word 'comunidad' seemed to be little used in indian parlance, except sometimes for cabildos.[2]

---

2   In an early article (1986 [1976, 1978, 1980]), I used the segmentary terminology as a matter of descriptive convenience; it was not meant to suggest a close theoretical or empirical coincidence with the segmentary *lineages* of the Nuer as described by E.E. Evans-Pritchard (1940). In the 1970s, and to some extent still today, the ayllus were segmentary *territorial*

Figure 7.2. The alferez [ritual sponsors] and company coming up to San Marcos for Corpus Christi, 1971. Photo: T. Platt.

I remember how, after a couple of months of learning little (except the need to bring up water early each morning from a hole down the hill before the animals muddied it, and pass it through the filter I had brought with me on the pack-mule), I got depressed as, instead of some exotic Andean organisation emerging, everything seemed framed by the 'canton', which at the time I considered boringly Napoleonic. I feared I might end up doing yet another local 'peasant community study', like so many others in Latin America, rather than finding traces of institutional and civilisational Otherness. However, one day a visitor said to me, 'you know, our highest authorities don't live down here, they are up on the puna.' He seemed uncertain if there were one or two headmen, whom he called *curacas*. Then he told me a story of three brothers, Macha, Pocoata and Laymi, who walked down from the puna with their llamas, passing the valleys of San Marcos and continuing down to the maize and red-pepper lands at Carasi. There Laymi's sandals broke, and he had to stay; but Macha and Pocoata carried on down until they reached the distant town of Misque, in the department of Cochabamba.

At this, I began to hear echoes of Murra and verticality. It seemed I had finally stumbled on an alternative set of social relationships that went way beyond communities or cabildos, cantons and provinces, and even departments. The story was vividly illustrated when, in May 1971, the llama-trains from

groups, though tendentially endogamous at each level. For the far more complex 16th-century forms of organisation, see Platt et al. (2011 [2006]).

Figure 7.3. Tinku in San Marcos for Corpus Christi, 1971. Photo: T. Platt.

Chayanta province began to appear in San Marcos, loaded with salt and other highland produce to exchange for maize. I and all the other valley-dwellers got really excited. Some *llameros* went on down towards Carasi, though I heard of none going further.

As I continued asking, the moiety division between *Alasaya* and *Majasaya* [upper and lower halves], and a confused tangle of smaller groups – minimal ayllus, together with the ten historic minor ayllus – began to emerge as fractions of a jatun ayllu called Macha. All expressed their alliances and enmities at the four ritual battles, or *tinkus*, held annually in San Marcos between the two moieties: Carnival, Corpus Christi (to replace Cruz on 3 May, as the priest only came once a year for Corpus), Todos Santos (All Saints' Day) and Navidad (Christmas) (see figure 7.2). At Corpus the puna llameros were also there to take part on the side of their respective ayllu and moiety. I began to realise that social violence organised from below was a fundamental aspect of defending land rights in the legal vacuum that seemed to characterise this part of Bolivia's countryside.

All this yielded rich ethnographic material to explore and work with, but clearly I could not understand what this supra-provincial social entity might be like without a visit to the puna.

At the end of my year's fieldwork in San Marcos, I took part in the Corpus Christi celebration in June 1971, at which many different ayllus and cabildos participated and there was a violent tinku (see figure 7.3).

The study of this fiesta (Platt, 1996 [1987]) showed the complex interplay of ayllus and cabildos in assuming ritual sponsorships, and the way in which extra-liturgical rituals can serve as an Andean 'commentary', or *apparatus criticus*, on the liturgical ritual of the Catholic church. I compared the 20th-century ethnography of the extra-liturgical fiesta I had witnessed with a late 18th-century summary of the Catholic rites given in a colonial *Libro de Fábrica* written by a San Marcos priest. I might perhaps have written up an account of this local parish, considered as the basis of the canton; only I now knew that, way beyond any local 'community', I was living in a maize-growing appendix to the main body of Macha society, which lay far away on the distant puna.

So in June 1971 I went back with my things by mule to San Pedro de Buena Vista, where I picked up Sancho (a broken back spring bound up with cowhide strips), and drove round by Llallagua, Uncia, Chuquiuta and Pocoata, through the high, bare, cold puna lands, until I reached the dreich-looking town of Macha, in the Chayanta province. It was some 3,550 metres above sea level, 1,500 metres higher than San Marcos, which was now far down the valleys of Charcas province on the other side of the provincial capital and the Colquechaca-Aullagas mining centre's towering mountains. For the Macha lands in both provinces were contiguous, forming a long vertical strip some 130 kilometres long, an immense area spread over two provinces and eight cantons, over which were scattered ten ayllus, some 50 cabildos, and hundreds of indian hamlets and villages. This was in addition to the mining capital of Colquechaca, on the borders between Macha and neighbouring Pocoata, and a few smaller mestizo towns.

At this point the corregidor of Macha town, Don Ricardo Arancibia (still remembered today for his inspired charango-playing), came to my rescue telling me I had to meet Agustín Carbajal, the Alasaya moiety's curaca. Here, it seemed, was one of the higher authorities. So half an hour's drive from Macha across the low puna in the direction of Cruce Culta we left the road and followed another stony riverbed to Liconi Pampa, where the Carbajal family lived.

I will always remember the astute and gently smiling face of Santiago Carbajal, don Agustín's eldest son. He listened attentively to what Ricardo and I told him, and cut the discussion short by inviting me to come immediately to stay with him and his family. 'It suits us to have someone who will explain our point of view to the outside world', he said, with instant understanding of one thing anthropology might be about, while laying on me a responsibility I could only try and fulfil.

During the next two months in Liconi Pampa I learned as much as I had in all the previous year in San Marcos. The old curaca Don Agustín Carbajal (1900–85) showed me documents from his archive, Santiago discussed Macha

Figure 7.4. Liconi Pampa, 2013. Photo: Fortunato Laura.

social organisation, religion, politics and dualism with me, his younger brother Gregorio showed me his iron-working and notarial skills, Santiago's wife Feliciana Cali brought us food and talked about weaving, and their children – six boys and four girls – accompanied me, told me stories and riddles, and demonstrated their skills and entertainments to me. Everyone was immensely kind, courteous and good-humoured; and all spoke entirely in Quechua. The extended family's other households lay scattered over the pampa. I tried to answer their many questions with tales of my own land.

Liconi Pampa was in cabildo Pichichua, ayllu Alacollana, moiety Alasaya (see figure 7.4). We went around, walking or in Sancho, visiting people in different hamlets, cabildos and ayllus, often participating in drunken fiestas where the chicha unlocked all tongues. I now realised why it had been so difficult for me to understand the ramifications of social organisation in the lowlands (much less detect a 'community'): not from lack of chicha, but because the valley-dwellers had forgotten much of it, and in any case they lived *chajrusqa* [mixed-up] in what Murra might call 'archipelagical' style, and no longer distinguished clearly between ayllu and cabildo (Platt, 2009b). On the puna, however, the traditional patterns, including each cabildo's rights to specific valley lands, were remembered more distinctly, although some puna dwellers did try to take advantage of the valley-dwellers' forgetfulness.[3] New social perspectives came

---

3 This contrast between valley and puna people was mentioned in a letter denouncing an intrusion in Jancoma Valley by a puna usurper: '*viendo que los campesinos del valle son escasos de memoria, y él es de puna entrador de todo*', corregidor of Surumi to the prefect

Figure 7.5. Carbajal patriclan members, 1971: Curaca Agustín Carbajal (extreme right), Gregorio and Santiago Carbajal (at centre, seated). Photo: T. Platt.

to enrich those I had learned in San Marcos; I explored highland ritual ideas and practices of the sacred, learning the denizens of a different, more powerful landscape. Santiago introduced me to a shaman (*yachaq*, 'one who knows'), and we arranged to hold a session (also called cabildo), where we conversed with a *jurq'u* [mountain spirit], in the invisible but audible form of a flapping condor. I was allowed to tape the proceedings which took place in pitch darkness (Platt, 1997). We also went to visit the miraculous image of Santiago at the Macha annex of Pumpuri, patron of lightning, shamanism and curing. The Pumpuri chapel was tended by a sacristan, a post rotating annually between two local cabildos belonging to Alasaya and Majasaya.

As we talked, chewed coca, drank chicha and visited, a new world of sociological, historical and religious ideas, as well as a new everyday normality, came to subvert and reorganise the dense layers of my academic formation and 'commonsense' expectations. It also led me to question some condescending urban and international assumptions about peasant 'poverty' and 'misery'. And with that experience began a series of visits to Liconi Pampa over the decades, during which local life changed dramatically for all of us, particularly in the 1980s–90s, as neoliberal economic policies invaded all our worlds.

---

of Potosí, Surumi, 25 May 1966, Archivo de la Vice-Presidencia. B-PO/ACMA C2-32.
The 'forgetfulness' may also have been due to the peasant unions in the valleys of Charcas province being so overbearing.

In the 1970s, people in the hamlet wore few imported clothes; the men wore *bayeta* trousers of homespun cloth woven from their own wool, they and the women spun and plied, knitting their own *chhulus* [woollen bonnets], making their own waistcoats and jackets, buying their sandals, made from rubber straps and old tyres, and their felt hats in the neighbouring town of Pocoata. Santiago and his younger brother Gregorio had an old Underwood typewriter and acted as scribes for their father Don Agustín (see figure 7.5); both wrote notarial Spanish, while preferring not to converse in Spanish. I began to realise that, far from being an 'oral society', Macha was permeated by the power of alphabetic writing (Platt, 1982; 1992).

Gregorio Carbajal was a skilful handyman; he had a forge and was the Carbajal family blacksmith, making iron tools and gun barrels. One of Santiago's sons was the local potter, who collected clay from deposits at a Macha annex, Qayne, and fashioned it into the different styles required by his exchange partners, in the lowlands as well as the highlands. Santiago's wife Feliciana and his daughters Julia and Paulina were superb weavers; and the designs of woven cloth, Gregorio told me, were the Chullpas' writing, the Chullpas being the people who had lived 'for 1,000 years' before the Incas, and whose tombs can still be seen in scattered corners of the landscape. The women still wove the marvellous designs for which the Macha are famous: superb striped ponchos for their husbands, beautiful *llijllas* [carrying cloths], and dazzling *ajsus* hanging down behind over their dresses. The latter were made from bayeta woven by the men, and embroidered by them too: at that time every self-respecting husband had his sewing machine (Santiago had an old Singer) to adorn his wife's dresses with threads representing multicoloured flowers and patterns. Both sexes used hard-woven *chumpis*, or belts; and the men carried *ch'uspas*, bags woven by the women for storing coca-leaf, with little pockets to hold the alcaline *llijt'a*, and also coins. They were adorned with *tullmas* [long tassels] and a narrow woven band with which to carry them. Great time and care was expended on dignifying a way of life still on the margins of consumer capitalism. I have sometimes wondered about the extent to which I myself – a city-dweller and a foreigner arriving with manufactured clothes, a Nissan, a Petromax lantern, plastic bowls and more – was a harbinger of future changes, unknown to myself at the time.

Clearly, I was not simply living in a local 'community', but in a complex Andean agropastural society with a strong ideal of gender complementarity made up of two extended vertical moieties, each with some 25 cabildos grouped into five ayllus, all dispersed across the landscape. The cabildo was the basic tributary unit of Macha society, the level at which contributions were collected from each tributary by the collectors and alcaldes, before delivery to the *jilancos* [ayllu chiefs] and thence to the moiety's curaca. But clearly, it was impossible to grasp Macha by limiting oneself to one local cabildo, as a 'community study' might require: to do so would be to silence the great ayllu's social and political complexity, which in turn affected the political relations of all the lower-level units.

Thus Yuqhuna, the little locality where I had been living in the valleys, turned out to be the valley lands of a cabildo of the same name on the puna, part of ayllu Majacollana, one of Majasaya's five ayllus. And Liconi Pampa, where I lived on the puna, was an estancia in the Pichichua cabildo, a sprawling territory divided into two parts, which was one of seven cabildos belonging to ayllu Alacollana, itself one of Alasaya's five ayllus. It turned out that the Pichichuas had their maize lands near the distant valley of Amutara, a hillside on the other side of the ravine from San Marcos, whose maize fields I had often watched glow yellow in the early morning sunlight from my little house in cabildo Yuqhuna's valley lands. In short, I had ended up (without planning it) living in two cabildos, one from each moiety, and each at opposite ends of Macha's long vertical territory. One was in the 'mixed-up' maize lands of Majasaya, the other at the centre of the administrative authority for Alasaya's 25 cabildos and five ayllus. From these accidental vantage points I looked out on the life of Macha society.

Inevitably, I wanted to discover the age of this complex social entity, and the historical processes underlying its formation. A first, flying visit to the Sucre archive showed me that the two moieties and their ten constituent ayllus had been known, with exactly the same names and a similar vertical distribution, in 1579. This gave Macha a paradigmatic value for the study of persistence and agency under colonialism, in relation to different sorts of state. And it opened the door to wider questions concerning the historic relations between the various great ayllus of Northern Potosí (see figure 7.6), and of these with the Inca and Spanish states.

The age of the cabildos was more difficult. While cabildo means 'council' and was part of the early modern local political formation brought by Spain in the 16th and 17th centuries, I have found no evidence of cabildos as territorial subdivisions of an ayllu before the 19th century. My present hunch is that these territories were created by ayllu members following the abolition in 1825 of their colonial councils and *municipios* by Simon Bolivar, who in 1828 at Cúcuta restored the 'little cabildos' to ensure the continued payment of the tribute, without which there could have been no Bolivian state. But I reached this view years later, when comparing the early republican history of Chayanta with that of the neighbouring Porco province (2009a).

What was common to my approach and that of 'community studies' was, no doubt, the ethnographic method, involving close conviviality with the heirs of a different cultural history, however much I would later choose to build bridges

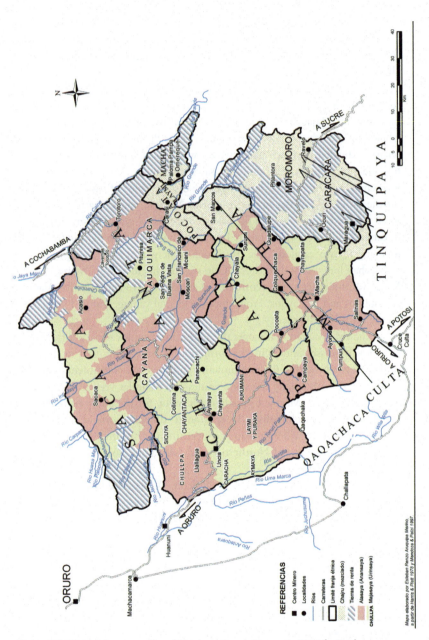

Figure 7.6. Map of the great ayllus of Northern Potosí. Drawn in 2015 by Esteban Renzo Aruquipa Merino (after Mendoza and Patzi, 1997; Harris and Platt, 1978)

across the divides, and develop a documented vision of connected histories. At that time, I was motivated by the search for direct relations with difference – exchanges, experiences, ideas, flavours and savours – while learning to speak a non-Indo-European language in the process. Later, I sought how to present my findings in texts that aimed at different audiences, while trying to be true to the push-and-pull of the testimonies, and of other imaginative identifications and points of view. And I was – and am – open to seeking answers as far back as the 16th century, or earlier.

Meanwhile it was becoming clear to me that Bolivian representative democracy (first the MNR, later the parties of both the left and the neoliberal right) tolerated the ayllus only with difficulty. They regarded them as primitive and wanted to replace them with a more modern and 'progressive' form of peasant political organisation: the rural sindicatos, or peasant unions, which they also saw as a handy means of mobilising mass support and votes. The unions were organised by federation, central, sub-central and dirigente, following the units of national administration. Moreover, in the mines of Siglo XX, the mining unions were then dominated by Trotskyist *obreristas*, for whom peasants were petty-bourgeois food pedlars, lacking true 'revolutionary consciousness'.[4] As such they had to be organised by union leaders – although many of these were mestizos from the local towns, thereby reproducing an old racialised hierarchy based on ethnic 'civilisational' difference as much as politico-economic stratification.

The project was growing, and I was lucky to find colleagues with whom to share it. The first was Olivia Harris, a family friend with a similar academic trajectory, whom I was able to interest, on my return to London in autumn 1971, in working in the society of another of the brothers who came down from the puna, but whose sandals had broken in Carasi: the Laymi.[5]

In 1971, after leaving Liconi Pampa but before leaving Bolivia, I also met two French colleagues, both historians but open to anthropology in the classic *Annales* tradition: Nathan Wachtel and Thierry Saignes. I first met Nathan in the Sucre archive, and we met again in Thierry's flat in La Paz in August, during General Banzer's bloody coup, carried out with the connivance of ex-president

---

4 In a Trotskyist joke that circulated at that time, a miner is pursued by the army, hides, takes refuge in the countryside, reaches an indian hamlet, tells his hosts of the horrors of military dictatorship, of the need for a class alliance between peasants and miners ... To which the peasant replies, 'All of this is most interesting, compañero, but I have just one question: what is today's rate of exchange with the dollar?'

5 Fieldwork in the lands of the third brother, Pocoata, has been carried out by Krista van Vleet, who worked in ayllu Sullkata, great ayllu Pocoata (van Vleet, 2008). This fine ethnography of linguistic performance and gossip is situated in a 'community', but without mentioning that this 'community' is part of a hierarchy of indigenous social units. Pocoata appears only as a 'provincial town', whereas historically (and to some extent ethnographically) it is a great ayllu divided, like Macha, into 2 moieties, and 11 minor ayllus with their cabildos. In 2013 I could still meet the moiety Curacas in the town of Pocoata.

Víctor Paz Estenssoro and the US Embassy. Santiago Carbajal had accompanied me from Macha to see La Paz, and was present in Thierry's flat to witness the coup. Thierry's sister Roselyne and the political reporter Bernard Poulet were also there. Together we sat out the three days, watching the planes dive down from El Alto to attack students resisting from the university monobloc, just opposite the flat. Sniper fire cracked from the rooftops close by.

Both Nathan and Thierry were colleagues in those early years when we shared the excitement of combining history with anthropology. Nathan was a pioneer of the new French Andean studies, and had begun to articulate Murra's ideas on the redistributive political economy of the Incas with Zuidema's Dutch structuralism, before publishing *The Vision of the Vanquished* (1971) and beginning his first fieldwork in Chipaya in 1973. In 1971 I took him to Macha, and later I visited him in Chipaya in August–September 1973. We were in Chipaya with Gilles Rivière on 11 September when a school teacher, escaping over the frontier, told us of President Allende's assassination in Santiago de Chile during General Augusto Pinochet's far more bloody and longer-lasting coup, also with US connivance.

During the years 1970 to 1971 Thierry was doing his military service by discovering Bolivia 'with his feet' (he was an ardent walker) and preparing his doctoral thesis on the Chiriguano in the Sucre archives. We became good friends and met up in Europe in 1972 before we both returned to the Andes.

To London and back again: a Chilean expansion, 1971–6

Having found such a field site, the next step might have been to write up a synchronic analysis, present a thesis, publish it and join the academic rat race. But I was not inclined to do that. Apart from anything else, I did not know enough of the history of this extended social unit called Macha, and I felt that to force what I knew into even a moderately synchronic 'community' model would be a distortion. I had to explore further the history, politics and ethnography of this complex social formation, if I wished to do it the justice that the curacas of Macha demanded.

It seemed pointless to stay in London, when I could learn more in the Andes; moreover, the people most interested in my findings lived over the ocean. So after a year of culture shock and writing up seminars at LSE in 1971–2, with welcome support from the Institute of Latin American Studies in Tavistock Square and its director R.A. Humphreys, I was keen to return. In May 1973, with a recommendation from the Peruvian anthropologist Fernando Fuenzalida, I took up a job in the Archaeological Museum of San Miguel de Azapa, which belonged to the Universidad del Norte in the porttown of Arica (Chile).

The museum was a research institute without regular teaching obligations, and it lay some 20 minutes by bus up the Azapa Valley. I always remember the gentle chortling of the irrigation canals and the bi-tonal calling of the cuculís amid the banana palms, olive trees and bourgainvilleas at the museum, where I worked with several Chilean colleagues, including Mario Rivera, Patricia Soto and Jorge Hidalgo, all of us obsessed with the Andes, its archaeology, history and civilisation, and surrounded by the silent, trembling desert.

In San Miguel de Azapa I finished writing a text in Spanish on *yanantin*, a key dualism in Macha and Andean thought and ritual practice, for publication in La Paz, Bolivia (1976). This was then reworked for the Andean special number of *Annales ESC*, published in Paris (1978), edited by Murra and Wachtel, and later brought out in English (Platt, 1986 [1976, 1978, 1980]). I had been thinking about this topic on and off since my discussions with Santiago Carbajal in July 1971 and, on passing through Ithaca in September that year, I had given a talk on Macha, verticality and yanantin amidst the peonies of Murra's garden in Ithaca.

But Arica also meant exposure to archaeology and to the Pacific Ocean. As an ethnographer, I was interested in the *chinchorros* of the fishermen, but also in a new agricultural settlement that was appearing in 1973-4 in the Azapa Valley's headwaters, using water diverted from the international river Lauca, which rose on the Chilean Altiplano bordering with Bolivia. This again led to a study of a 'vertical archipelago', for Pampa Algodonal was an archipelago in the making: four or five groups from different parts of the Altiplano, the pre-cordillera and a valley further south, had converged to render fruitful a stretch of desert in Azapa which the Chilean Agrarian Reform (CORA) had dismissed as 'uncultivable'. It was clear that the Andeans knew their land better than the *santiaguinos*.

One might call this work a 'community study', except that again, as in San Marcos, the components of the community combined horizontal neighbourly relations with vertical links to their dispersed places of origin. The political and land-holding situation was complicated, too, for if some supporters of Salvador Allende's elected government had favoured socialist collectivisation, Pinochet's dictatorship aimed to enforce alienable private ownership. Neither understood the careful balance between heritable possession and collective 'reversionary rights' (I used Gluckman's term) that characterises traditional south Andean land-holding.

In 1975 the study was published in *Chungará*, the museum's journal, and was later used by peasants to defend their autonomy in negotiations with CORA (whose santiaguinos now wished to claim credit for Andean success). A recent visit in January 2015, with Aymara spokeswoman Nancy Alanoca and members from two of the original families I had known, showed me how much has changed: all the different traditional methods of irrigation which I had described, each installed by a different group of settlers and suited to diverse plants and terrains, have today been replaced by Israeli drip-technology under acres of plastic. The increase in production has been exponential, and most families now live in Arica. But their wealth stems from the first founders' 'Andean' perception of a new agricultural opportunity, as those who remember the early days know full well.

From Arica I was able to travel to Iquique, Antofagasta and Atacama. My initial trip was to Antofagasta for the First Chilean Congress of Andean Humanity, organised in July 1973 by Freddy Taberna, Lautaro Nuñez and others. Their aim was to increase the visibility of the Chilean Norte Grande's Andean culture. Here I met with Gabriel Martínez and Verónica Cereceda, then engaged in an ethnographic and weaving project in Isluga on the Iquique Altiplano. Their theatrical experience, and Verónica's love of music, resonated with my father's lifelong operatic passion. Their warmth and enthusiasm, as well as their commitment to the Andes and to anthropology, founded on gripping earlier experiences in Oruro and Lunlaya (Bolivia), spoke both to me and John Murra who was also attending the Congress. John published Verónica's pioneering work on Isluga textiles, in French, in the 1978 *Annales*, and a later version in English in 1986; it did not appear in Spanish until the special number of the museum's journal *Chungará, Revista Antropológica Chilena*, which we compiled in John's memory in 2010 (volume 42, no. 1). Back in Arica, after Pinochet's coup, I used to visit them in Iquique, and sometimes accompanied them to Isluga.

But in January 1976 I was expelled from my Arica job as 'suspicious' (the military had decided I was a *correo comunista* doing subversive work on my trips to the Altiplano).[6] So I went to La Paz to find a new job, before visiting my family in England, where I worked with Olivia, now returned from the field, to produce the first map of the great ayllus of Northern Potosí, published in 1978 in Bolivia, and in *Annales*. Thierry joined us in London and so too did John Murra and Thérèse Bouysse-Cassagne, who was then preparing her thesis in Paris on the ethnohistory of the Bolivian Aymaras. In 1976 the seeds were being sown for our Franco-British ethnohistorical project on the Aymara-speaking confederation, Qaraqara-Charka.

---

6   The military planned to plant a false chauffeur in the university jeep I used, who would leap out just before sending the vehicle over a precipice with me inside it. Fortunately, the Rector Cnl. Hernán Danyau and the Vice-Rector Sergio Giaconi, unhappy with this plan, decided that the only solution was to fire me without explanation. See Sergio Giaconi, *La Universidad del Norte Sede Arica en el periodo 1973–1976. Recuerdos de una burbuja* (MS pdf).

La Paz, Lima, Sucre, Potosí: 1976–83

On returning to La Paz in September 1976, I worked for a year as research associate at the Museum of Ethnography and Folklore (MUSEF), thanks to its director, Hugo Daniel Ruiz. Eager to get back to the ethnohistory of Macha, I began writing an analysis of the *Memorial de Charcas*, an exceptional document published in 1969 by Waldemar Espinoza Soriano, in Chosica, Peru. This document yielded the first evidence that Macha had, in the 16th century, been the leading group in a whole federation of great ayllus (or *repartimientos*) that together composed the south Aymara-speaking Qaraqara 'nation'. This, as we later discovered, stretched from Chayanta to Chichas, and from Quillacas on the Altiplano to the coca fields of Chuquioma near Santa Cruz – an enormous reach. Moreover, it showed that Qaraqara had been closely related to a neighbouring federation called Charka, the capital of which was another historic great ayllu, Sacaca, which still exists today in Northern Potosí. Later we learned that ceremonial visits had been exchanged in the 16th century between the high moiety lords of Macha and Sacaca, each carried by their dependent ayllu headmen on litters.

These discoveries located field studies in Northern Potosí in an altogether wider and deeper historical and cultural context, at the same time as it provided a frame within which new ethnohistorical and field studies might be carried out and the ayllus' changing historical entanglements uncovered – today the research possibilities have increased exponentially due to the involvement of archaeological colleagues.

After our 1976 meeting in London Thierry and I, once back in Bolivia, made many trips together, including one to his own field site in Larecaja where he directed a project for the French Institute of Andean Studies (Lima-Paris) – its first incursion into Bolivia. The last expedition we made together, shortly before his return to Europe in 1979, was to the pre-Hispanic fortress of Oroncota, on Qaraqara's old south-western frontier with the Chiriwana, the latter being the theme of his first South American and Bolivian research.

Thierry was a veritable archive sleuth and bubbled with ideas. He discovered that in the 17th century islands of the Macha and Sacaca tributaries had been planted in Larecaja and Inquisivi in the La Paz department, again showing the interregional reach of Qaraqara and Charka. We debated whether these islands were settled before or under the Incas, or during the colonial period. Thus began our Franco-British effort to visibilise these two ancient confederated 'nations', which we discussed with Murra and Gunnar Mendoza, and which our group (two 'froggies' and two 'rosbifs', as we joked) undertook over the following two decades.

Throughout the 1970s, ethnohistorical initiatives in the southern Andes were stimulated initially by Murra's studies of Lake Titicaca's Lupaqa federation on the basis of the 16th-century *visitas* [colonial inspections]. In this he was joined by many colleagues, including the historian Franklin Pease and the archaeologist Luis Lumbreras in Lima, Udo Oberem and Frank Salomon in Quito, and the ethnohistorians Jorge Hidalgo and Agustín Llagosteras in Chile. In France at the same time Thérèse was working on the Collao federations, Thierry was deciphering the mitimaes and pie-de-monte groups of the eastern Cordillera, Antoinette Molinié was busy with her ethnography of Urubamba in Cuzco, and Nathan Wachtel was working on the Chipayas, while Carmen Bernand and Chantal Caillavet were also in Quito. New Bolivian discoveries were also being made in Pacajes and Carangas by Xavier Albó, Silvia Rivera and Teresa Gisbert, in dialogue with the work of the Bolivian historians Ramiro Condarco and Gunnar Mendoza. These efforts converged with the emerging density of the Qaraqara and Charka ayllus, which Olivia and I reconstructed ethnographically from the bottom up, within the emerging ethnic map of Charcas.

In La Paz in 1970, Marta González had introduced me to Ramiro Molina Barrios. We became good friends. Ramiro and his then wife, the poetess Blanca Wiethüchter, took me to meetings of the La Zona cultural tertulia, in the house of the young painter Juan Conitzer. Here I had met the essayist Juan Cristobal Urioste, the poetess Blanca, the poet Fernando Rosso, the sociologist Silvia Rivera and several others. Meanwhile, with Blanca and Ramiro, I began to visit the house of one of the most interesting contemporary Bolivian writers, the poet and novelist Jaime Saenz, a master of style and a devotee of throwing the dice.

On returning to La Paz in 1976, I talked to Silvia, who was tracing her own descent from the Cusicanquis of 16th-century Pacajes, about how to recover indian history in both the colonial and republican periods, in ways that might help change modes of self-identification in a highly racist Bolivia. In the case of the republican period, the path had been opened by the book by Ramiro Condarco Morales (1965) on the rôle of Zárate Willka and the ayllus during the 1899 Bolivian Civil War. At the same time, we wanted to incorporate the mestizo perspective, and the dimensions of a popular internal market. So in 1976-7 we formed the Avances research group in La Paz, together with Ramiro Molina Barrios, the Aymara historian Roberto Choque, René Arze Aguirre and others. We published two numbers of a short-lived but influential journal, *Avances* (its cover design was by Jaime Saenz). And I think it was in 1977-8 that John Murra also came to Bolivia for a few months, invited to the MUSEF by Hugo Daniel Ruiz. Shortly afterwards Silvia began her pioneering work with Aymara oral historians which led to the emergence of a new 20th-century Aymara ethnohistory (THOA, 1984; Mamani, 1991; Rivera-Cusicanqui, 1991).

My job at the MUSEF came to an end in mid 1977, so between then and 1979 I worked with a World Bank-funded project on the Northern Potosí tin mines at Siglo XX-Catavi, and their articulation with the great ayllus' peasant economies. This gave me and Ramiro, encouraged by our friend and project leader Antonio Birbuet, a chance to investigate peasants' seasonal labour in the tailings, *veneros* and drainage-canals of the mines; and also to run a survey of 500 households, drawn from several ayllus on the Northern Potosí puna, to generate statistical coverage of peasant family production, sales of labour and products, recruitment of extra-familial labour, vertical access to valley maize fields and so on. With this material I was able to show that puna farmers exercising traditional access to these maize fields were richer *and* had stronger market links than those without verticality. This, of course, had not dissuaded peasant unions in provincia Charcas, organised by province and canton by Banduriri near San Pedro de Buena Vista, from trying to detach the Macha valley-dwellers in San Marcos from their puna kin in provincia Chayanta so that they could dispose of their votes. And it must be recognised that they seem to have been largely successful in doing so.

The work with *Avances* also led to the opportunity to open up the new field of 19th-century ethnohistory, which was broached in the journal's second number. This, coupled with my experiences with peasants and miners in Northern Potosí, convinced Heraclio Bonilla, from Lima's Instituto de Estudios Peruanos (IEP), to invite me to join a project he was formulating with Carlos Sempat Assadourian on 'Mining and Economic Space in the Andes'; I was to be responsible for 19th-century Potosí. This was a chance to research the periods before and during the accentuation of internal colonialism in the second half of the century, when the ayllus began to feel the effects of the rise of European racism (Arthur de Gobineau, Herbert Spencer) as transmitted in Bolivia by the 'civilised' élites. At the same time, the 'liberal' shift was reflected in the economic ruin induced by free trade in an increasingly unprotected countryside. When créole plans for agrarian reform, beginning with the Law of Disentailment in 1874, threatened to dissolve the ayllus, a series of rebellions finally exploded in insurrection during the 1899 Bolivian Civil War, giving way to a 20th century marked by indigenous efforts to defend and recover control of their lands, threatened until 1952 by the expansion of the hacienda.

Heraclio suggested I should find a *chambita* [temporary job] while the project was gelling, so in 1979 I spoke to Angel Robles, the Mexican director of the La Paz United Nations office. A short contract gave me the opportunity to examine Northern Potosí indian land and fiscal history in the 19th to 20th centuries. This work, for which the support of the National Archive of Bolivia and its director Gunnar Mendoza was again indispensable, followed on naturally from my fieldwork carried out between 1970 and 1971 in San

Marcos and Liconi Pampa, and it led me to consider ayllu relations with the republican state, situating my ethnographic perspectives in an historical economic context, while the ethnography helped me better understand what was in – and missing from – the documents.

The relationship between the Macha ayllu and the state depended on what I called a 'pact', in which tribute and services were given in exchange for state recognition of indian possession of land. My first glimpse of this relationship had come from conversations with Agustin Carbajal in 1971, although I did not at the time understand the pre-revolutionary antecedents. When I asked him why he and his cabildos continued paying tribute and sending postillions to attend the Tambo in Macha, even though the latter was no longer obligatory by law, he replied: 'It is for our land'.[7] I showed the UN report, written in Spanish in the second half of 1980, to the IEP, where Christine Hunefeldt, Heraclio Bonilla and José Matos Mar encouraged me to publish it in the Institute's *Historia Andina* series. I called it *Estado boliviano y ayllu andino: tierra y tributo en el Norte de Potosí* (1982). A new edition was published in Bolivia in 2016.

Two more years of military dictatorship and narco-tyranny followed (1980–2), during which time I moved to Sucre where I was able to work in the Bolivian National Archive with the wise guidance of Gunnar Mendoza. At the end of each day, when everyone had left, I and Gunnar Mendoza would talk about the day's findings, and Gunnar would make observations and suggest new leads. His knowledge of the national archive, and his devotion to old books and papers, reminded me of my maternal grandfather; both were driven by great clarity of mind together with family, regional and national loyalty.

At that time, Carlos Sempat Assadourian's book on the colonial economic system (1982), gave me a rich new take on Andean colonial and 19th-century history, centred on mining demand, the circulation of silver and the importance of the Andean internal market. The methodological cross-fertilisation between Andean anthropology and economic history, so productive since the 1980s, was partly rooted in Sempat's work and his talks with anthropologists (including Murra) in Lima during our project with the IEP. I participated in these discussions from Sucre, where I worked in collaboration with Antonio Rojas, visiting Lima periodically.

In 1982, Olivia Harris and the historians Brooke Larson and Enrique Tandeter were inspired to plan the first of a series of three Andean conferences, supported by the New York SSRC, to take place in Sucre in 1983. The results of this conference, dedicated to indigenous participation in Andean markets, were published in Cochabamba in a benchmark essay collection (Harris et al. (eds.), 1987). My contribution (*in absentia*, as I moved back to Britain

---

7 Two expressions of this pact written by representatives from two cabildos of the Sullkavi ayllu (Salinas and Cariporco) have just been discovered in the old Curaca Archive (Platt, 2014). The postillion service was not suspended until 1974.

in January 1983) was an ethnohistorical analysis of calendrical movements, festive gatherings, market interventions and tribute payment ceremonies in 19th-century Lípez, on the high south-western Altiplano bordering with Chile, which was based mainly on new data I had found in the Historical Archive of Potosí (1987). This showed the southern limits of Murra's verticality model,[8] which pre-supposes *mitimaes*' [colonists'] direct access to land at different levels, because in Lípez long-distance displacements from the highlands to the Chaco in search of maize did not involve direct control of cultivable land, but were instead based on labour and exchange. Lípez pasturalists and arrieros could therefore be seen as a southern equivalent to the northern, Ecuadorean limits to the model, characterised as 'micro-verticality' by Udo Oberem (1976), and where microecological levels in close proximity could be linked by groups of *mindalaes* [intermediaries] and the use of *tianguis* [markets] (Salomon, 1978).

In relating my research on ayllus to the wider economy, both national and global, I was also influenced by the critique we had developed in 1972 with London colleagues Kate Young, Felicity Nock, Joel Kahn and Josep Llobera. This led to the formation of the London Alternative Anthropology Group that in turn gave rise to the journal *Critique of Anthropology*, based at Goldsmith's College, London. Equally, my connection with *History Workshop Journal*, which came about in 1984 through Olivia Harris, strengthened my understanding of 'history from below'. These critiques led me to research the wider contexts of Macha, Northern Potosí and the Southern Andes, both in the early colonial period and in the 19th and 20th centuries, by relating rural to mining histories, and connecting Andean anthropologies with global processes of capital accumulation and change.

Wales, Scotland, Spain and back to Bolivia, 1983-98

In 1983 I returned with my family to a cottage on the top of a Welsh mountain, which had been my mother's. There, I continued working and publishing on 19th-century Potosí, while supporting the Llangattock Hillside community's battles for a mains water supply and our resistance to being turned into a playground for city-dwellers. Looking into local and Welsh rural and mining history was a strange mirror in which to view Bolivian concerns; but we were there when Thatcher crushed the Miner's Strike in 1984-5, awakening echoes of violent Andean manifestations and repressions. I also discovered the existence of a Commoners' Association to regulate the use of collective summer pastures on the hilltop, under the aegis of the duke of Beaufort. It was intriguing to

---

8   Murra (1973) had invited researchers to determine his model's geopolitical limits, rather than simply providing counter-examples. From the coast, Maria Rostworowski (1972) had already introduced the idea of horizontal displacements to counter the highland emphasis on verticality.

find that a partial agrarian reform had been carried out in the 1920s giving the freehold to tenants while keeping rights to the subsoil in the duke's hands. I began to think about the meaning of *comunario* (a word sometimes used in Bolivia for an ayllu member or *tributario*). In the Welsh variant of verticality, a commoner had the right to summer pastures on the hilltop for as many sheep as he could winter in the valley below. At an annual dinner hosted by the duke, any commoner could stand up and report on what transpired in his neck of the woods. A commoner, it seemed, was a person who had a right to speak in communal assemblies and demand redress.

In 1984 I travelled from Wales to Quito to teach in the Andean master's programme run by the Facultad Latinoamericana de Ciencias Sociales (FLACSO). Here I met up with another good friend and colleague, Andrés Guerrero. Andrés had published in *Avances 2* an important essay on the decline of the pre-capitalist and capitalist hacienda in Otávalo (1978). I had heard him speak in 1982 at a seminar in the IEP, Lima. Since Quito, we have debated, on many occasions in Madrid, the power of the word, the reproduction of 'community' and the limits of 'domination'.

In 1985, while I was still living in Wales, the two froggies and two rosbifs won two years' Franco-British funding (ESRC-CNRS) to pursue our ethnohistorical studies of the Qaraqara and the Charka. Our aim was not simply to seek long-term 'continuities', but to recognise the profound historicity of populations living in time at every moment, and the way in which persistences may be combined with transformations and resignifications. But it was not until 14 years after Thierry's tragic death in 1992 that the three survivors of our group finally gave birth to a heavy collection of essays and source-documents: *Qaraqara-Charka* (Platt et al., 2011 [2006]).

This 1,000-page book investigated the formation and incorporation of the two federations into the Inca and Spanish empires, and includes previously unpublished early colonial documents on Sacaca, Macha and neighbouring groups, drawn from several international archives. The complexity and extent of South Andean social and religious organisation in the region of Qaraqara, Charka and the wider Inca Charcas province, before and after the Spanish invasion, was presented together with the hitherto-unknown evidence for it.[9]

My approach to Macha and the southern Andes thus became one of multiple takes, expressed in several partial studies, a procedure which has many epistemological advantages, in that it allows the researcher to escape the misleading, often ahistorical and inevitably ephemeral unity bestowed on 'communities' in most 'community studies'. Political accusations of essentialism

---

9   A second edition of *Qaraqara-Charka* was published in La Paz in 2011, shortly after another tragic death, that of Olivia Harris on 9 April 2009.

(fashionable in the 1990s, and still ongoing) are dispelled as soon as one brings different historical perspectives to bear on the picture.

I will mention one further piece of fieldwork I pursued in Macha in 1994-5, after I had joined the anthropology department at the University of St Andrews, Scotland, and was participating in a European Commission project in Bolivia (1994-5), designed by a feminist collective at Trinity College Dublin with the aim of studying traditional and appropriate methods of childbirth in the context of high rates of maternal mortality. Here, I was responsible for the rural Quechua-speaking component, with two native-speaking colleagues; and my friends at Liconi Pampa received us and facilitated a fine set of interviews.

This fieldwork differed from that which I had previously practised. It comprised a clear set of pre-defined research questions, 30+ Quechua-speaking interviewees, systematic taping of all interviewees with their background information, followed by the tricky but rewarding experience of transcribing the interviews into written Quechua (taking as a guide Dennis Tedlock and Dell Hymes's ethnopoetic formatting style), and then translating them into Andean Spanish to create parallel texts, with footnotes and vocabulary. This process yielded scholarly base materials for collation and interpretation. Though helped by native speakers, I found myself sometimes having to correct them as we listened to the tapes together. I realised, again, that it was necessary to know at least enough of the local language to be able to listen to and correct the transcriptions of native speakers, who are often tempted to transmit what they think the interviewee *should have said*, rather than what they have *actually* said.

Once again, in this project, there was little in the way of a 'community studies' dimension, since we talked only to those willing to pass on their knowledge and experience of childbirth; on the other hand, I had already done fieldwork there, and this project allowed a crucial (and generally omitted) aspect of cabildo life to be examined and contrasted with that in other parts of the country, with potentially significant implications for women's well-being. In-house seminars in Sucre expanded the focus by allowing different components of the macro-project to be presented and discussed; we were struck by the defence of caesareans given by one experienced nurse. The work produced a new perspective, that of Macha women struggling in childbirth, the practices of rural midwives, and the uneven, sometimes dangerous relationships of women with the foetus, with men, and with the state. Romantic assumptions of maternal universality were undermined, while articulating a wealth of specialised Quechua birthing language, practices and ideas in relation to other kinds of ethnographic and ethnohistorical discourse (particularly religious) with which I was already familiar (Platt, 2001).

Conclusion: the battle of the maps

Part of the *Avances* group's aim in La Paz during 1977 was to provide a space for reflection on the history of internal colonialism and of colonised peoples from their own points of view (they did not consider themselves 'colonised', rather victims of flagrant acts of injustice by lower-level officials). This allowed us to question the narrow Eurocentric and liberal-progressive (postcolonial) vision of the traditional créole guardians of the state. I will end with a practical illustration of this narrowness, because it leads to a wider consideration of a country which, although differing a great deal from Peru, is similar in the intensity of the social and political violence which has marked it (and to some extent still does).

The peasant *sindicatos* [rural trades-unions] that developed in rural Northern Potosí between 1952 and 1964 were MNR supporters. Some were inspired by the mining unions in Siglo XX, others by the Cochabamba peasant unions (the Agrarian Reform Law, which did not consider the ayllus, was signed in 1953 in Ucureña). In Macha and neighbouring ayllus the unions were often controlled by town mestizos, and tended to reproduce town attempts, prior to and since the 19th century, to dominate the ayllus which were far superior in numbers. Apart from the old silver-refining mills around Colquechaca, there were few haciendas in provincia Chayanta. Following on from earlier attempts at agrarian reform in the 19th century (Platt, 1982), many mestizos wanted to dissolve the ayllus, abolish their authorities and replace them with sindicatos controlled from the towns through the system of centrals, subcentrals and dirigentes. Between 1954 and 1961 don Agustín, who had hoped to continue collecting the tribute for the new revolutionary government (which the Carbajal family supported), was marginalised by the MNR local authorities (subprefect, corregidors and sindicatos), although he remained a widely respected elder, awaiting the ideal moment to return.

The curaca was brought back in 1961 by Paz Estenssoro and the Potosí prefect when it became evident that only he, and not the unions, commanded sufficient legitimacy among the ayllus to ensure the collection of the tribute; and his remit was once again to deliver the money to the departmental treasury, and not to the subprefects or sindicatos. Nevertheless, the curaca proceeded in 1963 to organise a written *Pronunciamiento de los campesinos de Macha* [Pronouncement by the Macha peasants], replete with the fingerprints of his supporting authorities, denouncing Paz Estenssoro and the flagrant corruption of the MNR dirigentes in Macha town. This move prepared local support for General René Barrientos Ortuño's coup in 1964, and then his candidature in 1966. The delivery of tribute to the Potosí treasury continued thereafter throughout Banzer's dictatorship (1971–8), and for several years after don Agustín's death in 1985 under the government of the new curaca, his son Gregorio Carbajal.

After 1976, towards the end of the Banzer regime, a new set of unions began to be fostered by the Movimiento de Izquierda Revolucionaria (Revolutionary Left Movement, MIR) in the mining town of Ocuri on the southern puna edge of ayllu Macha. With Belgian funding to support the Tomas Katari Polytechnic Institute (IPTK), a project which came to include the only hospital in the region equipped with an operating theatre, the MIR also wanted to mobilise votes during the elections held in 1978 and 1982. From 1985 a new split brought the Movimiento Bolivia Libre (Free Bolivia Movement, MBL) to power in Ocurí. Following the MNR's and MIR's examples, the MBL also aimed to replace the ayllus and cabildos with a syndical organisation based on the 'community'. So what did they understand by 'community'?

It so happens that I have a map of the region given me in the 1980s by two Belgian volunteers working with the IPTK. It shows the space occupied by the Macha ayllu without any moieties, ayllus or cabildos. The only indications of population are little black dots that represent named hamlets and individual houses. All these hamlets were given the label of 'community'! One might have expected them at least to have mapped the cabildos (sometimes referred to by the indians themselves as 'communities'). But no: the only communities recognised by this syndical organisation were those of the extended family.

In the context of a struggle to impose political control over the peasants, the situation is understandable. The cabildos were sites for reproducing the indian system of rural authorities, from the alcaldes and *cobradores* [collectors] of the cabildo to the jilancos of the ayllu and the curaca of the moiety. The alcaldes changed annually and the collectors every six months, and all landholders had to fulfil these services to the state and the cabildo to confirm their rights to cabildo land. Through this rotating system of *turnos forzosos* [obligatory turns] the cabildo remained sovereign within its territory, while the curaca mediated between the cabildos, the ayllus and the departmental treasury. In this direct democracy decisions were taken by local consensus and everyone had to take their turn at being a cabildo authority (Platt, 2014).

None of this interested the MBL in Ocuri, whose aim was for themselves to accumulate regional votes for their party through recruiting extended families into the sindicatos. In this way, they and their local dirigentes worked as part of a 'civilisational' mission to undermine the curaca's autonomy and the rural system of direct democracy. Their attempt to recruit the 18th-century indian leader Tomas Katari for their cause, by taking his name for their organisation, was given the lie when they attempted to ignore the ayllus that Katari himself had defended back in 1781.

In 1991, the MIR president Jaime Paz Zamora legally abolished payment of the tribute, though this did not take automatic effect in the countryside. But in 1994 don Gregorio Carbajal was forced by the MBL sindicatos in the municipal town of Colquechaca to resign from his post as curaca. Gregorio had taken over from his father Agustín before the latter's death (his elder brother Santiago had died in 1977), and he made a valiant effort to keep things going, as was confirmed in many interviews before his own death in December 2014, and by the documents in the Curacal archive which he maintained, following his father's example. His last receipts from the treasury, which continue up to 1987, show him paying big sums for an ever-shrinking number of cabildos. This was a time of colossal inflation, again under President Siles Suazo; in Leconi Pampa, long bundles of elasticated banknotes were piled into wheelbarrows for transportation.

The last straw was Gonzalo Sánchez de Lozada's 1994 Law of Popular Participation, a neoliberal decentralising measure which threw money and new rules at a complex situation without trying to understand it. Municipal authorities in Colquechaca, dominated by the parties, were strengthened at the cost of the rural authorities and their shrinking fiscal arrangement with the state. The convergence of the MIR's, MBL's and Goni's anti-ayllu policies, following in the early MNR's footsteps, is remarkable, and the explanation probably lies, at least in part, in the blind 'progressivism' shared from both the right and left by these disparate parties. To them, the ayllus represented a survival from a neocolonial, pre-revolutionary past. But what the curaca sought was not a party, but a state whose departmental authorities would be willing to receive the tribute he collected on behalf of his cabildos, in order to defend the ayllu's relative autonomy. Don Agustín was thus a force for state formation, consolidation and reproduction, on the basis of direct democracy; not for party rivalries in a system of representative democracy. The basis for misunderstanding between parties and ayllus was complete.

In response to the MBL's map, others were motivated to try and draw it differently, in a last-ditch attempt to gain recognition for the system of ayllus, cabildos and moieties, and the bottom-up form of direct popular democracy it represented. Diego Pacheco's unpublished map of Macha was drawn in the early 1990s: it was an attempt, on the basis of much careful fieldwork, to represent in two colour groups, each comprising five shaded colours, the distribution of the two moieties and the five ayllus in puna and valley.

Shortly afterwards another map was made with satellite precision by an EC-funded project carried out by Fernando Mendoza and Felix Patzi (1997) (see figure 7.7). This showed the long strip of territory making up the great Macha ayllu, with the moieties contrasted in orange and green, and the cabildo names sprinkled over it, sometimes with their boundaries included. Unfortunately, there is no sign on this map of the ten historic ayllus, five in each moiety, into which the cabildos are grouped.

In 2009 I published a detailed map of the mixed-up ayllu and cabildo holdings in San Marcos de Miraflores, a revised and redrawn version of

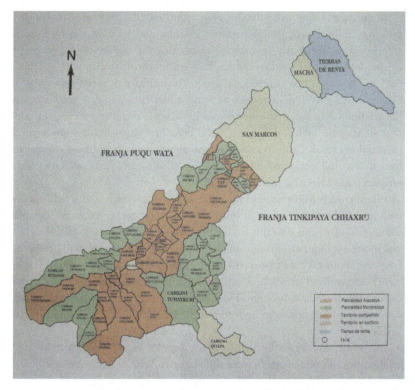

Figure 7.7. Map of Macha territory, with moieties and cabildos (Mendoza and Patzi, 1997)

one initially published in 1996, in which I combined information from my own fieldwork and that of Mendoza and Patzi (2009b). The data and their representation would be more precise if done by indigenous cartographers, although this version was as accurate as possible with all our data coming from conversations with local residents.

Maps are, of course, deeply political documents and they can have the disadvantage of fixing boundaries which would otherwise be flexible. What is included and what omitted also reveals their intentionality. Today the web carries hundreds of political maps of nation-states that obliterate alternative ways of representing their lands and populations. But regional and local maps can be equally misleading. The MBL map of Macha was an attempt to erase the complexities of a traditional organisation that the party thought impeded their own system of syndical organisation. Hence the importance of the efforts made in the 1990s by Pacheco, and by Mendoza and Patzi, even if there is still room for improvement – provided the MBL's misrepresentation of hamlets as 'communities' is left firmly to one side.

In the countryside today the discussion continues. In 2009 one of Santiago's sons was collector for the Pichichuwa cabildo, and he held the traditional tribute-paying ceremony in Liconi Pampa. But the money no longer went to the departmental treasury, which had relinquished its claim; it was now paid to the sindicatos controlled by the Movimiento al Socialismo (MAS). Yet the MAS government refuses to recognise or communicate directly with the traditional indian rural authorities in Macha, preferring to 'ensure' the peasant vote through loyal unions' local branches, whose leaders are beyond the cabildo's reach. In respect of peasant direct democracy, history seems to have turned full circle and returned to the MNR's early years, along with its offspring: the MIR, the MBL and Goni.

I have tried in this chapter to keep close to my experience as a fieldworker with the Macha people, while showing the reasons for my need to think 'beyond the community', and how this led me to situate historically the cabildos, ayllus and moieties of Qaraqara's old capital. This has led me to understand better the long-term political conflicts in which the ayllus of Macha and Northern Potosí have been involved in colonial, republican and post-revolutionary times, and the changes these have brought. However, I have not referred here to the work on money, mining and refining technologies that this research programme has involved.

It is worth noting, finally, that, over the decades, local people's own ideas of temporality and periodisation have also changed. When I first went to visit the Carbajales in 1971, several people told me the well-known legend of the three *tyimpus* [ages], probably influenced by Joachimism: 1) the ancestral Chullpas who lived under the moon; 2) the rise of the Inca and Christian sun under which we still live; and 3) the future age of the Holy Spirit, which many suspected would arrive in the year 2000. When I asked what would happen then, people were uncertain: the 'time of the ayllus' might be beginning, I was told, but the age might also bring in the 'time of the mestizos'. New miracles began to appear. Shortly after the year 2000, Goni was thrown out and in 2005 the sindicato leader Evo Morales came to power on the MAS's shoulders. And so in 2015, I was given a slightly different version of the present: another of Santiago Carbajal's sons told me that they now live in the 'time of the sindicatos'.

Visions of past and future change as time passes and history unfolds. The ayllus in Macha are today on the back foot, due to pressure from the sindicatos over so many decades. Yet, in neighbouring Tinkipaya, the ayllus are making a comeback (Nicolás, 2015). Perhaps the Macha cabildos will finally end up as 'communities', each under the control of a dirigente; perhaps the cabildos will fragment into kinship groups, to the sindicatos' satisfaction; or perhaps in some parts the traditional cabildo and ayllu authorities will persist in parallel. At present, however, it seems unlikely that the valley maize-lands in San Marcos and Carasi in Charcas province, where my long-term exploration of the ayllu began, will again depend on the ayllu authorities in Chayanta province. As the ayllu and cabildos become forgotten in San Marcos, will the canton finally morph into what, one day, some will want to call a 'community'?

8. In love with *comunidades*

Enrique Mayer

Part of my chapter title is borrowed from my friend Jaime Urrutia (1992) who used it in his article 'Comunidades campesinas y antropología: historia de un amor (casi) eterno', which demonstrates how the subject matter's trajectory and the political/ideological discussions around it are quite different from what the European-American ethnological community believes. In the 1920s it was infused with the intellectual political/cultural movement *indigenismo* together with the ideas of reform-minded lawyers who thought that with appropriate legislation they could resolve what was known as the problem of the indian. The Marxist awakenings in Peru accompanied musings on the possibilities that indigenous 'primitive' communities could convert into socialist cooperatives. The aftermath of the Mexican Revolution also had an impact when President Lázaro Cárdenas implemented the Mexican *ejido* [communal land] which Peruvians copied. The Mexican government also created an international organisation in 1940 called the Instituto Indigenista Interamericano for which I worked in Mexico from 1979–81. It had affiliates in all Latin American countries with significant indigenous populations. The Instituto Indigenista Peruano sponsored applied anthropology projects which sent Peruvian anthropologists to the field to write reports on indigenous peoples' living conditions in the 1950s. They were written in the style of bureaucratic positivism derived from design intervention programme guidelines.

The legislative background to the creation of *comunidades indígenas* comes with President Leguía and his 1929 Constitution, which granted them collective land in perpetuity. Dora Mayer (no relation, but the daughter of a Hamburg merchant resident in Callao) together with Pedro Zulen (a Chinese Peruvian) worked with the Asociación Pro Indígena to help indian villages achieve official recognition. Dora was an intellectual who became a supporter of José Carlos Mariátegui, the Peruvian Socialist party founder, whose seminal essays linking the 'problem of the *indio*' to that of the land were written in 1928 (1971). This piece became the political reference for a whole century. So much so, that the recent uprising of the Partido Comunista del Perú's Maoist faction considered itself to be following the '*Shining Path* that Mariátegui had laid out', a description which became its sinister nickname. Anthropology as an academic subject was a latecomer to these conversations starting in 1944 with volume two of the *Handbook of South American Indians* which covered the Andes (Steward (ed.), 1963). Its chapters were principally written by scholars in US universities. Luis E. Valcárcel, a Cuzco scholar, was instrumental in linking Peruvian institutions with US- and European-based academic interests in the peoples of the Andes (Rénique, 2013).

My participation in this bicultural milieu underscores a somewhat unique lifelong active involvement in that I have straddled both contexts. I worked in academic settings in Peru and the United States, debating with the Anglo-Saxon scholarly community while at the same time being involved in Peruvian perspectives. My publications are in both languages, although I daresay that different interpretations are possible depending on whether the reader is Peruvian or an American/English scholar.

Looking back on 45 years of research in the Andes I now assess how each of my studies provided a bridge for the next phase with new questions and different methodologies. My initiation to the profession was a year-long fieldwork venture in Tangor for my PhD thesis. For the next project, I constructed land use maps to help understand the dynamic relationships between comunidades in a regional context where environmental conditions play a significant role. I detailed how households and community manage their commons[1] and how they rule themselves. And I began to track how comunidades were affected by national policies; with the see-saw implementation of legislation, development projects, agrarian reforms and neoliberal transformations. In the 1980s, with Stephen Brush and Carl Zimmerer, the team assessed how genetic erosion of potato varieties is affected by environment, household consumption patterns and market forces. In the 1990s I dedicated a decade to studying the agrarian reform (the primary beneficiaries of this were the comunidades). Throughout all of this, my love for comunidades has stemmed from an admiration of what it is they can achieve as one of the world's examples of collective land holdings, a self-organised group that has developed long-term survival tactics.

How I was turned into an Andeanist

I was born in 1944 of German Jewish refugees from Hamburg, who settled in Huancayo, in Peru's central highlands. It was a thriving market town in the Mantaro Valley situated 3,200 metres above sea level at the end of the highest wide-gauge railroad in the world. To my parents, who constructed a modified foreign enclave version of their lives in Huancayo with father's hardware store, mother's lush vegetable garden, uncle's dairy farm and aunt's handicraft

---

1 Shared resources in which each stakeholder has an equal interest. Usage is derived from the English legal term for areas of common land, which are also known as 'commons' (source: Wikipedia).

workshop, the local social order was clear. The people they had to deal with – the town's merchants, lawyers, doctors, politicians, mechanics, carpenters, plumbers and city folk – were 'locals'. In German we called them *hiesigen* [those who are from here]. They spoke Spanish, called themselves *gente* or Peruvians and some were part of the town elite. Behind our backs they called us *gringos*, not always with hostility. They were not necessarily particularly welcome in our intimate German-speaking household, although our lunch table was always open to people my father had sought out, among them travelling salesmen, miners, engineers, foreign correspondents, priests and tourists picked up at the railway station. These people were foreigners like us. Our home was a cosmopolitan centre.

Then there were the indios, although we hardly ever used that term. The most immediate were our maids, washerwomen, gardeners and my uncle's farm workers or my aunt's skilled hand weavers. They wore distinctive peasant dresses and hats and spoke Quechua and Spanish. They treated us with great respect and we children responded politely and addressed them using the terms *don* or *doña*. They came from villages in the valley, had trades such as braiding our garden chairs with reeds collected from a lake, or they looked for temporary work. We liked the indios more than the town's gente, but they kept their distance and knew their place in the hierarchy. For that reason they aroused my curiosity. I would sit on the low garden wall separating our compound from the street and watch the indios' comings and goings for hours. On Sundays, when there was a huge fair in town, I observed from my perch how women coming in from the countryside would squat, take out shoes from their carrying cloths and put them on to enter the city. One could see this hurt their feet because they soon started hobbling.

After high school in Peru, my parents arranged for me to attend an English grammar school in a north London suburb, after which I studied anthropology and economics at the London School of Economics (LSE), 1963–6. I had already discovered anthropology in the public library and read with fascination about African, Asian, Himalayan, Middle Eastern peoples. At LSE I quickly realised that I was good at the technique of ethnographic observation and I was pleased when my professors and fellow students listened with interest to my descriptions of what I had seen in Huancayo. I was trained in structural functionalism; mainly, explaining observed customs in terms of their utility in the ethnographic present and not as fossil residues. At that time London had few options for Latin America and I therefore applied to universities in the United States and was happy when Cornell University in Ithaca, a small town in upstate New York, accepted my application and granted me a scholarship for graduate studies.

My stay in Cornell, 1966–74, coincided with that university's unprecedented interest in Peru. Professor Alan Holmberg had developed a project in Vicos, a hacienda that was being intensely studied but was also the site of a project to change dependent indio hacienda serfs into a free indigenous comunidad (Greaves et al. (eds.), 2010; Mayer, 2010). The Vicos Project in the department of Ancash was famous and I was keen to be part of it. But when I arrived in Cornell, I discovered that Professor Holmberg had died of leukaemia and the Vicos connection had been closed. A Yale graduate, Holmberg had done his first fieldwork with the Sirionó people in the Bolivian rainforest and surveyed the jungles in that country for potential rubber plantations for the US war effort. He had then worked in Peru and developed applied anthropology studies after the 1950s, based on the Vicos experience.

In 1968 Cornell hired John V. Murra to replace Holmberg. Murra and Holmberg could not have been more different in their approaches or orientations. Murra, a Jew born in Odessa, grew up in Romania where his family had fled the October Revolution. As a teenager he got into trouble for supporting his Marxist school teacher, was sent to Chicago and later joined the Lincoln Brigade of American Volunteers in the Spanish Civil War. Upon his return he earned a PhD from the University of Chicago with a famous study about the economic system of the Inca state. Unable to leave the US during the McCarthy period of communist witch hunts, he sat in New York's public library taking the most careful notes from the 16th-century Spanish chroniclers. His fluent Spanish, intuitive understanding of the chronicler's accounts of the Incas in the context within which they wrote, combined with his personal experience of Russian-Soviet imperialism, gave him an understanding of what it means to resist an European invasion and it coloured his approach.

Murra was behind the revival of studies that stressed the *longue durée* (Harris, 2000a, p. 7) of cultural continuities from the present all the way to pre-Hispanic times, a research strategy that Ferreira, following Harris, calls 'long-termist' approaches to Andean anthropology (2012, p. 27). Murra also used the term '*lo andino*' to express how a whole civilisation of people were resisting as best they could the European invasion, taxation, religious conversion and the reordering of their society, and this term had resonance in the 1970s among scholars, indigenous leaders and politicians. The discussion by Olivia Harris (2000a, p. 12) of how this approach became a politicised academic issue with pro and con positions provides an excellent background for understanding why this was 'hot stuff' in the 1970s.

Murra's skill as an ethnohistorian lay in the extraction from archival sources of new information on the Inca empire, their society, customs and mores combined with a Polanyist intepretation on the economies of early empires (1957) highlighting the role of reciprocity, tribute and redistribution over and above market mechanisms. In the 1960s Murra directed such a project in the region of Huánuco, because he had a detailed 16th-century village-by-village and house-to-house census, carried out in 1562, only 25 years after the conquest, recording taxation matters, rights, privileges and the obligations of *encomenderos* [Spaniards granted the right to receive tribute from indian subjects] tribute-paying labourers] *kurakas* [local chiefs] and the *runa* [common people]. That project conducted archaeological excavations of the Inca administrative centre of Huánuco Pampa, followed the Inca roads, and the bridges and *tambos* [way stations], and surveyed the villages subject to the *encomienda* [taxation in goods and labour], assisted by student social anthropologists who conducted fieldwork in villages that could be traced back to that document. Murra arrived in Cornell with César Fonseca, one of the students who became a good friend and colleague of mine. The decision that I would conduct fieldwork in that area for my PhD became obvious after listening to César's accounts. We were to work together for many years in various projects until his untimely death in an absurd accident at Cuzco airport in 1986.

An integral aspect of Murra's thinking at that time was the concept of 'verticality' (1972). By this, he meant that Andeans tended to colonise a maximum number of vertically stacked ecological niches for direct production, transportation and redistribution. His pre-Hispanic evidence showed that the model operated at the sub-Inca ethnic group level – *kurakazgos* or *señoríos* – such as the Chupaychu, Lupaqa, or Cantas. The main products were salt, cotton, capsicum peppers, coca, cotton fibre, wood and feathers – items not easily produced in their highland home territories. These items could also have been obtained through trade, but evidently were not. A paper I wrote for Murra's seminar concluded that verticality and trade had coexisted in pre-Hispanic times (2002, chapter 2; 2013). Armed with questions about verticality, I carried out my fieldwork in 1970–1, in the Tangor community situated in the *quebrada* [ravine] of Chaupiwaranga, Daniel Carrión province, department of Pasco in Peru's central highlands.

I came down from Tangor in August 1971 for the XXXIX Congress of Americanists in Lima, hosted by José Matos Mar from the Instituto de Estudios Peruanos (IEP) and inaugurated by President Juan Velasco Alvarado, the leftist general whose revolutionary military government undertook a series of programmes favouring the indigenous populations of the Andes including a radical agrarian reform. In a session organised by Billie Jean Isbell, at which I presented a paper on barter relationships between the villagers of Tangor and others in the region, Murra and R. Tom Zuidema were present. Also participating was Henri Favre, a French professor from the Centre National de la Recherche Scientifique (CNRS) in Paris. He critiqued our papers, accusing us of taking selective aspects from our field data as evidence for long-term continuities without proof or discussion of the mechanisms that might be at work. He also attacked us for ignoring other more recent aspects of historical change taking place in the Andes. Favre had in mind the revolutionary takeovers of land from haciendas and other aspects of modernisation, which he said were of high importance but did not hark back to pre-Hispanic times. Thus the battle grounds pro and anti 'lo andino' were already clearly drawn and continued to provoke debate for two decades. For me the situation was ambiguous. While enthused with Murra's ideas, I was not anti-modernisation nor, by implication, anti-revolutionary and intrigued by Velasco's agrarian reform. I thought that the dividing line was unimportant because, as I saw it, I could be in both camps.

My paper on bartering 'Un carnero por un saco de papas...' (2002, chapter 5; 1971) became an instant success. It was part of my village ethnography of Tangor, published by the Cornell Latin American Dissertation Series (1974). The dissertation satisfied the requirements of a community study in the tradition of cultural anthropology. While it pursued one line of research, namely reciprocity, I argued that it was so central to the community's structure that by following it through all levels, it would provide a holistic picture of the place (see figure 8.1). I also contributed to the historical continuities crusade with two articles. In 'Censos insensatos' I reviewed the practice of census taking in Inca, colonial and my contemporary field surveys (1972). Much later, I wrote an ethnographic analogy about Tangor projecting from the present back to the past, to the day in 1562 when the Spanish *visitador* inspected the same village (1984; 2002, chapter 3). It was a resourceful application of long-termist ethnographic writing because it used aspects of fiction by imagining monologues in attempts to overcome the 16th-century documentation's shortcomings. Its aim was to understand the transition from Inca times to Spanish encomienda rule.

In 1970 I was hired to teach at the Catholic University in Peru and invited to collaborate on publications with the IEP in Lima, which led to an edited volume in Spanish on reciprocity that included my own research as well as collaborations of other young anthropologists who had also done their community studies in various regions of Peru (Alberti and Mayer, 1974; Mayer, 2002, chapter 4). In another initiative, one focusing on kinship and marriage, Ralph Bolton and I coordinated a symposium on this topic at the 1972 American Anthropological Association (AAA) meetings, which was published in English (Bolton and Mayer (eds.), 1977) and Spanish (1980).

These publications served to underscore the commonalities and differences of aspects of Andean village life. Made possible by the boom in funding for young PhD candidates, a great wealth of detailed ethnographic description, analysis and interpretation was produced on many a community in the Andes.

Figure 8.1. Tangor carguyoj with his servant and friends carrying chicha to the plaza for distribution to the whole comuna, 1969. Photo: E. Mayer.

These works also helped in establishing for two decades the leading paradigms for Andean anthropology (Salomon, 1982). By paying close attention to the local details but with the optics of comparative work along common themes, our scholarly work was sustained and productive and helped establish our reputations and the Andes as a particularly interesting geographical area for research, comparable to Mesoamerica. We used to have Andean dinners as part of the AAA meetings, requiring restaurant reservations and long tables where on occasions arch rivals ended up sitting next to each other and were forced to engage in polite conversation. The whole event was cohesive, made sense and was great fun.

I would emphasise three particular features of that period: first, the Andean area included Ecuador, southern Colombia, Peru, Bolivia, northern Argentina and Chile. It looked for commonalities not only with the deep Inca past, but across a wider geographical area, defining and elaborating an Andean Culture Area in line with the *Handbook of South American Indians* (Steward (ed.), 1963 [1946–50]).

Second, each study was village-based but drew upon the others and each concluded with wider implications drawn by the scholars themselves focusing on the internal mechanisms of what was going on inside the villages at the time we were studying them. This approach did not deny or ignore outside influences but they were considered only when assessing what effects these may have had on the internal mechanisms.

Third, it stressed differences between what we saw and described and the surrounding and larger non-indigenous national Spanish-speaking cultures, whether or not we labelled them mestizo. Eventually this approach triggered a searing critique by Orin Starn (1991; 1992a) along with the corresponding rebukes it provoked (Starn 1992b; 1994; Roseberry, 1995). Starn began by acknowledging the power and influence of the Andeanist anthropology carried out by the generation preceding his own. His analogy of our Andeanism to Orientalism (Said, 1978) is contrived and unfair because our observations were the result of the painstaking minutiae of rigorous ethnography, while Said's work implied that Europeans saw only themselves darkly reflected in the looking glass of the essentialised Other. What brought his critique to the forefront was the Shining Path insurgency of the late 1980s, which Starn claimed we had missed (that is, the essentialising romantically blinkered Andeanists).

In my essay 'Peru in deep trouble: Mario Vargas Llosa's "Inquest in the Andes" reexamined' (1992; revised in Spanish in Mayer, 2012), I focused on the difficulties of essentialising indigenous village life, taking on the report by the famous writer, Mario Vargas Llosa (1983), about the events of that year in Uchuraccay, in the Ayacucho area. On 26 January eight journalists were killed by a bewildered crowd of comuneros because they confused the journalists clad in western clothing with Shining Path guerrillas coming to attack their village to avenge the executions of Shining Path members carried out a few days previously. Vargas Llosa used the phrase *Perú profundo* [deep Peru] – code for the prejudiced view of the indians as ignorant, cornered, persecuted and discriminated against – that nonetheless represented Peru's profound 'salt of the earth' identity. This, according to him, was quite different from *Perú oficial* [official Peru] – code for civilised, Hispanic and with a modern identity. With these words he implied that the comunidad of Uchuraccay members should be commiserated with and forgiven. I also argued in that article that Starn's criticism of Andeanist anthropologists and Vargas Llosa shared the same essentialising tendencies about indians but from opposite ends of a value scale. Starn accused American Andeanists of essentialising due to our admiration of indigenousness, while Vargas Llosa did so because he condescendingly commiserated with them. Few people realised at the time, that the actions of the Uchuraccay comuneros were the first organised bellicose and consensually agreed-upon *rondas campesinas* [peasant self-defence], and these defences eventually defeated – with the help of the armed forces – the Shining Path insurgency. In *Night Watch* (1999), Starn's own ethnographic study of similar peasant defences in a town in northern Peru, he painted this picture in present-day needs and actions. As far as the essentialisms critiqued in that article, the argument also implied that romantic involvement with the peoples under study was incompatible with the objectivity that the title of this chapter denies.

Agriculture, maps and local history

My next research project took me back to the basics of 'verticality' along the ecological gradient of the Andes characterised by a rapid succession of altitudinal ecological zones. César Fonseca and I studied the Cañete Valley from its source in the highlands to its estuary in the Pacific in 1979. Comunidades were located in the middle altitude 2,000 to 3,800 metres above sea level. They were created in the 16th century by the Spanish administration as *reducciones de indios* from what were probably scattered settlements. There was another set of pastoralists' comunidades above the limits of agriculture who originated from the more recent breakaway herder developments. These herders were seeking independence from their mother communities from around 1900. Similarly, other breakaway communities in the lowland areas near the main river's banks sought to obtain greater control over irrigation water to respond to a developing fruit and vegetable market in Lima. (In the Cañete Valley each original comunidad was coterminous with the smaller tributary that emptied into the Cañete collector on the right and left sides as the river flowed south-westwards down towards the sea).

In that study we defined the agricultural systems for the whole valley. We measured their upper and lower limits, studied production techniques and paid attention to communal control over production. Using low-altitude black-and-white aerial photographs, we created a land use map of agricultural zones for the whole valley (see figure 8.2). The quantum jump from studying one comunidad in the valley to 49 allowed a comparative approach. Each comunidad had high puna pastures, higher zone potato fields, lower zone *mahuay* potato fields which were rapid maturing, and most important, fantastic maize terraces and fruit orchards. They had complex communal irrigation systems. The comunidad controlled production in higher zones through rules and regulations that are similar to the management of a commons (Ostrom, 1990) but the degree of communal intervention varied from tight control and highly communal agricultural rules to relaxed supervision and near-complete private property relations. These changed according to the ecological gradient – the higher zones were more communal, the lower ones less so (like Switzerland, studied by Netting, 1976). We also found that communal control over scarce water controlled what was grown in the irrigated fields. In some respects these systems could be related to long-term domestication processes including the adaptation of European vegetable and animal species (Gade, 1967), especially alfalfa. Our study helped underpin the long-term infrastructure management of their agricultural systems which served to regulate a subsistence base of the population.

Shorter-term aspects of change became evident as well. The high quality maize terraces – the most productive but expensive pieces of agricultural

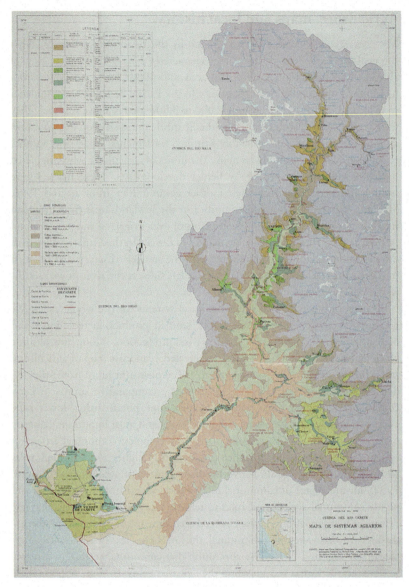

Figure 8.2. Map of Cañete Valley (Lima, Peru) agricultural zones (Mayer and Fonseca, 1979; 1988, no page number)

Ecological zones key (see opposite page for **Production zones key**)

White = nival permanent snow > 5,000 m.
Pale purple = subalpine humid tundra 4–5,000 m.
Pale beige = montane steppe 3–4,000 m.
Pale green = lower montane scrub 2–3,000 m.
Pale orange = semi-arid subtropical scrub desert, 1–2,000 m.
Pale yellow = semi-arid subtropical desert, 0–1,000 m.

IN LOVE WITH *COMUNIDADES* 243

Agriculture		Symbols	Production zones	Type of field	Altitude (m.)		Surface (ha)	
Type	Frequency				Minimum	Maximum	Partial	Total
Rainfed	Seasonal	brown	Sectorial fallow under communal control	Slope terraces	3,000	4,000	7,814	
	Seasonal	light green	Individual farmer rotation in the same field	Open Fields on hillside	2,400	3,950	12,950	20,764
Irrigated	Seasonal	dark green	Maize terraces (moyas)	Terraces for maize	2,200	3,600	2,586	
	Permanent	light blue	Higland crops in rotation with Alfalfa	Converted terraces to meadows	1,300	3,500	7,679	
		green	Alfafa zone	Walled sloping meadows	1,200	3,500	4,613	
		pink	Apple orchards	Intercropped with annual crops	1,150	3,200	774	
		orange	Wine orchards	Intercropped with annual crops	200	1,400	1,174	47,825
		blue	Coastal crops	Walled field with rapid sucession of single crops & cotton	50	1,400	6,045	
		light orange	Citrus orchards	Walled fields with citrus trees	50	150	1,417	
		light green	Agroindustrial zone	Large cotton tractor driven fields	50	150	23,537	
				Grand Total				68,589

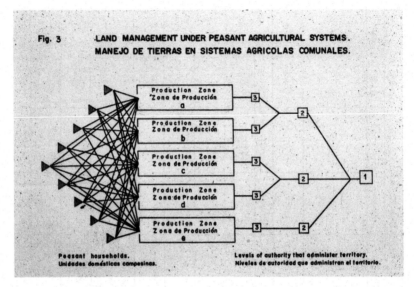

Figure 8.3. Diagram of land management by production zones, Cañete Valley (Mayer, 1985; 2002, p. 389)

construction in the Andes – were taken apart to construct sloping meadows so that cows, whose milk was made into cheese for sale in the Lima market, could graze on alfalfa fields. The water regime was altered to irrigate more frequently than was done in the watering schedule for maize. Maize fields in the lower parts were converted to apple orchards in response to market opportunities. We observed how the Cañete gorge's desert sections were being colonised by the expansion of small irrigation systems to develop highly productive orchards.

The map, 'Sistemas agrarios y ecología en la cuenca del Río Cañete' (Mayer and Fonseca, 1979; 1988), was published by the Peruvian Oficina Nacional de Evaluación de Recursos Naturales (Office of Natural Resource Management, ONERN). The theoretical article and ethnographic report appeared as 'Production zones', published by Tokyo University Press (Mayer, 1985; 2002, chapter 8). It linked individual family-oriented production with communal decision making, that is, an administrative body which regulated production decisions in a system specialising in production zones according to the climatic, slope and altitudinal conditions of open field agriculture, in conjunction with households benefiting from diversified and non-specialised access to fields in these zones, a microversion of Murra's verticality at the local level (see figure 8.3).

My chapter also stressed that aspects of this system was not unique to the Andes but a highly effective adaptation to the ecological conditions of mountain systems. They provided interesting examples for comparison with

Figure 8.4. Maize terraces in Laraos (Lima, Peru). Photo: E. Mayer.

the Swiss Alps and the Himalayan mountain ranges (Rhoades and Thompson, 1975; Guillet, 1983; Netting, 1993).

My publication coincided with the years when a group of foreign scholars intensively studied the agronomy practised by peasants in the high Andes. Insights such as why terracing was effective (Donkin, 1979; Treacy, 1994; Denevan, 1987) and how irrigation systems worked (Mitchell, 1976; Valderrama and Escalante, 1988; Boelens, 2008). A group of French agronomists (Morlon et al., 1982; Eresue and Brougère, 1988) considered microlevel technological adaptations in the quotidian practices of peasant agriculture in great painstaking detail, measuring, for example, how stone walls surrounding small fields absorb heat from the sun during the day, and release it slowly during the night, thus mitigating the effects of frost. Or, that irrigation immediately after a frost attack helps the plants affected by the consequent dehydration to survive. Pierre Morlon (1996) published a compendium of what he considered to be the positive adaptive technological aspects of the agricultural and pastoral practices he and other scholars had observed in the mountainous areas, a jewel of a book that should be reprinted. John Earls (1992; 2006) applied sophisticated ecology, climatology and systems theory to Andean agriculture, relating ancient terrace formations to agricultural practices. Felix Palacios-Rios (1977) and Jorge Flores-Ochoa (1977) published ethnographic studies about how herders in the high punas extended the flood plain areas to create managed, pond-like microenvironments known as *bofedales* [peat bogs], which modified the plant communities with aquatic plants suitable for alpaca grazing in the dry season.

These studies underscored the point that Andean peasants in their comunidades were doing the right thing. Intellectually we were cultural ecologists stressing adaptations and the collective wisdom of communal management over the long term. I provided a summary of all the wonderful scholarly work done on cultural ecological/agronomic/ aspects for a biannual Peruvian agrarian seminar (Seminario Permanente de Investigación Agraria, SEPIA) in Arequipa in which I also took issue with another aspect of essentialising (1994).

A group of Peruvian scholars: agronomists and sociologists gathered under the umbrella of the Proyecto andino de tecnologías campesinas (PRATEC), a non-governmental organisation (NGO), took an extremist stance, arguing vehemently against any form of technological importation and heaping unstinted praise on Andean local peasant practices supposedly derived from the caring relationship peasant indians have with the Earth Mother, Pachamama. This form of ultra-greenness associated with an anti-neocolonialist stance was echoed in the United States by Frédérique Apffel Marglin (1988). Her efforts to make PRATEC's views available to an English reading public includes an introduction in which she further elucidated my debate in Arequipa with Eduardo Grillo-Fernández (1994), PRATEC's most articulate spokesperson. I find her defence stemming from a position advocating a postcolonial-western-anti-western stance one swing of the pendulum too far. The Proyecto influenced agronomists in provincial technical colleges ideologically to form a distinct sect-like group of professionals whose indigenous formulation encompassing Quechua and Aymara concepts of subsistence-oriented ideas has recently been enshrined in the '*buen vivir*' [living well] goal in the constitutions of Bolivia and Ecuador (Gudynas, 2011). I stay away from fundamentalist formulations that equate indigenous identity and culture with automatic good stewardship of their environment, but I did argue at the Arequipa meeting that comunidades do make good territorial and collective units for environmental management, reiterating that 'Andean villagers and Indigenous populations in the tropics may find that in undertaking projects of cultural revitalization and ethnic reaffirmation they can actually reaffirm their cultures through efforts at regenerating their own degraded natural resources' (2002, p. 330). This is close enough but not identical to the position that PRATEC takes.

Although we did not always underline the survival of the Incas, finding maize terraces in Laraos that have been cultivated continuously for a millennium certainly played on that note (see figure 8.4). The Cañete Valley study helped us understand why comunidades tended to bunch together at certain altitudes of the mountain range since their territories were characterised by a sharper and more variable environmental gradient compared with more homogeneous environments such as the coastal plains or the high grasslands. Here, capitalist sheep ranches in the highland puna and cotton estates in the coastal plains had displaced traditional herders and small family farms. Our map also showed that on the margins of the coastal cotton plantations small-scale, intensively worked, diversified cropping systems encroached on the desert and, when it could, onto the cotton estates. Tractor-driven, irrigated, cotton monocropping on the coast was seen as progressive, while the intensely worked smallholder multicrop fruit, vegetable and chilli pepper horticulture it displaced was seen as underdeveloped. Leftist and conservative thinkers alike preached that technological innovations were needed to overcome underdevelopment.

In between these homogeneous extremes, the diversified and broken environment of the mountain slopes was occupied by the complex agricultural systems that sustained its members and produced marketable crops. Modernisation theorists regarded this mid-range region as the realm of underdevelopment because of their rudimentary technology, and as a consequence, their people were supposedly mired in poverty and ignorance. Our map instead clearly exposed ecological realities showing a much more diverse and complex world of agro-pastoral production operated by comunidades in conjunction with its peasant household operations.

We also became acutely aware that comunidades were conscious of making their own history, keeping their own records to underwrite the communal authority and to litigate with other communities, private landholders or the state with documentation that supported claim and counterclaim. My study of how the Laraos comunidad changed its agricultural systems from highly communal to very private and, 50 years later, reverted to a more communal organisation, was made possible by local intellectuals who shared with me their documentary sources dating from 1900–76. It was first published as 'Tenencia y control comunal de la tierra: caso de Laraos' (1977; 2002, chapter 9). That article demonstrated that comunidades understand the wider-scale issues that affect their interests, and therefore keep their own records. They are aware of the historical change that they themselves create, maintain and interpret, adding an important dimension to the issue of continuities from the past and what had become a research subject under the name of resistance (Scott, 1985; Rivera Cusicanqui, 1982; Schwartz and Salomon, 1999).

Members of the Laraos intellectual elite had commissioned topographers to map their territory accurately in order to defend its lands from hacienda encroachment long before I arrived, and they had on their own initiative deposited the most important colonial documents in the Lima National Archive to prevent misuse or fraud. The mayor of Laraos, a topographer, made a sketch map of the Laraos production zones published in my reports, and

Ezequiel Beltrán, son of the schoolmaster and a trained historian, interpreted the information for me and later also joined my seminar at the Catholic University.

My article on land tenure and communal control in Laraos belongs to a tradition and research strategy of writing and interpreting the history of the comunidades. It combines ethnographic fieldwork with archival records, oral tradition, folkloric festival and the divergent views of factionalised membership within each comunidad's population. On a larger scale, put briefly, such work can encompass a river basin, region or department. The school teachers of the Yauyos province had, in the 1940s and 1950s, encouraged self-awareness of an *indigenista* slant publishing in each issue of their *Revista Yauyos* a complete monograph about each comunidad. Struck by the fact that everyone in Laraos repeated the same myths in identical ways, I stumbled on the fact that Brígido Varillas (1965), one of their teachers, had published a folklore collection which was taught in the school and which was memorised by the children.

As for the comunidades today they form part of North Yauyos's Tourist and Landscape National Park. They have built hostels and restored some of their terraces, they have become even more self-conscious in their practice of festivals and rituals, and are, no doubt, proficient in explaining the ancient Inca survivals still practised today to their guests. There is also a t-shirt for sale adorned with pictures of Laraos men wielding their *chaquitacllas* (foot-ploughs).

The Cañete Valley field techniques and mapping exercise interested the Centro Internacional de la Papa (International Potato Centre, CIP), whose potato gene bank was located near Huancayo. They commissioned me to repeat my mapping exercise in respect of the Mantaro Valley, which brought me back to my home territory. As in the Cañete, comunidades occupied distinct ecologically determined areas of the valley. They were the result of a historical process involving splitting off from older colonial mother comunidades and recreating themselves as functioning institutions in higher ecological zones. This process manifested itself as an upward movement. Comunidades reproduced their form and governance as the older and more original ones tended to decline. In this process certain zones split off from their mother comunidad to become independent but recreated the structure on a smaller scale (Alberti and Sánchez, 1974). This process, combined with aspects of modernisation, market penetration and development, was mixed, scattered and dotted over our land-use map for the Mantaro Valley. Overall, the comunidades in this region had begun a process of agricultural intensification, at the expense of fallowing, which led to a trend of land privatisation and the development of a different and unexpected response to commercial production compared with the models of mono-crop agribusiness and capitalist development (Long and Roberts, 1978; 1984; Lehman, 1982, for Carchi, Ecuador). Different because the large, private estate-like commercial farms or haciendas did not come to dominate the valley floor, the homogeneous low zone. Instead one could see the predominance of small or even micro-land holdings, split by inheritance patterns into what agronomists disdainfully called *minifundios*. The CIP published the map and the report as *Land Use in the Andes: Ecology and Agriculture in Mantaro Valley of Peru with Special Reference to Potatoes* (Mayer, 1979) and distributed it widely as part of the technical literature devoted to development. It became internationally famous as part of Peru's Farming Systems Approach.

By focusing on production issues, the role played by comunidades in the valley and their own historical evolution, whether involution or dissolution, also helped other scholars locate and evaluate diachronic processes and their effects on productive systems in the valley (Mallon, 1983; Manrique, 1987). The emphasis was on emigration in order to work in mines (Laite, 1981) or the eastern lowland coffee farms and coca production areas (Shoemaker, 1981; Lund Skar, 1994; Kernaghan, 2009). There was also a high level of emigration to the coastal cotton plantations in order to undertake seasonal labour (Favre, 1977) and to trade in Lima's informal sector (Smith, 1989), and also abroad (Paerregaard, 1997; de Vries, 2015).

The Mantaro Valley map was useful in locating areas where high biodiversity in potato agriculture, in what became popularly known as 'native' varieties, was practised in the highest agricultural zones. It prompted attempts to study them as part of the endeavour to stem the process of genetic erosion. As improved high yielding varieties replace the locally domesticated land ones, the survival of the gene pool, upon which future combinations depend, is threatened. Scholars and scientists therefore began to search for native potato and maize varieties and to develop techniques to conserve them (Brush et al., 1981; Zimmerer, 1988; 1996; de Haan, 2009; 2006; Scurrah et al., 2012), such as in situ conservation practices, in collaboration with the local farming population and their supporting NGOs (Brush, 2004; 2000).

The map also identified the places where commercial potato agriculture was concentrated including the production of high levels of fertiliser and hybrid varieties. That study served both interests, the developmentalists and the biological conservationists, by highlighting individual and collective strategies involved in potato production. Their distribution in space according to climatic variability is an expression of environmental constraints and of family strategies for taking care of subsistence and marketing needs. Also relevant in a historical dynamic is the farmer's relationship to evolving regional economic structures and capitalist development in the valley.

Today I can Google the Laraos maize fields and watch that crop grow from my computer in Rio de Janeiro whenever I wish. Back in 1974 when Richard Shea, then a Fulbright undergraduate fellow at the Catholic University, became enthused with the mapping idea, map-making technology was primitive and laborious. The United States had endowed ONERN and the Servicio Aerofotográfico Nacional (National Aerial Photographic Service) with map-making technology and facilities to aid them in monitoring coca production in the *montaña* but also in producing an ecological map for the whole country. We were allowed to use their facilities and given technical training. The air force's low-altitude aerial photographs and our own fieldwork and notes permitted us to accurately delimit the production zones for the whole valley on a 1/100,000 scale map available through the Instituto Geográfico Militar. Each production zone was allocated a colour code which needed to be superimposed on the base map using plastic sheets. All the coloured zones were cut out with an X-Acto knife. The printing was done using a four-colour offset process. In the case of the Mantaro Valley we had to lump production zones into what we called agro-life zones because there was too much small-scale variation which could not be visually transferred on to a single map. Budgetary constraints imposed by the CIP limited us to a two-colour scheme (orange representing commercial, green for areas where subsistence was important) with hatchings to differentiate zones for the final printing. The difference between our maps and today's remote sensing technology is that our maps were 100 per cent ground-proofed and emically accurate (that is, we painted maize fields and production zones as perceived by the locals and interpreted by us). As remote sensing and GPS navigation systems have become easily available, the mapping task is easier, and its reproduction on a computer screen makes it accessible, modifiable and capable of monitoring diachronic changes. Our handcrafted maps, on the other hand, were expensive to produce, difficult to reproduce, and even harder to distribute. But in 1979 they were a sensation among agronomists, social scientists and development specialists. When the offset plates rusted, the maps could no longer be printed. As inserts in their respective reports many maps have been stolen from libraries. The original Mongol pencil-coloured map and the printed ONERN Cañete one, along with the Mantaro Valley map are now deposited in Yale University's map collection.

My maps were the predecessors of the idea of mapping local scenarios, aided by local people, that is known as community participatory mapping. This is a recognised tool for research, community empowerment, development projects and conservation work (di Gessa et al., 2008). Its practice is effective and underscores aspects of communal consensus making in a way that is visible and often more meaningful to NGO supervisors than to the local farmers. Although they know every inch of their territory, passing this knowledge on through the generations (once a year young men walk around the Tangor territory boundaries memorising them), and they have other non-visual, non-paper or electronic ways of representing it to themselves, their methods are somewhat opaque to ethnographers.

Agrarian reform: from hacienda to comunidad

During my entire university career I ended every term paper with passionate statements like: 'Without a thorough agrarian reform program Peru's peasant population will continue to live in poverty and submission.' I landed in Peru in 1969 the year that Juan Velasco Alvarado began what was then considered to be an extremely radical agrarian reform. Radical, because it was drastic in terms of the speed and number of expropriated properties. I lived through this process and had many chances to observe how the reform was affecting comunidades. Five aspects need to be considered: 1) Antecedents leading up to the reform, followed by the three parts of the reform itself: 2) Expropriation; 3) Adjudication; 4) Implementation; and finally 5) The aftermath of the reform which includes the collapse of the cooperatives of various types created by that agrarian reform, and the consequent redistribution of the adjudicated land among individuals or comunidades. The end result was an indisputable strengthening of the comunidades as organisations and a growth in their numbers and the portion of territory they occupied in the sierra. In the 1994 Agricultural Census, as reported by Valera Moreno (1998) and Trivelli (1992), the number of recognised comunidades campesinas was 5,680. They harboured 711,571 rural families, reaching an estimated three million people, 43 per cent of the rural population in the country. The rate of official recognition of communities grew exponentially during the regimes of Fernando Belaúnde Terry (both the first and second time he was in power), Juan Velasco Alvarado, Francisco Morales Bermúdez and Alan García Pérez during the years of the agrarian reform and its aftermath. This growth more than doubled the number of comunidades. The same census also indicates that the total territory these comunidades occupied adds up to 18 million hectares – a third of the country's total agricultural land and half the total land in production. More than three-quarters of natural pastures in the high punas are also controlled by comunidades. In the departments of Puno, Apurimac, Junín and Huancavelica lands under the comunidad regime comprise more than 60 per cent of the total (Mayer, 2002, pp. 36-7). The trend continues with the 2012 Agricultural Census showing a total of 6,227 comunidades (Agronoticias, 2013).

The 1966 Belaúnde and 1970 Velasco Agrarian Reforms stipulated that the first priority must be that expropriated hacienda lands should benefit the resident worker, *yanacona* and *colono* populations. The second priority was that neighbouring comunidades, who could demonstrate that they had suffered land loss due to hacienda expansion, should benefit. Land expropriated would be adjudicated in the form of cooperatives and assistance provided with introducing technologically advanced production methods in respect of the newly adjudicated lands to take advantage of economies of scale. Comunidades members would gain through profit sharing and development assistance. With regard to adjudication, the land reform changed property regimes, created institutions that were under government control and did not – as far as possible – distribute any land to individuals. When the agrarian reform collapsed, political acts of defiance then took that land from the state. However, it should also be noted that this land was not privatised in the strictest sense of individual private property plots, but, under the comunidad campesina system, is legally and socially under collective property regimes. On the coast, land taken from cooperatives was distributed to individuals as private property.

Puna sheep ranches (Atocsayco)

Haciendas were not all the same, nor did they carry the same negative ideological weight justifying their expropriation. They had different dynamics of expansion and decline. As César Fonseca and I had concluded in our Cañete and Mantaro studies, hacienda enclosures with their concomitant expulsion of peasant populations from their lands took place primarily in extensive homogeneous environments because the technology these enterprises implemented did not rely on peasant techniques, wisdom or control. They were associated in the sierra with the high puna pastures where improved breeds of sheep grazed for the world's wool market.

With the agrarian reform of the 1970s, the owners were expropriated but the aim was to leave intact the technology, installations and improved herds managed by professionals by creating super-cooperatives in the territory of the expropriated enterprise (the technical name was Sociedades Agrarias de Interés Social, SAIS). The communities that had historical claims to those lands became shareholders in these corporations and participants in the profits that these enterprises generated. When, 20 years later, these enterprises were in economic and political crisis, the partner comunidades reacted by renewing their political activism and organised a second wave of land invasions on the cooperative lands. Once captured, those lands were then divided among the participating peasant communities and among newly created comunidades campesinas.

The comunidad campesina San Juan de Ondores is also a district capital in the high punas of the Pampa de Junín in central Peru. The economy of the Pampa is dominated by mining and wool production. Sheep ranching was under the control of an American corporation, the Division Ganadera de la

Cerro de Pasco Mining Corporation. The Pampa had experienced a wave of land invasions as rural unrest and electoral politics were agitating for agrarian reform during the 1960s (Handelman, 1975). To thwart these, Fernando Belaúnde Terry, then candidate for Acción Popular, had promised to implement an agrarian reform policy, which he did in 1963, and when he was deposed by Juan Velasco Alvarado, the lands of the Cerro de Pasco Corporation were expropriated in 1969. The whole complex of many *haciendas ganaderas* was integrated into a single management converted into the SAIS Túpac Amaru I, and Ondores became a shareholding member. Looking for documentation in the library of the University of Huancayo, I came across a thesis, the story of which is summarised below (Valerio Laureano, 1985). It tells how the lands of Atocsayco were taken from the administration of the SAIS Tupac Amaru I.

According to Jonatán Valerio Laureano, a University of Huancayo sociology graduate of 1978, Miguel Valerio Ordoñez (a close relative of Jonatán) was elected president of the Ondores community with a slate of seasoned leftist trade union leaders. A section of the puna lands known as Atocsayco had once belonged to the communidad, but had passed in late colonial times to private hands, and from there to the Cerro de Pasco Corporation. Subsequently it became part of SAIS Tupac Amaru I. Ondores wanted its lands back.

The leaders worked on two fronts: 1) litigation: the services of Genaro Ledesma Izquieta were retained (the maverick leftist ex-mayor of the city of Cerro de Pasco, senator in the Constituent Assembly and presidential hopeful); and 2) in great secrecy they began preparations to occupy Atocsayco, collecting money, provisions, organising people into groups, and assigning to them the best places for rounding up animals and driving them on to the contested lands.

Víctor Caballero, my friend and the legal adviser of Confederación Campesina del Perú (CCP), the leftist opposition peasant league remembers the case's legal complexities very well. When I interviewed him in 1994 he said that:

> The lands did belong to the community which was in an old lease/mortgage situation since colonial times. Ondores had litigated for the return of these lands since 1927 and kept getting favourable judgements as they moved up in the courts. By 1967 they were clear, but they never managed to get a judge to adjudicate the lands. When the Velasco reform came, Ondores was joined to the SAIS. For ten years, the comuneros resigned themselves to being part of the SAIS, but the SAIS retained the land, it did not provide the people of Ondores with work opportunities. They were unhappy with the profit-sharing scheme. So they started the law suit again. But the legal situation was complicated. The local judges no longer had jurisdiction. They told them that they must sue the SAIS. The SAIS administrators said 'the lands are not ours, they belong to the state until we finish paying the agrarian debt, so you sue them.'

As legal advisers of the CCP got involved, we found that one could cut through all this garbage by having a judge adjudicate the lands to Ondores in an on-site legal ceremony called a *ministración* on the basis of past rulings in Ondores' favour. So we found a willing judge. He did it. Well, that judge did not last two days in his post after he did that.

According to Jonatán's account, by September everyone in Ondores was eagerly awaiting the marching orders, code-named 'the travelling day', which was announced on a provincial radio station at 6am on 5 September 1997, disguised as an urgent message that a certain woman in the community was sick and urgently requested that her sons come home. Despite freezing rain hundreds of comuneros marched to the Atocsayco boundary with provisions on their backs and building materials loaded on to donkeys and mules. They drove their sheep and llamas and bore banners stating 'Fear stops here'. Once they had arrived at the wire fence, the CCP president, Andrés Luna Vargas, gave a fiery speech. They then elected peasant guards and to top it all a musical group performed traditional dances and songs. Then they ceremoniously cut the fence and marched on to Atocsayco lands. The comuneros immediately began setting up their huts and establishing the animals on the grazing lands. At 10am the next day Judge Guillermo Carbajal, chauffeured in the community vehicle, arrived at the Atocsayco casa hacienda accompanied by eight policemen. The judge performed the ministración legal ceremony in the presence of community officials and some highly reluctant SAIS employees. Ondores had accomplished 'its peaceful and legal possession of the land' (Valerio Laureano, 1985, p. 106). Respectfully they separated the SAIS's animals from their own and left all hacienda installations intact.

The SAIS quickly mobilised to repel them. Two nights later when more than one hundred horsemen attacked a group of comuneros, SAIS employees blocked roads and looted the invaders' possessions. The SAIS chief executive officer mobilised its partner communities, requesting that ten men from each community help form posses and, according to Ondores versions of the confrontation, he hired mercenaries as well. He also got the government to annul the ministración and later to obtain an eviction order.

The people of Ondores stayed on, receiving support from neighbouring communities and opposition groups. Progressive doctors and relatives of the comuneros in Lima, Huancayo and the mining camps provided materials and money. A replay in reverse occurred on 19 October when SAIS officials and horsemen, accompanied by a different judge armed this time with an eviction order, made a second attempt to dislodge the people of Ondores,. They were backed up by policemen, who were transported to the same place, this time on SAIS trucks. The order was fiercely resisted by the invaders and the judge left the premises having been unable to accomplish his mission. Ondores also sued the SAIS for theft and disturbing the peace, and sought interdiction orders in the courts.

In Jonatán's version of the dispute, the Ondores community tried to gain support from the sister villages in the SAIS, but the day before the scheduled meeting, the administration convened a delegates meeting which expelled Ondores from SAIS membership. This took place under intimidating conditions. Not one delegate from any of the communities spoke against the motion. The SAIS also gained support from the government, which supplied them with three hundred Peruvian crack anti-riot police. On 18 December 1979, the troops brutally drove out the people of Atocsayco, leaving three dead, four wounded, substantial destruction of property and animals, and over 40 people arrested. Luna Vargas was arrested in Lima the same day. For Jonatán, this was 'a confrontation of antagonic social classes with remnants of semifeudality which still subsist in our society' (Valerio Laureano, 1985, p. 120).

In November 1980 the members of the Fourth Russell Tribunal met in Rotterdam, Holland to hold (quasi-legal) moral trials hearing native peoples' accusations of mistreatment and dispossession throughout the world. The people of Ondores presented their case to this tribunal. It found the Peruvian government guilty of violating its own constitution, agrarian reform laws, and scores of international conventions on political rights including those on racial discrimination and the universal declaration of human rights (Ismaelillo and Wright, 1982).

The final irony: these actions took place in an electoral year. The military were about to hand over the government to an elected president, who turned out to be none other than an older, but not necessarily wiser, Fernando Belaúnde Terry, doing what he always enjoyed most. On 9 May 1980, campaigning in the town of Junín, he promised he would 'return the lands of Atocsayco to the *comunidad* of Ondores as soon as he assumed power' (Valerio Laureano, 1985, p. 144). A year later, with him in power, nothing had happened, and Ondores' leaders, now severely divided between leftists and pro-Belaúnde factions, again organised the exhausted people of Ondores to push their animals and carry their provisions and pro-Belaúnde placards across the boundary on to the contested territory. And one last time, SAIS employees mobilised to repel them. But the combative spirit was gone and in the end Ondores kept part of Atocsayco for good.

Valley agricultural haciendas (Paucartambo)

Below the puna pastures, in the agricultural sierra's traditional hacienda with 'feudal' structures, the resident colono population of peasants had usufruct rights to produce crops for their own subsistence in exchange for work on the owner's plots. Unlike the sheep ranches, the agricultural technology there was peasant-like, with labour-intensive skills and was controlled by the peasants. It should be noted that, in contrast to the puna ranches, these haciendas were already in secular decline throughout the latter part of the 20th century (Caballero, 1981). Many a hacienda became completely dominated by colonos, with the owner producing little. Hacienda owners began a process of selling off the plots they had allocated to their colonos, which in effect was a transfer of usufruct rights to permanent ownership and a cancellation of the labour obligations (in local parlance, the colonos were liberated). In Cajamarca, the owners sold off poor lands on hilly, rain-fed slopes to their colonos, but kept a small area of flat, irrigated pastureland for dairy production (Deere, 1990). Owners also tried to reduce the size of their property in order to fall within the limits of what the reform considered to be the minimum amount of land that they should be allowed to keep *mínimo inafectable* by subdividing the lands among their heirs. Many became absentee landowners with other interests in towns and cities, leaving their lands in benign neglect. All sought to convert their animal stocks to cash. With little land to physically expropriate in these areas, the state's attempt to establish cooperatives was a miserable failure. The transition from hacienda to comunidad in the agricultural areas was more direct and rapid.

In 1985 César Fonseca did fieldwork in the Paucartambo province of the Cuzco department, an area where the traditional 'feudal' hacienda had predominated. I summarise from the field notes which I published after his death (Fonseca and Mayer, 1988).

In the 1961 census in the department of Cuzco's Paucartambo province, there were 169 haciendas and 24 comunidades. The reform created four agrarian cooperatives, 47 new comunidades campesinas and 26 grupos campesinos. By 1985, the four cooperatives were about to dissolve. They had sold their tractors, had serious liquidity problems and had not planted any crops. Soon afterwards their lands were allocated among neighbouring communities and the cooperative's ex-workers. Twenty-four original comunidades were located in territories that did not have any haciendas to be expropriated and thus they did not receive additional land. Eighteen pre-existing comunidades did benefit from more land allocation on which they could supposedly farm collectively, using modern technology, but instead distributed them among themselves. And the 26 *grupos campesinos* were, in effect, ex-haciendas on their way to becoming new comunidades since they were already functioning as such and only awaited legal recognition. Adding them together, the number of communities grew from 24 to 68, while the 164 haciendas shrank to zero. Not a single hacienda was left in the whole valley.

Before the reform hacendados, when they were on their properties, lived in their casa haciendas, located in the lower milder climatic areas, surrounded by eucalyptus groves, orchards, stables and paddocks for their horses. They were attended by indian servants, some permanently attached to the household, others recruited by turns from among the resident colono population. Many a hacienda house was in actual fact not as sumptuous or ostentatious as the myth would like us to believe. On his property he was owner and master, and his power was absolute, but the despotism was constrained by a series of reciprocal obligations coated with an etiquette of relationships with his indigenous serfs. These were strongly tinged with condescending tones which treated the indian as childlike, to which the indian responded with extreme servility but also with Andean versions of James C. Scott's descriptions of foot-dragging, resistance and feigned obtuseness. In reality, if the situation is analysed more carefully, the despotic hacendado was more the pawn of his colono serfs, who were organised into the 'captive' communities already noted by Mario Vázquez (1961) following the Vicos case. In that case, the serfs were organised and functioned as self-governing hierarchical systems, took their own decisions, made rules, and policed and punished offenders using the civil religious hierarchies of rotating civic offices and fiesta sponsorship. They were part of various *cargo* systems such as the guarding of the fields from damage by stray animals or from theft. They managed the sectorial fallow procedures, maintained the irrigation systems, distributed water and land as it came out of the fallow phase and had mechanisms to resolve conflicts and disputes among themselves. It is true they also had to be obedient to the wishes and commands of the hacienda owner and his manager, and they had to work hard in exchange for their right to use land on the hacienda.

When the reform came, and if the peasants were savvy enough to convince the agrarian reform agents, the hacienda quickly became a community. The plots worked by the owner became part of its communal allocation, the usufruct plots of the peasants continued as before, and a new set of elected authorities became the official representatives of a resurrected comunidad. All that was needed was the Agrarian Reform office's official recognition of the land transfer and the Dirección de Comunidades Campesinas's acceptance (under the Sistema Nacional de Apoyo a la Mobilización Social, SINAMOS) of their incorporation into the register.

Even before the reform, hacienda territory was subdivided into production zones, the high puna for pasture, the high potato zone with extensive fallow, the sectorial rotation one for tubers and barley, and a lower more permanent one for maize. The serfs and the owner jointly rotated and fallowed their fields in the same sectors. Together, the owner and a comunidad representative participated in the *suertes* [annual distribution of plots], ensuring that the owner reserved the best ones for himself, called *hacienda mañay*. Serfs with full-use rights to one or two suertes were called *mañayruna*, which was an inherited right. The owner could, if he so wished, increase, decrease, exchange or cancel such rights depending on how well and loyal he thought this serf had behaved. The hacienda mañay was worked first before the ordinary runa could work on their allotments. Similarly, irrigation distributions followed hierarchical rules of privilege, priorities and leftover distributions.

The mañayruna remembered their obligations to the owner. On one hacienda they worked three five-day weeks (Monday to Friday) per month. They earned an almost fictional 'wage' of one sol in 1965 that rose to two, then five and then went up to 15 just before the reform. In addition, the runa vividly remember that the most onerous obligation was the transport of the harvest to the town of Paucartambo. Each mañayruna was responsible for delivering ten *cargas* of potatoes. To do this the runa had to procure their own borrowed or rented pack animals.

The serfs did not all have the same rights and obligations as a tripartite segmentation was in place. The most privileged, the mañayruna, were able to secure a fair amount of land by joining plots together from different suertes. Then there were the *yanapakojruna* who received half the allotment and had to fulfil half the obligations owed to the owner. They often helped the main mañayruna to discharge their commitments, sharing access to plots with them. *Yanapakojruna* were docile and obedient hoping that their good behaviour would result in better land allocations next time the suertes were distributed. There were also some landless servants called *puchuruna* attached to the owner's household, who were fed and housed in and around the casa hacienda and had no land to work for themselves. Such divisions persisted on the ex-haciendas that César had visited. The mañayruna became full comuneros while the yanapakojkuna and puchuruna were classed as unmarried sons of comuneros not yet allotted land, or men who had married into the comunidad and newcomers who, through friendship or kinship ties, had flocked to areas where additional land might soon become available as the news of expropriations spread in the region. The Quechua terms of yanapakojruna and puchuruna had their bureaucratic equivalent in Spanish: the comunero *calificado* and the comunero *no calificado* in the officially sanctioned list of comuneros.

To everyone's great relief the obligations to the owner were immediately abolished after the reform was instituted. Free time was dedicated to an expansion of commercial potato production on individual family plots in the higher rotating sectors, and in places where water trickled out of the mountainside, creating humid soil conditions for *mahuay* [early maturing potatoes] which could be sold for better prices in the Cuzco market. Obligatory communal *faena* work only took place on rare occasions and was much less onerous than the requirements they had to fulfil with the owner. The population on one ex-hacienda doubled from 38 to 72 families in the intervening years following the reform. César chronicled expanded consumption of durable goods in the region. Among the more amusing ones was the fashion of buying record-players with amplifiers to play loud *huayno* music. These were powered by car batteries, laboriously carried up and down the mountains whenever they needed to be recharged in the market towns of Paucartambo, Challabamba or Colquepata.

With the return to electoral regimes and the world's conversion to neoliberalism that followed the collapse of the Berlin Wall, the agrarian reform bureaucracy was shut down and the land institutions created by it were reconverted. Under Fujimori's ten-year reign (1990-2000) anything that smacked of collectivism was described as a failed leftist Velasquista communist project. In new legislation, land could be freely bought and sold; there were to be no limits to the size of the property a legal person or corporation could hold. The exception was the comunidad campesina whose collective land was inalienably protected by several constitutions. With World Bank financial support a titling programme was implemented mainly to regularise the de facto possessions. In comunidades, the programme first settled the boundaries of the comunidades in order to later attempt to individualise the family holdings situated on myriads of small plots (del Castillo, 1997; 2003). The intent was to prepare the way towards dissolving the comunidades, again copying the Mexican example where privatisation of ejido collective lands has also floundered (Cornelius and Myre, 1998).

Peru's current national experts on comunidades include anthropologist Alejandro Diez Hurtado (1999a; 1999b; 2003; 2012). Diez studied communities in Piura, and more recently Peruvian and Bolivian communal organisations. He notes increased responsibilities for the comunidad leadership, coupled with new sources of income and conflicts between municipal and comunidad organisations. Ferreira (2012) reports greater state services (health, education, infrastructure) in the comunidad he studied. Lawyer Laureano del Castillo (1997; 2003; 2008) keeps track of the legal imbroglios whereby neoliberals attempt to bypass older constitutional collective guarantees of comunidades campesinas for the benefit of mining concessions. The complete compendium, pertaining to comunidades of all laws made in the past and present centuries, is by Robles Mendoza (2002).

Making the agrarian reform and the whole country into a research subject posed methodological challenges for me. I used similar tactics to those acquired in fieldwork, combined with those of an investigative reporter. Here and in the next paragraph I sum up the methodological points that are detailed in my book, *Ugly Stories of the Peruvian Agrarian Reform* (2009, pp. 2–5). During 1995-6, I travelled all over Peru with Danny Pinedo, armed with a small battery-powered tape recorder, to interview people who had lived through the agrarian reform. I selected places that I remembered due to their notoriety as emblems of the reform process, or because I was familiar with the area from previous fieldwork. In each place, Danny and I reviewed the area's local history and completed a bibliographic search in local university libraries. We then identified potential subjects and, after tracking them down and getting them to agree to tell us their stories, we carried out the interviews. We tried to gather as many versions from as many perspectives as possible. Separately, we interviewed the ex-landlords, expropriators, government officials, local politicians, peasant leaders, activists, officials of the cooperatives and the farming families in each region.

My recordings were not open-ended or free-flowing. I sometimes asked tough questions and I used a loose structure following the agrarian reform's principal events to get the narrator to move on to other topics. Not one of the stories I gathered was neutral about the agrarian reform. It would be naïve to believe that the people told me the dry and factual truth, and even more simple-minded to have personal experiences stand for larger social processes, unleashed by the massive process of expropriation and redistribution. The people I interviewed mixed personal memories, shared experiences, popular opinions from the time or collectively elaborated afterwards, apt examples kept in mind as cautionary tales, unconfirmed gossip and political opinions. All of these were shaken together into a cocktail of interpretations which poured into the tape recorder. Finding it impossible and unnecessary to sort them out, or to separate truth from exaggeration, I paid more attention to the narrative quality and what it sought to illustrate.

When it came to editing, I attempted to put the elements together so that each chapter became a story in a particularly literal way. I constructed the stories from the interviews/memories/reports from my fieldwork and scholarly works into larger wholes. For each tale I roughly followed the chronological sequence of the reform process, intertwining the various points of view of my interviewees and my own scholarly comments and memories. Thus the 'ugly' agrarian reform 'stories' of my book's title (2009). I believe such tales are an apt concept for researching memories about the larger processes that people have lived through. My book stitched it all together. Some reviewers (Kay, 2011; Mitchell, 2010; Antrosio, 2011) have quibbled about the word 'ugly', pointing either to the fact that I may have twisted the intent of the story in a particular way (I do not deny it in the sense that any journalistic account has a 'line'); or that I ironically meant exactly the opposite. I hoped that every reader, no matter what his or her current political position or received wisdom about the agrarian reform, could empathise with one or several of its personal stories.

In doing this, I was inspired by Studs Terkel, whose books based on radio interviews about memories, such as *Hard Times* (1970) on the subject of the USA's Great Depression, added atmosphere, colour and human content to large-scale events. Like him, my intention was to stitch individual memories together into a larger narrative; also like him, the overall tone of the book belies its title. Terkel is a great practitioner of oral history, and reading him is indeed inspiring. In three chapters of my book on the agrarian reform, I tell interesting tales about how specific comunidades recovered lands from the state-imposed institutions after adjudication. I have included the case of Atocsayco here, which I had to cut from my book as it would have made that chapter excessively long.

Conclusion

My rather resigned conclusions about the prospects of indigenous revitalisation, through the environmental practice mentioned above, needs to be revised. When I was doing fieldwork, open-pit mining in the high Andes was not yet booming like it is today for the foreign corporations that leave gigantic holes where mountains used to be and pollute watercourses. Nor did I anticipate that peasants and comunidades would react against this, mobilising so strongly in defence of their resources. I have followed this new development through the internet and activist networks, but see Bebbington (2011) and Scurrah (2008) for two examples of the growing scholarly literature on this issue. The level of conflict and high-stakes protest certainly mark a new chapter in comunidades history.

Another important issue I have not researched myself, but am greatly aware of, is migration and the relationship that migrants maintain with their comunidades and vice versa: how comunidades are affected by what it is that migrants do or do not do. Already by 1969 half of Tangor's population lived in Lima's shanty towns. On Sundays, when I accompanied Tangorinos to the market town in Parcoy, I watched how they would pick up *giros* [remittances] and encomiendas, sent by relatives in Lima, from the bus company. Families in Tangor fortunate enough to have such relatives were better off than those without.

The family I lived with in Tangor had a grandson who was born and raised in Lima. His father had hit hard times so the boy was sent to live with his grandparents in Tangor. The boy was lonely, moody and had many chores to do. I offered to take him to Lima to visit his parents, stopped on the way so he could eat *pollo a la brasa* in a restaurant in Yanahuanca, and then dropped him off in the miserable, foggy, sandy hills of one of the Cono Norte's *pueblos jóvenes*. On the day appointed for me to pick him up, his father told me the child would not be returning to his grandparents. Jessaca Leineaweaver's apt title for this phenomenon is the *Circulation of Children* (2009). Based in Ayacucho, her study is concerned with the effects on families in the region when members become victims of violence, but the implications of her book go way beyond the specific aspects of the violence to deal with how kinship gets restructured over long distances. *Mediated Migrations: Race, Mobility, and Personhood in Peru and the US*, by Ulla Berg (2015), looks at the relationships between families in the Mantaro Valley comunidades and their migrants in the greater New York area. She describes situations where the mother is an illegal in the United States and cannot get back, even for a short visit, to the village where she left her son in the care of her parents because of US immigration laws. Cell phones and videos attempt to replace the absence of face-to-face interactions. At the same time it is the migrants who, when they finally obtain their green cards, return to the village to finance sumptuous fiestas and help out comunero members who get into difficulties, legal or otherwise.

Ethnographic writing is a learned skill, a method and a vocation. Looking back as a practitioner of this craft, I find that vivid description and the portrayal of my impressions of real people during fieldwork make ethnological topics come alive. I have also found that describing processes, rather than merely describing their practices, enlivens the narration and enhances the value of the ways of life I am trying to convey. Process allows the delineation of context and of place in dynamic ways and leaves plenty of room to thicken the descriptions as recommended by Geertz (1973). It allows the writer great freedom to use, as in my particular case, the tools of fiction writing to infuse agency and drama into the description. And it foregrounds people over theory. It stays close to the ground and avoids the postmodern tendency to use dense, pun-ridden exegesis.

As I moved from one project to the next, my methods changed. In efforts to scale upwards from village to valley to nation, I strove to retain the people-oriented aspects I wished to highlight in my research. Even with map-making in the Cañete and Mantaro valleys, what I tried to portray is the somewhat invisible but nonetheless real collective process of communal creations. I was concerned with the administration of the infrastructure which produces the food, sustenance and money that touches on basic human needs. As I put it in the chapter on production zones:

> There is a dynamic, symbolic and conflict-ridden relationship between the constituent households at one level and the community at the other. The households are the autonomous production and consumption units, and the community comprises the association of households in a territory administered by them as a unit. This dynamic relationship manifests itself in a constant tension between the interests of the households, which push for as much autonomy and independence as possible, and the communal aspects of their own collective selves, which impose restrictions and controls. (2002, pp. 248–9)

That tension generates a variation in outcomes: in one comunidad enforcement is strict, in another it is lax. It generates history: there is a before and an after, and a process that leads from one to the other in, say, the decision to build a new irrigation canal to open up new lands. There are leaders and those who oppose them. There are alternative pathways, factions, accusations of fraud and corruption. There are enthusiastic forward spurts and despondent periods of no progress. Accidents happen, unity and discord alternate and the process is rife with politics. The desired outcome is always uncertain, the unfolding of events is more open-ended. When researching these, there are scars in the natural landscape, traces within archaeological evidence, documents, key informants, witnesses, women's and men's views of the matter, pressures from inside the comunidad and from outside agencies, gossip, jokes, stories and myths to gather. One can record, one can photograph, and one can dance and drink at public events. There are many field techniques ranging from interviews and key informants to surveys, town meetings and quiet observation, and, above all, there is serendipity if the researcher is attuned into noticing the unexpected. From Laraos's intellectuals, I found out how important it is to let them teach me. Recovering hacienda lands from the defunct agrarian reform institutions is as much a collective project as is opening an irrigation canal. Picking a topic that people want to talk about is also the key to success.

I never returned to Tangor and here's why. In 1973, feeling heady as a new and popular professor in the Catholic University, and noticing that it had acquired a brand new Toyota Land Cruiser, I requested it to 'do fieldwork' and took off to Tangor. I travelled via Huánuco, where I rescued 100 copies of Murra's *Visita de la Provincia de León de Huánuco* volume 2, which its publishers, the local university administration, were too timid to release without the authorisation I had brought with me. In Tangor I was given so many breakfasts to feast on that I became rather sick. I asked my friend Don Víctor Lucas if he would read the coca leaves for me later in the evening. Ensconced beside candlelight and the embers of his kitchen, Don Víctor blew on the coca leaves, asked in mumbled Quechua the questions I had put to him, shook them in his cupped hands, opening them up to read the results from the position of the leaves. His wife, sitting next to him, looked over his shoulder at his open hand and exclaimed: 'Accident!' Don Victor was embarrassed and told her to be quiet. He continued to examine them for some time while thinking hard about what to say: 'You will get to Yanahuanca safely', he finally declared; and I did. But on the way to Lima I took a detour. Driving over a 5,000 metre-high pass on a little-used road, I misjudged a curve, and the car tumbled down the hillside. Several flips later it landed on its roof. I had a broken foot, my assistant a deep gash in hers, and the hundred volumes of Murra's *Visita*, splattered with mud and blood, were scattered across the rainy puna. We spent a miserable night up there until we were rescued the following day by a passing truck, which picked us up and gathered the *Visitas* into a sleeping bag. In Lima, after my assistant's wound had been stitched up and my foot put in a cast, I paid a printer to reassemble the books.

References

Abercrombie, T.A. (1998) *Pathways of Memory and Power: Ethnography and History Among an Andean People* (Madison, WI: University of Wisconsin Press).

Adams, R.N. (1968 [1959]) *A Community in the Andes: Problems and Progress in Muquiyauyo* (Seattle, WA and London: University of Washington Press).

Agronoticias (2013) 'Las comunidades campesinas y nativas del país, según el IV CENAGRO y el Ministro de Agricultura', *Agronoticas: revista para el desarrollo*, 31 Oct., pp. 14–20.

Alber, E. (1999 [1993]) *¿Migración o movilidad en Huayopampa?: nuevos temas y tendencias en la discusión sobre la comunidad campesina en los Andes* (Lima: Instituto de Estudios Peruanos).

Alberti, G. and E. Mayer (eds.) (1974) *Reciprocidad e intercambio en los Andes Peruanos* (Lima: Instituto de Estudios Peruanos).

Alberti, G. and R. Sánchez (1974) *Poder y conflicto social en el valle del Mantaro, 1900–1974* (Lima: Instituto de Estudios Peruanos).

Allen, C.J. (1981) 'To be Quechua: the symbolism of coca chewing in highland Peru', *American Ethnologist* 8 (1): 157–71.

— (1988) *The Hold Life Has: Coca and Cultural Identity in an Andean Community* (Washington DC and London: Smithsonian Institution Press).

— (2002 [1988]) *The Hold Life Has: Coca and Cultural Identity in an Andean Community* (Washington DC and London: Smithsonian Institution Press).

— (2008 [1988]) *La Coca Sabe: Coca e identidad cultural en una comunidad andina* (Cuzco: Centro Bartolomé de las Casas).

— (2011) *Foxboy: Intimacy and Aesthetics in Andean Stories* (Austin, TX: University of Texas Press).

— (2014) 'The whole world is watching: New perspectives on Andean animism', in T. Bray (ed.), *The Archaeology of Wak'as: Explorations of the Sacred in the Pre-Columbian Andes* (Boulder, CO: University Press of Colorado).

Allen, C.J. and N. Garner (1996) *Condor Qatay: Anthropology in Performance* (Prospect Heights, IL: Waveland Press).

Allison, A and C. Piot (2014) 'Editors' note on "neoliberal futures"', *Cultural Anthropology* 29, pp. 3–7.

D'Amico, L. (2011) *Otavalan Women, Ethnicity, and Globalization* (Albuquerque, NM: University of New Mexico Press).

Anderson, P.S.D. and D. Salomon (2010) *The Architecture of Patterns* (New York, NY: Norton).

Antrosio, J. (2011) 'Review of Enrique Mayer's *Ugly Stories of the Peruvian Agrarian Reform*', *American Ethnologist* 38, pp. 592–4.

Apffel-Marglin, F. and PRATEC (eds.) (1988) *The Spirit of Regeneration: Andean Culture Confronting Western Notions of Development* (London: Zed Books).

Ardite, B. (2008) 'Arguments about the left turns in Latin America: A post-liberal politics?', *Latin America Research Review* 43, pp. 59–81.

Arguedas, J.M. (1956) 'Puquio, una cultura en proceso de cambio', *Revista del Museo Nacional* 25: 5–53.

— (1971) 'No soy un aculturado', 1968 Inca Garcilaso de la Vega Prize acceptance speech. In appendix to *El zorro de arriba y el zorro de abajo* (Buenos Aires: Losada).

— (1978 [1968]) *Las comunidades de España y del Perú* (Madrid: Instituto de Cooperación Iberoamericana).

Arguedas, J.M. (trans.), P. Duviols and F. de Ávila (1966 [1598–1608]) *Dioses y hombres de Huarochiri* (Lima: Museo Nacional de Historia, Instituto de Estudios Peruanos).

Arnold, D. (1997) *Más Allá del Silencio: Las Fronteras de Genero en Los Andes* (La Paz: Instituto de Lengua y Cultura Aymara, CIASE).

Assadourian, C.S. (1982) *El Sistema de la Economía Colonial* (Lima: Instituto de Estudios Peruanos).

Ávila, J. (2000a) 'Entre archivos y trabajo de campo: La etnohistoria en el Perú', in C.I. Degregori (ed.), *No hay país más diverso: compendio de antropología peruana* (Lima: Red Para el Desarrollo de las Ciencias Sociales en el Perú), pp. 180–203.

— (2000b) 'Los dilemas del desarrollo: Antropología y promoción en el Perú', in C.I. Degregori (ed.), pp. 413–42.

Bastien, J.W. (1978) *Mountain of the Condor: Metaphor and Ritual in an Andean Ayllu* (St Paul, MN, New York, NY, Los Angeles and San Francisco, CA: West Publishing Company).

Baudin, L. (1961 [1928]) *A Socialist Empire: The Incas of Peru* (Princeton, NJ and New York, NY: D. Van Nostrand Co).

Bebbington, A. (ed.) (2011) *Social Conflict, Economic Development and the Extractive Industry: Evidence from South America* (Milton Park: Routledge).

Benavides, M.A. (1986) 'Cambios en la tenencia y el uso de tierras desde el siglo XVI hasta el presente en el Valle del Colca (Caylloma, Arequipa)', in W. Denevan (ed.), *The Cultural Ecology, Archaeology, and History of Terracing and Terrace Abandonment in the Colca Valley of Southern Peru*, vol. 1 (Madison, WI: University of Wisconsin), pp. 509-24.

Benjamin, W. (1969 [1940]) 'Thesis on the philosophy of history', in H. Arendt (ed.), *Illuminations: Essays and Reflections* (New York, NY: Schocken Books), pp. 253-64.

Berg, U.D. (2015) *Mediated Migrations: Race, Mobility, and Personhood in Peru and the US* (New York, NY: New York University).

van den Berghe, P. and G. Primov (1978) *Inequality in the Peruvian Andes: Class and Ethnicity in Cuzco* (Columbia, MO: University of Missouri Press).

Bernal, C.A. (2010) *Metodología de la Investigación* (Mexico City: Pearson Education).

Bertram, G. (2002 [1991]) 'Perú, 1930-1960', in L. Bethell (ed.), *Historia de América Latina*, 8 (Barcelona: Crítica), pp. 3-58.

Blaser, M. (2009) 'The political ontology of a sustainable hunting program', *American Anthropologist* 111, pp. 10-20.

Boas, F. (1955 [1927]) *Primitive Art* (New York, NY: Dover Publications).

Boelens, R. (2008) *The Rules of the Game and the Game of the Rules: Normalization and Resistance in Andean Water Control* (Wageningen: Wageningen University).

Bolin, I. (1998) *Rituals of Respect: The Secret of Survival in the High Peruvian Andes* (Austin, TX: University of Texas Press).

— (2009) 'The glaciers of the Andes are melting: indigenous and anthropological knowledge merge in restoring water resources', in S. Crate and M. Nuttal (eds.), *Anthropology and Climate Change: From Encounter to Actions* (Walnut Creek, CA: Left Coast Press), pp. 228-39.

Bolton, R. and E. Mayer (eds.) (1977) *Andean Kinship and Marriage* (Washington DC: American Anthropological Association).

Borges, J.L. (1949 [1947]) *El inmortal* and *La busca de Averroes*, in *El Aleph* (Buenos Aires: Editorial Losada).

— (1960) *El hacedor* (Madrid: Alianza Editorial).

Bourdieu, P. (1977) *Outline of a Theory of Practice* (Cambridge: Cambridge University Press).

— (1990) *The Logic of Practice* (Stanford, CA.: Stanford University Press).

Brougère, A.M. (1980) *Traditions, changements et ecologie dans des communantes paysannes Andines* (Paris: Université de Paris).

Brush, S.B. (2004) *Farmers' Bounty: Locating Crop Diversity in the Contemporary World* (New Haven, CN: Yale University Press).

Brush, S.B. (ed.) (2000) *Genes in the Field: On-Farm Conservation of Crop Diversity* (Boca Raton, FL: Lewis Publishers).

Brush, S.B., H.J. Carney and Z. Huamán (1981) 'Dynamics of Andean potato agriculture', *Economic Botany* 35, pp. 70–85.

Buitrón, A. (1947) 'Situación económica y social del indio Otavaleño', *America Indígena* 7, pp. 45–67.

— (1962) 'Panorama de la aculturacion en Otavalo, Ecuador', *America Indigena* 26, pp. 53–79.

Buitrón, A. and B. Barbara (1945) 'Indios, blancos, y mestizos en Otavalo, Ecuador', *Acta Americana* 3, pp. 190–216.

van Buren, M. (1996) 'Rethinking the vertical archipelago: ethnicity, exchange, and history in the south central Andes', *American Anthropologists* 98, pp. 338–51.

Burkett, P. (1999) *Marx and Nature: A Red and Green Perspective* (New York, NY: St. Martin's Press).

Caballero, J.M. (1981) *Economía agraria de la sierra peruana antes de la reforma agraria de 1969* (Lima: Instituto de Estudios Peruanos).

de la Cadena, M. (2010) 'Indigenous cosmopolitics in the Andes: conceptual reflections beyond "politics"', *Cultural Anthropology* 25, pp. 334–70.

— (2015) *Earth Beings: Ecologies of Practice Across Andean Worlds* (Durham, NC: Duke University Press).

Canessa, A. (2012) *Intimate Indigeneities: Race, Sex, and History in the Small Spaces of Andean Life* (Durham, NC and London: Duke University Press).

Carey, M. (2010) *In the Shadow of Melting Glaciers: Climate Change and Andean Society* (New York, NY: Oxford University Press).

Casaverde, J. (1970) 'El mundo sobrenatural en una comunidad', *Allpanchis* 2, pp. 121–244.

del Castillo, L. (1997) 'Propiedad rural, titulación de tierras y propiedad comunal', *Debate Agrario* 26, pp. 59–80.

— (2003) 'Titulación de comunidades campesinas: CEPES, Allpa y problemática comunal', *Debate Agrario* 36, pp. 89–104.

— (2008) 'Comunidades, tierras, recursos naturales y desarrollo incluyente', in M. Bustamante-Olivares (ed.), *38 años de la reforma agraria* (Lima: Fundación Manuel J. Bustamante De la Fuente, Instituto Riva Agüero), pp. 83–146.

Castillo-Fernández, M. (2004) 'Comunidades Campesinas del Perú: Más cantidad, menos comunidad, y más diversidad en el último medio siglo', in A. Laos F. (ed.), *Las comunidades campesinas en el siglo XXI: Situación actual y cambio normativo* (Lima: Grupo ALLPA), pp. 15–63.

Castro-Pozo, H. (1979 [1924]) *Nuestra comunidad indígena* (Lima: Castro Pozo Editor).

Chan, A.S. (2011) 'Competitive tradition: intellectual property and New Millenial craft', *Anthropology of Work Review* 32, pp. 90–102.

Chibnik, M. (2003) *Crafting Tradition: The Making and Marketing of Oaxacan Wood Carvings* (Austin, TX.: University of Texas Press).

Clay, C.T. with W. Farrer (2013 [1914–1965]) *Early Yorkshire Charters* (Cambridge: Cambridge University Press), 13 vols.

Clifford, J. (1988) *The Predicament of Culture: Twentieth-Century Ethnography, Literature and Art* (Cambridge, MA and London: Harvard University Press).

Collier, J. and A. Buitron (1949) *The Awakening Valley* (Chicago, IL: University of Chicago Press).

Colloredo-Mansfeld, R.J. (1999) *The Native Leisure Class: Consumption and Cultural Creativity in the Andes* (Chicago, IL and London: University of Chicago Press).

— (2009) *Fighting Like a Community: Andean Civil Society in an Era of Indian Uprising* (Chicago, IL & London: University of Chicago Press).

— (2011) '"Don't be lazy, don't lie, don't steal": Community justice in the neoliberal Andes', *American Ethnologist* 29, pp. 637–62.

Colloredo-Mansfeld, R.J. and J. Antrosio (2015) *Fast Easy and In Cash: Artisan Hardship and Hope in the Global Economy* (Chicago, IL and London: University of Chicago Press).

Comisión de la Verdad y la Reconciliación (1994) *Informe Final* (Lima: Universidad Nacional Mayor de San Marcos, Pontificia Universidad Católica del Perú), 9 vols.

Cook, N.D. (1982) *People of the Colca Valley: A Population Study* (Boulder, CO: Westview Press).

— (ed.) (1975) *Tasa de la Visita General de Francisco de Toledo* (Lima: Universidad Nacional Mayor de San Marcos).

Cornelius, W. and D. Myre (eds.) (1998) *The Transformation of Rural Mexico: Reforming the Ejido Sector* (San Diego, CA: University of California).

Costin, C.L. and T.K. Earle (1989) 'Status distinction and legitimation of power as reflected in changing patterns of consumption in late pre-Hispanic Peru', *American Antiquity* 54, pp. 691–714.

Deere, C.D. (1990) *Household and Class Relations: Peasants and Landlords in Northern Peru* (Berkeley, CA: University of California Press).

Degregori, C.I. (ed.) (1990-1) 'A dwarf star', *NACLA Report on the Americas* 24, p. 14.

— (ed.) (2000) *No hay país más diverso: Compendio de antropología peruana* (Lima: Red Para el Desarrollo de las Ciencias Sociales en el Perú).

— (2000a) 'Panorama de la antropología en el Perú: del estudio del otro a la construcción de un nosotros diverso', in C.I. Degregori (ed.), *No hay país más diverso: Compendio de antropología peruana* (Lima: Red Para el Desarrollo de las Ciencias Sociales en el Perú), pp. 20–73.

— (2000b) 'Presentación', in C.I. Degregori (ed.), *No hay país más diverso: Compendio de antropología peruana* (Lima: Red Para el Desarrollo de las Ciencias Sociales en el Perú), pp. 13–19.

Degregori, C.I. and P. Sandoval (2008) 'Peru: From Otherness to a shared diversity', in D. Poole (ed.), *A Companion to Latin American Anthropology* (Malden, MA. and Oxford: Blackwell), pp. 150–74.

Degregori, C.I., J. Coronel, P. del Pino and O. Starn (1996) *Las rondas campesinas y la derrota de Sendero Luminoso* (Lima: Instituto de Estudios Peruanos).

Degregori, C.I. and J. Golte (1973) *Dependencia y desintegración estructural en la comunidad de Pacaraos* (Lima: Instituto de Estudios Peruanos).

Denevan, W.M. (1987) 'Abandono de terrazas en el Perú andino: Extensión, causas y propuestas de restauración', in C. de la Torre and M. Burga (eds.), *Andenes y camellones en el Peru andino* (Lima: CONCYTEC), pp. 255–9.

— (ed.) (1986) *The Cultural Ecology, Archaeology, and History of Terracing and Terrace Abandonment in the Colca Valley of Southern Peru*. Technical Report to the National Science Foundation and National Geographic Society, vol. 1 (Madison, WI: University of Wisconsin).

Dias, N. (2008) 'Double erasures: Rewriting the past at the Musée du Quai Branley', *Social Anthropology* 16 (3): 300–11.

Díaz-Martínez, A. (1985 [1969]) *Ayacucho: Hambre y esperanza* (Lima: Mosca Azul Editores).

Diez-Hurtado, A. (1999a) *Comunidades mestizas: Tierras, elecciones y rituales en la sierra de Pacaipampa, Piura* (Lima: Pontificia Universidad Católica del Perú).

— (1999b) 'Diversidades, alternativas y ambigüedades: Instituciones, comportamientos y mentalidades en la sociedad rural', in V. Agreda and M. Glave (eds.), *Perú. El problema agrario en debate: SEPIA VII* (Lima: Seminario Permanente de Investigación Agraria; ITDG), pp. 247-326.

— (2003) 'Interculturalidad y comunidades: Propiedad colectiva y propiedad individual', *Debate Agrario* 36, pp. 71-88.

— (2012) *Tensiones y transformaciones en comunidades campesinas* (Lima: CISEPA, Pontificia Universidad Católica del Perú).

Dobyns, H.F. (1970) *Comunidades campesinas del Perú* (Lima: Editorial Estudios Andinos). Actualised and expanded Spanish version of *The Social Matrix of Peruvian Indigenous Communities* (Ithaca, NY: Cornell University Press, 1964).

Donkin, R.A. (1979) *Agricultural Terracing in the Aboriginal New World* (Tucson, AZ: University of Arizona Press).

Doughty, P.L. (1968) *Huaylas: An Andean District in Search of Progress* (Ithaca & New York: Cornell University Press).

Duranti, A. (1994) *From Grammar to Politics: Linguistic Anthropology in a Western Samoan Village* (Berkeley & Los Angeles, CA: University of California Press).

Duranti, A. and C. Goodwin (eds.) (1992) *Rethinking Context: Language as an Interactive Phenomenon* (New York, NY: Cambridge University Press).

Duviols, P. (1973) 'Huari y Llacuaz: Agricultores y pastores, un dualismo prehispánico de oposición y complementariedad', *Revista del Museo Nacional* 39, pp. 153-91.

Earls, J. (1969) 'The organization of power in Quechua mythology', *Steward Journal of Anthropology* 1, pp. 63-82.

— (1992) 'Viabilidad productiva de la comunidad andina', in CIPCA (ed.), *Futuro de la comunidad campesina* (La Paz: Centro de Investigación y Promoción del Campesinado), pp. 155-72.

— (2006) *La agricultura andina ante una globalización en desplome* (Lima: Pontificia Universidad Católica del Perú, Centro de Investigaciones Sociológicas, Económicas, Políticas y Antropológicas).

Eresue, M. and A.M. Brougère (eds.) (1988) *Políticas agrarias y estrategias campesinas en la cuenca del Cañete* (Lima: Universidad Nacional Agraria, Instituto Francés de Estudios Andinos).

Eribon D., C. Lévi-Strauss and T.P. Wissing (1988) *Conversations with Claude Lévi-Strauss* (Chicago, IL: University of Chicago Press).

Erickson, P.A. and L.D. Murphy (1998) *A History of Anthropological Theory* (Peterborough: Broadview Press).

Escalante, C. (2010) *Huancavelica: Etnicidad y ciudadanía. Visión de los comuneros sobre la época de la violencia (1980–2000)*, PhD dissertation (Pontificia Universidad Católica del Perú).

Espósito, R. (2010 [1998]) *Communitas: The origin and destiny of community* (Stanford, CA: Stanford University Press).

Evans-Pritchard, E.E. (1940) *The Nuer: A Description of the Modes of Livelihood and Political Institutions of a Nilotic People* (Oxford: Clarendon Press).

Favre, H. (1977) 'The dynamics of Indian peasant society and migration to coastal plantations in central Peru', in K. Duncan and I. Rutledge (eds.), *Land and Labour in Latin America: Essays on the Development of Agrarian Capitalism in the Nineteenth and Twentieth Centuries* (Cambridge: Cambridge University Press), pp. 253–68.

— (1967) 'Tayta Wamani: Le culte des montagnes dans le centre sud des Andes Péruviennes', in *Colloque D'Études Péruviennes*, Publications des Annales de la Faculté des Lettres, N.S. 61 (Aix-en-Provence: Éditions Ophrys), pp. 121–40.

Feldman, J.P. (2015) Review of *Art from a Fractured Past: Memory and Truth-telling in Post-Shining Path Peru*, *The Americas* 72, pp. 500–2.

— (2012) 'Exhibiting conflict: History and politics at the Museo de la Memoria de ANFASEP in Ayacucho, Peru', *Anthropological Quarterly* 85, pp. 487–518.

Ferreira, F. (2012) *Back to the Village? An Ethnographic Study of an Andean Community in the Early Twenty-first Century* (PhD dissertation, Royal Holloway University of London).

— (2014) 'Ritual mixing: An ethnographic approach to the combination of soils from different origins in Inca *Ushnu* platforms', in F. Meddens, C. McEwan, K. Willis and N. Branch (eds.), *Inca Sacred Space: Landscape, Site and Symbol in the Andes* (London: Archetype Press), pp. 119–26.

Field, L.W. (1994) 'Who are the Indians? Reconceptualizing indigenous identity, resistance, and the role of the social sciences', *Latin American Research Review* 29, pp. 237–48.

Figueroa, A (1984) *Capitalist Development and the Peasant Economy in Peru* (Cambridge: Cambridge University Press).

Fischer, E.F. and P. Benson (2006) *Broccoli and Desire: Global Connections and Maya Struggles in Postwar Guatemala* (Stanford, CA: Stanford University Press).

Flores-Ochoa, J. (ed.) (1977) *Pastores de la puna* (Lima: Instituto de Estudios Peruanos).

Flyvbjerg, B. (2006) 'Five misunderstandings about case-study research', *Qualitative Inquiry* 12, pp. 219–45.

Fonseca, C. (1985) 'Estudios antropológicos sobre comunidades campesinas', in H. Rodríguez-Pastor (ed.), *La antropología en el Perú* (Lima: Consejo nacional de Ciencia y Tecnología), pp. 71–95.

Fonseca, C. and E. Mayer (1979) 'Sistemas agrarios y ecología en la cuenca del Río Cañete', *Debates en Antropología* 2, pp. 25–51.

— (2015) *Kausanamunay: Queriendo la Vida. Sistemas económicos en las comunidades campesinas* (Lima: Fondo Editorial del Congreso).

— (eds.) (1988) *Comunidad y producción en la agricultura andina* (Lima: Asociación para el Fomento de las Ciencias Sociales en el Perú).

Foster, J.B. (2000) *Marx's Ecology: Materialism and Nature* (New York, NY: Monthly Review Press).

Foster, J.B., B. Clark and R. York (2010) *The Ecological Rift: Capitalism's War on the Earth* (New York, NY: Monthly Review Press).

Foucault, M. (1982) 'The subject and power', *Critical Enquiry* 8, pp. 777–95, https://www.jstor.org/stable/1343197?seq=1#page_scan_tab_contents

Fuenzalida-Vollmar, F. (1976 [1969]) 'Estructura de la comunidad de indígenas tradicional: Una hipótesis de trabajo', in J. Matos Mar (ed.), *Hacienda, comunidad y campesinado en Perú* (Lima: Instituto de Estudios Peruanos), pp. 219–63.

Gadamer, H.G. (1975) *Truth and Method*, 2nd revd. edn. (New York, NY: Continuum).

— (1981) *Science in the Age of Reason* (Cambridge, MA: MIT Press).

Gade, D. (1967) *Plant Use and Folk Agriculture in the Vilcanota Valley of Peru: A Cultural-Historical Geography of Plant Resources* (PhD dissertation, University of Wisconsin).

García-Canclini, N. (2000 [1992]) *Culturas híbridas: Estrategias para entrar y salir de la modernidad* (Barcelona: Gedisa).

Geertz, C. (1973) *The Interpretation of Culture* (Boston, MA: Beacon Books).

Gelles, P.H. (1990) *Channels of Power, Fields of Contention. The Politics and Ideology of Irrigation in an Andean Peasant Community* (PhD dissertation. Harvard University).

— (2002 [2000]) *Agua y poder en la sierra peruana: La historia y política cultural del riego, rito y desarrollo* (Lima: Pontificia Universidad Católica del Perú).

de Gerando, M.J. (1800) *Considération sur les diverses méthodes a la suivre dans l'observation des peuples sauvages* (Paris: Société des Observateurs de L'Homme).

di Gessa, S., P. Poole and P. Bending (2008) *Participatory Mapping: A Tool for Empowerment: Experiences and Lessons Learned from the ILC network. International Land Coalition* (Rome: International Land Coalition).

Godelier, M. (1972) *Rationality and Irrationality in Economics* (London: New Left Books).

— (1973) *Horizons, trajets en anthropologie* (Paris: Maspero).

Goffman, E. (1967) *Relations in Public: Essays on Face-to-Face Behavior* (Garden City, NY: Anchor Books).

Golte, J. (2000) 'Economía, ecología, redes. Campo y ciudad en los análisis antropológicos', in C.I. Degregori (ed.), *No hay país más diverso: Compendio de antropología peruana* (Lima: Red Para el Desarrollo de las Ciencias Sociales en el Perú), pp. 204-34.

González, O.M. (2012) *Unveiling Secrets of War in the Peruvian Highlands* (Chicago, IL and London: University of Chicago Press).

Gornick, V. (2001) *The Situation and the Story: The Art of Personal Narrative* (New York, NY: Farrar Strauss and Giroux).

Gose, P. (1986) 'Sacrifice and the commodity form in the Andes', *Man* 21, pp. 296-310.

— (1988) 'Labour and the materiality of the sign: beyond dualist theories of culture', *Dialectical Anthropology* 13, pp. 103-21.

— (1993) 'Segmentary state formation and the ritual control of water under the Incas', *Comparative Studies in Society and History* 35, pp. 480-514.

— (1994) *Deathly Waters and Hungry Mountains: Agrarian Ritual and Class Formation in an Andean Town* (Toronto: University of Toronto Press).

— (1995) 'Contra Pascual Haro: un proceso de idolatrías, Cuzco 1697', *Ciencias Sociales* 1, pp. 203-18.

— (1996) 'Oracles, mummies, and political representation in the Inka State', *Ethnohistory* 43, pp. 1-33.

— (2000) 'The state as a chosen woman: Bride service and the feeding of tributaries in the Inka Empire', *American Anthropologist* 102, pp. 84–97.

— (2001 [1994]) *Aguas mortíferas y cierros hambrientos: Rito agrario y formación de clases en un pueblo andino* (La Paz: Mama Huaco).

— (2004 [1994]) *Aguas mortíferas y cierros hambrientos: Rito agrario y formación de clases en un pueblo andino* (Quito: Aba Yala).

— (2008) *Invaders as Ancestors: On the Intercultural Making and Unmaking of Spanish Colonialism in the Andes* (Toronto: University of Toronto Press).

Gow, D. (1980) 'The roles of Christ and Inkarrí in Andean religion', *Journal of Latin American Lore* 6, pp. 279–98.

Gow, R. (1982) 'Inkarrí and revolutionary leadership in the southern Andes', *Journal of Latin American Lore* 8, pp. 197–223.

Gramsci, A. (1971 [1948–51]) *The Prison Notebooks* (New York, NY: International Publishers).

Greaves, T., R. Bolton and F. Zapata (eds.) (2010) *Vicos and Beyond: A Half Century of Applying Anthropology in Peru* (Lanham, MD: Altamira Press).

Grillo-Fernández, E, V. Quiso-Choque, G. Rengifo-Vásquez and J. Valladolid-Rivera (eds.) (1994) *Crianza Andina de la chacra* (Lima: Proyecto Andino de Tecnolgías Campesinas).

Gudynas, E. (2011) 'Buen vivir: Today's tomorrow', *Development* 54, pp. 441–7.

Guerrero, A. (1978) 'Renta diferencial y vías de disolución de la Hacienda pre-capitalista en el Ecuador', *Avances* 28, pp. 47–72.

Guillet, D. (1983) 'Toward a cultural ecology of mountains: The Andes and the Himalayas compared', *Current Anthropology* 24, pp. 561–74.

de Haan, S. (2006) *Catálogo de variedades de papa nativa de Huancavelica-Perú* (Lima: Centro Internacional de la Papa, CIP, Federación Departamental de Comunidades Campesinas, FEDECH).

— and M. Bonierbale, H. Juarez, J. Poma and E. Salas (2009) 'Annual spatial management of potato diversity in Peru's central Andes', in S. de Haan, *Potato Diversity at Height: Multiple Dimensions of Farmer-driven in-situ Conservation in the Andes* (PhD dissertation, Wageningen University), pp. 91–116.

Handelman, H. (1975) *Struggle in the Andes: Peasant Political Mobilization in Peru* (Austin, TX: University of Texas Press).

Harris, O. (1980) 'The power of signs: Gender, culture and the wild in the Bolivian Andes', in C. MacCormack and M. Strathern (eds.), *Nature, Culture and Gender* (Cambridge: Cambridge University Press), pp. 70–94.

— (2000a) 'Andean anthropology in the fulcrum of history', in Harris (2000b) (London: Institute of Latin American Studies), pp. 1–24.

— (2000b) *To Make the Earth Bear Fruit: Ethnographic Essays on Fertility, Work and Gender in Highland Bolivia* (London: Institute of Latin American Studies).

— (2009) Leaflet handed out at the Bolivian Forum conference, Newcastle University, 4 Feb. (two pages).

Harris, O., B. Larson and E. Tandeter (eds.) (1987) *La participación indígena en los mercados surandinos* (La Paz: CERES).

Heaney, S. (2014) *New Selected Poems 1988–2013* (London: Faber & Faber Ltd).

Hemming, J. (1970) *Conquest of the Incas* (New York, NY: Harcourt Brace Jovanovich).

Hernández-Príncipe, R. (1923 [1621–2]) 'Mitología Andina', *Inca* 1, pp. 7–56.

Hite, K. (2012) *Politics and the Art of Commeration* (New York, NY: Routledge).

Hoetmer, R., M. Castro, M. Daza, J. de Echave and C. Ruiz (2013) *Minería y movimientos sociales en el Perú: Instrumentos y propuestas para la defensa de la vida, el agua y los territorios* (Lima: Programa Democracia y Transformación Global).

Hurtado, G.H. (1974) *Formación de las comunidades campesinas en el Perú* (Lima: Tercer Mundo).

Irigaray, L. (1977) *This Sex Which Is Not One* (Paris: Les Editions de Minuit).

Isbell, B.J. (1972) 'Acquisition of Quechua morphology: An application of the Berko Test', *Papers in Andean Linguistics* 1, pp. 79–129.

— (1973) *Andean Structures and Activities: Towards a Study of Transformations of Traditional Concepts in a Central Highland Peasant Community* (PhD dissertation, University of Illinois).

— (1974) 'Parentesco andino y reciprocidad: Kuyaq – los que nos aman', in G. Alberti and E. Mayer (eds.) *Reciprocidad e intercambio en los Andes Peruanos* (Lima: Instituto de Estudios Peruanos), pp. 110–52.

— (1976) 'La otra mitad esencial: Un estudio de complementariedad sexual en los Andes', *Estudios Andinos*, pp. 37–56.

— (1978) *To Defend Ourselves: Ecology and Ritual in an Andean Village* (Austin, TX: Institute of Latin American Studies, University of Texas at Austin: distributed by University of Texas Press).

— (1985 [1978]) *To Defend Ourselves: Ecology and Ritual in an Andean Village* (Prospect Heights, IL: Waveland Press).

— (1994) 'Shining Path and peasant responses in rural Ayacucho', in D.S. Palmer (ed.), *Shining Path of Peru* (New York, NY: St Martin's), pp. 59–82.

— (1997) 'De inmaduro a duro: Lo simbolico femenino y los esquemas Andinos de genero', in C. Lutz and L. Abu-Lughod (eds.), *Mas Alla del Silencio: Las Fronteras de Genero en Los Andes* (La Paz: Instituto de Lengua y Cultura Aymara, CIASE), pp. 253–301.

— (1998) 'Violence in Peru: Performances and dialogues', *American Anthropologist* 100, pp. 283–92.

— (2004) 'Protest arts from Ayacucho, Peru: Song and visual artworks as validation of experience', in G. Delgado and J.M. Schechter (eds.), *Quechua expresivo quechua: La inscripción de voces andinas* (Bonn: Bonn Americanist Studies), pp. 237–62.

— (2005 [1978]) *Para defendernos: Ecología y ritual en un pueblo andino (To Defend Ourselves: Ecology and Ritual in an Andean Village)* (Cuzco: Centro de Estudios Regionales Andinos Bartolomé de las Casas).

— (2009a) *Finding Cholita* (Urbana and Chicago, IL: University of Illinois Press).

— (2009b) 'Written on my body', in P. Ghassem-Fachandi (ed.), *Violence: Ethnographic Encounters* (Oxford and New York, NY: Berg), pp. 15–34.

— (2010) 'El retorno de Cornell a Vicos, 2005', in R. Bolton, T. Greaves and F. Zapata (eds.), *50 Años de Antropología Aplicada en el Perú. Vicos y otras experiencias* (Lima: Instituto de Estudios Peruanos), pp. 371–410.

— (2011) 'Cornell returns to Vicos, 2005', in T.C. Greaves, R. Bolton and F. Zapata (eds.), *Vicos and Beyond: a Half Century of Applying Anthropology in Peru* (Lanham, MD: AltaMira Press), pp. 283–308.

Isbell, B.J. and F.A. Roncalla-Fernández (1977) 'The ontogenesis of metaphor: Riddle games among Quechua speakers seen as cognitive discovery procedures', *Journal of Latin American Lore* 3, pp. 19–49.

Ismaelillo, S. and R. Wright (eds.) (1982) *Native People in Struggle: Russell Tribunal of the Religious Rights of the Indians of the Americas* (Bombay, NY: ERIN Publications, Boston, MA: Anthropology Resource Center).

Jaffee, D. (2007) *Brewing Justice: Fair Trade Coffee, Sustainability and Survival* (Berkeley, CA: University of California Press).

Johnson, A.W. (1978) *Quantification in Cultural Anthropology: An Introduction to Research Design* (Stanford, CA: Stanford University Press).

Kahn, P. (2012) 'Centennial sauvage: The survival of *Tristes Tropiques*', *Cerise Press* 4, pp. 1–15.

Kay, C. (2011) 'Reseña, Enrique Mayer: *Ugly Stories of the Peruvian Agrarian Reform*', *Estudios Interdisciplinarios de America Latina y el Caribe* 22, pp. 125–8.

Keesing, R.M. and A.I. Strathern (1998 [1976]) *Cultural Anthropology: A Contemporary Perspective* (Fort Worth, TX and London: Harcourt Brace College Publishers).

Kernaghan, R. (2009) *Coca's Gone: Of Might and Right in the Huallaga Post Boom* (Palo Alto, CA: Stanford University).

Laguna, P. (2011) *Mayas y Flujos: Acción colectiva, cambio social, quinua y desarrollo regional indígena en los Andes Bolivianos* (Wageningen: Wageningen University).

Laite, J. (1981) *Industrial Development and Migrant Labour in Latin America* (Austin, TX: University of Texas Press).

Latour, B. (1993) *We Have Never been Modern* (Cambridge, MA: Harvard University Press).

Laurenson, D. (ed.) (1978) 'The sociology of literature: Applied studies (with a memorial by Claire Bland)', *The Sociological Review*, special issue, 26.

Leach, E. (1976) *Culture and Communication: The logic by which symbols are connected* (Cambridge: Cambridge University Press).

Lehman, D. (1982) 'After Chayanov and Lenin: New paths of agrarian capitalism', *Journal of Development Economics* 11, pp. 133–61.

Leinaweaver, J. (2009) *The Circulation of Children: Kinship, Adoption, and Morality in Andean Peru* (Durham, NC: Duke University).

Lévi-Strauss, C. (1955) *Tristes Tropiques* (Paris: Plon).

— (1961 [1955]) *A World on the Wane* (New York, NY: Criterion Books).

— (1963 [1958]) *Structural Anthropology* (New York, NY: Basic).

— (1964) *Le Cru et le Cuit, Mythologiques* series, vol. 1 (Paris: Plon).

— (1969 [1962]) *The Savage Mind (Nature of Human Sociology)* (New York, NY: Harper Row).

— (1969 [1949]) *The Elementary Structures of Kinship* (Boston, MA: Beacon Press).

— (1973 [1955]) *Tristes Tropiques* (trans. J. and D. Weightman) (New York: Penguin).

Li, F. (2013) 'Relating divergent worlds: Mines, aquifers and sacred mountains in Peru', *Anthropologica* 55, pp. 399–411.

Long, N. and B. Roberts (1978) *Peasant Cooperation and Capitalist Expansion in Central Peru* (Austin, TX: University of Texas Press).

— (1984) *Miners, Peasants and Entrepeneurs: Regional Development in the Central Highlands of Peru* (Cambridge: Cambridge University Press).

Lukács, G. (1971) *History and Class Consciousness: Studies in Marxist Dialectics* (Boston, MA: MIT Press).

Lund-Skar, S. (1994) *Lives Together-Worlds Apart: Quechua Colonization in Jungle and City* (Oslo: Scandinavian University Press Book).

Málaga, A.M. (1977) 'Los collaguas en la historia de Arequipa en el siglo XVI', in F. Pease (ed.), *Collaguas I* (Lima: Pontificia Universidad Católica del Perú), pp. 93-130.

Malinowski, B. (1922) *Argonauts of the Western Pacific* (London: George Routledge and Sons).

Mallon, F. (1983) *The Defense of Community in Peru's Central Highlands: Peasant Struggle and Capitalist Transition, 1840-1940* (Palo Alto, CA: Stanford University Press).

Mamani, C. (1991) *Taraqu. 1866-1935. Masacre, guerra y "renovación" en la biografía de Eduardo L. Nina Qhispi* (La Paz: Ediciones Aruwiyiri).

Manrique, N. (1986) *Colonialismo y pobreza campesina* (Lima: DESCO).

— (1987) *Mercado interno y región: La sierra Central 1820-1930* (Lima: DESCO).

Mariátegui, J.C. (1971[1928]) *Seven Interpretative Essays on Peruvian Reality* (Austin, TX: University of Texas Press).

— (2005 [1928]) *Siete ensayos de interpretación de la realidad peruana* (Lima: Biblioteca Amauta).

Markowitz, L. (2006) '¿Cómo ganarse la vida? Estrategias de los alpaqueros de Caylloma', in C. Reniere, E. Frank and O. Toro (eds.), *Camélidos Sudamericanos Domésticos* (Lima: DESCO), pp. 334-55.

Marx, K. (1964 [1844]) *The Economic and Philosophical Manuscripts of 1844* (New York, NY: International Publishers).

Matos Mar, J. (ed.) (1958) *Las actuales comunidades de indígenas: Huarochiri en 1955* (Lima: Universidad Nacional Mayor de San Marcos, Instituto de Etnología y Arqueología).

Matos Mar, J. (1965) 'Algunas características generales de las comunidades de indígenas del área andina', *Cuadernos de Antropología* 8, pp. 1-12.

Mayer, E. (1971) 'Un carnero por un saco de papas: Aspectos del trueque en la zona de Chaupiwaranga (Pasco)', *Revista del Museo Nacional* 37, pp. 184-96.

— (1972) 'Censos insensatos: Evaluación de los censos campesinos en la historia de Tangor', in J.V. Murra (ed.), *Visita de la Provincia de León de Huánuco en 1562* (Iñigo Ortiz de Zúñiga, visitador) (Huánuco: Universidad Nacional Hermilio Valdizán), pp. 339-66.

— (1974) *Reciprocity, Self-Sufficiency and Market Relations in a Contemporary Community in the Central Andes of Peru* (Ithaca, NY: Cornell University. Cornell Latin American Dissertation Series, vol. 72).

— (1977) 'Tenencia y control comunal de la tierra: El caso de Laraos (Yauyos)', *Cuadernos del Consejo Nacional de la Universidad Peruana* 24, pp. 59-72.

— (1979) *Land Use in the Andes: Ecology and Agriculture in Mantaro Valley of Peru with Special Reference to Potatoes* (Lima: Social Science Unit Publication, International Potato Center).

— (1984) 'A tribute to the household: Domestic economy and the encomienda in colonial Peru', in R.T. Smith (ed.), *Kinship Ideology and Practice in Latin America* (Chapel Hill, NC: University of North Carolina Press), pp. 85-118.

— (1985) 'Production zones', in S. Masuda, I. Shimada, and C. Morris (eds.), *Andean Ecology and Civilization: An Interdisciplinary Perspective on Andean Ecological Complementarity* (Tokyo: University of Tokyo Press), pp. 45-84.

— (1992) 'Peru in deep trouble: Mario Vargas Llosa's "Inquest in the Andes" reexamined', in G. Marcus (ed.), *Rereading Cultural Anthropology* (Durham, NC: Duke University Press), pp. 181-219.

— (1994) 'Recursos naturales, medio ambiente, tecnología y desarrollo', in V.O. Dancourt, E. Mayer and C. Monge (eds.), *Perú: El problema agrario en debate* (Lima: Seminario Permanente de Investigación Agraria), pp. 479-533.

— (2002) *The Articulated Peasant: Household Economies in the Andes* (Boulder, CO: Westview Press).

— (2005) 'Prólogo a la edición en español', in B.J. Isbell, *Para defendernos: ecología y ritual en un pueblo andino* (Cuzco: Centro de Estudios Regionales Andinos Bartolomé de las Casas), pp. 11-15.

— (2009) *Ugly Stories of the Peruvian Agrarian Reform* (Durham, NC: Duke University Press).

— (2010) 'Vicos as a model: A retrospective', in T. Greaves, R. Bolton and F. Zapata (eds.), *Vicos and Beyond: A Half Century of Applying Anthropology in Peru* (Walnut Creek, CA: Altamira Press), pp. 163-92.

— (2012) 'Uchuraccay y el Perú profundo de Mario Vargas Llosa', in C.I. Degregori, P.F. Sendón and P.E. Sandoval (eds.), N*o hay país más diverso II, Compendio de Antropologia Peruana* (Lima: Instituto de Estudios Peruanos), pp. 146-88 .

— (2013) 'In the realm of the Incas', in J. Pillsbury, K.G. Hirth, D. Beliaev and R.E. Blanton (eds.), *Merchants, Trade and Exchange in the Pre-Columbian World* (Washington DC: Dunbarton Oaks), pp. 311-19.

Mayer, E. and R. Bolton (eds.) (1980) *Parentesco y matrimonio en los Andes* (Lima: Pontificia Universedad Católica del Perú).

Mayer, E. and C. Fonseca (1979) *Sistemas agrarios en la cuenca del río Cañete* (Lima: Oficina Nacional de Evaluación de Recursos Naturales).

Meisch, L. (2002) *Andean Entrepreneurs: Otavalo Merchants and Musicians in the Global Arena* (Austin, TX: University of Texas Press).

Mendoza, F. and F. Patzi (1997) *Atlas de los Ayllus del Norte de Potosí* (Potosí: Comisión Europea, Programa de Autodesarrollo Campesino).

Merleau Ponty, M. (1945) *Phenomenology of Perception* (Paris: Editions Gallimard)

Miller, D. (1995) 'Consumption studies as the transformation of anthropology', in D. Miller (ed.), *Acknowledging Consumption* (New York, NY: Routledge), pp. 264-95.

Milton, C. (2014) *Art from a Fractured Past: Memory and Truth Telling in Post-Shining Path Peru* (Durham, NC: Duke University Press).

Mintz, S.W. (1985) *Sweetness and Power: The Place of Sugar in Modern History* (New York, NY: Penguin).

Mishkin, B. (1946) 'The contemporary Quechua', in J.H. Steward (ed.), *Handbook of South American Indians*, 2 (Washington DC: Smithsonian Institution), pp.411-70.

Mitchell, W.P. (1976) 'Irrigation and community in the central Peruvian highlands', *American Anthropologist* 78, pp. 25-44.

— (2010) 'Review of Enrique Mayer's *Ugly Stories of the Peruvian Agrarian Reform*', *Journal of Latin American Studies* 15, pp. 483-4.

Morales, R.C. (1965) *Zarate, el Temible Willka* (La Paz: Talleres Gráficos Bolivianos).

Morissette, J. and L. Racine (1973) 'La hiérarchie des Wamaní: Essai sur la pensée classificatoire Quechua', *Recherches Amérindiennes au Québec* 3, pp. 167-88.

Morlon, P. (ed.) (1996) *Comprender la agricultura campesina en los Andes Centrales, Perú-Bolivia* (Lima and Cuzco: Instituto Francés de Estudios

Andinos, Centro de Estudios Regionales Andinos Bartolomé de las Casas).

Morlon, P., B. Orlove and A. Hibon (1982) *Tecnologías agricolas tradicionales en los Andes Centrales: Perspectivas para el desarrollo* (Lima: UNESCO, PNUD, COFIDE).

Morris, C. (1938) *Foundations of the Theory of Signs* (Chicago, IL: University of Chicago Press).

Müller-Wille, S. (2010) 'Claude Lévi-Strauss on race, history and genetics', *Bio-societies* 5, pp. 330–47.

Murra, J.V. (1972) 'El "control vertical" de un máximo de pisos ecológicos en la economía de las sociedades andinas', in J.V. Murra (ed.), *Visita de la Provincia de León de Huánuco en 1562 (Iñigo Ortíz de Zúñiga, visitador)* (Huánuco: Universidad Nacional Hermilio Valdizán), pp. 427–76.

— (1973) 'Los límites y las limitaciones del archipiélago vertical en los Andes', *Avances* 1, pp. 75–80.

— (1975) *Formaciones económicas y políticas del mundo andino* (Lima: Instituto de Estudios Peruanos).

— (2005 [1972]) 'El "control vertical" de un máximo de pisos ecológicos en la economía de las sociedades andinas', in *El Mundo Andino* (Lima: Pontificia Universidad Católica del Perú), pp. 59–115.

Murra, J.V. et al. (1966) *Cuadernos de Investigación Huánuco* (Huánuco: Universidad H. Valdazán).

Nader, L. (1965) 'Perspectives gained from field work', in S. Tax (ed.), *Horizons of Anthropology* (London: Georges Allen and Unwin Ltd), pp. 148–59.

Narayan, K. (1993) 'How native is a "native" anthropologist?', *American Anthropologist*, n.s., 95, pp. 671–86.

— (2007) 'Tools to shape texts: What creative nonfiction can offer ethnography', *Anthropology and Humanism* 32, pp. 130–44.

Nash, J. (1993 [1979]) *We Eat the Mines and the Mines Eat Us: Dependency and Exploitation in Bolivian Tin Mines* (New York, NY: Columbia University Press).

Netting, R. McC. (1976) 'What alpine peasants have in common: Observations on communal tenure in a Swiss village', *Human Ecology* 4, pp. 135–46.

— (1993) *Smallholders, Householders: Farm Families and the Ecology of Intensive, Sustainable Agriculture* (Palo Alto, CA: Stanford University Press).

Nicolás, V. (2015) *Los ayllus de Tinguipaya: Ensayos de historia a varias voces* (La Paz: Plural Editores).

Núñez del Prado, J. (1970) 'El mundo sobrenatural de los Quechuas del Sur del Perú a través de la comunidad de Qotobamba', *Allpanchis* 2, pp. 57-119.

Oberem, U. (1976) 'El acceso a recursos naturales de diferentes ecologías en la sierra ecuatoriana, siglo XVI', in J. Flores-Ochoa (ed.), *Organización social y complimentaridad económica en los Andes centrales*, 4 (Paris: Actes XLII International Congress of Americanists), pp. 51-64.

Orlove, B.S. and H.J. Rutz (1989) 'Thinking about consumption: A social economy approach', in H.J. Rutz and B.S. Orlove (eds.), *The Social Economy of Consumption* (Lanham, MD: University Press of America), pp. 1-57.

Ortiz, A. (1980) *Huarochirí, 400 Años Después* (Lima: Pontificia Universidad Católica del Perú).

Ortiz de Zuñiga (ed. J.V. Murra, 1972) *Visita de la Provincia de León de Huánuco en 1562* (Huánuco: Universidad Nacional Hermilio Valdizan).

Osterling, J.P. and H. Martínez (1983) 'Notes for a history of Peruvian social anthropology, 1940-80', *Current Anthropology* 24, pp. 343-60.

Ostrom, E. (1990) *Governing the Commons: The Evolution of Institutions for Collective Action* (Cambridge: Cambridge University Press).

Paerregaard, K. (1991) 'Más allá del dinero: Trueque y economía categorial en un distrito del Valle de Colca'. Manuscript of the article published in *Anthropologica* 11, pp. 209-51.

— (1997) *Linking Separate Worlds: Urban Migrants and Rural Lives in Peru* (Oxford: Berg).

Pajuelo, R. (2000) 'Imágenes de la comunidad. Indígenas, campesinos y antropólogos en el Perú', in C.I. Degregori (ed.), *No hay país más diverso: compendio de antropología peruana* (Lima: Red Para el Desarrollo de las Ciencias Sociales en el Perú), pp. 123-79.

Palacios-Ríos, F. (1977) 'Pastizales de regadío para alpacas', in J. Flores Ochoa (ed.), *Pastores de la puna* (Lima: Instituto de Estudios Peruanos), pp. 155-70.

Palomino-Flores, S. (1984 [1970]) *El sistema de oposiciones en la comunidad de Sarhua*, BA dissertation, Universidad Nacional de San Cristóbal de Huamanga) (Lima: Pueblo Indio).

Parsons, E.C. (1945) *Peguche: A Study of Andean Indians* (Chicago, IL: University of Chicago Press).

Partridge, W.L. (1982) 'Community studies in Latin America', *American Anthropologist* 84, pp. 130-3.

Paul, B.D. (1953) 'Interview techniques and field relationships', in A.L. Kroeber (ed.), *Anthropology Today* (Chicago, IL: University of Chicago Press), pp. 430-51.

Pease F.G.Y. (ed.) (1977a) *Collaguas I. Yanque Collaguas: Sociedad, economía y población. 1604-1617* (Arequipa: Fondo Editorial PUCP).

— (ed.) (1977b) *Collaguas II. Yanque Collaguas: Sociedad, economía y población. 1604-1617* (Arequipa: Fondo Editorial PUCP).

Pelto, J.P. and H.P. Pelto (1973) 'Ethnography: The fieldwork enterprise', in J.J. Honigmann (ed.), *Handbook of Social and Cultural Anthropology* (Chicago, IL: Rand McNally and Co), pp. 241-88.

Pérez-Galán, B. (2004) *Somos como Incas: Autoridades tradicionales en los Andes Peruanos* (Cuzco, Madrid and Frankfurt: Iberoamericana/Vervuert).

Platt, N. (2001) *Making Music* (Ashford: Pembles Publications).

Platt, T. (1975) 'Experiencia y experimentación: Los asentamientos andinos en las cabeceras del valle de Azapa', *Chungará* 5, pp. 33-60.

— (1983) 'Conciencia Andina y conciencia proletaria: Qhuyaruna y ayllu en el norte de Potosí', *HISLA: Revista Latinoamericana de Historia Económica y Social* 2, pp. 47-73.

— (1986 [1976, 1978, 1980]) 'Mirrors and maize: The concept of *yanantin* among the Macha of Bolivia', in J. Murra, N. Wachtel and J. Revel (eds.), *Anthropological History of Andean Polities* (Cambridge: Cambridge University Press), pp. 228-59.

— (1987) 'Calendarios tributarios e intervención mercantil: Racionalidades estacionales entre los ayllus de Lipez (Potosí) en el siglo XIX', in O. Harris, B. Larson and E. Tandeter (eds.), *Participación indígena en los mercados surandinos* (Cochabamba: Centro de Estudios de la Realidad Social).

— (1992) 'Writing, shamanism and identity: Voices from Abya-Yala', *History Workshop Journal* 34, pp. 148-58.

— (1996 [1987]) *Los guerreros de Cristo: Cofradías, misa solar y guerra regenerativa en una doctrina surandina (siglos XVIII–XX)* (Sucre and La Paz: Ediciones ASUR no 5 – PLURAL).

— (1997) 'The sound of light: Emergent communication through Quechua shamanic dialogue', in R. Howard-Malverde (ed.), *Creating Context in Andean Cultures* (Oxford University Press: Oxford Studies in Anthropology Linguistics no. 6), pp. 195-226.

— (2001) 'El feto agresivo. Parto, formación de la persona y mitohistoria en los Andes', in *Anuario de Estudios Americanos* (Seville) 58, pp. 633–78.

— (2009a) 'Tributo y ciudadanía en Potosí, Bolivia. Consentimiento y libertad entre los Ayllus de la Provincia de Porco, 1830-1840', in P. García-Jordán (ed.), *Dinámicas de poder local en América Latina, siglos XIX-XXI* (Barcelona: Universitat de Barcelona).

— (2009b) '"From the island's point of view". Warfare and transformation in an Andean vertical archipelago', *Journal de la Société des Américanistes* 95, pp. 33–70.

— (2014) 'Un archivo campesino como "acontecimiento de terreno". Los nuevos papeles del Curaca de Macha (Alasaya)', *Revista Fuentes* 33, pp. 6-18.

— (2016 [1982]) *Estado boliviano y ayllu andino: Tierra y tributo en el Norte de Potosí* (Lima: Instituto de Estudios Peruanos).

Platt, T., T. Bouysse-Cassagne, O. Harris and T. Saignes (2011 [2006]) *Qaraqara-Charka. Mallku, Inka y Rey en la Provincia de Charcas. Historia antropológica de una confederación aymara (siglos XV-XVII)* (La Paz: Institut Français d'Études Andines, Plural Editores, University of St Andrews, University of London).

Platt, T. et al. (eds.) (2010) *Chungará. Revista Antropológica Chilena* (special number in memory of John Murra) 42.

Polanyi, K. (1944) *The Great Transformation* (New York, NY: Farrar and Rinehart).

Polanyi, K., C.M. Arensberg and H.W. Pearson (eds.) (1957) *Trade and Market in the Early Empires: Economies in History and Theory* (Glencoe, IL: The Free Press).

Poole, D. (ed.) (2008) *A Companion to Latin American Anthropology* (Malden, MA, and Oxford: Blackwell).

Postero, N. (2010) 'The struggle to create a radical democracy in Bolivia', *Latin American Research Review* 45 (4): 60-78.

Quispe-Mejía, U. (1969 [1968]) *La herranza en las comunidades de Choque Huarcaya y Huancasancos*, BA dissertation, Universidad Nacional de San Cristóbal de Huamanga (Lima: Instituto Indigenista Peruano).

Ramberg, L. (2014) *Given to the Goddess: South Indian Devadasis and the Sexuality of Religion* (Durham, NC and London: Duke University Press).

Rappaport, J. (1998 [1990]) *The Politics of Memory: Native Historical Interpretation in the Colombian Andes* (Durham, NC: Duke University Press).

Rasmussen, M.B. (2015) *Andean Waterways: Resource Politics in Highland Peru* (Seattle, WA: University of Washington Press).

Rasnake, R. (1989 [1988]) *Autoridad y poder en los Andes. Los Kuraqkuna de Yura* (La Paz: HISBOL).

Ravi-Mumford, J. (2012) *Vertical Empire: The General Resettlement of Indians in the Colonial Andes* (Durham, NC and London: Duke University Press).

Redfield, R. (1956) *The Little Community* (Chicago, IL: University of Chicago Press.

Rénique, J.L. (2013) 'Estudio preliminar', in J.L. Rénique (ed.), *Luis E. Valcárcel: del indigenismo cusqueño a la antropología peruana (textos esenciales)* (Lima: Ediciones COPE-PETROPERU, Fondo Editorial del Congreso del Peru, Instituto de Estudios Peruanos), pp. 15–82.

Rhoades, R. and S.I. Thompson (1975) 'Adaptive strategies in alpine environments. Beyond ecological particularism', *American Ethnologist* 2, pp. 535–51.

Ricard-Lanata, X. (ed.) (2005) *Vigencia de lo andino en los albores del siglo XXI: Una mirada desde el Perú y Bolivia* (Cuzco: Centro de Estudios Regionales Andinos Bartolomé de las Casas) esp. 'Introducción', pp. 9–21.

Rivera-Andía, J. (2014) *Comprender los rituales ganaderos en los Andes y más allá: Etnografías de lidias, herranzas y arrierias* (Aachen: Shaker Verlag).

Rivera-Cusicanqui, S. (1972) 'Las etnias de Chillón', *Revista del Museo Nacional* 38, pp. 250–314.

— (1982) *Ayllus y proyectos de desarrollo en el Norte de Potosí* (La Paz: Aruwiyiri).

— (1991) '"Pedimos la revisión de límites": Un episodio de incomunicación de castas en el movimiento de caciques-apoderados de los Andes Bolivianos, 1919–1921', in S. Moreno and F. Salomon (eds.), *Reproducción y Transformación de las Sociedades Andinas, Siglos XVI–XX*, 1 (Quito: Ediciones Abya-Yala and Movimiento Laicos para América Latina), pp. 603–52.

Robinson, D.J. (ed.) (2006) *Collaguas III. Yanque Collagua: Sociedad, economía y población. 1604–1617* (Lima: Ediciones PUCP).

— (ed.) (2009) *Collaguas IV. Cabanaconde: Sociedad, economía y población. 1604–1617* (Lima: Ediciones PUCP).

— (2012) *Collaguas: Visitas de Yanque-Collaguas 1591, y documentos asociados* (Lima: Ediciones PUCP).

Robles-Mendoza, R. (2002) *Legislación peruana sobre comunidades campesinas* (Lima: Fondo Editorial de la Facultad de Ciencias Sociales, Universidad Nacional Mayor de San Marcos).

Roel-Mendizábal, P. (2000) 'De folklore a culturas híbridas: rescatando raíces, redefiniendo fronteras entre nos/otros', in C.I. Degregori (ed.), *No hay país más diverso: Compendio de antropología peruana* (Lima: Red Para el Desarrollo de las Ciencias Sociales en el Perú), pp. 74-122.

Roseberry, W. (1995) 'Latin American studies in a "post colonial" era', *Journal of Latin American Anthropology* 1, pp. 150-77.

Rostworowski de Diez Canseco, M. (1972) 'Las etnias de Chillón', *Revista del Museo Nacional* 38, pp. 250-314.

— (1977) *Etnía y sociedad: Costa peruana prehispánica* (Lima: Instituto de Estudios Peruanos).

— (1988) *Historia del Tahuantinsuyu* (Lima: Instituto de Estudios Peruanos).

Rowe, J. (1946) 'Inca culture at the time of the Spanish conquest', in J.H. Steward (ed.), *Handbook of South American Indians*, 2 (Washington DC: Smithsonian Institution), pp. 183-330.

Rubio-Orbe, G. (1956) *Punyaro, estudio de antropologia social y cultural de una communidad indigena y mestiza* (Quito: Casa de la Cultura Ecuatoriana).

Ruíz-Estrada, A. (1981) *Los quipos de Rapaz* (Huacho: Centro de Investigación de Ciencia y Tecnología de Huacho).

Rulfo, J. (1955) *Pedro Páramo* (Fondo de Cultura Económica, Mexico).

Russell, J. (1961) *A World on the Wane* (London: Criterion).

Saavedra, B. (1903) *El Ayllu* (La Paz: Velarde).

Sahlins, M. (1976) *Culture and Practical Reason* (Chicago, IL: University of Chicago Press).

Said, E.W. (1978) *Orientalism* (New York, NY: Vintage Books).

Salas-Carreño (2012) 'Entre les mineurs, les grands propriétaires terriens et l'État: Les allégeances des montagnes dans le sud des Andes péruviennes (1930-2012)', *Recherches Amérindiennes au Quebec* 42, pp. 25-37.

Sallnow, M.J. (1987) *Pilgrims of the Andes: Regional Cults in Cusco* (Washington DC and London: Smithsonian Institution Press).

Salomon, F. (1981) 'Weavers of Otavalo', in N.E. Whitten (ed.), *Cultural Transformations and Ethnicity in Modern Ecuador* (Urbana, IL: University of Illinois Press), pp. 420-49.

— (1982) 'Andean ethnology in the 1970s: A retrospective', *Latin American Research Review* 17, pp. 75-128.

— (1985) 'The dynamic potential of the complementarity concept', in S. Masuda, I. Shimada and C. Morris (eds.), *Andean Ecology and Civilization: An Interdisciplinary Perspective on Andean Ecological Complementarity* (Tokyo: University of Tokyo Press), pp. 511-33.

— (1986 [1978]) 'Vertical politics on the Inca frontier', in J. Murra, N. Wachtel and J. Revel (eds.), *Anthropological History of Andean Polities* (Cambridge: Cambridge University Press), pp. 89-118.

— (2002) 'Unethnic ethnohistory: On Peruvian peasant historiography and ideas of autochthony', *Ethnohistory* 49, pp. 475-506.

— (2004) *The Cord Keepers: Khipus and Cultural Life in a Peruvian Village* (Durham, NC: Duke University Press).

Salomon, F. and M. Niño-Murcia (2011) *The Lettered Mountain: A Peruvian Village's Way with Writing* (Durham, NC: Duke University Press).

Salomon, F. and G. Urioste (eds. and trans.) (1991) *The Huarochirí Manuscript, a Testament of Ancient and Colonial Andean Religion* (Austin, TX: University of Texas Press).

Sandoval, P. (2000) 'Los rostros cambiantes de la ciudad: Cultura urbana y antropología en el Perú', in C.I. Degregori (ed.), *No hay país más diverso: Compendio de antropología peruana* (Lima: Red Para el Desarrollo de las Ciencias Sociales en el Perú), pp. 278-329.

Sangren, S. (1988) 'Rhetoric and the authority of ethnography: "Postmodernism" and the social reproduction of texts', *Current Anthropology* 29, pp. 405-35.

Schwartz, S. and F. Salomon (1999) 'New peoples and new kinds of people: Adaptation, readjustment, and ethnogenesis in South American indigenous societies (colonial era)', in S. Schwartz and F. Salomon (eds.), *Cambridge History of the Native Peoples of the Americas*, 3(New York, NY and Cambridge: Cambridge University Press), pp. 443-501.

Scott, J.C. (1985) *Weapons of the Weak: Everyday Forms of Peasant Resistance* (New Haven, CT: Yale University Press).

Scurrah, M. (ed.) (2008) *Defendiendo derechos y promoviendo cambios: El estado, las empresas extractivas y las comunidades locales en el Perú* (Lima: Instituto de Estudios Peruanos, Oxfam Internacional, Instituto de Bien Comun).

Scurrah, M., S. de Haan, E. Olivera, R. Ccanto, H. Creed, M. Carrasco, E. Veres and C. Barahona (2012) 'Ricos en agrobiodiversidad, pero pobres en nutrición: Seguridad alimentaria en comunidades de Chopcca, Huancavelica', *Revista Agraria* 13, pp. 8-9.

Seligmann, L. (1995) *Between Reform and Revolution: Political Struggles in the Peruvian Andes, 1969–1991* (Stanford, CA: Stanford University Press).

— (2008) 'Agrarian reform and peasant studies: The Peruvian case', in D. Poole (ed.), *A Companion to Latin American Anthropology* (Malden, MA and Oxford: Blackwell), pp. 325–51.

Sendón, P.F. (2006) 'Ecología, ritual y parentesco en los Andes: Notas a un debate no derimido', *Debate Agrario*, 40–1, pp. 273–97.

Shoemaker, R. (1981) *The Peasants of El Dorado: Conflict and Contradiction in a Peruvian Frontier Settlement* (Ithaca, NY: Cornell University Press).

Smith, G. (1989) *Livelihood and Resistance: Peasants and the Politics of Land in Peru* (Berkeley, CA: University of California Press).

Sontag, S. (1994) 'The anthropologist as hero', in *Against Interpretation* (London: Vintage), pp. 69–81.

Spalding, K. (1970) 'Social climbers: Changing patterns of mobility among the Indians of colonial Peru', *Hispanic American Historical Review* 50, pp. 645–64.

Stanish, C. (2001) 'The origin of state societies in South America', *Annual Review of Anthropology* 30, pp. 41–64.

Starn, O. (1991) 'Missing the Revolution: Anthropologists and the war in Peru', *Cultural Anthropology* 6, pp. 63–91.

— (1992a) 'Antropología andina, "andinismo" y Sendero Luminoso', *Allpanchis* 39, pp. 15–72 (article), pp. 123–9 (final comments).

— (1992b) 'Missing the Revolution: anthropologists and the war in Peru', in G.E. Marcus (ed.), *Rereading Cultural Anthropology* (Durham, NC: Duke University Press), pp. 152–80.

— (1994) 'Rethinking the politics of anthropology: The case of the Andes', *Current Anthropology* 35, pp. 13–27 (article), pp. 27–33 (comments), pp. 33–35 (reply).

— (1995) 'Maoism in the Andes: The Communist Party of Peru-Shining Path and the refusal of history', *Journal of Latin American Studies* 27, pp. 399–422.

— (1999) *Nightwatch: The Politics of Protest in the Andes* (Durham, NC: Duke University Press).

Stearman, A.M. (1973) *San Rafael: Camba Town* (Gainesville, FL: The University of Florida Press).

Steward, J.H. (ed.) (1963 [1946–50]) *Handbook of South American Indians* (New York, NY: Cooper Square Publishers).

Stobart, H. (2006) *Music and the Poetics of Production in the Bolivian Andes* (Aldershot: Ashgate).

Tambiah, S. (1985) *Culture, Thought, and Social Action* (Cambridge, MA: Harvard University Press).

Taussig, M. (1999) *Defacement: Public Secrecy and the Labor of the Negative* (Stanford, CA: University of Stanford Press).

— (1980) *The Devil and Commodity Fetishism in South America* (Chapel Hill, NC: University of North Carolina Press).

Taylor, G. (ed. and trans.) with A. Acosta (1987) *Ritos y tradiciones de Huarochirí del siglo XVII* (Lima: Instituto de Estudios Peruanos, Instituto Francés de Estudios Andinos).

Terkel, S. (1970) *Hard Times: An Oral History of the Great Depression* (New York, NY: Avon).

THOA: Taller de Historia Oral Andina (1984) *El Indio Santos Marka T'ula, Cacique Principal de los ayllus de Qallapa y Apoderado General de las Comunidades Originarias de la República* (La Paz: Universidad Mayor de San Andrés).

Thompson, E.P. (1963) *The Making of the English Working Class* (New York, NY: Vintage).

Treacy, J. (1994) *Las chacras de Coporaque: Andenería y riego en el valle del Colca* (Lima: Instituto de Estudios Peruanos).

Trivelli, C. (1992) 'Reconocimiento legal de comunidades campesinas: Una revisión estadística', *Debate Agrario* 14, pp. 23–39.

Tschopik, H. Jnr. (1955) 'At home in the high Andes', *National Geographic Magazine*, Jan., pp. 133–46.

Tsing, A. (2004) *Friction: An Ethnography of Global Connection* (Princeton, NJ: Princeton University Press).

Urrutia, J. (1992) 'Comunidades campesinas y antropología: Historia de un amor (casi) eterno', *Debate Agrario* 14, 1–16.

Urton, G. (1981) *At the Crossroads of the Earth and the Sky: An Andean Cosmology* (Austin, TX: University of Texas Press).

— (1984) 'Chuta: El espacio de la práctica social en Pacariqtambo, Perú', *Revista Andina* 2, pp. 7–56.

— (1990) *The History of Myth: Pacariqtambo and the Origin of the Inkas* (Austin, TX: University of Texas Press).

Valcárcel, L.E. (1985 [1980]) 'Inicios de la etnología en el Perú', in H. Rodríguez-Pastor (ed.), *La antropología en el Perú* (Lima: Consejo nacional de Ciencia y Tecnología), pp. 15-28. Extracts from the author's autobiography: *Memorias* (Lima: IEP).

Valderrama, R. (2012) *Pastores, pastos y rebaños en la provincia de Caylloma (Arequipa)*, PhD dissertation (Pontificia Universidad Católica del Perú).

Valderrama, R. and C. Escalante (1977) *Gregorio Condori Mamani. Autobiografía* (Cuzco: Centro de Estudios Rurales Andinos Bartolomé de las Casas).

— (1983) 'Testimonio de un pongo huancavelicano', *Oralidad* 1, pp. 40-4.

— (1988) *Del Tata Mallku a la Mamapacha. Riego, sociedad y ritual en los Andes Peruanos* (Lima: DESCO).

— (1992) *Nosotros los humanos: Testimonios de los quechuas del siglo XX. Ñuqanchis runakuna* (Cuzco: Centro de Estudios Regionales Andinos Bartolomé de Las Casas).

— (1997) *La Doncella Sacrificada. Mitología del Valle del Colca* (Lima: UNSAA, IFEA).

— (2012) 'Pastores, pastos y Rebaños en la provincia de Caylloma (Arequipa)', in J. Flores-Ochoa (ed.), *El pastoreo Altoandino. Origen, desarrollo y situación actual*. Works presented at the RUR 6 Symposium (Cuzco: CEAC), pp. 29-38.

Valera-Moreno, G. (1998) *Las comunidades en el Peru: Una visión nacional desde las series departamentales* (Lima: Instituto Rural del Perú).

Valerio Laureano, J.H. (1985) 'Revindicación de tierras de la comunidad campesina de San Juan de Ondores, 1979-1980', BA thesis (Huancayo: Departamento de Sociología, Universidad Nacional del Centro del Perú).

Vallee, L. and S. Palomino (1973) 'Quelques elements d'ethnographie du "nakaq"', *Bulletin de l'Institut Francais d'Etudes Andines* 2, pp. 9-19.

Vargas-Llosa, M., A. Gúzman-Figueroa and M. Castro-Arenas (1983) *Informe de la Comisión Investigadora de los Sucesos de Uchuraccay* (Lima: Editora Perú).

Varillas-Gallardo, B. (1965) *Apuntes para el folklore de Yauyos* (Lima: Litografía Huascarán).

Vázquez, M. (1961) *Hacienda, peonaje y servidumbre en los Andes Peruanos* (Lima: Editorial Estudios Andinos).

Velasco-de-Tord, E. (1978) 'La K'apakocha: sacrificios humanos en el Incario', in M. Koth-De-Paredes and A. Castelli (eds.), *Etnohistoria y Antropología Andina* (Lima: Museo Nacional de Historia), pp. 193-9.

de la Vera Cruz, P. (1987) 'Cambios en los patrones de asentamiento y el uso y abandono de los andenes en Cabanaconde, valle del Colca,

Perú', in W.M. Denevan, K. Mathewson and G. Knapp (eds.), *Pre-Hispanic Agricultural Fields in the Andean Region. Part I* (Oxford: British Archaeological Reports. International Series), pp. 89–128.

Vincent, J. (1974) 'The structuring of ethnicity', *Human Organization* 33, pp. 375–9.

Viveiros de Castro, E.B. (2004) 'Exchanging perspectives: The transformation of objects into subjects in Amerindian ontologies', *Common Knowledge* 10, pp. 463–84.

— (1998) 'Cosmological deixis and Amerindian perspectivism', *Journal of the Royal Anthropological Institute* 4, pp. 469–88.

van Vleet, K. (2008) *Performing Kinship. Narrative, Gender and the Intimacies of Power* (Austin, TX: Texas University Press).

de Vries, P. (2015) 'The real of community, the desire for development and the performance of egalitarianism in the Peruvian Andes: A materialist–Utopian account', *Journal of Agrarian Change* 15 (1): 65–88.

Wachtel, N. (1971) *La vision des vaincus* (Paris: Gallimard), trans. (1977) B. and S. Reynolds as *The Vision of the Vanquished* (Hassocks: Harvester).

Weismantel, M. (1988) *Food, Gender, and Poverty in the Ecuadorian Andes* (Philadelphia, PA: University of Pennsylvania Press).

— (1989) 'Making breakfast and raising babies', in R. Wilk (ed.), *The Household Economy: Reconsidering the Domestic Mode of Production* (Boulder, CO: Westview Press), pp. 55–72.

Willerslev, R. (2007) *Soul Hunters: Hunting, Animism and Personhood among the Siberian Yukaghirs* (Berkeley, CA: University of California Press).

Williams, W.C. (1995 [1946]) *Paterson. Revised Edition* (New York, NY: New Directions).

Wolf, E.R. (1955) 'Types of Latin American peasantry: A preliminary discussion', *American Anthropologist* 57, pp. 452–71.

— (1957) 'Closed Corporate Peasant Communities in Mesoamerica and Central Java', *Southwestern Journal of Anthropology* 13, pp. 1–18.

— (1982) *Europe and the Peoples without History* (Berkeley & Los Angeles, CA: University of California Press).

— (1986) 'The vicissitudes of the closed corporate peasant community', *American Ethnologist* 13, pp. 325–9.

Wolfe, T. (2011 [1940]) *You Can't Go Home Again* (New York, NY: Scribner) (original copyright 1940, Harper & Rowe, NY).

Zimmerer, K.S. (1988) 'The ecogeography of Andean potatoes', *BioScience* 84, pp. 445–54.

— (1996) *Changing Fortunes: Biodiversity and Peasant Livlihood in the Peruvian Andes* (Berkeley, CA: University of California Press).

Zuidema, R.T. (1964) *The Zeque System of Cuzco: The Social Organization of the Capital of the Inca* (Leiden: E.J. Brill).

— (1989) *Reyes y guerreros: Ensayos de cultura Andina* (ed. M. Burga) (Lima: Grandes estudios Andinos).

— (2011) *El calendario Inca: Tiempo y espacio en la organizacion ritual del Cusco. La idea del pasado* (Lima: Fondo Editorial del Congreso del Perú).

— (2014) 'Hacer calendarios en quipus y tejidos', *Actas del Simposio Internacional, Lima 15-17 de Enero de 2009* (Lima: Ministerio de Cultura), pp. 397-444.

Index

academia, 8, 17, 21, 28, 50
acculturation/acculturated, 18, 19, 25, 49, 146
agrarian reform (*see also* land reform), 42, 54, 55, 74, 86, 166, 188, 217, 221, 224, 226, 234, 237, 238, 251–3, 255, 257, 259, 260, 261, 263
agriculture/agricultural, 5, 6, 10, 15, 26, 27, 39, 49, 51, 58, 97, 82, 84, 94, 109, 112, 127–29, 131, 133, 134, 138, 149, 151, 152, 160, 162, 217, 218, 241, 244, 245, 247–9, 251, 255, 256
Allen, Catherine J., ix, 4, 26, 38, 39, 69–91, 96
Ancash, 14, 18, 236
Andeanism (*see also* lo andino), 29, 31, 32, 105, 240
applied anthropology, 17, 18, 233, 236
Apurímac, 27, 39, 64, 93, 125, 138, 141, 251
apus (*see also* mountain spirits), 119–21, 130
archaeology/archaeological, 6, 9, 20, 69, 71, 76, 90, 127–9, 145, 171, 177, 183, 186, 187, 201, 216, 217, 219, 237, 263
Arequipa, 27, 28, 39, 72, 108, 125, 126, 127, 129, 138, 139–41, 143, 146, 147, 246
Arguedas, José M., 19, 146, 170
armed conflict/s, 7, 10, 28, 29, 32, 36, 38–40, 43, 65, 85, 137

astronomy/astronomical, 26, 27, 47, 136
authority/authorities, 1, 26–8, 35, 49, 56, 63, 74, 75, 95, 96, 101, 125, 132–4, 138, 140, 149, 161, 162, 188, 207, 209, 213, 226–8, 230, 231, 247, 257
Ayacucho (*see also* Huamanga), 1, 4, 6, 7, 9, 19, 26, 29, 36, 38, 45, 46, 48, 53–6, 58–61, 64, 65, 67, 108, 130, 137–40, 240, 261
ayllu/s, 15, 21, 25–7, 34, 41, 74, 75, 80, 82, 84, 86, 87, 102, 119, 121, 172, 173, 175, 178, 179, 182, 183, 185, 195, 199, 203–6, 208–10, 212, 213, 215, 218–24, 226–8, 230, 231
Aymara/s, 19, 36, 89, 127, 187, 199, 200, 217–20, 246
ayni, 21, 85, 94, 95, 121
(de) Ávila, Francisco, 14, 170, 173

Bateson, Gregory, 53, 70, 202
Belaúnde Terry, Fernando, 188, 251, 253, 255
Boas, Franz, 17, 23, 70
Bolivia/n, 5, 7, 12, 14, 16–20, 27, 33–6, 41–3, 97, 105, 121, 122, 136, 140, 170, 199–202, 204, 206, 208, 213, 215–27, 236, 239, 246, 259
Bourdieu, Pierre, 70, 79, 80, 98, 157

cabildo/s, 206–13, 215, 222, 225, 227, 228, 230, 231

Cañete Valley, 241, 244, 246, 248, 250, 252, 262
capitalism, 24, 113, 118, 156, 166, 212
cargo systems, 75, 142, 152, 154, 257
Charcas province, 204, 205, 209, 211, 219–21, 224, 231
Chile, 60, 136, 216, 217, 220, 223, 239
closed corporate community, 25, 26, 29, 30, 86
coca, 4, 26, 32, 39, 64, 76, 77, 78–81, 87, 89, 151, 186, 191, 196, 206, 211, 212, 219, 237, 249, 250, 263
Colca Valley/River, 27, 28, 39, 125, 127, 128–30, 132–4, 137, 138, 141, 146, 151, 159
Colombia, 7, 45, 136, 152, 154, 239
colonialism, 30, 48, 86, 102–4, 117, 200, 213, 221, 226
Colloredo-Mansfeld, Rudi, ix, 33, 40, 149–67
communism/communist, 53, 54, 203, 206, 236, 259
compadrazgo, 49, 74, 130
comunero/s, 26, 27, 31, 54, 55, 57, 59, 63, 94, 105, 132–9, 141, 144, 146, 173, 174, 196, 197, 240, 253, 254, 258, 262
comunidad/es campesina/s (*see also* peasant community/ies), 74, 108, 111, 173, 174, 185, 233, 251, 252, 256, 257, 259
consumption studies, 33, 158, 165
Cornell University, 16, 18, 25, 43, 50, 60, 65, 72, 169, 170, 203, 204, 235–8
cosmovision/cosmology, 32, 33, 97
curaca/s (*see also kuraka/s*), 207, 209, 212, 215, 216, 222, 226–8

Cuzco, 1, 19, 22, 26, 27, 34, 35, 38, 47, 64, 72, 74, 76, 80, 81, 85, 88–100, 106, 108, 119, 121, 125, 126, 130, 132, 134, 138, 141–3, 170, 203, 220, 234, 237, 256, 258

Degregori, Carlos Iván, 13, 17–19, 21, 24, 25, 28, 58, 59
democracy, 7, 143, 215, 227, 228, 230
development, 8, 18, 23, 33, 35, 40, 64, 68, 85, 125–7, 130, 132, 133, 136, 138, 141, 149, 151, 153, 156, 163, 166, 167, 188, 234, 248–50, 252
dualism, 26, 202, 210, 217

ecological adaptation, 11, 20–2, 25, 30, 42
ecology, 21, 40, 133, 134, 136, 149, 151, 166, 245
Ecuador, 5, 12, 14, 16, 19, 33, 36, 40, 43, 105, 136, 140, 152, 154, 162, 239, 246, 249.
Escalante, Carmen, x, 27, 39, 40, 42, 125–47
essentialism/essentialisation, 29, 30, 224, 240
ethnic, 1, 12, 14, 15, 22, 26, 27, 34, 68, 94, 95, 110, 127, 134, 150, 157, 159, 160, 162, 163, 201, 206, 215, 220, 237, 246
ethnicity, 30, 40, 117, 149, 152, 157, 171, 202
ethnohistory, 20, 23, 24, 26, 27, 41, 169, 171, 197, 218–21
evangelism/evangelical/evangelic, 34, 82, 87, 88, 183, 196
exoticism/exoticising, 29, 32, 52, 91, 117, 118

INDEX

Favre, Henri, 23, 237, 238
Ferreira, Francisco, x, 1, 69, 199, 236, 259
Field, Les W., 22, 23, 30
folklore, 17, 115, 188, 219, 248
Fonseca, Cesar, 25, 133, 203, 237, 241, 256

Geertz, Clifford J., 70, 80, 90, 96, 163, 167, 262
gender, 35, 50, 51, 67, 68, 87, 101, 131, 133, 135, 201, 202, 212
globalisation, 28, 30, 117
Gonzalez, Olga M., 36, 61, 66
Gose, Peter, x, 26, 27, 93–123, 197
guerrilla/s, 7, 85, 137, 138–41, 188, 206, 240

hacienda/s, 14, 18, 54, 74, 86, 97, 119, 188, 221, 224, 226, 236, 238, 247, 249, 251 252, 253, 254, 255, 256, 257, 258, 263
Handbook of South American Indians, 16, 19, 234, 239
Harris, Olivia, 8, 13, 19–23, 27, 121, 122, 167, 215, 222–4, 236
herding/herders, 34, 49, 67, 100, 108, 112, 113, 125, 129, 132, 133, 139, 144, 241, 245, 247
historical continuities, 8, 18, 19, 21, 22, 23, 29, 35, 167, 238
historiography, 19, 172, 201
Huamanga (*see also* Ayacucho), 6, 9, 46, 47, 53, 54, 56, 64, 140
Huancavelica, 125, 138, 251
Huancayo, 234, 235, 248, 253, 254
Huánuco, 14, 126, 237, 263
Huarochirí, 3, 17, 34, 41, 170–6, 186, 220
hybridity/hybrid, 8, 11, 30, 35, 111, 249

identity/identities, 11, 23, 29, 30, 33, 35, 36, 67, 68, 101, 117, 118, 125, 128, 136, 146, 147, 152, 156-8, 161, 164, 165, 195, 240, 246
Inca/Inka, 5, 6, 8, 9, 19, 20, 22, 27, 34, 40, 47, 48, 56, 69-71, 76, 77, 82, 87, 100-2, 127-9, 132, 135, 140, 173, 175, 180, 182, 183, 185, 195, 196, 199, 200-3, 205, 212, 213, 216, 219, 224, 230, 236-9, 248
Indian/s/*indio/s*, 16, 17, 30, 104, 105, 115, 146, 186, 170, 171, 201, 206, 209, 215, 220-2, 227, 230, 233, 234, 235, 236, 237, 240, 241, 246, 257
indigenism/st (*indigenismo*), 14–16, 173, 197, 233, 248
indigenous, 3, 13–17, 21–3, 26, 30, 32-4, 36, 39, 40, 64, 74, 78, 84, 90, 94, 95, 101-6, 115, 118, 120-2, 136, 149, 150, 152, 154-7, 159, 162, 164, 170, 171, 215, 221, 222, 229, 233, 236, 237, 240, 246, 257, 261
Instituto de Estudios Peruanos (IEP), 25, 221, 237
irrigation, 27, 28, 39, 125-8, 130-7, 145, 146, 151, 159, 217, 218, 241, 244, 245, 257, 258, 262, 263
Isbell, Billie Jean, xi, 4, 23, 26, 29, 31, 32, 38, 45-68, 72, 125, 128, 130, 133, 237

Junín, 15, 18, 25, 126, 129, 251, 252, 255

khipu/s, 34, 40, 41, 175–80, 182–9, 191–3, 195–7

kinship, 15, 19, 22, 26, 49, 50, 74, 86, 102, 103, 130, 131, 140, 145, 150, 153, 202, 230, 238, 258, 261
kurakals (*see also curacals*), 101, 102, 104, 132, 237

La Paz, 36, 201, 204, 206, 215–21, 224, 226
Lake Titicaca, 19, 199, 219
land reform (*see also* agrarian reform), 20, 21, 23, 137, 252
Lévi-Strauss, Claude, 22, 47–53, 70, 80, 202
Lima, 1, 13, 20, 23, 25, 31–4, 40, 41, 54–6, 58–61, 63, 65, 72, 101, 107, 108, 126, 128, 131, 133, 134, 138, 139, 145–7, 166, 169, 170, 172, 173, 183–9, 204, 219–22, 224, 237, 238, 241, 244, 247, 249, 254–6, 261, 263
literacy, 34, 35, 41, 64
llacta/kuna, 170–2, 174
lo andino (*see also* Andeanism), 22, 236, 238
London School of Economics (LSE), 100, 200, 202, 235
long-termism/-termist, 8, 9, 11, 18, 19, 23, 24, 26, 29, 30–5, 37, 39

Macha, 41, 205, 206, 207–9, 211–13, 215–17, 219, 221–30
maize, 71, 127, 130, 132, 133, 146, 207–9, 213, 221, 223, 230, 241, 244, 246, 249, 250, 257
Malinowski, Bronislaw, 15, 77, 91, 202
Mariátegui, José Carlos, 25, 53, 233

Marxism/Marxists, 21, 23–5, 27, 31, 39, 54, 96, 98, 202, 233, 236
Mayer, Enrique, xi, 23, 41, 42, 133, 204, 233–63
memory, 34–6, 49, 51, 52, 65, 66, 69, 103, 127, 172, 183, 218
Mendoza, Gunnar, 219–22, 229
methodology/methodological/ly, 3, 5, 6, 8, 17, 28, 29, 30, 32, 34, 36, 37, 40, 43, 50, 52, 68, 130, 131, 135, 136, 144, 145, 177, 222, 234, 259
migration, 10, 14, 20, 21, 31, 33, 35, 81, 115, 149, 166, 249, 261, 262
minga/minka, 150, 154, 156, 160–2, 167
mining, 32, 90, 110–16, 118, 123, 197, 200, 209, 215, 221–3, 226, 230, 252–4, 259, 261
modernisation, 21, 25, 111, 118, 238, 247, 248
modernist, 120, 183, 188, 195
modernity, 20, 32, 117, 119, 120, 172
moiety/moities, 49, 58, 185, 206, 208–10, 212, 213, 215, 219, 227, 228, 230
mountain spirits (*see also* a*pus*), 28, 101, 102, 113, 114, 118
multidisciplinary, 5, 19, 20, 133, 145
Murra, John V., 8, 16, 17, 20–3, 25, 26, 30, 43, 133, 169, 170, 199, 203, 204, 207, 210, 216, 218–20, 222, 223, 236–8, 244, 263
museification, 183, 184, 196

myth/s/mythology, 13, 14, 22, 27, 47, 48, 50, 125, 127, 130, 132, 134, 170-4, 248, 257, 263
Mythologiques, 47, 48, 50

neoliberalism/neoliberal, 11, 24, 28, 36, 39, 42, 96, 100, 105, 110, 117, 118, 149, 211, 215, 228, 234, 259
non-governmental organisation/s (NGO/s), 35, 40, 67, 141, 153, 154, 162, 163, 174, 188, 246, 249, 250
Northern Potosí, 27, 35, 199, 213, 218, 219, 221, 223, 226, 230

ontology/ontological, 80, 90, 118-21
Orientalism, 29, 105, 240
Otávalo, 17, 33, 40, 149, 150, 152-4, 160-4, 224

paccha/s, 71, 72, 75, 76
Pajuelo, Ramón, 13, 15-17, 23, 24
participant observation, 6, 17, 90
Pasco, 42, 126, 142, 189, 237, 253
Paz Estenssoro, Víctor, 201, 216, 226
peasant community/ies (*see also comunidad/es campesina/s*), 1, 9, 20, 21, 46, 74, 127, 144, 157, 162, 174, 199, 207, 252
peasant patrol/s (*see also ronda/s campesina/s*), 32, 119, 137
peasants, 7, 17, 19, 21, 22, 24, 28, 29, 40, 53, 104, 133, 141, 149, 157, 199, 202, 203, 215, 217, 221, 226, 227, 245, 246, 255-7, 261
Pease, Franklin, 129, 203, 220

Peru, 1, 5, 7, 9, 12-14, 16, 18-21, 28, 32, 34, 37-40, 42, 43, 45, 47, 52-5, 59, 60, 62, 65, 66, 68, 69, 72, 76, 77, 80, 84, 85, 93, 97, 100, 104, 110, 117, 118, 125-8, 136, 138, 140, 145, 151, 152, 172, 183, 185, 219, 226, 233-40, 249, 251-3, 259, 262
pilgrimage/s, 26, 27, 65, 73, 75, 87, 125.
Platt, Tristan, xii, 7, 16-17, 24, 41, 42, 102, 104, 120, 199-231
Polanyi, Karl, 20, 21, 236
political economy, 24, 96, 157, 166, 216
postcolonial, 28, 32, 40, 117, 149, 226, 246
postmodernism/postmodern, 3, 24, 28, 29, 31, 35, 91, 106, 119, 149, 157, 158, 262
poststructuralism/poststructural, 32, 117, 156
poverty, 48, 64, 85, 138, 141, 161, 170, 211, 247, 251
pre-Hispanic, 13-15, 25, 127, 128, 134, 173, 219, 236, 237, 238
processual, 8, 11, 30, 68
protestantism/protestant, 82, 86-8, 183, 196
puna, 9, 45, 54, 59, 67, 74, 89, 100, 108, 109, 112, 132, 139, 191, 204, 206-10, 213, 215, 221, 227, 228, 241, 245, 247, 251-3, 255-7, 263
Puno, 19, 64, 108, 138, 139, 251

Qoyllur Rit'I, 73, 75, 87
Quechua/Quichua, 3, 7, 13, 35, 40, 41, 45, 46, 49, 51, 60, 62, 64, 67, 69, 72-7, 89, 95, 98, 125,

127, 128, 130, 136, 139, 141,
143, 144, 146, 150, 152, 153,
155, 159, 160, 165, 169, 170,
172, 173, 175, 185, 189, 199,
200, 203–6, 210, 225, 235, 246,
258, 263
Quito, 152–5, 159, 160, 162, 220,
224

reciprocity/reciprocal, 11, 21, 26,
33, 42, 49, 50, 57, 58, 85, 96,
149, 236, 238, 257
redistribution, 11, 20, 21, 236, 237,
251, 260
reflexivity/reflective, 3, 28, 43, 77,
91, 97, 106
religion/religiosity, 11, 14, 23, 27,
35, 87, 171, 210
revisionism/revisionist, 3, 8, 9, 23,
28, 29–33, 35, 37, 38, 40
ritual/s/ritualistic, 4–6, 10, 11, 19,
23, 26–8, 31, 34, 35, 38–40,
47, 49, 51, 54, 56, 58, 67, 71,
72, 75–7, 87, 94–9, 101, 102,
104–6, 113–16, 121, 122, 125,
126, 128, 130–2, 134, 136, 140,
142, 144, 145, 149, 166, 167,
170, 175, 180, 183, 185, 188,
189, 191, 193, 208, 209, 211,
217, 248
ronda/s campesina/s (*see also* peasant
patrol/s), 32, 119, 240
Rowe, John H., 8, 16, 20, 203
rural, 2, 3, 5, 6, 13, 17, 20, 29, 34,
35, 37, 40, 53, 61, 63, 74, 84,
104, 126, 127, 130, 136, 141,
144, 149, 152, 153, 157, 163,
165, 166, 186, 206, 215, 223,
225–8, 230, 251, 253

Salomon, Frank, xii, 16, 19, 21, 30,
33, 34, 40–2, 103, 152, 159,
163, 169–97, 174, 192, 204,
220
Scott, James, 149, 157, 257
sector/s, 33, 153–5, 159–62, 165,
167, 175
Sendero Luminoso/Shining Path, 7,
29, 38, 51–4, 61–6, 68, 85, 100,
106–8, 117, 129, 137–41, 146,
172, 188, 233, 240
short-termism/-termist, 8, 23, 25,
33, 35, 40, 167
Sistema Nacional de Apoyo
a la Mobilización Social
(SINAMOS), 54, 55, 188, 257
social change, 8, 11, 18–21, 23,
25–7, 31, 35, 36, 167
sociology/sociologist, 138, 142, 169,
170, 200, 220, 253, 246
Spalding, Karen, 24, 170, 172
Starn, Orin, 16, 22, 29–31, 105,
240
state, 7, 9, 11, 19, 26, 28, 30, 45,
47, 57, 64, 75, 86, 95–8, 136,
138, 141, 149, 162, 172, 183,
184, 188, 197, 199, 213, 222,
225–9, 236, 257, 252, 253, 256,
259, 261
structural functionalism, 23, 166,
235
structuralism, 9, 20–2, 26, 38,
46–50, 52, 53, 71, 101, 134, 216

The Hold Life Has, 4, 74, 78, 81, 82,
87–91
To Defend Ourselves, 4, 46, 128
(de) Toledo, Francisco, 1, 127, 128,
206

tourism/tourist, 27, 32, 35, 119, 123, 127, 128, 142-4, 178, 183, 195, 235, 248
transnationalisation/transnational, 28, 117, 163
Truth and Reconciliation Commission (TRC), 7, 59, 62, 65, 137, 138

University of Huamanga (UNSCH), 6, 9, 46, 47, 53, 56, 64, 140
University of Illinois, 46, 69, 71, 72
University of San Marcos (UNMSM), 16-18, 43, 185
urban, 1, 10, 14, 20, 33, 34, 48, 53, 63, 78, 81, 104, 108, 110, 118, 125, 149, 152, 183, 188, 211
Urton, Gary, 26, 27, 72, 188

Valcárcel, Luis E., 14, 16, 18, 19, 234
Valderrama, Ricardo, xiii, 27, 39, 40, 42, 125-47

vecinos, 26, 27, 94
Velasco Alvarado, Juan, 21, 74, 75, 188, 237, 238, 251, 253
verticality, 203, 207, 217, 221, 223, 224, 237, 241, 244
Vicos project, 18, 43, 68, 236, 257
violence, 7, 28, 31, 34, 35, 38, 54, 56, 59, 60, 62, 66, 85, 117, 137, 138, 141, 188, 208, 226, 261
visita/s/visitador, 14, 55, 220, 238, 263

Wachtel, Nathan, 20, 134, 215, 217, 220
Weismantel, Mary, 152, 156-8
Wolf, Eric R., 19, 20, 25, 26, 30, 157, 169

Zuidema, R. Tom, 8, 9, 20, 22, 23, 26, 27, 38, 43, 46-8, 50, 53, 57, 70-2, 76, 77, 134, 203, 216, 237

Founded in 1965, the Institute of Latin American Studies (ILAS) forms part of the University of London's School of Advanced Study, based in Senate House, London. Between 2004 and 2013, ILAS formed part of the Institute for the Study of the Americas.

ILAS occupies a unique position at the core of academic study of the region in the UK. Internationally recognised as a centre of excellence for research facilitation, it serves the wider community through organising academic events, providing online research resources, publishing scholarly writings and hosting visiting fellows. It possesses a world-class library dedicated to the study of Latin America and is the administrative home of the highly respected *Journal of Latin American Studies*. The Institute supports scholarship across a wide range of subject fields in the humanities and cognate social sciences and actively maintains and builds ties with cultural, diplomatic and business organisations with interests in Latin America, including the Caribbean.

As an integral part of the School of Advanced Study, ILAS has a mission to foster scholarly initiatives and develop networks of Latin Americanists and Caribbeanists at a national level, as well as to promote the participation of UK scholars in the international study of Latin America.

The Institute currently publishes in the disciplines of history, politics, economics, sociology, anthropology, geography and environment, development, culture and literature, and on the countries and regions of Latin America and the Caribbean.

Full details about the Institute's publications, events, postgraduate courses and other activities are available on the web at http://ilas.sas.ac.uk.

Institute of Latin American Studies
School of Advanced Study, University of London
Senate House, Malet Street, London WC1E 7HU

Tel 020 7862 8844, Fax 020 7862 8886, Email ilas@sas.ac.uk
Web http://ilas.sas.ac.uk

Recent and forthcoming titles published by the Institute of Latin American Studies:

Organized Labour and Politics in Mexico: Changes, Continuities and Contradictions (2012)
Graciela Bensusán & Kevin J. Middlebrook

Traslados/Translations: Essays on Latin America in Honour of Jason Wilson (2012)
edited by Claire Lindsay

Broken Government? American Politics in the Obama Era (2012)
edited by Iwan Morgan & Philip John Davies

Democracy in Mexico: Attitudes and Perceptions of Citizens at National and Local Level (2014)
edited by Salvador Martí i Puig, Reynaldo Yunuen Ortega Ortiz & Mª Fernanda Somuano Ventura

Recasting Commodity and Spectacle in the Indigenous Americas (2014)
edited by Helen Gilbert & Charlotte Gleghorn

Obama's Washington: Political Leadership in a Partisan Era (2014)
edited by Clodagh Harrington

A Liberal Tide? Immigration and Asylum Law and Policy in Latin America (2015)
edited by David James Cantor, Luisa Feline Freier & Jean-Pierre Gauci

Provincialising Nature: Multidisciplinary Approaches to the Politics of the Environment in Latin America (2016)
edited by Michela Coletta & Malayna Raftopoulos

The New Refugees: Crime and Forced Displacement in Latin America (Spanish edition 2015; English edition 2016)
edited by David James Cantor & Nicolás Rodríguez Serna

Understanding ALBA: the progress, problems and prospects of alternative regionalism in Latin America and the Caribbean (forthcoming 2017)
edited by Asa Cusack